Legal Aspects of Cryptocurrency in the UK

Legal Aspects of Cryptocurrency in the UK

Blake O'Donnell BCL (NUI), LLM (U of Minn), MPhil (Cantab)

Bloomsbury Professional

LONDON • DUBLIN • EDINBURGH • NEW YORK • NEW DELHI • SYDNEY

BLOOMSBURY PROFESSIONAL

Bloomsbury Publishing Plc
50 Bedford Square, London, WC1B 3DP, UK
1385 Broadway, New York, NY 10018, USA
29 Earlsfort Terrace, Dublin 2, Ireland

BLOOMSBURY and the Diana logo are trademarks of Bloomsbury Publishing Plc

British Library Cataloguing-in-Publication Data

A catalogue record for this book is available from the British Library.

ISBN: PB 978-1-52652-890-2
ePDF 978-1-52652-892-6
ePub 978-1-52652-891-9

Typeset by Evolution Design & Digital Ltd (Kent)
Printed and bound by CPI Group (UK) Ltd, Croydon, CR0 4YY

Preface

Welcome to *Legal Aspects of Cryptocurrency in the UK*. In navigating the intricate landscape of cryptocurrencies, this book aims to provide a comprehensive understanding of the legal framework surrounding these digital assets and distributed ledger technology within the UK.

The advent of cryptocurrency and blockchain has ushered in a new era of financial possibilities and technologies, challenging traditional norms and reshaping the legal terrain. As the interest in and application of cryptocurrencies continues to grow, so does the need for a nuanced holistic understanding of the legal system that governs their use and abuse.

In drafting this text, my goal was to unravel the complexities of the law, offering legal practitioners, market participants, policymakers, regulators, academics, and enthusiasts a thorough exploration of the key facets shaping the UK's crypto legal landscape: from the foundational principles underpinning existing treatment of digital assets to the evolving regulatory measures being developed by institutions nationally and internationally.

As the crypto landscape continues to evolve, so will the legal considerations that accompany it. This book is a snapshot of the current legal environment and hopefully will become a dynamic resource that adapts to the ever-changing nature of crypto law with future editions. Between the time of submitting the final draft of this book in early October 2023 and the writing of this preface, there have been a few regulatory updates which I will briefly summarise below.

On 30 October 2023, HM Treasury released updates on its plans to regulate fiat-backed stablecoins, certain classes of cryptoassets, and cryptoasset activities. In the government's update on plans to regulate fiat backed stable coins, the focus is on bringing stability to payment chains involving these stablecoins, aligning them with existing financial service standards.[1] The Financial Services and Markets Act 2023, introduced in July 2022, grants regulatory oversight to HM Treasury, the Bank of England, and the Payment Systems Regulator for fiat-backed stablecoin activities within the financial services regulatory framework.[2]

HM Treasury is set to present secondary legislation by early 2024 to integrate fiat-backed stablecoin activities into the regulatory scope of the Financial Conduct Authority. The plan involves a two-phase approach. Phase 1 focuses on fiat-backed stablecoins, while Phase 2 encompasses a broader range of cryptoassets,

1 HM Treasury, 'Update on Plans for the Regulation of Fiat-backed Stablecoins Plans' (October 2023) https://assets.publishing.service.gov.uk/media/653a82b7e6c968000daa9bdd/Update_on_Plans_for_Regulation_of_Fiat-backed_Stablecoins_13.10.23_FINAL.pdf [accessed 25 November 2023].

2 See **3.17–3.25**, **14.14–14.17**.

including algorithmic stablecoins and commodity-backed tokens. Additionally, Phase 2 addresses various cryptoasset activities such as trading venues, custody, lending platforms, market abuse, and public offerings of cryptoassets, as detailed in the February 2023 consultation.[3]

In February 2023, HM Treasury proposed regulating certain classes of cryptoassets and activities in the future.[4] Feedback from the consultation was published on 30 October 2023 wherein the government indicated that they intend to proceed largely in line with their guidance on Phase 2 of their regulatory approach.[5]

On 10 November 2023, the UK Government in a joint statement with other members of the Organisation for Economic Cooperation and Development announced they would work towards the automatic exchange of information between tax authorities on crypto exchanges to combat offshore tax avoidance and evasion.[6] They aim to swiftly transpose the Crypto-Asset Reporting Framework into domestic law and activate exchange agreements in time for exchanges to commence by 2027, subject to national legislative procedures.[7]

With the preceding clarified, I invite you to explore the fascinating realm where law and crypto intersect.

I extend my gratitude to Andy Hill, Head of Practitioner Publishing at Bloomsbury, and Paul Crick, Editor, for their invaluable contributions to bringing this book to fruition.

Blake O'Donnell
30 November 2023

3 See **3.18**, **19.9–19.11**.
4 *Ibid.*
5 HM Treasury, 'Future financial services regulatory regime for cryptoassets: Response to the consultation and call for evidence' (October 2023) https://assets.publishing.service.gov.uk/media/653bd1a180884d0013f71cca/Future_financial_services_regulatory_regime_for_cryptoassets_RESPONSE.pdf [accessed 27 November 2023].
6 HM Treasury, 'Collective engagement to implement the Crypto-Asset Reporting Framework' (Policy Paper, 10 November 2023) www.gov.uk/government/publications/international-joint-statement-on-the-crypto-asset-reporting-framework/collective-engagement-to-implement-the-crypto-asset-reporting-framework [accessed 25 November 2023].
7 For further information see **19.53–19.57**.

Contents

Table of Statutes

References are to paragraph number.

Table of Statutory Instruments

References are to paragraph number.

Table of Cases

References are to paragraph number.

Part I

Introduction to Cryptocurrency

Chapter 1

History and Overview of Cryptocurrency

HISTORICAL CONTEXT

1.1 The concept of digital currency has been around since the early days of the internet, but it was not until 2009 that the first decentralised cryptocurrency, Bitcoin,[1] was created by an unknown person or group using the pseudonym Satoshi Nakamoto. The white paper was the culmination of work done over many years by a loose collection of computer programmers known as the 'Cypherpunks'. The manifesto of the group was published by Eric Hughes in 1992.[2] A mailing list was set up for discussion among the community and culminated in a number of software projects.[3] The White Paper entitled 'Bitcoin: A Peer-to-Peer Electronic Cash System'[4] was first published at www.bitcoin.org on 1 November 2008 against the backdrop of the global financial crisis. On 3 January 2009, Bitcoin was launched.[5]

1.2 Bitcoin was designed to be a peer-to-peer electronic cash system that would allow people to send and receive payments without the need for a central authority like a bank. Transactions are verified by network nodes through cryptography and recorded on a decentralised public ledger called the blockchain. It resembles a shared spreadsheet that is copied and stored on many computers. Changes to the blockchain can be made if the majority of users agree.[6] This system does not rely on a central authority like a bank because transactions are conducted directly between peers.[7] There is no central bank, government or centralised structure that manages the system.[8]

1 Ticker Symbol: BTC.
2 Eric Hughes, 'A Cypherpunk's Manifesto' (*activism*, 9 March 2023) www.activism.net/cypherpunk/manifesto.html [accessed 25 September 2023].
3 Ivan Cryptoslav, 'Crypto Basics: Who are the Cypherpunks?' *CoinMarketCap* https://coinmarketcap.com/academy/article/who-are-the-cypherpunks [accessed 25 September 2023].
4 Satoshi Nakamoto, 'Bitcoin: A Peer-to-Peer Electronic Cash System' (2008) Sathoshi Nakamoto Institute https://nakamotoinstitute.org/bitcoin/ [accessed 8 October 2023].
5 Brian Nibley, 'Bitcoin Price History: 2009–2023' (*SoFi Technologies*, 1 March 2023) www.sofi.com/learn/content/bitcoin-price-history/ [accessed 24 September 2023].
6 Cryptoslav, 'Crypto Basics: Who are the Cypherpunks?' (n 3 above).
7 Justin Steffen and Ellen Pactor, 'Deconstructing the digital dollar: protecting financial privacy from surveillance capital' (2021) 2 IBLJ, 255, 257.
8 Department for Business & Trade and others, 'Economic Crime and Corporate Transparency Bill 2022, Factsheet: cryptoassets – legislation' (20 June 2023) www.gov.uk/government/publications/economic-crime-and-corporate-transparency-bill-2022-factsheets/fact-sheet-cryptoassets-legislation [accessed 24 September 2023].

1.3 Transactions are identified by public keys, which are visible to everyone on the network. To control or use the Bitcoin associated with a public key, the owner needs a private key, which acts like a ticket granting access. Bitcoin transactions are considered 'pseudo-anonymous' because they are linked to public keys, not individuals. Some transactions may not be recorded on the public blockchain, and certain exchanges keep intra-exchange transactions off-chain, at least temporarily.[9]

1.4 Transactions are added to the blockchain through a process called 'mining'. Miners compete to solve a complex mathematical problem, and the first one to solve it gets to add a block of transactions to the blockchain. The winning miner receives a reward in the form of new Bitcoin. Bitcoin was the first cryptocurrency, but there are now other digital assets and protocols created by modifying Bitcoin's source code.[10]

1.5 For example, Zcash[11] uses zero knowledge proofs to enable proving the truth of a mathematical statement without revealing all the details. In Zcash transactions, holders can prove ownership and proper transfer of funds without disclosing transaction details or participant identities, known as 'shielded' transactions. Alternatively, holders can choose 'transparent' or unshielded transactions. Even for shielded transactions, users can selectively share transaction details using viewing keys.[12]

1.6 Users typically store cryptocurrencies in digital wallets. There are hosted wallets (eg blockchain.com, Coinbase) and un-hosted (personal) wallets. Hosted wallets manage private keys, while un-hosted wallets allow users to store their own keys. Hardware devices like Trezor can also store private keys. Some individuals print their keys on paper. The choice of storage method involves financial privacy and security considerations, as some hosted wallets have been hacked.[13]

1.7 Bitcoin, Zcash, Ethereum,[14] and other protocols are decentralised, with no individual controlling the transaction ledger. However, there are more centralised variants like Central Bank Digital Currencies (CBDCs), which are issued, controlled, and often tracked by governments or central banks. For example, the digital Yuan allows the Chinese Central Bank to monitor user transactions.[15]

1.8 Cryptocurrency is not a one-size-fits-all innovation. Each protocol has unique attributes, and developers can customise their tokens by emphasising,

9 Bank for International Settlements, 'The crypto ecosystem: key elements and risks' (Report submitted to the G20 Finance Ministers and Central Bank Governors, July 2023) Bank for International Settlements [2.1] www.bis.org/publ/othp72.pdf [accessed 8 October 2023].
10 Steffen and Pactor, 'Deconstructing the digital dollar' (n 7 above).
11 Ticker Symbol: ZEC.
12 Steffen and Pactor, 'Deconstructing the digital dollar' (n 7 above).
13 *Ibid* 258.
14 Ticker Symbol: ETH.
15 Steffen and Pactor, 'Deconstructing the digital dollar' (n 7 above), 258.

deemphasising, or eliminating specific features. Consequently, the governing rules of each protocol can enhance or diminish privacy.[16]

1.9 After Bitcoin's success, several other cryptocurrencies emerged, each with their own unique features and purposes. In 2011, Litecoin[17] was created by Charlie Lee, a former Google employee. It was designed to be a faster and more efficient version of Bitcoin, with a different hashing algorithm and a higher maximum number of coins.[18]

1.10 In 2015, Ethereum was created by Vitalik Buterin, which allowed developers to create smart contracts and decentralised applications (DApps) on top of its blockchain. Smart contracts are computer programs which automatically execute certain actions when specified conditions are met without relying on a trusted third party. The code itself enforces the contract, meaning parties to the contract only need to trust the contract's code rather than each other.[19] This innovation opened up a whole new world of possibilities for blockchain technology beyond just financial transactions.[20]

1.11 Since then, there have been thousands of new cryptocurrencies created, each with its own use case and philosophy. Some, like Ripple,[21] are focused on streamlining international payments,[22] while others, like Dogecoin,[23] were created as a light-hearted alternative to the larger cryptocurrencies[24] but have gained significant popularity through social media.[25]

1.12 Today, cryptocurrencies are traded on a number of exchanges and have become an increasingly popular investment vehicle and attracting institutional investors. In recent years, the landscape of cryptocurrency has witnessed remarkable advancements, particularly in the realms of non-fungible tokens (NFTs), decentralised finance (DeFi), and decentralised autonomous organisations (DAOs). These innovations have ushered in a new era of financial

16 *Ibid.*
17 Ticker Symbol: LTC.
18 CMC Markets, 'What is litecoin?' www.cmcmarkets.com/en/learn-cryptocurrencies/what-is-litecoin [accessed 6 November 2023].
19 Department for Business & Trade and others, 'Economic Crime and Corporate Transparency Bill 2022' (n 8 above).
20 CMC Markets, 'What is ethereum?' www.cmcmarkets.com/en-au/learn-cryptocurrencies/what-is-ethereum#:~:text=Ethereum%20is%20an%20open%20software,used%20on%20the%20Ethereum%20network. [accessed 6 November 2023].
21 Ticker Symbol: XRP.
22 CMC Markets, 'What is ripple?' *CMC Markets* www.cmcmarkets.com/en-ie/learn-cryptocurrencies/what-is-ripple [accessed 25 September 2023].
23 Ticker Symbol: DOGE.
24 CMC Markets, 'Alternative cryptocurrencies' www.cmcmarkets.com/en-ie/learn-cryptocurrencies/alternative-cryptocurrencies [accessed 25 September 2023].
25 CoinTelegraph, 'DOGE price surge: The power of memes and social media on full display' (29 January 2021) *CoinTelegraph* https://cointelegraph.com/news/doge-price-surge-the-power-of-memes-and-social-media-on-full-display [accessed 25 August 2023].

and technological possibilities, prompting legal scholars and practitioners to grapple with novel legal and regulatory challenges.

1.13 NFTs, a significant innovation within the crypto space, bringing a seismic shift in the concept of ownership and provenance. NFTs are digital assets that are unique, verifiable ownership records on the blockchain, and have found applications across art, music, collectibles, and even virtual real estate.[26]

1.14 DeFi is an emerging ecosystem of cryptocurrency financial products and services. Rather than relying on intermediaries, these products and services are delivered through applications built on the blockchain using smart contracts.[27] DeFi platforms leverage smart contracts to provide open, permissionless, and automated financial services, such as lending, borrowing, trading, and yield farming.[28] The legal implications surrounding DeFi are multifaceted, encompassing issues of regulatory compliance, investor protection, and potential liability in cases of smart contract vulnerabilities.

1.15 DAOs represent an innovative model of decentralised decision-making and governance. DAOs are structured entities that operate based on predefined rules encoded in smart contracts, allowing for transparent and democratic management. The legal landscape around DAOs involves considerations of liability, accountability, and fiduciary duty, as the traditional corporate framework may not easily apply to these decentralised entities.[29]

1.16 The evolution of cryptocurrency has sparked discussions on intellectual property, data privacy and taxation, necessitating legal frameworks that adapt quickly to the distinctive natures of these innovations.

1.17 The technology continues to evolve and attract new users and investors. El Salvador has decided to adopt Bitcoin as legal tender and has issued Bitcoin Denominated Sovereign Bonds.[30] The Central African Republic has also adopted Bitcoin as legal tender.[31]

26 Hanna Shnaider, 'The Rise of NFTs: Exploring the Future of Digital Ownership' (5 July 2023) *FourtySeven* https://fortyseven47.com/blog/the-rise-of-nfts-exploring-the-future-of-digital-ownership/ [accessed 25 September 2023[.

27 Department for Business & Trade and others, 'Economic Crime and Corporate Transparency Bill 2022' (n 8 above).

28 Cointelegraph, 'What is DeFi? A beginner's guide to decentralized finance' *Cointelegraph* https://cointelegraph.com/learn/defi-a-comprehensive-guide-to-decentralized-finance [accessed 25 September 2023].

29 Cointelegraph, 'What is a decentralized autonomous organization, and how does a DAO work?' *Cointelegraph* https://cointelegraph.com/learn/what-is-a-dao [accessed 25 September 2023].

30 Henri Arslanian, Robert Donvan, Matthew Blumenfeld and Antony Zamore, 'El Salvador's law: a meaningful test for Bitcoin' (October 2021) *PWC* www.pwc.com/gx/en/financial-services/pdf/el-salvadors-law-a-meaningful-test-for-bitcoin.pdf [accessed 25 September 2023].

31 Ryan Browne, 'Central African Republic Becomes Second Country to Adopt Bitcoin as Legal Tender' (28 April 2022) *CNBC* www.cnbc.com/2022/04/28/central-african-republic-adopts-bitcoin-as-legal-tender.html [accessed 25 September 2023].

1.18 The rise of Bitcoin and other cryptocurrencies prompted central banks to re-evaluate their monetary policies and explore the concept of CBDCs. Several motivations influenced their decisions including:[32]

(a) **Quicker payments**: CBDCs could enhance the speed, security, and cost-effectiveness of domestic and cross-border transactions.

(b) **Financial inclusion**: CBDCs aim to provide broader access to financial services, particularly in regions with limited banking infrastructure.

(c) **Direct transmission of monetary policy**: CBDCs present an opportunity for central banks to leverage distributed ledger technologies to allow them to be more responsive to economic challenges and transmit monetary policy changes more efficiently.

1.19 Various countries and regions have made significant progress in researching and developing CBDCs. Notable examples include:

(a) **The Bahamas**: The Central Bank of The Bahamas launched the Sand Dollar, a CBDC pegged to the Bahamian dollar, in October 2020, becoming one of the first countries to introduce a nationwide digital currency.[33]

(b) **China**: The People's Bank of China (PBOC) has been at the forefront of CBDC development, piloting the digital yuan (also known as the digital currency electronic payment or DCEP) across several cities since November 2020.[34]

(c) **Eastern Caribbean Currency Union:** The currency union comprising Anguilla, Antigua and Barbuda, Dominica, Grenada, Montserrat, Saint Kitts and Nevis, Saint Lucia and Saint Vincent and the Grenadines uses the Eastern Caribbean Dollar supervised by the Eastern Caribbean Central Bank, which launched the Dcash pilot on 31 March 2021, pegged to the Eastern Caribbean dollar.[35]

(d) **The European Union**: The ECB has been actively researching a digital euro, conducting experiments and engaging with the public and stakeholders to assess its potential implementation.[36]

32 See **18.4**.

33 Central Bank of Bahamas, 'Digital Bahamian Dollar' *Sand Dollar* www.sanddollar.bs/ [accessed 25 September 2023].

34 Working Group on E-CNY Research and Development of the People's Bank of China, 'Progress of Research & Development of E-CNY in China' (July 2021) *People's Bank of China 13-14* www.pbc.gov.cn/en/3688110/3688172/4157443/4293696/2021071614584691871.pdf [accessed 25 September 2023].

35 Eastern Caribbean Central Bank, 'About the project' *DCash* www.dcashec.com/about/ [accessed 25 September 2023].

36 European Central Bank, 'Digital euro' www.ecb.europa.eu/paym/digital_euro/html/index.en.html [accessed 25 September 2023].

(e) **Jamaica**: Bank of Jamaica launched its CBDC knowns as the JAM-DEX in July 2022 which is pegged to the Jamaican dollar.[37]

(f) **Nigeria**: The Central Bank of Nigeria with launched the eNaira in October 2021 pegged to the naira.[38]

(g) **Sweden**: The Sveriges Riksbank has been exploring the concept of an e-krona since 2017, aiming to address the decline in cash usage and ensure a resilient payment system.[39]

(h) **Switzerland**: The Swiss National Bank is set to launch a pilot of a wholesale CBDC.[40]

(i) **United States**: The Federal Reserve is engaged in a number of experiments related to digital currencies, including a hypothetical CBDC and engaging with the public and stakeholders to assess its potential implementation.[41]

1.20 The development of CBDCs raises various implications and challenges for the financial ecosystem, such as:[42]

(a) **Data collection and privacy concerns**: The design and implementation of CBDCs require careful consideration of privacy concerns and the balance between surveillance capabilities and individual freedoms.

(b) **Monetary policy and financial stability**: CBDCs may impact traditional monetary policy tools, increasing central banks' power and may cause unforeseen consequences on financial stability in a digital era.

(c) **Cybersecurity, interoperability and standardisation**: The digitised nature of CBDCs could be a single point of failure for a cyber attack or technical malfunction. The interoperability of CBDCs with existing payment systems and the establishment of common standards pose significant technical challenges.

1.21 International organisations, such as the International Monetary Fund (IMF) and the Bank for International Settlements (BIS), are actively engaged in studying and facilitating dialogue on CBDCs to promote cooperation among central banks and financial institutions. It is important to note that while some countries are actively pursuing CBDC development, others are adopting a

37 Bank of Jamaica, 'CBDC FAQs' https://boj.org.jm/core-functions/currency/cbdc/cbdc-faqs/ [accessed 25 September 2023].

38 Central Bank of Nigeria, 'eNaira' *eNaira* https://enaira.gov.ng/ [accessed 25 September 2023].

39 Sveriges Riksbank, 'E-krona' iksbank www.riksbank.se/en-gb/payments--cash/e-krona/ [accessed 25 September 2023].

40 Noele Illien and John Revill, 'SNB to launch digital currency pilot' (26 June 2023) *Reuters* www.reuters.com/markets/currencies/snb-launch-digital-currency-pilot-chairman-2023-06-26/ [accessed 25 September 2023].

41 US Federal Reserve, 'Central Bank Digital Currency (CBDC): Frequently Asked Questions' www.federalreserve.gov/cbdc-faqs.htm [accessed 25 September 2023].

42 See **18.8**.

cautious approach, considering the potential risks and challenges associated with implementation.

BLOCKCHAIN/DISTRIBUTED LEDGER TECHNOLOGY

1.22 Originally created to support Bitcoin, blockchain technology is a distributed database that allows multiple parties to maintain a shared and secure ledger of transactions. Blockchain has since become a widely applicable technology with many potential use cases beyond digital currencies. This makes it an ideal technology for financial transactions, supply chain management, and other use cases where security and transparency are important.

1.23 The basic idea of blockchain is that it creates a decentralised, tamper-proof database that is secured by cryptography. Rather than relying on a central authority to manage the database which may be vulnerable, each node in the network maintains a copy of the ledger. Each transaction is verified by the network and recorded on the ledger, making it impossible to alter past transactions without being detected. In the case of cryptocurrencies, ownership can typically only be transferred using a private key.

1.24 The ledger is maintained using a consensus algorithm that determines how transactions are validated and recorded. There are different consensus algorithms used in different blockchains, including proof of work (PoW), proof of stake (PoS) and proof of authority (PoA):

(a) PoW is the original consensus algorithm used by Bitcoin, and it requires nodes in the network to solve complex mathematical puzzles in order to validate transactions. This process, known as mining, is energy-intensive and has been criticised for its environmental impact.

(b) PoS requires nodes to put up a stake of the blockchain's native cryptocurrency in order to validate transactions. This reduces the energy consumption required for validation.

(c) PoA transactions involve approved accounts known as 'validators' who run automated software to validate blocks.

1.25 One of the key benefits of blockchain technology is its transparency and security. As the ledger is maintained by multiple parties and each transaction is recorded in a tamper-proof manner, it is difficult to alter the records without being detected. Another benefit of blockchain is its potential for decentralisation and disintermediation. By removing the need for a central authority to manage the database, blockchain can allow for peer-to-peer transactions and eliminate the need for intermediaries. This can reduce costs and increase efficiency in many industries, such as finance and real estate.

1.26 DLT is the general term for blockchain-like technology. It is important to note that blockchain is a type of DLT, but not the only one, despite being commonly used interchangeably. Similarly cryptocurrencies are a category of the broader term 'cryptoassets', and the two terms are commonly used interchangeably. Cryptoassets rely on DLT for security and functionality. A key feature of DLT is that it allows the record of token ownership to be distributed across the network, preventing double spending, and ensuring a secure ownership record.

1.27 DLT operates differently from traditional transaction recording methods, where a trusted entity maintains a centralised database or ledger. In a DLT system, the ledger is comprehensive and real-time, distributed among participants, and combined with security measures. Key characteristics of DLT include:[43]

(a) distributed nature of the ledger;

(b) consensus mechanism; and

(c) cryptographic mechanisms.

1.28 Despite its potential benefits, blockchain/DLT is still in its early stages and faces several challenges. The technology requires interoperability, standardisation, significant energy consumption, and questions regarding its use at scale.[44] Additionally, there are regulatory and legal concerns surrounding the use of DLT in financial transactions and managing personal data. While there are still challenges to be addressed, the technology continues to evolve and attract interest from a wide range of industries and stakeholders.

EXCHANGES AND WALLETS

1.29 Cryptoasset exchanges are online platforms (whether a firm or sole practitioner) that provide one or more of the following services:[45]

(a) exchanging, or arranging or making arrangements with a view to the exchange of, cryptoassets for money or money for cryptoassets or one cryptoasset for another;

(b) operating a machine which utilises automated processes to exchange cryptoassets for money or money for cryptoassets; or

43 World Bank, 'Distributed Ledger Technology (DLT) and Blockchain' (FinTech Note No. 1, 2017), 5–9 https://documents1.worldbank.org/curated/en/177911513714062215/pdf/122140-WP-PUBLIC-Distributed-Ledger-Technology-and-Blockchain-Fintech-Notes.pdf [accessed 25 September 2023].

44 Soundarya Jayaraman, 'Distributed Ledger Technology: Its Promises and Potential' (31 August 2023) *G2* https://learn.g2.com/distributed-ledger-technology [accessed 25 September 2023].

45 Department for Business & Trade and others, 'Economic Crime and Corporate Transparency Bill 2022, Factsheet: cryptoassets – key terms and definitions' (20 June 2023) www.gov.uk/government/publications/economic-crime-and-corporate-transparency-bill-2022-factsheets/factsheet-cryptoassets-key-terms-and-definitions [accessed 8 October 2023].

(c) holding private cryptographic keys on behalf of its customers in order to hold, store and transfer cryptoassets.

1.30 To securely hold and transfer cryptoassets, various 'wallets' have been developed. The wallet stores a combination of cryptographic public and private keys. The type of wallet can differ based on the method and location of storage. Internet connectivity defines whether a cryptoasset wallet is 'hot' or 'cold'.[46] The loss of a private key to a wallet does not affect the existence of the tokens which can be recovered by use of seed phrase.[47]

1.31 Hot wallets are connected to the internet and are therefore less secure and more susceptible to hacks. These wallets are akin to online bank accounts and usually used for storage of sums of money for shorter periods of time, similar to a bank 'current account'. Hot wallets are straightforward to set up, and the cryptoassets held in them are easily accessible.[48] These services are often offered by cryptoasset exchanges

1.32 Cold wallets store users' private keys offline (eg on a USB stick or paper) and do not require internet connectivity, thereby lessening security risks. Cold wallets are analogous to a safe or a vault, where more substantial sums of money can be stored for longer periods of time.[49]

1.33 Hosted wallets are software or hardware that enables a third party to store or transfer cryptoassets for an individual. With a hosted wallet, private cryptographic keys are stored with the third party and the wallet provides for the backup and security of funds.[50]

1.34 Unhosted wallets are software or hardware that enables a person to store and transfer cryptoassets on their own behalf. They administer their own private cryptographic key.[51]

1.35 A custodian wallet provider is a business providing services to safeguard and/or administer cryptoassets on behalf of its customers, or private cryptographic keys on behalf of its customers in order to hold, store, and transfer cryptoassets generally via a hot wallet. A Cryptoasset service provider is a term used to describe both custodian wallet providers and a cryptoasset exchanges.[52]

46 *Ibid.*

47 Robert Stevens, 'Your First Crypto Wallet: What Is a Crypto Wallet and How to Use It' (11 May 2023) *CoinDesk* www.coindesk.com/learn/your-first-crypto-wallet-how-to-use-it-and-why-you-need-one/ [accessed 8 October 2023].

48 *Ibid.*

49 *Ibid.*

50 *Ibid.*

51 *Ibid.*

52 *Ibid.*

1.36 Wallets can serve as transaction and balance records, assisting taxpayers in meeting tax record-keeping obligations. HM Revenue and Customs (HMRC) may request access to wallets to provide evidence of gains. If an exchange does not retain transaction records, taxpayers must ensure they retain enough information (eg, dates, times, and values of transfers) to identify their transactions.[53]

TYPES OF CRYPTOCURRENCIES

1.37 While Bitcoin was the first and most well-known cryptocurrency, there are now thousands of different cryptocurrencies with various features and use cases. Here are some of the most common types and categories of cryptocurrency:

1.38 **Bitcoin**: Created in 2009, Bitcoin is the first and most well-known cryptocurrency. It uses a PoW consensus algorithm to validate transactions and has a maximum supply of 21 million coins.

1.39 **Altcoins**: Any cryptocurrency other than Bitcoin. There are many different altcoins, each with its own unique features and use cases. Some popular altcoins include Ethereum, Litecoin, and Ripple.

1.40 **Stablecoins**: Cryptoassets with their value pegged to specific government-issued fiat currencies or precious metals.[54] These may be backed by reserves of the fiat currencies themselves, by other cryptoassets, by specific commodities, or their value may be determined algorithmically.[55] For example, Tether[56] and USD Coin[57] are pegged to the US dollar.

1.41 **E-money**: Tokens that meet the definition of electronic money (e-money) under the Electronic Money Regulations 2011 (EMRs) are subject to regulation by the Financial Conduct Authority (FCA). E-money is electronically stored monetary value representing a claim on the issuer, which is issued on receipt of funds for the purpose of making payment transactions and which is accepted by a person other than the issuer. Some examples of e-money include stablecoins, which are tokens that attempt to offer some degree of price stability by pegging their value to an external reference such as a fiat currency or the value of a commodity. However, not all stablecoins will fall within the regulated

53 HMRC, HMRC internal manual: Cryptoassets Manual (30 March 2021, updated 21 August 2023) CRYPTO10400 www.gov.uk/hmrc-internal-manuals/cryptoassets-manual [accessed 9 October 2023]. Please note sections in the Cryptoassets Manual follow the format of 'CRYPTO' followed by identifying numbers. For ease of reference, when this notation is used in this book it refers to the Cryptoassets Manual. The same citation method will apply for other relevant HMRC internal manuals where referenced.

54 *Ibid* CRYPTO10100.

55 Department for Business & Trade and others, 'Factsheet: cryptoassets – key terms and definitions' (n 45 above).

56 Ticker Symbol: USDT.

57 Ticker Symbol: USDC.

environment. The FCA will assess each product on a case-by-case basis to determine whether it meets the definition of e-money.[58]

1.42 **Privacy coins:** These are cryptoassets aimed at preserving their users' anonymity. They generally do not have public blockchains and the details of each transaction are hidden from public view, including the transfer amount and users' wallet addresses.[59] Examples include such as Dash,[60] Monero,[61] and Zcash. They use advanced cryptography to keep transactions private and untraceable, and often use alternative consensus algorithms, such as PoS.

1.43 **Utility tokens**: Utility tokens provide the holder with access to particular goods or services on a platform such as cloud storage space or cryptoasset trading, usually using DLT. A business or group of businesses will normally issue the tokens and commit to accepting the tokens as payment for the particular goods or services in question. In addition, utility tokens may be traded on exchanges or in peer-to-peer transactions in same way as exchange tokens.[62] Examples include Binance Coin[63] and Ethereum.

1.44 **Exchange tokens**: Tokens that are intended to be used as a means of payment and are increasingly popular as an investment due to potential increases in value. Bitcoin is an example of an exchange token.[64] These tokens typically have limited or no rights for holders, and there is usually no single issuer responsible for enforcing rights. Exchange tokens function as a medium of exchange, similar to currency, but they are not generally accepted as legal tender. They operate independently from a platform and use DLT for recording ownership and transfers. Unlike utility or security tokens, exchange tokens do not grant any rights or access to goods or services. Their value is primarily based on their use as a means of exchange or investment, without any underlying person, state, group, or asset supporting them. Exchange tokens can be traded on exchanges for currency and are also used for purchasing goods and services, with some shops and retail chains accepting them as payment. They are often highly volatile in value, which can limit their acceptance as a widely recognised medium of exchange.[65]

1.45 **Security tokens**: Tokens are issued by businesses and represent ownership interests in the business, such as debt rights or a share of profits. Security tokens are commonly used by companies to raise funds through ICOs or

58 See **3.4–3.7**.
59 Department for Business & Trade and others, 'Factsheet: cryptoassets – key terms and definitions' (n 45 above).
60 Ticker Symbol: DASH.
61 Ticker Symbol: XMR.
62 CRYPTO10100.
63 Ticker Symbol: BNB.
64 CRYPTO10100.
65 Mary Young and Jill Lorimer, 'Developments in the UK crypto-asset landscape', (2021) 2 IBLJ 241–254, 243.

security token offerings (STOs). These tokens are issued to investors in exchange for cash or cryptoassets. The nature of the tokens, whether they represent securities or provide other rights, depends on the specific rights associated with them. They are subject to securities regulations and are often used to raise capital for startups.[66] Examples include:

(a) tZERO: tZERO is a security token trading platform and subsidiary of Overstock.com. They issued a security token called TZROP,[67] which represents ownership in tZERO and entitles holders to a share in the company's profits.[68]

(b) Spice VC: Spice VC is a venture capital fund that tokenised its shares as security tokens. The SPICE token[69] represents ownership in the fund and provides potential profit-sharing rights.[70]

(c) Blockchain Capital: Blockchain Capital is a venture capital firm focused on blockchain and crypto-related investments. They issued BCAP,[71] a security token that represents shares in their fund and gives token holders economic rights and voting power.[72]

1.46 **DeFi tokens**: Digital assets that serve as integral components of decentralised financial applications built on DLT platforms. These tokens power various functionalities within DeFi protocols, including lending, borrowing, trading, and yield farming. DeFi tokens often provide holders with access to specific services, governance participation, or revenue-sharing mechanisms within the decentralised ecosystem.[73]

1.47 **DAO tokens**: Digital assets issued by blockchain-based organisations that operate through smart contracts and decentralised governance mechanisms, without the need for traditional centralised management. DAO tokens represent ownership, participation, or voting rights within these organisations, granting holders a stake in decision-making processes and potentially a share of the organisation's resources or profits.[74]

1.48 **NFTs**: These are a cryptographic token of a particular asset (it can be either physical or digital), which cannot be swapped directly for other NFTs (ie they are non-fungible). They allow owners to cryptographically prove the

66 See **3.4–3.7**.
67 Ticker Symbol: TZROP https://stomarket.com/sto/tZERO [accessed 25 September 2023].
68 www.tzero.com/ [accessed 25 September 2023].
69 Ticker Symbol: SPICE https://stomarket.com/sto/spice-vc-spice [accessed 25 September 2023].
70 https://spicevc.com/ [accessed 25 September 2023].
71 Ticker Symbol: BCAP https://stomarket.com/sto/blockchain-capital-bcap [accessed 25 September 2023].
72 www.blockchaincapital.com/ [accessed 25 September 2023].
73 Ekin Genç, 'What Are DeFi Tokens?' (16 November 2022) *CoinDesk* www.coindesk.com/learn/what-are-defi-tokens/ [accessed 25 September 2023].
74 Alyssa Hertig, 'What Is a DAO?' (17 January 2023) *CoinDesk* www.coindesk.com/learn/what-is-a-dao/[accessed 25 September 2023].

authenticity of their asset and their ownership of it through the blockchain, giving it a perceived value. NFTs can digitally represent any asset.[75] Examples include a piece of content, intellectual property, artwork, real estate or collectibles on a blockchain. Unlike traditional cryptocurrencies such as Bitcoin or Ethereum, which are interchangeable and hold equal value, NFTs are indivisible and distinct, making them particularly suited for representing rare or one-of-a-kind digital assets.

1.49 **CBDC**: CBDC is digital money that a country's central bank can issue. It is called digital (or electronic) because it is not physical money like notes and coins and is held in the form of an amount on a computer or similar device.[76] Internationally, the concept of CBDCs is gaining popularity, with the ECB also considering its own digital currency. On 19 April 2021, the Bank of England (BoE) and HM Treasury announced a joint taskforce to explore the possibility of a UK central bank digital currency.[77] Unlike typical cryptocurrencies, this 'digital currency' would be issued by the BoE and would coexist with cash and bank deposits, rather than replacing them, and be a fiat currency.

1.50 In conclusion, there are many different types of cryptoassets with various features and use cases. While Bitcoin remains the most well-known and widely used cryptocurrency, there are many alternatives that offer unique advantages and benefits. The introduction of CBDCs is potentially an important moment in the evolution of money.

75 Department for Business & Trade and others, 'Factsheet: cryptoassets – key terms and definitions' (n 45 above).

76 BoE, 'What is central bank digital currency?' (7 February 2023) www.bankofengland.co.uk/explainers/what-is-a-central-bank-digital-currency [accessed 25 September 2023].

77 BoE, 'Bank of England statement on Central Bank Digital Currency' (19 April 2021) www.bankofengland.co.uk/news/2021/april/bank-of-england-statement-on-central-bank-digital-currency [accessed 29 November 2023].

Chapter 2

Definition of Cryptocurrency

INTRODUCTION

2.1 Financial Services and Markets Act 2023 (FSMA 2023), s 69(4) amends Financial Services and Markets Act 2000 (FSMA 2000), s 417, introducing a definition of 'cryptoassets':

> 'In this Act—
>
> [...]
>
> "cryptoasset" means any cryptographically secured digital representation of value or contractual rights that—
>
> (a) can be transferred, stored or traded electronically, and
>
> (b) that uses technology supporting the recording or storage of data (which may include distributed ledger technology).'

Section 69(4)(b) also grants power to the Treasury to amend the definition of 'cryptoasset' by regulations.

2.2 In investment terminology a cryptocurrency is a digital currency which is held and exchanged on a decentralised electronic ledger. They can broadly be described as a digital asset that is secured by cryptography and used as a medium of exchange. Cryptocurrencies can be decentralised or centralised.

2.3 A question that often arises is whether cryptocurrency is 'money'. Public international law does not have an independent or self-standing definition or conception of money and simply recognises States have the sovereign right to issue and regulate their own currency.[1] In terms of UK law, cryptocurrency is not legal tender recognised by statute and therefore not a currency. In certain jurisdictions,[2] Bitcoin is legal tender; however, cryptocurrencies are not legal tender in any major financial jurisdiction. The public can however use cryptocurrencies to make payments to a private vendor or business if the party chooses to accept it as a form of payment.

2.4 European law recently came up with a definition of 'virtual money':[3]

1 David Fox and Sarah Green, *Cryptocurrencies in Public and Private Law* (1st edn, Oxford University Press, 2022), [3.16]–[3.17].

2 See **1.17**.

3 Council Directive (EU) 2018/843 of 30 May 2018 amending Directive (EU) 2015/849 on the prevention of the use of the financial system for the purposes of money laundering or terrorist financing, and amending Directives 2009/138/EC and 2013/36/EU [2018] OJ L156/43, Art 2(d).

> '"Virtual currencies" means a digital representation of value that is not issued or guaranteed by a central bank or a public authority, is not necessarily attached to a legally established currency and does not possess a legal status of currency or money, but is accepted by natural or legal persons as a means of exchange and which can be transferred, stored and traded electronically.'

It is to be noted that, from a terminological point of view, 'currency' is not the best choice of wording as, traditionally speaking, a currency is a means of exchange issued and controlled by a government, or a central bank.

2.5 The US Commodity Futures Trading Commission (CFTC) has defined Bitcoin and other virtual currencies as commodities under s 1a(9) of the US Commodity Exchange Act (CEA).[4] In its settlement order the CFTC applied the broad definition of commodity as laid out in the CEA and found that the scope of that definition included Bitcoin: 'The definition of a "commodity" is broad [...] Bitcoin and other virtual currencies are encompassed in the definition and properly defined as commodities.'[5] Depending on the attributes of the cryptocurrency they may qualify as a security and subject to regulation by the Securities and Exchange Commission (SEC).[6]

2.6 As outlined above, from the perspective of UK law cryptoassets are not legal tender but can be used as a medium of exchange in the context of relationships regulated by private law. In the event that the UK introduces its CBDC, the digital pound, a form of cryptoasset, will be considered 'money'.[7]

CRYPTOASSETS AS PROPERTY

2.7 The UK's legal approach is that cryptoassets are a form of property rather than a 'currency' or 'commodity'. With the advent of the internet and the digital age, the question arises: can data, especially digital data like cryptoassets, be considered something that can be owned? While traditional banking involves a legal relationship between the depositor and the bank, cryptoassets operate differently, lacking a creditor-debtor arrangement. While banks have moved away from cash towards electronic bank-created scriptural money, statistically representing the majority of all transactions, they are a series creditor-debtor book transfers.[8]

4 *In the Matter of: Coinflip, Inc., d/b/a Derivabit, and Francisco Riordan,* CFTC Docket No 15-29 2015 WL 5535736 (17 September 2015).
5 *Ibid*, Legal Discussion [A].
6 See **13.1–13.4**.
7 See **18.22–18.31**.
8 Michael McLeay, Amar Radia and Ryland Thomas, '*Quarterly Bulletin Q1: Money Creation in the Modern Economy*' (2014) BoE www.bankofengland.co.uk/quarterly-bulletin/2014/q1/money-creation-in-the-modern-economy [accessed 11 August 2023].

2.8 A cryptoasset fraction is data saved on a computer, held by the beneficiary or a third-party service provider: there is no creditor and no debtor. It is submitted that the cryptocurrency design reflects more the common person's understanding of what money is: an object of value without a creditor-debtor relationship. This, however, causes major issues for legal categorisation.

2.9 There is no consensus on the issue of whether digital data or goods (by essence intangible) are things subject to common law ownership rights, or whether other legal regimes apply, such as intellectual property law. Pure information is not property, although there may be rights associated with information that are proprietary.[9] Whether the UK courts treat a novel cryptoasset as property ultimately depends on the nature of the asset and the rules of the ecosystem in which it exists. Cryptoassets are usually more than just information. However, private keys are pure information and would not, therefore, be property for English law purposes.

2.10 There has been an ongoing debate in the UK as to cryptoasset categorisation which has been resolved in favour of classification as property. Currently English law only recognises two forms of property: (i) choses in possession, and (ii) choses in action.[10] Since cryptoassets are intangible and not tangible objects, they cannot be classified as things in possession. The criminal law, however, is wider and the Theft Act 1968 defines 'property' in relation to 'theft' as 'including things in action and other intangible property'.[11] The classification of cryptoassets as things in action is more complex, as it typically refers to enforceable rights such as debts or contractual rights. However, participants in DLT networks usually do not assume legal obligations toward each other.

2.11 The UK Jurisdiction Taskforce (UKJT) set up by LawTech UK, a government-backed initiative to examine legal technology issues, published its influential 'Legal statement on cryptoassets and smart contract' in November 2019.[12] UKJT concluded that cryptoassets possess all the legal attributes of property and should generally be treated as such under English law. Rather than providing a legal definition of cryptoassets, the UKJT focused on identifying their principal unique features, which include:[13]

9 See, eg *Your Response Ltd v Datateam Business Media Ltd* [2014] EWCA Civ 281.

10 UKJT, 'Legal statement on cryptoassets and smart contracts' (November 2019), The LawTech Delivery Panel, [66]–[84] www.blockchain4europe.eu/wp-content/uploads/2021/05/6.6056_JO_Cryptocurrencies_Statement_FINAL_WEB_111119-1.pdf [accessed 26 September 2023]. See also *Colonial Bank v Witney* (1885) LR 30 Ch 261, 285–86 (Fry LJ, adopted (1886) LR 11 App Cas 426 (HL). For a discussion of this, see, for example, Professor Michael Bridge, Professor Louise Gullifer, Professor Gerard McMeel, Professor Kelvin F K Low, *The Law of Personal Property* (2nd edn, Sweet and Maxwell, 2017), Chapter 4: Debts and Things in Action.

11 Theft Act 1968, s 4. Similar definition applies in relation to identifying a gain or loss under the Fraud Act 2006, s 5.

12 UKJT, Legal statement on cryptoassets (n 10 above).

13 *Ibid* [31].

(a) intangibility;

(b) cryptographic authentication;

(c) use of distributed transaction ledger;

(d) decentralisation; and

(e) rule by consensus.

2.12 Of these features, the analysis hinges on the fact that a cryptoasset typically consists of a pair of data parameters: a public parameter accessible to all participants, containing information like asset ownership, value, and transaction history, and a private parameter (private key).[14] The private key enables cryptographic authentication of transfers or other dealings in the cryptoasset. Ultimately, control and ownership of the asset lie with the individual who possesses the private key.[15]

2.13 The UKJT identified several key features of property that apply to cryptoassets:

(a) They are definable and certain because the public parameter sufficiently defines the asset.[16]

(b) They are controlled exclusively by the holder of the private key.[17]

(c) They can be owned and potentially transferred or assigned, albeit in unconventional ways.[18]

(d) They exhibit a level of permanence or stability similar to other financial assets until they are cancelled, redeemed, repaid, or exercised.[19]

(e) The UKJT clarified that although cryptoassets involve information, their commercial value does not lie solely in the data itself. The data enables transaction authentication.[20]

2.14 The UKJT found precedents in statutes and case law where unique forms of intangible assets were treated as property. For instance, the Patents Act 1977 deems a patent or patent application as personal property (without being a thing in action). In *Armstrong DLW GmbH v Winnington Networks Ltd*,[21] the court recognised an EU carbon emissions allowance as a type of 'other intangible property' in a tracing action, despite not fitting the criteria of things in possession

14 *Ibid* [28].
15 *Ibid* [43].
16 *Ibid* [49].
17 *Ibid* [50].
18 *Ibid* [51].
19 *Ibid* [52].
20 *Ibid* [59]–[65].
21 [2012] EWHC 10 (Ch).

or things in action. This has subsequently been recognised by the English High Court in *AA v Persons Unknown*.[22]

2.15 Considering such examples, the UKJT concluded that a cryptoasset may not fit the narrow definition of a thing in action, but it can still be treated as property,[23] and typically have the indicia of property.[24] Looking at cryptoassets generally, the UKJT statement considers that they are however capable of being intangible property (choses in action).[25] It was recognised that this conclusion was likely to have important consequences in areas relating to: [26]

(a) succession on death;

(b) vesting of property in personal bankruptcy;

(c) rights of liquidators in corporate insolvency;

(d) fraud;

(e) theft; or

(f) breach of trust.

2.16 Other implications of UKJT's conclusions are that cryptoassets:

(a) do not constitute 'goods' for the purposes of the Sale of Goods Act 1979, which operates on the assumption that 'goods' are capable of being possessed;[27]

(b) cannot be the object of a bailment because, by nature, bailment requires the transfer of possession;[28]

(c) are limited in terms of what types of security can be granted over them. Pledges and liens can only be created if it is possible to transfer possession of the asset, meaning that cryptoassets cannot be the object of a pledge or lien;[29] and

(d) do not meet the definition of 'instruments' under the Bills of Exchange Act 1882 (as physical possession is required), and are not considered documents of title or negotiable instruments.[30]

Ultimately, the UKJT recommends that it would be preferable for cryptoassets to be classed as a third kind of property, and that this would be something for Parliament to legislate.[31]

22 [2019] EWHC 3556 (Comm)
23 UKJT, 'Legal statement on cryptoassets' (n 10 above) [84].
24 *Ibid* [15].
25 *Ibid* [58].
26 *Ibid* [16].
27 *Ibid* [130].
28 *Ibid* [17].
29 *Ibid* [102].
30 *Ibid* [17].
31 *Ibid* [86].

2.17 On 27 June 2023, the Law Commission issued its final report on digital assets, recommending law reform for digital assets so that they become a separate third category of personal property.[32] They indicated that it is not necessary, conceptually coherent or helpful for cryptoassets to be categorised as choses in action.[33] The Law Commission recommended confirmatory legislation to indicate a third category of property exists.[34] They indicate the common law position and that it is not necessary or appropriate to define in statute the hard boundaries of this third category of things. They concluded the common law is the better vehicle for determining those things that properly can (and should) be objects of the third category of personal property rights.[35]

2.18 The Law Commission's previous consultation paper suggested that a digital asset should only qualify as a 'data object' if it met all of the following criteria:[36]

(a) it is composed of data represented in an electronic medium, including in the form of computer code, electronic, digital or analogue signals;

(b) it exists independently of persons and the legal system; and

(c) it is 'rivalrous' (its consumption by one consumer prevents simultaneous consumption by other consumers).

2.19 The final report concludes that these criteria are best used as indicia to guide the incremental population of the third category of thing to which personal property rights can relate, rather than as hard exclusionary boundaries that, over time, are likely to become less effective.[37]

2.20 The final report discusses various issues around cryptoassets, including control, transfers, intermediate holding arrangements, collateral arrangements, causes of action and associated remedies. They recommend the Financial Collateral Arrangements (No 2) Regulations 2003 (FCARs) be amended to clarify the extent to which cryptoassets meet the statutory definition of cash, to confirm that a financial instrument or credit claim will be unaffected by being recorded or registered by DLT, and confirm that a financial instrument or credit claim stapled or linked to a crypto-token satisfies the FCARs definition.[38] They also recommend that laws relating to UK companies should be reviewed and potentially amended to allow the use of crypto token networks for the issuance and transfer of equity and registered corporate securities.[39]

32 Law Commission, 'Digital Assets: Final report' (Law Com No 412, 2023).
33 *Ibid* [2.49].
34 *Ibid* [2.53].
35 *Ibid* [2.46].
36 *Ibid* [4.5].
37 *Ibid* [4.71].
38 *Ibid* [10.4].
39 *Ibid* [10.5].

2.21 It should be noted that, as a new species of property, cryptoassets are entitled to a degree of recognition and protection under international law as they are a means of exchange and therefore must be treated as a form of property or possession. They therefore are protected under Art 1 of the First Protocol of the European Convention on Human Rights and the Human Rights Act 1998. Limitation or restriction of the use of cryptoassets, would have to be proportionate to desired objectives, such as, financial stability, anti-money laundering, and payment of taxes.[40]

JUDICIAL TREATMENT OF CRYPTOCURRENCY

2.22 The question of whether cryptocurrency was a chose in action (and, therefore, property) was considered by the High Court in *AA v Persons Unknown*.[41]

2.23 The court considered whether Bitcoin was property and could, therefore, be the subject of a proprietary injunction. Bryan J held that although cryptocurrencies did not fall within either of these two categories, as they are virtual, intangible and cannot be possessed, and do not embody any right capable of being enforced by action, they nevertheless constituted a form of property (and were thus capable of being the subject of a proprietary injunction).[42] Referring to the reasoning set out in the UKJT statement, Bryan J adopted the analysis in the UKJT statement, and concluded that cryptoassets like Bitcoin are property.[43] Bryan J went on to say that cryptocurrencies meet the four criteria set out in Lord Wilberforce's definition of property in *National Provincial Bank v Ainsworth*[44] as being definable, identifiable by third parties, capable in their nature of assumption by third parties, and having some degree of permanence.

2.24 In *Reyes v Persons Unknown* [45]and *Fetch.ai Ltd and another v Persons Unknown*,[46] HHJ Pelling KC also held that cryptocurrencies constituted property, but did so on the basis that they did fall within the category of choses in action. In the later cases of *Danisz v Persons Unknown*[47] and *Jones v Persons Unknown*,[48] both of which do not refer to the decisions in either *Reyes* or *Fetch.ai*, the respective judges agreed with and followed Bryan J's judgment in *AA*.[49]

40 Fox and Green (n 1 above), [3.21]–[3.22].
41 See n 22 above.
42 *Ibid* [55], [59], and [61].
43 *Ibid* [57]–[59].
44 [1965] AC 1175.
45 [2021] EWHC 1938 (Comm) [12].
46 [2021] EWHC 2254 (Comm) [9].
47 [2022] EWHC 280 (QB).
48 [2022] EWHC 2543 (Comm).
49 See also *Vorotyntseva v Money-4 Ltd, trading as Nebeus.com* [2018] EWHC 2596 (Ch) and *Liam David Robertson v Persons Unknown* (unreported), 15 July 2019 (Commercial Court).

2.25 In the recent judgment in *Tulip Trading Ltd v Van der Laan,*[50] the Court of Appeal did not engage with the property debate in any detail, as the point was not in dispute. However, Birss LJ, who gave the leading judgment, did confirm that a cryptoasset was property, referring with apparent approval to the relevant passage in Bryan J's judgment in *AA*. In light of the Law Commission's final report, it is likely that the judicial treatment of cryptoassets will be altered in due course to recognise them as a third form of property.

2.26 Reasoned decisions of the courts of Singapore[51] and New Zealand provide additional support for the notion that cryptoassets qualify as property for the purposes of English law. The most extensive treatment of the subject is to be found in *Ruscoe v Cryptopia Ltd (in Liquidation)*,[52] a decision of the High Court of New Zealand. In that case, Gendall J cited relevant English cases[53] and the UK Jurisdiction Taskforce's Legal Statement on Cryptoassets and Smart Contracts[54] with approval, applied the *Ainsworth* test,[55] and held that cryptoassets were property for the purposes of s 2 of New Zealand's Companies Act 1993 (the relevant statutory provision in terms of the pool of assets available for distribution on liquidation).

SITUS OF CRYPTOASSETS

2.27 As mentioned above, cryptoassets are often held on decentralised ledger, where such register exists simultaneously in several locations, often without any single identifiable location. In such circumstances, cryptoassets can thus be effectively everywhere and nowhere at the same time.

2.28 In *Ion Science v Persons Unknown*,[56] Butcher J stated that the lex situs of a cryptoasset is the place where the person or company who owns it is domiciled. HHJ Pelling KC followed this approach in *Fetch.ai*.[57] This approach thus differs from that applicable to 'ordinary' money held in a bank account, which is a debt owed by the bank to the customer, where the debt is considered to be situated in the county where the debtor, ie the bank or branch where the account is kept, resides.[58] In those debt cases, the focus is thus on the debtor, and not on the owner or creditor.

50 [2023] EWCA Civ 83, [2023] 4 WLR 16.
51 *Quoine Pte Ltd v B2C2 Ltd* [2020] SGCA(I) 02.
52 [2020] NZHC 728.
53 *AA v Persons Unknown* (n 22) at [55]–[61] and *Ion Science Limited & another v Persons Unknown* (21 December 2020, Butcher J).
54 UKJT, 'Legal Statement on Cryptoassets' (n 10 above).
55 *National Provincial Bank Ltd v Ainsworth* [1965] AC 1175 (HL) at 1247–1248.
56 (Unreported) (21 December 2020) (para 13).
57 *Fetch Ai v Persons Unknown* (n 46 above).
58 *Dicey, Morris & Collins on the Conflict of Laws* (16th edn, Sweet and Maxwell, London 2022), [23-026]–[23-029].

2.29 In the recent case of *Tulip Trading Ltd v Bitcoin Association for BSV*,[59] the court's response to ambitious legal arguments revealed a shift in perspective on the legal situs of cryptoassets. In this regard, the court favoured residency over domicile as the determining factor.

2.30 Once the lex situs of a cryptocurrency is established as the place where the person or company who owns it is resident, the English courts can determine that English law applies pursuant to Article 4.1 of Rome II,[60] where it is the law of the country in which the damage occurred, and that they have jurisdiction over cryptocurrency-related fraud claims, where the owner and thus the property in question was is resident in England and the damage was suffered within the jurisdiction.[61]

2.31 In response to the Cryptoassets Manual, the Society of Trust and Estates Practitioners (STEP) issued a Guidance Note: 'Location of Cryptocurrencies – an alternative view' that proposes an alternative stance on the situs (location) of exchange tokens. STEP suggests that the situs of exchange tokens should be determined by where they can be effectively managed.[62] Their argument revolves around the central role of the private key in controlling exchange tokens. STEP asserts that the location of exchange tokens should be linked to either (i) the location of the private key, or (ii) the person who holds control over the private key, even if not the beneficial owner.[63]

2.32 In *The Taxation of Non-Residents and Foreign Domiciliaries*, James Kessler KC argues that the private key is essentially computer code, devoid of a physical location.[64] He emphasises that while the private key might be stored in a physical hardware device, this device is merely recording the private key rather than housing the key itself. According to Kessler, the rights associated with the hard drive are separate from those tied to the private key.

2.33 Kessler points out that there are scenarios where cryptoassets can only be accessed through a cold wallet, and some argue that the location of the cold wallet should determine the asset's location. However, Kessler opines that English courts are unlikely to favour this perspective due to the potential it offers non-domiciled individuals to choose the location of their cryptoassets.[65]

59 [2022] EWHC 667 (Ch).

60 Council Regulation (EC) No 864/2007 of 11 July 2007 on the law applicable to non-contractual obligations (Rome II) [2007] OJ L199/40.

61 For further discussion, see **9.2–9.18**.

62 (3 September 2021) STEP www.step.org/system/files/media/files/2021-09/step_note_location_of_cryptocurrencies-an_alternative_view_0.pdf?LinkSource=PassleApp [accessed 8 October 2023].

63 *Ibid* 3. STEP cites UKJT's 'Legal Statement on Cryptoassets' (n 10 above), [99(c)] which suggests that the location of a cryptoasset's control (eg private key storage) should be a relevant factor in determining the applicable law for cryptoasset dealings.

64 James Kessler KC, *The Taxation of Non-Residents and Foreign Domiciliaries* (21st edn, Key Haven Publications PLC, 2022), Ch 93 [A.6.4].

65 *Ibid* Ch 93 [A.6.4].

2.34 It is important to note that STEP's view on situs does not account for the use of multi-signature (MultiSig) wallets. MultiSig wallets require multiple private keys to authorise a crypto transaction making it difficult to determine where multiple keys are held by various participants in different locations.[66]

GOVERNMENT AND REGULATORY TREATMENT OF CRYPTOCURRENCY

2.35 The UK Government and regulators have recognised cryptocurrencies as cryptoassets and have taken steps to regulate them. As mentioned earlier, FSMA 2023, s 69(4) introduced a definition of cryptoasset as:

> 'any cryptographically secured digital representation of value or contractual rights that can be transferred, stored or traded electronically, and that uses technology supporting the recording or storage of data (which may include distributed ledger technology).'

2.36 In January 2020, the FCA became the anti-money laundering (AML) and counter-terrorist financing (CTF) supervisor for UK cryptoasset businesses under the Money Laundering, Terrorist Financing and Transfer of Funds (Information on the Payer) Regulations 2017 as amended by the Money Laundering and Terrorist Financing (Amendment) Regulations 2019 (MLRs).[67]

2.37 The FCA define cryptoassets similarly to FSMA 2023 as:

> 'cryptographically secured digital representations of value or contractual rights that use some type of distributed ledger technology (DLT) and can be transferred, stored or traded electronically'.[68]

2.38 The legal treatment of cryptocurrencies in the UK depends on their classification and the circumstances in which they are used or traded. The FCA has introduced a regulatory framework for cryptoassets, which classifies cryptoassets into regulated and unrelated tokens. Regulated tokens include security tokens and e-money tokens. Unregulated tokens are tokens that do not meet the security token or e-money token criteria such as utility tokens and exchange tokens (ie Bitcoin, Litecoin and equivalents). Security tokens are tokens that have features that mean they meet the definition of a specified investment, such as shares or debt instruments. Utility tokens are tokens that provide access to a specific product or service.[69] It is important to note that cryptoasset activities are now closely regulated by the FCA. This will be discussed further in the next chapter.

66 Ethan (Ho-Ning) Yu, 'Locating the Ethereal: the situs of cryptoassets reexamined' (2022) 6 PCB, 220–226, 225.

67 Department of Treasury and Home Office, *Economic Crime Plan, 2019 to 2022* (updated 4 May 2021) [1.40] Action 37 www.gov.uk/government/publications/economic-crime-plan-2019-to-2022/economic-crime-plan-2019-to-2022-accessible-version [accessed 25 September 2023].

68 FCA, 'Crypto assets: our work' (23 February 2023) www.fca.org.uk/firms/cryptoassets [accessed 25 September 2023].

69 *Ibid.*

Part II

Regulatory Framework

Chapter 3

Overview of UK Regulatory Framework for Cryptocurrency

3.1 Cryptocurrency has gained significant attention in recent years as the popularity and adoption of cryptocurrencies, such as Bitcoin, Ethereum, and Tether, continue to rise. With the advent of DeFi, governments around the world are grappling with the need to develop regulatory frameworks to address various concerns, including consumer protection, money laundering, and financial stability.

FINANCIAL CONDUCT AUTHORITY

Overview

3.2 The Financial Conduct Authority (FCA) is an independent regulatory authority that operates under the purview of the UK government's Treasury. Its main objectives include ensuring the integrity of the financial markets, promoting competition, and protecting consumers' interests. To achieve these goals, the FCA supervises and regulates various financial activities, including cryptocurrencies. The FCA is governed by the Financial Services and Markets Act 2000 (FSMA 2000) and Financial Services and Markets Act 2023 (FSMA 2023) (collectively, FSMA).

3.3 The FCA is the primary regulatory body overseeing the cryptoassets industry in the UK. Its mandate is to ensure market confidence, financial stability, public awareness, protection of consumers, reduction of financial crime and enhancing public understanding of financial matters.[1] The FCA has taken a proactive approach to cryptocurrency regulation and has implemented a registration regime for cryptoasset businesses.[2]

3.4 The FCA recognises the potential benefits and risks associated with this emerging asset class and seeks to strike a balance between fostering innovation and safeguarding consumer protection.[3] The FCA considers itself a technology-neutral regulator. Rather than introducing new legislation specifically for

1 FSMA 2000, ss 3–6A.

2 FCA, 'Cryptoassets: AML/CTF regime – Registering with the FCA' (22 March 2023, updated 18 August 2023) www.fca.org.uk/firms/cryptoassets-aml-ctf-regime/registering [accessed 26 September 2023].

3 FCA, 'Guidance on Cryptoassets' (CP19/3, January 2019), [5.4] www.fca.org.uk/publication/consultation/cp19-03.pdf [accessed 21 August 2023].

cryptoassets, the FCA applies existing regulations to crypto-related activities. This means that it does not regulate specific types of technology, but rather the activities and products that these technologies facilitate and the firms that carry out the activities.[4]

3.5 In theory, this approach allows the FCA to develop a principle-based system of regulation that can withstand the challenges of constantly evolving technological innovation. However, it also means that there is often scope for legitimate disagreement as to whether a particular product falls inside or outside the FCA's regulatory perimeter.[5]

3.6 The FCA has taken a cautiously welcoming stance to cryptoassets to date. It has adopted a consultative and collaborative approach to the development of its approach and has worked closely with market participants and other stakeholders to develop guidance as to whether certain cryptoassets fall within or outside the FCA's regulatory perimeter. The FCA as part of the UK Cryptoassets Taskforce (CATF) has identified three types of token: exchange tokens, security tokens, and utility tokens. The FCA subsequently identified a fourth type of token, electronic money tokens (e-money tokens) that meet the definition of e-money under the EMRs.[6] The FCA has subsequently decided to reframe the taxonomy of tokens as:[7]

(a) **Regulated:**

   (i) **Security tokens** – tokens that provide rights and obligations akin to specified investments as set out in The Financial Services and Markets Act 2000 (Regulated Activities) Order 2001,[8] excluding e-money. Examples of specified investments include debt instruments like debentures and shares in a company. Security tokens are within the regulatory perimeter.

   (ii) **E-money tokens** – tokens that reach the definition of e-money.[9] These tokens are subject to the EMRs and are regulated. This category formerly sat within the utility tokens category.

(b) **Unregulated tokens** – any token that does not meet the definition of e-money or provide the same rights as other specified investments under the RAO. This includes tokens referred to as utility tokens, and exchange tokens.

4 *Ibid* [1.5].

5 Mary Young and Jill Lorimer, 'Developments in the UK crypto-asset landscape' (2021) 2 IBLJ 241, 243.

6 FCA, 'Guidance on Cryptoassets' (n 3 above).

7 *Ibid* [2.25].

8 SI 2001/544 (RAO).

9 EMRs, reg 2(1) defines 'electronic money' as: 'electronically (including magnetically) stored monetary value as represented by a claim on the electronic money issuer which—(a) is issued on receipt of funds for the purpose of making payment transactions; (b) is accepted by a person other than the electronic money issuer; and (c) is not excluded by regulation 3'.

3.7 The FCA considers the security token and e-money tokens to be subject to regulation, potentially under secondary legislation, such as the MiFID II legislation for transferable securities and financial instruments[10] or the Payment Services Regulations 2017[11] (PSR 2017).[12]

3.8 Under FSMA 2023, cryptoassets are subject to the regulated activities and financial promotion orders. Section 69 of FSMA 2023 amends the definition of 'investment' to include, 'where an asset, right or interest is, or comprises or represents, a cryptoasset,' in ss 21 (Restrictions on Financial Promotions) and 22 (Regulated Activities) of FSMA 2000. This is discussed further below.

3.9 As mentioned previously, 'cryptoasset' is defined under s 69(4) of FSMA 2023 as follows:

> '"Cryptoasset" means any cryptographically secured digital representation of value or contractual rights that—
>
> (a) can be transferred, stored or traded electronically, and
>
> (b) uses technology supporting the recording or storage of data (which may include distributed ledger technology).'

3.10 This definition has a broad application due to the description of the underlying technology and is similar to that used in the EU's Markets in Crypto-Assets Regulation (MiCA)[13] in line with the Financial Action Task Force's (FATF) recommended definition of 'virtual asset.'[14] In recognition of the changing technological landscape, the definition is accompanied by a power to update the definition through secondary legislation if and when required.

3.11 Firms marketing regulated activities to UK consumers are required to have a UK establishment and be authorised in the UK. Unauthorised firms intending to undertake cryptoasset activities constituting a regulated activity must first apply for permission from the FCA, and authorised firms will need to apply to vary their permission accordingly.

10 Council Directive 2014/65/EU of 15 May 2014 on markets in financial instruments and amending Directive 2002/92/EC and Directive 2011/61/EU (recast) [2014] OJ L173/349; The definition of 'transferable security' is defined at MIFID II, Art 4(1)(44) and 'financial instrument' is defined at MIFID II, Annex 1, Sch C.

11 SI 2017/752.

12 For guidance in relation to the FCA's role under EMRs and PSR 2017, see FCA, 'Payment Services and Electronic Money – Our Approach, The FCA's role under the Payment Services Regulations 2017 and the Electronic Money Regulations 2011' (Version 5, November 2021 www.fca.org.uk/publication/finalised-guidance/fca-approach-payment-services-electronic-money-2017.pdf [accessed 4 October 2023].

13 Council Regulation (EU) 2023/1114 of 31 May 2023 on markets in crypto-assets, and amending Regulations (EU) No 1093/2010 and (EU) No 1095/2010 and Directives 2013/36/EU and (EU) 2019/1937 [2023] OJ L150/40.

14 FATF, 'International Standards on Combating Money Laundering and the Financing of Terrorism & Proliferation' (Paris France 2012–2023), 135 www.fatf-gafi.org/content/dam/fatf-gafi/recommendations/FATF%20Recommendations%202012.pdf.coredownload.inline.pdf [accessed 26 September 2023].

3.12 Regulated firms involved in cryptoasset-related activities must comply with regulatory provisions in the FCA's Handbook, such as the Principles for Business, Senior Managers and Certification Regime, Systems and Controls Provisions, and Financial Promotions rules, which can also apply to unregulated activities in specific cases:[15]

(a) The Principles for Business consist of 12 high-level rules applicable to all FCA-regulated firms. Three of these principles – related to financial resources (Principle 4), systems and controls (Principle 3), and cooperation with the FCA – may extend to unregulated activities carried out by regulated firms.[16]

(b) The Senior Managers and Certification Regime enables the FCA to hold senior management accountable for unregulated activities. The FCA expects these principles to apply to unregulated cryptoasset-related business conducted by regulated firms.[17]

(c) The Systems and Controls Provisions encompass organisational requirements, risk control, record keeping, and employee obligations.[18] The FCA has previously taken action against regulated firms for breaches in systems and controls while carrying out unregulated activities.[19]

(d) Financial Promotions rules placed on regulated firms state that financial promotions must: be fair, clear, and not misleading; give a balanced impression of the product or service; and not disguise and diminish important warning statements.[20]

Regulated activities

3.13 The RAO specifies regulated activities and investments under FSMA. Regulated activities are specified activities related to specific investments carried on as a business in the UK. The RAO is periodically updated to reflect changes in financial services regulation, introducing new specified activities and investments. Additionally, FSMA designates certain RAO activities as Prudential

15 HM Treasury, FCA and BoE, 'Cryptoassets Taskforce: final report' (October 2018), [2.29]–[2.30] https://assets.publishing.service.gov.uk/media/5bd6d6f0e5274a6e11247059/cryptoassets_taskforce_final_report_final_web.pdf [accessed 26 September 2023].

16 FCA, *FCA Handbook* (31 July 2023), PRIN 2.1 www.handbook.fca.org.uk/handbook/PRIN/2/?view=chapter [accessed 8 October 2023].

17 FCA. *FCA Handbook* (Release 31, October 2023), SYSC 23–27 www.handbook.fca.org.uk/handbook/SYSC.pdf [accessed 26 September 2023].

18 *Ibid*. The FCA's systems and controls provisions are primarily in the Senior Management Arrangements, Systems and Controls (SYSC) section of the FCA Handbook.

19 FCA, 'FCA fines five banks £1.1 billion for FX failings and announces industry-wide remediation programme' (12 November 2014, updated 4 November 2019) www.fca.org.uk/news/press-releases/fca-fines-five-banks-%C2%A311-billion-fx-failings-and-announces-industry-wide [accessed 26 September 2023].

20 FCA, *FCA Handbook*, PERG 8 www.handbook.fca.org.uk/handbook/PERG/8/?view=chapter [accessed 26 September 2023].

Regulation Authority (PRA) regulated activities, subjecting firms to regulation by both the FCA and the PRA.

3.14 Specified activities under Part II of the RAO include various financial activities like accepting deposits, issuing electronic money, insurance-related activities, investment activities (such as dealing, advising, managing investments), mortgage-related activities, consumer credit regulated activities, and more.

3.15 Specified investments under Part III of the RAO encompass various financial instruments like deposits, shares, bonds, government securities, units in a collective investment scheme, options, futures, contracts for differences (CFDs), and more.

3.16 Certain exemptions are available for regulated activities, which means that a person falling within the scope of an exemption is not required to obtain authorisation under FSMA. It is essential to differentiate between an exemption and an exclusion – an exclusion removes an activity from being regulated, while an exemption simply exempts it from regulation. These activities that would normally be regulated are unregulated, such as certain overseas activities and those where potential customers are introduced to firms. There are two types of exclusions in the RAO:[21]

(a) exclusions specific to particular regulated activities, listed after each activity in the RAO; and

(b) general exclusions applicable to several regulated activities under certain circumstances.

Designated activities regime

3.17 A new designated activities regime (DAR) has been introduced under s 8 of FSMA 2023. Activities falling within DAR will be subject to requirements set out in the FCA Rulebook or by HM Treasury in secondary legislation. However, such activities will not require prior authorisation as for regulated activities.

3.18 As shown by the examples of activities listed in Sch 3 to FSMA 2023, DAR has initially been used to capture activities regulated under retained EU laws. HM Treasury also issued guidance in February 2023 on proposed activity categories to be regulated, including:[22]

(a) issuance activities;

21 FCA, *FCA Handbook,* PERG 2.8-2.9 www.handbook.fca.org.uk/handbook/PERG/2/?view=chapter [accessed 26 September 2023].

22 HM Treasury, 'Consultation and call for Evidence: Future financial services regulatory regime for cryptoassets' (February 2023), [4.8] Table 4.A https://assets.publishing.service.gov.uk/government/uploads/system/uploads/attachment_data/file/1133404/TR_Privacy_edits_Future_financial_services_regulatory_regime_for_cryptoassets_vP.pdf [accessed 26 September 2023].

(b) payment activities;

(c) exchange activities;

(d) investment and risk management activities;

(e) lending, borrowing and leverage activities;

(f) safeguarding and/or administration (including custody) activities; and

(g) validation and governance (including mining) activities.

3.19 Firms engaged in cryptoasset activities should monitor the activities designated by HM Treasury to understand whether their activities will fall under DAR and what regulations will apply. Entities combining designated and/or regulated activities will need to comply with all relevant rules. Cryptoasset businesses registered with the FCA pursuant to the MLRs will need to re-register under the new regime.[23]

Payment stablecoins

3.20 New provisions under FSMA 2023 also specifically address payment stablecoins through the introduction of digital settlement assets (DSA). Section 23(2) of FSMA 2023 defines a DSA as a digital representation of value or rights, whether or not cryptographically secured, which:

(a) can be used for settlement of payment obligations;

(b) can be transferred, stored or traded electronically; and

(c) uses technology supporting the recording or storage of data.

3.21 The explanatory notes to FSMA 2023 clarify that the definition is intended to encompass a range of digital assets.[24] HM Treasury also has the power to amend the definition to reflect changes to attributes, underlying technology, and/or the usage of DSAs.[25] The new regulations encompass stablecoins which reference fiat currencies and/or instruments with the same effect.[26]

3.22 FSMA 2023 empowers HM Treasury to regulate:[27]

(a) payments which include DSAs;

(b) payment systems using DSAs;

23 *Ibid* [3.9]. See also FCA, Registering with the FCA (n 2 above).

24 HM Treasury, *Explanatory Notes: Financial Services and Markets Act 2023 Chapter 29* (Stationary Office, August 2023), [215]–[229] www.legislation.gov.uk/ukpga/2023/29/pdfs/ukpgaen_20230029_en.pdf [accessed 8 October 2023].

25 FSMA 2023, s 23(5).

26 HM Treasury, Explanatory Notes (n 24 above), [215]–[221].

27 FSMA 2023, s 23(1).

(c) recognised DSA service providers;

(d) service providers connected with or related to the aforementioned systems and providers; and

(e) restructuring, administration and insolvency arrangements in respect of the above systems and providers.

3.23 Such regulations may include:[28]

(a) extending the regulation of electronic money and payments to DSAs;

(b) extending legislation in relation to insolvency arrangements to DSA systems and providers;

(c) conferring powers in the Treasury (including the power to legislate);

(d) conferring powers, or imposing duties, on a relevant regulator;

(e) recognition orders and recognition criteria under Pt 5 of the Banking Act 2009;

(f) enforcement of obligations pursuant to the regulations;

(g) appeals of decisions made pursuant to the regulations; or

(h) sharing of information.

3.24 Before making such regulations, HM Treasury must consult the FCA, the BoE, and in relation to regulations that refer to the PRA or to the Payment Systems Regulator, those bodies.[29]

3.25 FSMA gives the HM Treasury powers to amend insolvency and administration procedures as they apply to the operators of recognised payment systems and recognised service providers that use digital settlement (under Pt 5 of the Banking Act 2009) allowing HM Treasury to amend existing special administration regimes (SARs) by way of secondary legislation, to apply to such firms, to prepare for their possible failure. SARs provide for bespoke insolvency provision where the general administration process is not considered to be in the public interest. The financial market infrastructure (FMI) SAR[30] imposes an objective on administrators to ensure that a failed payment system in scope of the regime continues to be maintained and operated as an efficient and effective system, effectively prioritising its operation ahead of the interests of creditors. The Treasury intends to develop and bring forward a statutory instrument to amend the FMI SAR to ensure it can effectively be applied to digital settlement.[31]

28 FSMA 2023, s 23(3).
29 FSMA 2023, s 23(8).
30 Provided for in Pt 6 of Financial Services (Banking Reform) Act 2013.
31 HM Treasury, Explanatory Notes (n 24 above), [698].

ANTI-MONEY LAUNDERING AND COUNTER-TERRORIST FINANCING

3.26 The UK's AML framework is primarily governed by the Money Laundering, Terrorist Financing, and Transfer of Funds (Information on the Payer) Regulations 2017 (MLR 2017), as amended in recent years by the Money Laundering and Terrorist Financing (Amendment) Regulations 2019, the Money Laundering and Terrorist Financing (Amendment) (EU Exit) Regulations 2020, the Money Laundering and Terrorist Financing (Amendment) Regulations 2022, and the Money Laundering and Terrorist Financing (Amendment) (No 2) Regulations 2022 (collectively, MLR).

3.27 The MLR includes provisions that explicitly apply to cryptocurrency-related businesses and activities. Cryptocurrency exchanges, custodian wallet providers, and other relevant entities are classified as 'cryptoasset businesses'[32] and are subject to AML obligations. 'Cryptoasset' is defined as 'a cryptographically secured digital representation of value or contractual rights that uses a form of distributed ledger technology and can be transferred, stored or traded electronically'.[33]

3.28 The supplementary legislation to MLR 2017 has implemented the Fifth EU Money Laundering Directive[34] (5EUMLD),[35] implemented further changes regarding customer due diligence, beneficial ownership and trusts,[36] and extended the 'Travel Rule' to cryptoasset transfers.[37]

3.29 Under MLR, cryptoasset businesses must register with the FCA to operate legally in the UK. Registration involves undergoing stringent due diligence checks and demonstrating compliance with AML and CTF measures.

32 MLR 2017, Pt 7A inserted by The Money Laundering and Terrorist Financing (Amendment) (No 2) Regulations 2022, reg 5(5).

33 MLR 2017, reg 14A(3)(a) inserted by The Money Laundering and Terrorist Financing (Amendment) Regulations 2019, reg 4(7).

34 Directive (EU) 2018/843 of 30 May 2018 amending Directive (EU) 2015/849 on the prevention of the use of the financial system for the purposes of money laundering or terrorist financing and amending Directives 2009/138/EC and 2013/36/EU [2018] OJ L156/43.

35 5EUMLD implemented by Money Laundering and Terrorist Financing (Amendment) Regulations 2019.

36 The Money Laundering and Terrorist Financing (Amendment) (EU Exit) Regulations 2020.

37 The Money Laundering and Terrorist Financing (Amendment) (No 2) Regulations 2022, reg 5(5), inserted a new Pt 7A which implements Recommendation 16 of FATF, International Standards on Combating Money Laundering (n 13 above). The Travel Rule is a requirement for financial institutions to share identifying information about the sender and recipient (payer and payee) of a wire transfer, in the payment message. From 1 September 2023 cryptoasset businesses will have to comply with the rule. See FCA, 'FCA sets out expectations for UK cryptoasset businesses complying with the Travel Rule' (17 August 2023) www.fca.org.uk/news/statements/fca-sets-out-expectations-uk-cryptoasset-businesses-complying-travel-rule [accessed 26 September 2023].

Failure to register or comply with regulatory requirements can result in significant penalties or criminal prosecution.[38]

3.30 The MLR back up the criminal money laundering and terrorist financing provisions in the Proceeds of Crime Act 2002 (POCA), Pt 7 and the Terrorism Act 2000 (TACT), Pt 3 respectively. Core money laundering offences are contained at ss 327 and 328 of POCA.

3.31 Broadly the obligations for UK cryptoasset businesses under MLR are as follows:[39]

(a) If they intend to provide in-regulated services while acting in the course of business, they must be registered with the FCA before they begin.

(b) They must take appropriate steps to identify and assess the risks of money laundering, proliferation financing and terrorist financing which the business is subject to.

(c) They must assess the money laundering, terrorist financing and proliferation financing risks related to any new technologies prior to launch and take appropriate measures to manage and mitigate those risks.

(d) They must have in place policies, systems and controls appropriate to mitigate the risk of the business being used for the purposes of money laundering, terrorist financing and proliferation financing. This risk-based approach should seek to mitigate the risks identified in the business's risk assessment.

(e) Where appropriate, for the size and nature of its business, they must appoint an individual who is a member of the board or senior management to be responsible for compliance with the MLRs and the nominated officer. The nominated officer is also the person responsible for reporting suspicious activity to the National Crime Agency (NCA) under Pt 7 of POCA.

(f) Where appropriate, for the size and nature of its business, they must establish an independent internal audit function with responsibility for examining and evaluating the adequacy and effectiveness of the policies, controls and procedures, and making recommendations, as well as monitoring the controls.

(g) They must undertake screening of employees.

(h) They must undertake customer due diligence when entering into a business relationship or occasional transactions.

(i) They must apply enhanced due diligence, when dealing with customers who may present a higher money laundering, terrorist financing and proliferation

38 MLR 2017, reg 14A, inserted by The Money Laundering and Terrorist Financing (Amendment) Regulations 2019, reg 4(7).

39 FCA, 'Cryptoassets: AML / CTF regime' (22 October 2019, updated 22 March 2023) www.fca.org.uk/firms/financial-crime/cryptoassets-aml-ctf-regime [accessed 26 September 2023].

financing risk. This includes customers who meet the definition of a politically exposed person.

(j) They must undertake ongoing monitoring of all customers to ensure that transactions are consistent with the business' knowledge of its customer, the customer's business and risk profile.

(k) The UK AML regime adopts a risk-based approach, whereby businesses are expected to assess and mitigate the risks associated with their activities. This includes conducting risk assessments, implementing appropriate controls, and maintaining comprehensive AML policies and procedures specific to cryptocurrency-related risks.

(l) They must collect, verify and share information about cryptoasset transfers, known as the 'Travel Rule'.[40]

3.32 Overall, the AML/CTF regime represents a significant strengthening of measures to prevent illicit activities within the crypto industry in the UK. Cryptoasset businesses operating in this field should be aware of their obligations under these regulations and take appropriate actions to ensure compliance.

3.33 In relation to seeking authorisation from the FCA, the Upper Tribunal recently examined the FCA decision regarding the registration of a company as a cryptoasset exchange provider and custodian wallet provider under MLR 2017. In *Moneybrain Ltd v Financial Conduct Authority*,[41] a company applied for registration to perform activities related to the exchange of fiat currencies and cryptoassets in the UK. However, the FCA refused the application, stating that the owner was not a fit and proper person. The FCA cited misleading marketing and promotional material published on a website about its cryptocurrency called BiPS Tokens as the reason for the refusal. The tribunal upheld the FCA's refusal, dismissing the appeal. It was determined that the FCA has the authority to consider non-financial misconduct in assessing a person's fit and proper status. The misleading statements on the website were relevant because they were closely related to its business and potentially misleading to consumers. A similar decision was also made by the Upper Tribunal in *Vladimir Consulting Limited v The Financial Conduct Authority*.[42]

CONSUMER PROTECTION

3.34 The FCA places a strong emphasis on protecting consumers participating in the cryptocurrency market. It has issued warnings to investors about the risks

40 FCA, 'FCA sets out expectations for UK cryptoasset businesses complying with the Travel Rule' (17 August 2023, updated 1 September 2023) www.fca.org.uk/news/statements/fca-sets-out-expectations-uk-cryptoasset-businesses-complying-travel-rule [accessed 27 September 2023].

41 [2022] UKUT 257, [2022] UKUT 269, [2022] UKUT 308.

42 [2022] UKUT 168 (TCC), [2022] WLUK 478.

associated with cryptocurrencies,[43] including market volatility and the potential for fraud.[44] The FCA has also banned the sale of certain cryptocurrency derivatives to retail consumers due to their complex and high-risk nature.[45] FCA's financial promotions rules are imposed on regulated firms, however there are broader legal restrictions encompassing unregulated firms.[46]

3.35 Section 21 of FSMA 2023 sets out the restrictions on the making of 'financial promotions' (Financial Promotion Restrictions) stating that, in the course of business, it is a criminal offence to communicate an invitation or inducement to engage in investment activity unless the firm is authorised by the FCA (an authorised person), the promotion has been approved by the authorised person or falls under an exemption. The Financial Services and Markets Act 2000 (Financial Promotion) (Amendment) Order 2023,[47] brings cryptoassets within the scope of rules that regulate the marketing of financial products. The statutory instrument amends the Financial Services and Markets Act (Financial Promotion) Order 2005,[48] extending it to cryptoassets with effect from 8 October 2023. The FCA has announced that a short extension to 8 January 2024 may be granted.[49]

3.36 In line with cryptoassets being placed within the scope of Financial Promotion Restrictions, the FCA has announced new marketing rules which will require those marketing cryptoassets to UK consumers to introduce a cooling off period for first time investors. The new rules mean crypto firms must ensure that people have the appropriate knowledge and experience to invest in cryptoassets. Those promoting crypto will also be required to put in place clear risk warnings and ensure advertisements are clear, fair and not misleading. As part of a package of measures designed to ensure those who buy crypto understand the risk, 'refer a friend' bonuses will also be banned. Additionally, communicating an invitation or inducement to engage in investment activity in the UK, or in a way that may affect the UK, is prohibited unless the person making the promotion is authorised by the FCA or exempt.[50]

43 FCA, 'Investing in crypto' www.fca.org.uk/investsmart/investing-crypto [accessed 27 September 2023].

44 FCA, 'Crypto: The basics' www.fca.org.uk/investsmart/crypto-basics [accessed 27 September 2023].

45 FCA, 'FCA bans the sale of crypto-derivatives to retail consumers' (6 October 2020) www.fca.org.uk/news/press-releases/fca-bans-sale-crypto-derivatives-retail-consumers [accessed 27 September 2023].

46 FCA, 'FCA Approving financial promotions' (16 November 2019, last updated 15 March 2023) www.fca.org.uk/firms/financial-promotions-and-adverts/approving-financial-promotions [accessed 27 September 2023]; FCA, *FCA Handbook,* COBS 4, COBS 5 and COBS 6 www.handbook.fca.org.uk/handbook/COBS/3/ [accessed 8 October 2023].

47 SI 2023/612.

48 SI 2005/1529 (FPO).

49 FCA, 'FCA sets expectations ahead of incoming crypto marketing rules' (7 September 2023) www.fca.org.uk/news/press-releases/fca-sets-expectations-ahead-incoming-crypto-marketing-rules [accessed 27 September 2023].

50 FCA, 'Financial promotion rules for cryptoassets' (PS23/6) www.fca.org.uk/publication/policy/ps23-6.pdf [accessed 27 September 2023].

3.37 FCA authorised firms are subject to the remit of the Financial Ombudsman Service (FOS) which deals with, inter alia, complaints by consumers, micro-enterprises, and small businesses.[51] While eligible complaints do not reference cryptoassets, a regulated firm's conduct may entitle a complainant to compensation.[52] FOS has in the past ordered regulated financial institutions to compensate customers for crypto-related fraud and scams where they have not intervened in relation to suspicious transactions.[53]

3.38 Before the FCA's remit was expanded to include financial promotions for crypto products and services, the Advertising Standards Authority (ASA) had banned several crypto firms' promotions for being misleading and irresponsible:

(a) Coinbase's Facebook ad included text which stated '£5 in #Bitcoin in 2010 would be worth over £100,000 in January 2021. Don't miss out on the next decade – get started on Coinbase today … Buy bitcoin in 5 minutes with as little as £25', as well as claims that the 'competition' was unregulated when they were also unregulated for cryptocurrency services.[54]

(b) Luno's out of home billboards told people it's time to buy Bitcoin without a clear risk warning.[55]

(c) Arsenal Football Club's promotion of its fan token with partner Socios on its website and Facebook was deemed by the ASA to have trivialised investing in crypto.[56]

The ASA has also issued 50 enforcement notices against companies which advertise cryptocurrencies, instructing them to review their ads and to ensure they understand and are complying with the rules so that consumers are treated fairly.[57] The FCA and the ASA collaborate in relation to their regulatory functions and have entered into a memorandum of understanding setting out their respective roles.[58]

51 FCA, *FCA Handbook,* DISP 2.7.3 www.handbook.fca.org.uk/handbook/DISP/2/?view=chapter accessed 29 August 2023.

52 *Ibid*, DISP 2.7.6.

53 For example, see FOS, 'Consumer contacts us to complain after a cryptocurrency investment scam' www.financial-ombudsman.org.uk/decisions-case-studies/case-studies/consumer-contacts-us-complain-cryptocurrency-investment-scam [accessed 29 August 2023].

54 ASA, 'ASA Ruling on Coinbase Europe Ltd t/a Coinbase' (15 December 2021) www.asa.org.uk/rulings/coinbase-europe-ltd-a21-1123058-coinbase-europe-ltd.html [accessed 27 September 2023].

55 ASA, 'ASA Ruling on Luno Money Ltd t/a Luno' (26 May 2021) www.asa.org.uk/rulings/luno-money-ltd-g21-1101558-luno-pte-ltd.html [accessed 27 September 2023].

56 ASA, 'ASA Ruling on Arsenal Football Club plc' (10 August 2022) www.asa.org.uk/rulings/arsenal-football-club-plc-a21-1121873-arsenal-football-club-plc-1.html [accessed 27 September 2023].

57 ASA, 'ASA Enforcement Notice continues clampdown on misleading and irresponsible crypto ads' (22 March 2022) www.asa.org.uk/news/asa-enforcement-notice-continues-clampdown-on-misleading-and-irresponsible-crypto-ads.html [accessed 27 September 2023].

58 Memorandum of Understanding between the Financial Conduct Authority and Advertising Standards Authority dated 3 December 2014 www.fca.org.uk/publication/mou/mou-fca-asa.pdf [accessed 27 September 2023].

3.39 Individuals or businesses actively marketing unregulated cryptoassets in the UK must comply with the rules set by the ASA. Advertisements should meet the following requirements:[59]

(a) clearly and prominently state that cryptoassets are not regulated by the FCA and are not protected by financial compensation schemes;

(b) avoid taking advantage of consumers' inexperience or credulity;

(c) include all material information relevant to the cryptoasset being advertised;

(d) make clear that value can go down as well as up;

(e) state the basis used to calculate any projections or forecasts; and

(f) make clear that past performance is not a guide for future performance.

ICOS AND TOKEN OFFERINGS

3.40 ICOs and token offerings are fundraising methods used by cryptocurrency projects. Challenges with regulation of ICOs arise due to lack of harmonisation in categorising tokens and their regulatory treatment on an international and regional level. The cross-border nature of ICOs and DLT also raise conflict of law issues.[60]

3.41 The FCA provides guidance on the regulatory treatment of ICOs, depending on the specific characteristics of the tokens involved. Exchange and utility tokens, may fall outside the regulated space, others, such as security tokens that exhibit features similar to traditional financial instruments may be subject to additional regulations under the existing framework. The regulatory status of an ICO depends on the nature of the tokens issued, and each ICO must be assessed individually. The FCA warns that ICOs may have similarities to initial public offerings (IPOs), private placements, crowdfunding, or collective investment schemes, which fall under existing legislative regimes.[61] Further specified investments that a token could represent include, alternative investment funds and electronic money.

59 ASA, 'Financial products and services: Cryptoassets' (3 October 2022) www.asa.org.uk/advice-online/financial-products-and-services-cryptoassets.html [accessed 27 September 2023].

60 Financial Markets Law Committee, 'Initial Coin Offerings: Issues of Legal Uncertainty' (July 2019) http://fmlc.org/wp-content/uploads/2019/07/ICOs-paper.pdf [accessed 27 September 2023].

61 FCA, 'Initial Coin Offerings' (12 September 2017, updated 27 February 2019) www.fca.org.uk/news/statements/initial-coin-offerings [accessed 27 September 2023]; For detailed information, refer to FCA, 'Guidance on Cryptoassets: Feedback and Final Guidance to CP 19/3' (Policy Statement PS19/22, July 2019) www.fca.org.uk/publication/policy/ps19-22.pdf [accessed 27 September 2023].

3.42 Examples of ICOs that have been held to fall within the ambit of collective investment schemes[62] are set out below:[63]

(a) purchases of real estate interests by individuals under an understanding that there would be a centrally managed process to secure planning and development permission;[64]

(b) purchases of sub-lease interests in foreign real estate for the purposes of securing income generated by the land in terms of agricultural or carbon credit income;[65]

(c) services organised to place horse-racing bets on behalf of subscribers;[66]

(d) collective financing of a film venture;[67] and

(e) collective financing to acquire patent rights.[68]

3.43 According to s 85 of FSMA 2000, an approved prospectus is necessary for an issuer to offer transferable securities to the public in the UK, with breach of this section being a criminal offence. To avoid the need for publishing a prospectus, ICOs are often structured accordingly. The key factor determining the need for a prospectus is whether the tokens fall within the definition of 'transferable securities' as per UK MiFIR, Art 2(1), (24), (25).[69] Tokens resembling shares in companies or depositary receipts for shares are likely to be deemed securities. Exclusions and exemptions from prospectus publication exist, such as offers addressed to fewer than 150 persons or qualified investors, as well as cases where the quantum of securities offered falls below a certain threshold.[70]

3.44 Under s 21 of FSMA 2000, promoting an ICO involving securities or contract-based investments requires authorisation or exemption. Unauthorised financial promotions are unenforceable, and their communication is a criminal offence. If the token is a specified investment,[71] Financial Services Act 2012, ss 89 and 90 apply. Issuers can face criminal liability for false/misleading statements or creating deceptive impressions to induce investments. Even if not a specified investment, issuers are liable for untrue/misleading statements or omissions

62 FSMA 2000, s 235.

63 Iris H-Y Chiu, 'Decoupling tokens from trading: reaching beyond investment regulation for regulatory policy in initial coin offerings', (2018) 3 IBLJ, 265–287, 275.

64 *In re Sky Land Consultants Plc* [2010] EWHC 399 (Ch); *FSA v Asset LI Inc* [2014] EWCA Civ 435, affirmed in the Supreme Court, *Asset Land Investment Plc and another (Appellants) v The Financial Conduct Authority (Respondent)* [2016] UKSC 17.

65 *FCA v Capital Alternatives Ltd and Ors* [2014] EWHC 144 (Ch); [2015] EWCA Civ 284.

66 *Financial Services Authority v Fradley* [2005] EWCA Civ 1183 CA.

67 *Raymond Bieber v Teathers Ltd (in liquidation)* [2012] EWHC 190 (Ch).

68 *Brown 7 Ors v Innovator One Plc and Ors* [2012] EWHC 1321.

69 Council Regulation (EU) No 600/2014 of 15 May 2014 on markets in financial instruments and amending Regulation (EU) No 648/2012 [2014] OJ L173/84.

70 For further information on prospectus requirements, see FCA, *The FCA Handbook* (August 2023) PRR www.handbook.fca.org.uk/handbook/PRR.pdf [accessed 27 September 2023].

71 FCA, *FCA Handbook* Glossary, specified investment www.handbook.fca.org.uk/handbook/glossary/G1117.html [accessed 27 September 2023].

in marketing materials. A verification process similar to IPOs is advisable to minimise risk. Token issuers should consider if the UK's MLR apply to them. If so, they must register, conduct due diligence on customers, implement controls for money laundering and terrorist financing risk, and report suspicious activity.

3.45 The FCA has cautioned consumers about the risks associated with ICOs. ICOs are deemed highly speculative and high-risk investments due to their price volatility, lack of access to UK regulatory protections like the Financial Services Compensation Scheme (FSCS) and if unauthorised, FOS. ICOs have the potential for fraud, and inadequate documentation.[72]

3.46 In FS17/4, the FCA addressed the regulatory position on ICOs and highlighted a limited number of ICOs that engaged with its Innovation Hub as part of innovative business propositions with potential consumer benefits. For access to hub facilities, the ICO must meet one of these criteria:[73]

(a) the ICO must fall within the FCA regulatory perimeter and be fully compliant with UK and other relevant regimes; or

(b) if outside our regulatory perimeter, designed, promoted and governed in line with best practice, so that potential acquirers are properly informed about the proposition that is being marketed to them.

3.47 The FCA emphasised the importance of a well-functioning ICO market, where issuers are attentive to regulatory obligations and manage risks to protect the public and the markets. However, the FCA cautioned that ICO promoters must enable fully informed decision-making by potential token acquirers.

DERIVATIVES AND EXCHANGE TRADED NOTES

3.48 Cryptocurrency derivatives and exchange-traded notes (ETNs) have gained significant attention as financial instruments that allow investors to gain exposure to cryptoassets without directly owning them. Cryptocurrency derivatives are financial contracts whose value is derived from an underlying cryptocurrency asset, such as Bitcoin or Ethereum. They include futures contracts, options, CFDs, and other similar instruments. ETNs, on the other hand, are debt securities that track the performance of an underlying cryptocurrency or a basket of cryptocurrencies. Some businesses provide individuals and companies with the opportunity to participate in the cryptocurrency markets through derivative contracts.

72 FCA, 'Consumer warning about the risks of Initial Coin Offerings' (12 September 2017, updated 27 February 2019) www.fca.org.uk/news/statements/initial-coin-offerings [accessed 27 September 2023].

73 FCA, 'Distributed Ledger Technology: Feedback Statement on Discussion Paper 17/03' (FS17/4, December 2017) www.fca.org.uk/publication/feedback/fs17-04.pdf [accessed 8 October 2023].

3.49 The FCA has implemented regulations and guidelines that apply to cryptocurrency derivatives and ETNs to ensure investor protection and market integrity. The FCA places a strong emphasis on investor protection when it comes to cryptocurrency derivatives and ETNs and has banned the sale of such products to consumers.[74]

3.50 The following are the regulatory requirements for businesses offering cryptoasset derivatives and ETNs:

(a) **Registration and authorisation**: Companies issuing or trading cryptocurrency derivatives and ETNs must be registered with the FCA and obtain the necessary authorisation. This process involves meeting specific criteria, including compliance with AML/CTF and investor protection regulations.

(b) **Investor suitability**: Companies must assess the suitability of investors for trading cryptocurrency derivatives and ETNs. They are required to conduct proper due diligence and provide adequate risk warnings to ensure that investors understand the risks involved.

(c) **Risk disclosure and transparency**: Companies offering cryptocurrency derivatives and ETNs must provide clear and comprehensive risk disclosures, including information on the underlying assets, pricing, and potential market risks. Transparent and accurate pricing mechanisms should be established.

(d) **Margin requirements**: Margin trading, where investors trade with borrowed funds, is subject to specific margin requirements to ensure financial stability and investor protection. The FCA may impose limitations on leverage and margin ratios.

(e) **Market abuse and manipulation**: Companies and individuals involved in trading cryptocurrency derivatives and ETNs must adhere to rules prohibiting market abuse, insider trading, and market manipulation. Robust surveillance and reporting mechanisms are necessary to detect and prevent these activities.[75]

3.51 The regulatory landscape surrounding cryptoasset derivatives and ETNs is constantly evolving. The FCA and other regulatory bodies continue to monitor the market and may introduce further regulations or guidance to address emerging risks and ensure investor protection.

74 FCA, 'PS20/10:Prohibiting the sale to retail clients of investment products that reference cryptoassets' (6 October 2020, updated 9 October 2020) www.fca.org.uk/publications/policy-statements/ps20-10-prohibiting-sale-retail-clients-investment-products-reference-cryptoassets [accessed 27 September 2023]; FCA, 'Prohibiting the sale to retail clients of investment products that reference cryptoassets' (PS20/10, October 2020) www.fca.org.uk/publication/policy/ps20-10.pdf [accessed 27 September 2023].

75 FCA, *FCA Handbook,* MAR1 www.handbook.fca.org.uk/handbook/MAR/1/?view=chapter [accessed 27 September 2023].

INNOVATION HUB AND REGULATORY SANDBOXES

3.52 Recognising the importance of fostering innovation, the FCA operates a regulatory sandbox[76] within the innovation hub.[77] The innovation hub provides support and guidance to fintech firms, including those working with cryptocurrencies. The sandbox allows businesses to test innovative products and services in a controlled environment. These initiatives aim to promote responsible innovation while ensuring compliance with regulatory requirements.

HM Treasury also has the power to establish financial markets infrastructure (FMI) sandboxes under FSMA 2023, s 13. The first to be established under this new power will be the digital securities sandbox (DSS).[78] The consultation on the DSS closed on 22 August 2023, and is intended to be finalised late 2023. The DSS aims to:[79]

(a) test how existing UK legislation needs to change to accommodate digital asset technology and the new practices associated with it;

(b) enabling the financial sector to test and adopt digital asset technology in FMIs; and

(c) testing the use of FMI sandboxes as a policymaking concept.

3.53 Under HM Treasury's proposals, firms established in the UK may apply to participate in the DSS to test the use of digital asset technology. The key features include:[80]

(a) modified legislation and rules that remove barriers to the performance of notary, trading, settlement and maintenance in relation to digital securities, while maintaining the principle of 'same risk, same regulatory outcome;

(b) a range of securities, both systemic and non-systemic, to be in scope. This is expected to include a subset of 'financial instruments' as defined in the RAO and include digital bonds and equities, as well as digital versions of assets such as money market instruments;

(c) regulator-set limits on participating entities, particularly on the amount of digital securities in scope;

(d) both existing authorised firms and new entrants can apply to operate an FMI in the DSS;

76 FCA, 'Regulatory Sandbox' (27 March 2022, updated 1 August 2023) www.fca.org.uk/firms/innovation/regulatory-sandbox [accessed 27 September 2023].

77 FCA, 'Innovation Hub' www.fca.org.uk/firms/innovation [accessed 27 September 2023].

78 HM Treasury, 'Consultation on the first Financial Market Infrastructure Sandbox: The Digital Securities Sandbox' (July 2023) https://assets.publishing.service.gov.uk/government/uploads/system/uploads/attachment_data/file/1168457/Consultation_on_Digital_Securities_Sandbox.pdf [accessed 27 September 2023].

79 *Ibid* at [2.3].

80 *Ibid* at 12.

(e) after assessing the operation of modified legislation/regulation in the DSS and reported to Parliament, HM Treasury can make permanent changes to legislation to facilitate digital assets via statutory instrument; and

(f) successful entities should be able to move to performing unrestricted activity outside the DSS, without any regulatory cliff-edges.

INTERNATIONAL COOPERATION

3.54 The UK recognises the global nature of the cryptocurrency industry and actively participates in international initiatives aimed at promoting cooperation and consistent regulatory standards. It works closely with international organisations,[81] such as the FATF, International Financial Consumer Protection Organisation, Financial Stability Board (FSB), International Organisation of Securities Commissions (IOSC), European Securities and Markets Authority, and European Banking Authority, and has entered into many multilateral and bilateral memoranda of understanding and agreements with overseas regulators enabling them to coordinate, cooperate and exchange information.[82]

CONCLUSION

3.55 The regulatory framework for cryptocurrencies in the UK is evolving to address the challenges and risks posed by this emerging asset class. The FCA plays a crucial role in overseeing and regulating crypto asset businesses to protect consumers and maintain the integrity of the financial system. Continued collaboration between regulators, industry participants, and international organisations will be essential to ensure effective regulation and foster innovation in the cryptocurrency space.

81 FCA, 'International standards and regulations' (18 April 2021, updated 20 July 2022) www.fca.org.uk/about/how-we-regulate/international-standards-regulations [accessed 23 August 2023].

82 FCA, 'Agreements with overseas regulators' (8 July 2021, updated 17 March 2023) www.fca.org.uk/about/how-we-regulate/international-standards-regulations/agreements-overseas-regulators accessed 23 August 2023.

Chapter 4

Cryptoassets and Banking

UK BANKING STANDARDS

4.1 The UK brought in reforms to regulation in the wake of the 2008 global financial crisis in the form of the Financial Services Act 2012 (FSA 2012). An independent Financial Policy Committee (FPC) was created at the Bank of England (BoE) with a new prudential regulator, the Prudential Regulation Authority (PRA), created as a subsidiary of the BoE. The BoE took over new responsibilities for supervising financial market infrastructure providers.

4.2 On the 24 March 2022 Sam Woods, CEO of the PRA, issued a 'Dear CEO' letter discussing the regulator's approach to existing or planned exposure to cryptoassets in the context of increasing growth and innovation in the industry.[1] The letter was intended to outline the PRA's expectations around risk management and measurement against the existing prudential framework until the cryptoasset banking supervision standards of the Bank for International Settlements Basel Committee on Banking Supervision (BCBS) were announced.

4.3 The letter outlines a number of tangible measures that firms must take when gaining exposure to cryptoassets and should be considered by firms in relation to risk management systems and capital adequacy calculations going forward. Firms were advised to take specific actions to address crypto-related risks:

(a) **Strengthen risk controls**: firms must uphold their obligations under the PRA's Fundamental Rules and effective risk management systems are required along with transparency with the PRA about business activities. Crypto risks should be elevated to the board and senior management, especially those performing PRA-approved Senior Management Functions (SMF). SMFs should actively review and approve risk assessment frameworks for crypto exposure. Adaptation of risk management systems is necessary, including more frequent monitoring, accounting for uncertainty, and adjusting risk tolerance. Stress tests should be employed to capture increasing uncertainty. Firms should also ensure compliance with KYC and AML regulations for interactions with cryptoasset businesses.

1 PRA, 'Dear CEO, Existing or planned exposure to cryptoassets' (24 March 2023) www.bankofengland.co.uk/-/media/boe/files/prudential-regulation/letter/2022/march/existing-or-planned-exposure-to-cryptoassets.pdf [accessed 27 September 2023].

(b) **Prudential framework**: Firms should consider the full prudential framework, encompassing Fundamental Rules, Pillar 1, Internal Capital Adequacy Assessment Process (ICAAP), and related Pillar 2 capital considerations. The PRA will scrutinise Pillar 2 processes and disclosures for firms significantly exposed to cryptoassets. While the PRA has not identified specific prudential requirement changes for cryptoassets, firms must comply fully with the existing framework, particularly addressing custody activities and interactions with unregulated providers.

(c) **Pillar 1**: Crypto activities fall under the full Pillar 1 framework, but certain unique risks like market risk and counterparty credit risk require recalibration and additional capital. Direct holdings of certain cryptoassets classified as intangible assets may lead to capital deductions under Capital Requirements Regulation (CRR). The PRA suggests a capital requirement of 100% for many cryptoassets due to lack of comparability. Conservative approaches are recommended for diversification and hedging, considering potential relationship deterioration in stress. Some netting of long and short derivative positions for the same cryptoasset is allowed. Counterparty credit risk under standardised approach to counterparty credit risk (SA-CCR) should follow stricter netting provisions for 'other risks' categories.

(d) **Pillar 2**: the Pillar 2 framework addresses risks beyond Pillar 1. Firms should assess market, credit, counterparty credit, and operational risks related to crypto activities. Focus on operational risks including fraud and cyber risks is required.

4.4 In tandem, the BoE published its response to new forms of digital money[2] along with its FPC report on cryptoassets and decentralised finance.[3]

INTERNATIONAL BANKING STANDARDS

Introduction

4.5 The Basel Committee on Banking Supervision (BCBS) is composed of 28 member state governors of Central Banks and Heads of Supervision, including the UK.[4] BCBS recognises that the growing presence of cryptoassets and related services can pose financial stability concerns and increase risks for banks. To address these issues, the BCBS is introducing formal standards for the prudential treatment of internationally active banks' exposures to cryptoassets. These standards, published on 16 December 2022, will be incorporated as a

2 BoE, 'Responses to the Bank of England's Discussion Paper on new forms of digital money' (March 2022) www.bankofengland.co.uk/paper/2022/responses-to-the-bank-of-englands-discussion-paper-on-new-forms-of-digital-money [accessed 27 September 2023].

3 FPC, 'Financial Policy Committee, Financial Stability in Focus: Cryptoassets and decentralised finance' (March 2022) www.bankofengland.co.uk/-/media/boe/files/financial-stability-in-focus/2022/cryptoassets-and-decentralised-finance.pdf [accessed 27 September 2023].

4 BIS, 'Basel Committee membership' (21 July 2022) www.bis.org/bcbs/membership.htm?m=3071 [accessed 27 September 2023].

new chapter, SCO60 (Cryptoasset exposures), within the Scope and definitions standard (SCO) of the Basel framework. The BCBS expects its member jurisdictions to implement SCO60 by 1 January 2025 and will become a new chapter of the consolidated Basel Framework.[5] Bank exposures to cryptoassets, as defined in SCO60, encompass both on- and off-balance sheet amounts that give rise to credit, market, operational, or liquidity risks.[6]

4.6 The BCBS conducted an analysis in December 2019, outlined in BCBS490,[7] to identify the potential ways in which banks could be exposed to cryptoassets, either directly or indirectly. These channels include issuing cryptoassets, owning them as investments, holding products with underlying cryptoassets (eg ETFs), providing loans to individuals or institutions for cryptoasset investments, accepting cryptoassets as collateral, and engaging in proprietary trading or trading on behalf of clients. The BCBS also highlighted the risks associated with banks' exposures to cryptoassets, for example:[8]

(a) **Liquidity risk**: banks may face challenges converting cryptoassets into fiat currency in private markets without significant loss of value.

(b) **Market risk**: the volatile nature of cryptoassets' valuation and pricing may lead to mark-to-market losses for banks.

(c) **Credit and counterparty credit risk**: holding cryptoassets that constitute a legal obligation between issuer and holder may expose banks to credit risk related to those assets.

(d) **Cyber and operational risks**: technological vulnerabilities, cyber-attacks, network governance issues, and operational reliability concerns pose risks to banks dealing with cryptoassets.

(e) **Legal risks**: uncertainties surrounding the legal status of cryptoassets may lead to various risks, including those related to consumer protection, safeguarding client cryptoassets, and compliance with anti-money laundering and terrorist financing regulations.

(f) **Third-party risks**: Banks relying on third parties for cryptoasset-related activities may face disruptions in operations and services provided by such counterparties.

4.7 To mitigate these risks, the BCBS has developed standards for the prudential treatment of banks' exposures to cryptoassets. These standards aim to address the challenges posed by cryptoassets and promote financial stability in the banking sector.

5 BCBS, 'SCO60 – Cryptoasset exposures' (BIS, 16 December 2022, Effective 1 January 2025) www.bis.org/basel_framework/chapter/SCO/60.htm?inforce=20250101&published=20221216 [accessed 27 September 2023].

6 *Ibid* SCO60.4.

7 BCBS, 'Designing a prudential treatment for cryptoassets' (BIS, December 2019) www.bis.org/bcbs/publ/d490.pdf [accessed 27 September 2023].

8 *Ibid* 10.

4.8 The BCBS has specific expectations for banks regarding their exposures to cryptoassets and related services, aiming to address the risks associated with such exposures. These expectations were communicated in a statement published in March 2019 directed at member jurisdictions permitting these activities.[9] For banks that decide to acquire cryptoasset exposures or provide related services, the BCBS expects them to follow these minimum requirements:[10]

(a) **Due diligence**: before acquiring cryptoasset exposures or offering related services, the bank must conduct comprehensive risk analyses related to cryptoassets. The bank should possess the necessary technical expertise to assess these risks adequately.

(b) **Governance and risk management**: banks must establish a clear and robust risk management framework tailored to the risks associated with their cryptoasset exposures and services. The bank's boards and senior management should be provided with timely and relevant information about the bank's cryptoasset risk profile. Internal capital and liquidity adequacy assessment processes should include an evaluation of these risks.

(c) **Disclosure**: banks must publicly disclose any significant cryptoasset exposures or related services as part of their regular financial disclosures. They should also specify the accounting treatment for these exposures.

(d) **Supervisory dialogue**: banks should promptly inform their supervisors of actual and planned cryptoasset exposure or activities. They should assure the supervisor that they have fully assessed the permissibility of these activities and the associated risks and have taken measures to mitigate these risks.

4.9 The BCBS intends SCO60 to be the minimum standard for internationally active banks, and jurisdictions have the flexibility to add more conservative measures if needed. If a jurisdiction prohibits its banks from having any exposures to cryptoassets, it will be considered compliant with the standards.

4.10 The standards are set out at SCO60.5:[11]

(a) classification conditions;

(b) banking/trading book boundary, use of internal models and accounting classification;

(c) minimum capital requirements for credit risk for Group 1 cryptoassets;

(d) minimum capital requirements for market risk for Group 1 cryptoassets;

(e) add-on for infrastructure risk for Group 1 cryptoassets;

(f) minimum capital requirements for Group 2 cryptoassets;

9 BCBS, 'Statement on cryptoassets' (19 March 2019) www.bis.org/publ/bcbs_nl21.htm [accessed 27 September 2023].

10 *Ibid.*

11 BCBS, *SCO60 – Cryptoasset exposures* (n 5 above) SCO60.6 to SCO60.131.

(g) minimum capital requirements for credit valuation adjustment (CVA) risk;

(h) minimum capital requirements for counterparty credit risk;

(i) minimum capital requirements for operational risk;

(j) minimum liquidity risk requirements;

(k) leverage ratio requirements;

(l) large exposure requirements;

(m) group 2 exposure limit;

(n) bank risk management and supervisory review;

(o) disclosure requirements; and

(p) definitions.

Classification of cryptoassets

4.11 Cryptoassets for the purposes of SCO60 are stated to be private digital assets that rely on cryptography and DLT or similar technologies, investment, or accessing goods/services. Digital assets are a digital representation of value, which can be used for payment or investment purposes or to access a good or service. Dematerialised securities using electronic versions of traditional registers and databases centrally administered are not classified as cryptoassets.[12]

4.12 The BCBS classifies cryptoassets into two groups: Group 1 and Group 2.[13]

4.13 Group 1 cryptoassets meet all classification conditions set in SCO60 and are subdivided into:

(a) **Group 1a cryptoassets**: tokenised traditional assets representing ownership of assets captured within the Basel framework (eg cash, bonds, commodities, equities).

(b) **Group 1b cryptoassets**: cryptoassets with effective stabilisation mechanisms, including certain stablecoins. These must pass a redemption risk test, ensuring sufficient reserve assets for redeeming during stress periods, and be supervised and regulated by a prudential authority.[14]

Algorithm-based stablecoins are not eligible for Group 1.

4.14 Group 2 cryptoassets fail to meet any classification conditions and are considered higher risk, including unbacked cryptoassets, certain tokenised traditional assets, and unstable stablecoins.

12 *Ibid* SCO60.1.
13 *Ibid* SCO60.6 to SCO60.22.
14 *Ibid* SCO60.12.

(a) **Group 2a cryptoassets**: cryptoassets (including tokenised traditional assets, stablecoins and unbacked cryptoassets) that fail to meet the classification conditions, but pass the Group 2a hedging recognition criteria.

(b) **Group 2b cryptoassets**: all other cryptoassets (ie tokenised traditional assets, stablecoins and unbacked cryptoassets that fail to meet the classification conditions and fail the Group 2a hedging recognition criteria). Bitcoin falls under Group 2.

4.15 To be eligible for Group 1 classification, a cryptoasset must meet four classification conditions:[15]

(a) The cryptoasset is either a tokenised traditional asset or has an effective stabilising mechanism linking its value to an underlying traditional asset or a pool of traditional assets.

(b) All rights, obligations, and interests arising from the cryptoasset arrangement are clearly defined and legally enforceable in all jurisdictions where the asset is issued and redeemed, with settlement finality ensured.

(c) The cryptoasset's functions and the network it operates on, including the distributed ledger or similar technology, are designed to sufficiently mitigate and manage any significant risks.

(d) Entities executing redemptions, transfers, storage, or settlement finality of the cryptoasset, or managing or investing reserve assets, must be regulated, supervised, or subject to appropriate risk management standards, and they must have a comprehensive governance framework.

4.16 Banks must continually assess the classification of their exposed cryptoassets. They should have appropriate risk management policies, procedures, governance, and IT capabilities to evaluate cryptoasset risks. They must document the information used for classification compliance and provide it to supervisors when requested. Banks should inform their supervisor of the classification assessment before acquiring cryptoassets, allowing time for the supervisor to review and potentially override the decision.[16] Supervisors are responsible for reviewing and assessing banks' risk management approaches and classification decisions.[17]

Capital requirements for credit and market risk

4.17 SCO60 focuses on risk-based capital requirements for credit and market risk regarding exposures to cryptoassets. Unlike other elements of the Basel framework, SCO60 provides specific requirements for credit and market risk concerning cryptoassets.

15 *Ibid* SCO60.8 to SCO60.19.
16 *Ibid* SCO60.20.
17 *Ibid* SCO60.21.

4.18 The allocation of assets to a bank's banking book or trading book affects risk-weight calculations. Credit and equity positions in the trading book face market risk-based capital charges, while those in the banking book face credit risk-based charges. Rules governing asset allocation are set out in the Risk-based capital requirements standard (RBC) at RBC25.[18] These rules apply to cryptoassets' allocation to the banking and trading books, with some variations based on the type of cryptoasset (Group 1a, Group 1b, Group 2a, or Group 2b). Minimum capital requirements for credit and market risk in relation to Group 1 and Group 2 cryptoassets are set out at SCO60.26 to SCO60.92.

4.19 There is no new prescribed regulatory treatment for applying risk-based capital requirements for counterparty credit risk (CCR) to derivatives referencing cryptoassets. Existing standards should be applied.[19] The approach used for CCR depends on the classification of the cryptoasset referenced by the derivative. Only Group 1a cryptoassets that are tokenised versions of instruments eligible as financial collateral may qualify for recognition as eligible collateral.[20]

Other prudential requirements

4.20 A bank's total exposure to Group 2 cryptoassets should generally not exceed 1 per cent of its Tier 1 capital and must not go beyond 2 per cent. If a bank breaches the 1 per cent limit, it must notify its supervisor immediately and rectify the breach rapidly. Exposures exceeding the threshold will be subject to the capital requirements for Group 2b cryptoasset exposures until the 1 per cent limit is restored.[21]

Operational risk

4.21 The BCBS has not introduced a new regulatory treatment for cryptoassets under the operational risk framework (OPE) and should generally be captured by OPE25,[22] utilising the business indicator and internal loss multiplier. The guidance on applying the existing framework to cryptoassets is detailed at SCO60.100.

18 BCBS, *RBC25: Boundary between the banking book and the trading book* (27 March 2023, effective 1 January 2023) www.bis.org/basel_framework/chapter/RBC/25.htm?inforce=20230101&published=20200327 [accessed 27 September 2023].

19 BCBS, *SCO60 – Cryptoasset exposures* (n 5 above), SCO60.93 to SCO60.99.

20 *Ibid* SCO60.102.

21 *Ibid* SCO.60.116 to SCO60.119.

22 BCBS, *OPE25: Standarised approach* (30 Mar 2023, effective 1 January 2023) www.bis.org/basel_framework/chapter/OPE/25.htm [accessed 27 September 2023].

Liquidity

4.22 The regulatory treatment for cryptoassets under the liquidity framework is specified at SCO60.101 to SCO60.112. For the liquidity coverage ratio (LCR) and net stable funding ratio (NSFR) requirements, cryptoasset exposures should generally follow treatments consistent with existing approaches for traditional exposures with equivalent risks.[23] Group 1b and Group 2 cryptoassets will not qualify as high-quality liquid assets (HQLA).[24] Holdings of Group 1a cryptoassets will be eligible for HQLA if they meet specific criteria.[25] The application of LCR and NSFR frameworks varies depending on the type of cryptoassets.

Leverage

4.23 The BCBS has not introduced a new regulatory treatment for cryptoassets under the leverage ratio framework.[26] Cryptoassets should be included in the leverage ratio exposure measure based on their value for financial reporting purposes, using the applicable accounting treatment. Cryptoasset derivatives should follow the treatment of the risk-based capital framework.

Large exposures

4.24 The BCBS has not introduced a new regulatory treatment for cryptoassets under the large exposures framework. Guidance on applying the existing framework to cryptoassets is provided at SCO60.115.

4.25 Banks' exposures to cryptoassets will be subject to the large exposure limits specified in the large exposures standard (LEX). Cryptoasset exposures with credit risk exposure will be included in the large exposure measure based on their accounting value.

Other issues

4.26 **Bank risk management**: the BCBS' expectations for banks' risk management regarding cryptoassets are outlined in SCO60.121 to SCO60.125.

(a) Banks with direct or indirect exposures to cryptoassets or providing related services must establish policies and procedures to identify, assess, and mitigate risks related to cryptoassets on an ongoing basis.

23 BCBS, *SCO60 – Cryptoasset exposures* (n 5 above) SCO60.101.
24 *Ibid* SCO60.103.
25 *Ibid* SCO60.102.
26 *Ibid* SCO60.113 to SCO60.114.

(b) Banks should conduct a prudent assessment of any intended cryptoasset exposures and ensure the adequacy of existing risk management processes.

(c) A sound risk management approach, including limits and hedging strategies, should be in place, with clear responsibilities assigned for managing these risks.

(d) Banks must inform supervisors of their policies, assessment results, and actual and planned cryptoasset exposures or activities in a timely manner.

(e) Risks to consider include cryptoasset technology, general information and communication technology (ICT) and cyber risks, legal risks, money laundering and terrorist financing risks, and valuation risks.

4.27 **Supervisory review**: the BCBS' expectations on how supervisors should assess and review banks' cryptoasset activities are specified in SCO60.126 to SCO60.127.

(a) Supervisors should review the appropriateness of banks' policies and procedures for identifying and assessing cryptoasset risks and the adequacy of assessment results.

(b) They have the authority to require banks to address deficiencies in identifying or assessing cryptoasset risks.

(c) If capital inadequacies or risk management shortcomings are identified, supervisors may take supervisory actions, such as additional capital charges, provisioning for losses related to cryptoassets, or imposing internal limits to contain risks.

4.28 **Disclosures**: the BCBS' expectations on disclosures regarding cryptoassets and related activities are presented in SCO60.128 to SCO60.130.

(a) Banks must follow five general guiding principles for disclosures: clarity, comprehensiveness, meaningfulness to users, consistency over time, and comparability across banks (as specified in the Disclosure requirements standards – DIS10[27]).

(b) Banks should disclose information about material cryptoasset exposures regularly.

(c) Exposures to Group 1 cryptoassets should be included in the relevant existing disclosure templates for traditional assets.

4.29 **Potential revisions to standards**: in BCBS545, the BCBS made it clear that it will closely monitor the implementation and impact of SCO60 and is open

27 BCBS, *DIS10: Disclosure requirements* (26 November 2020, effective 1 January 2023) BIS www.bis.org/basel_framework/chapter/DIS/10.htm?inforce=20230101&published=20201126 [accessed 27 September 2023].

to issuing further refinements and clarifications to the standards. Specific areas that the BCBS intends to monitor and review include:[28]

(a) statistical tests and redemption risk test;

(b) permissionless blockchains;

(c) group 1b cryptoassets as collateral;

(d) group 2a criteria and hedge recognition; and

(e) calibration of the group 2 exposure limit.

4.30 In March 2023, the BCBS approved a work plan to further assess and address risks posed by cryptoassets to the global banking system. This plan includes targeted reviews of the prudential treatment of cryptoasset exposures, particularly focusing on permissionless blockchains and the eligibility criteria for Group 1 stablecoins. The BCBS will also continue monitoring banks' cryptoasset activities and exposures, including their potential role as issuers of stablecoins and custodians of cryptoassets, as well as their interconnections with other nodes in the cryptoasset ecosystem.[29]

LENDING PRACTICE

Good practice measures for banks

4.31 In June 2018, the FCA issued a warning to bank CEOs about the potential risks of abuse associated with cryptoassets, including their anonymity and cross-border movement capabilities. Banks were advised to take reasonable and proportionate measures to mitigate the risk of facilitating financial crimes related to cryptoassets.[30] The FCA highlighted that retail customers contributing large sums to ICOs are at higher risk of investment fraud. They directed banks to refer to a previous review conducted in 2012 on how banks handled investment fraud risk, which contains relevant good and poor practices applicable to ICOs as well.[31]

4.32 For banks offering services related to cryptoassets to clients, the FCA recommended increasing scrutiny on clients engaged in significant crypto-related activities, such as cryptoasset exchanges, trading with crypto-derived wealth, and involvement in ICOs. A risk-based approach is expected, recognising the

28 BCBS, *Prudential treatment of cryptoasset exposures* (BCBS545, December 2022) 4, www.bis.org/bcbs/publ/d545.pdf [accessed 27 September 2023].

29 BCBS, 'Basel Committee to review recent market developments, advances work on climate-related financial risks, and reviews Basel Core Principles' (*BIS*, 23 March 2023) www.bis.org/press/p230323a.htm [accessed 27 September 2023].

30 FCA, 'Dear CEO, Cryptoassets and financial crime' (11 June 2018) www.fca.org.uk/publication/correspondence/dear-ceo-letter-cryptoassets-financial-crime.pdf [accessed 27 September 2023].

31 FCA, 'Banks' defences against investment fraud' (June 2012) www.fca.org.uk/publication/archive/banks-defences-against-investment-fraud.pdf [accessed 29 November 2023].

varying risk levels within broad categories of business relationships. The FCA emphasised the importance of exercising particular care when evidence trails behind cryptoasset transactions are weaker.

4.33 Banks were also advised to be cautious of customers using state-sponsored cryptoassets to evade international financial sanctions, as it could be a high-risk indicator.

4.34 The FCA have outlined several good practice measures that banks could adopt concerning cryptoassets, as detailed below.[32]

(a) **Staff knowledge**: develop staff expertise on cryptoassets to identify high-risk clients and activities related to financial crime.

(b) **Updated frameworks**: ensure financial crime frameworks reflect the firm's involvement in crypto-related activities and can keep pace with fast-moving developments.

(c) **Client engagement**: understand the nature of clients' businesses and associated risks, including the source of customer wealth or funds. Apply the same risk-based assessment criteria for customers with cryptoasset-derived wealth as for other sources.

(d) **Know your customer**: conduct due diligence on key individuals in client businesses, considering any adverse intelligence.

(e) **Crypto-exchange services**: assess the adequacy of clients' due diligence arrangements for those offering crypto-exchange services.

(f) **ICOs**: for clients involved in ICOs, consider factors like investor-base, organisers, token functionality (including intended use), and jurisdiction.

4.35 The FCA followed up their 2018 'Dear CEO' Letter with a 'Notice to all FCA regulated firms with exposure to cryptoassets' in March 2022 indicating that the use of cryptoassets in financial services brings benefits like cost reduction but also risks such as market integrity, consumer confusion, financial crime, and money laundering. Firms must have proper systems, controls, and customer clarity.[33]

4.36 Broadly, the FCA indicated:[34]

(a) Cryptoasset businesses need to register and comply with AML.

(b) Firms interacting with cryptoassets must have due diligence and money laundering controls.

32 PRA, Dear CEO (n 1 above).

33 FCA, 'Notice to all FCA regulated firms with exposure to cryptoassets' (24 March 2022) www.fca.org.uk/news/statements/notice-regulated-firms-exposure-cryptoassets [accessed 27 September 2023].

34 *Ibid.*

(c) Adaptation to risks when clients deal with cryptoassets is expected of regulated firms.

(d) Prudential considerations apply to cryptoassets, and custody of security tokens may fall under specified rules.

4.37 The FCA indicated that international cooperation and engagement are crucial for responsible innovation and consumer protection,[35] as well as engagement with the industry participants.[36]

Margin lending

4.38 In simple terms, a margin loan is a type of credit offered to individuals or companies, backed by assets like cash, shares, or other tradable items. These assets serve as collateral. Margin loans can be set up for a fixed period or as a revolving credit line, and they can be either guaranteed or not guaranteed. They can also be structured as loans where the borrower is responsible for repayment, or where the lender bears more risk. Lending against cryptoassets is known as digital asset margin lending (DAML).

4.39 What is important is that the ability to borrow money depends on the quality of the assets you have, the loan-to-value ratio (LTV), specific margin requirements, and conditions for repayment. If you cannot repay the loan, the lender can claim your collateral. Even though you use the collateral, you still retain ownership rights like receiving dividends and voting.[37]

4.40 A margin loan is a tailor-made over-the-counter (OTC) transaction with a lot of flexibility that enables different investment strategies:[38]

(a) earning more from assets;

(b) protecting their value;

(c) fixing future selling prices;

(d) selling assets in a planned way; and

(e) locking in financing to purchase relevant assets. This type of lending is also called 'American-style' margin lending or Lombard loans, and they are commonly used even by regular investors.

4.41 Lenders assess the risk they are willing to take based on the LTV and the portfolio's valuation used as collateral, known as the haircut. Throughout

35 Specifically mentioned are the IOSCO, FSB, the FATF and the CATF.

36 *Ibid.*

37 Michael Huertas, 'The need for greater regulation of the margin lending market in crypto-assets – still an issue in 2020 and the outlook ahead?', (2020) 35(12) JIBLR 521–527, 523–524.

38 *Ibid* 524.

the loan's duration, the borrower needs to maintain an agreed-upon security-to-collateral coverage ratio. This means the portfolio's market value must be several times higher than the loan amount (adjusted for asset volatility). If this ratio is breached, the borrower receives a margin call. After being notified, the borrower must either repay a portion of the loan, the entire loan, or provide more collateral.

4.42 Failing to meet the margin call gives the lender the right to sell portfolio assets (acting on behalf of the borrower or through financial collateral arrangements) and use the proceeds to repay the owed amount. In many cases, margin calls hold the borrower fully accountable. This means even if the collateral's value drops to zero, the borrower still owes the full outstanding amount.

4.43 The risk increases when the loan is 'on-demand,' meaning the lender can request repayment anytime. In contrast, 'limited recourse' loans only allow the lender access to the secured portfolio. These limited recourse deals are generally not available to smaller investors. Such transactions require a more thorough lender assessment of the provided assets, detailed deal structuring, and well-defined exit and enforcement plans. Borrowers in margin loans should closely monitor the collateral's value, their available cash flow, and the impact of variable interest rates.[39]

Taking security over cryptoassets

4.44 The type of security that can be created over a cryptoasset depends on its nature and how it is held. Typically, intangible assets like virtual currencies are secured through a charge, similar to securing a bank account or shares. If a cryptoasset represents bearer securities, it may be possible to create a mortgage over them, requiring a transfer to the mortgagee. However, not all types of security are applicable to cryptoassets. For instance, creating a pledge or lien over a cryptoasset is not possible due to its intangible nature. As regulations surrounding DLT and cryptoassets are still developing, the viability of current security structures may change as the industry evolves.

4.45 Some companies offer customers the option to secure loans using cryptoassets like Bitcoin. To do so, the cryptoassets must be transferred to the lender's or a custodian's wallet. However, the documentation varies from lender to lender and enforceability of these arrangements remain unclear. These transactions may resemble a purchase of the cryptoasset with an agreement or option to sell it back, rather than a traditional security interest. Additionally, these companies often operate as peer-to-peer lending platforms, and they might not directly issue the loans themselves. Some of these companies are relatively

39 *Ibid.*

new in the market.[40] There have been a number of high-profile collapses of crypto lenders in recent years such as Cred,[41] BlockFi,[42] and Genesis.[43]

4.46 Under current UK law, there are broadly two ways in which a collateral taker can acquire a proprietary interest in the relevant assets used for collateral. A collateral taker either acquires an absolute interest in those assets ('title transfer collateral arrangements') or is granted a security interest in them ('security-based collateral arrangements').[44]

4.47 In a title transfer collateral arrangement, the party providing collateral fully transfers their rights in the collateral assets to the receiving party. In return, the receiving party commits to transferring back the full interest in the assets (or equivalent assets) to the provider once the secured obligations are completely fulfilled.[45]

4.48 Regarding crypto tokens, the Law Commission have indicated that they can, in principle, be used as subjects for title transfer collateral arrangements without requiring changes to the existing laws.[46]

4.49 However, although such arrangements are legally viable, the Law Commission expects that most participants in the market will not commonly opt for title transfer collateral arrangements, particularly because in the case that the receiving party faces insolvency, the collateral provider would have an unsecured claim only for amount constituting surplus proceeds, rather than a proprietary claim to the assets.[47] The risk of unsecured surplus is more pronounced in crypto-token collateral arrangements due to the substantial price volatility and changing liquidity seen in crypto-token markets. Consequently, participants in the market who aim to minimise their exposure to unsecured surplus risk are likely to find this concern more significant in the context of crypto-token collateral arrangements.[48]

4.50 The common law of England and Wales recognises two broad categories of consensual security:[49]

40 Jacqui Hatfield and Rebecca Kellner, 'Taking security over cryptoassets' *Practical Law UK* (13 December 2019), 7.

41 Jessica Klien, 'Crypto lender Cred collapsed in 2020 after pulling in $135 million from customers. Its shady dealings foreshadowed FTX's downfall—but regulators didn't notice' (6 July 2023) *Fortune* https://fortune.com/2023/07/06/crypto-lender-cred-bankruptcy-earnity-ftx/ [accessed 27 September 2023].

42 Natalie Sherman, 'Crypto firm BlockFi files for bankruptcy after FTX collapse' (28 November 2022) www.bbc.co.uk/news/business-63786201 [accessed 27 September 2023].

43 Kevin Simauchi, Suvashree Ghosh, and Joanna Ossinger, 'Crypto Lender Genesis Files for Bankruptcy as Crisis Spreads' (20 January 2023) www.bloomberg.com/news/articles/2023-01-20/crypto-lender-genesis-files-for-bankruptcy-as-crisis-spreads [accessed 27 September 2023].

44 Law Commission, 'Digital Assets: Final report' (Law Com No 412, 2023). [8.18].

45 *Ibid* [8.19].

46 *Ibid* [8.20].

47 *Ibid* [8.21].

48 *Ibid* [8.22].

49 *Ibid* [8.23].

(a) non-possessory security arrangements: mortgage and equitable charge; and

(b) possessory security arrangements: pledge and contractual lien.

Non-possessory security arrangements

Mortgage and equitable charge[50]

4.51 A mortgage involves transferring ownership of an asset as security, with the understanding that ownership will revert to the one providing collateral when the secured obligation is fulfilled. Unlike outright title transfers, mortgages allow the collateral provider to keep an 'equity of redemption.' This means they possess a proprietary right to reclaim the asset when the obligation is met, as opposed to a contractual right to the asset's value.

4.52 On the other hand, a charge does not entail transferring ownership. It establishes a legally enforceable right, established by trust or contract, to use a designated asset or group of assets to settle a specific debt. This right is fulfilled by selling the asset and using the proceeds.

4.53 In the context of unregulated cryptoassets, both these security-based arrangements, which do not involve physical possession, can be established without needing legal changes.

4.54 These non-possessory security-based arrangements have advantages. Both mortgages and charges can be applied to entitlements in an unspecified portion of a group of intangible, interchangeable assets. Since possession is not required, they are not limited to assets that can be physically held. They can be applied to assets governed by varying holding arrangements, involving multiple parties and automated processes.

4.55 Mortgages and charges are also useful for collateral providers dealing in unregulated cryptoassets aiming to manage credit risk. Unlike outright transfers, these arrangements let the collateral provider maintain a proprietary right to regain the assets after fulfilling the obligation, including any surplus value left after enforcing the security interest.

Possessory security arrangements

Pledge and contractual lien[51]

4.56 A possessory security arrangement involves the party securing the assets by physically holding or planning to hold them. However, because crypto tokens do not have a physical form, they cannot be included in a valid possessory

50 *Ibid* [8.24]–[8.28].
51 *Ibid* [8.32]–[8.35].

security arrangement. The Law Commission explored the possibility of extending the concept of possessory security arrangements to a third category of assets—specifically, a pledge or a similar arrangement based on control. However, implementing this would require changing existing legal norms and concluded it would not be practical and would lead to issues. They opted instead to focus on legal reform regarding arrangements that capitalise on and improve the inherent flexibility of non-possessory security interests.

Perfecting security

4.57 Perfecting a security interest is crucial to ensure its validity against relevant third parties and to establish its intended priority over other creditors of the security provider. Perfection methods for cryptoassets may include the following:[52]

(a) **Notice of security**: if the security taken is a charge over a chose in action (certain types of cryptoassets may fall under this category), notice of the security must be given to third parties. This step ensures that other parties are aware of the security interest.

(b) **Registration at Companies House**: if the security is created by a company or limited liability partnership, registration of the security at Companies House is necessary. This step is essential to establish the security's validity.

(c) **Transfer of possession**: for security taken over a bearer instrument, such as a token representing a bearer share or security, transfer of possession of the cryptoasset to the security taker is required. This step ensures control over the asset, providing additional assurance to the secured party.

4.58 Noting a charge or encumbrance on the ledger governing the ownership of the cryptoasset is not currently feasible in open source cryptoassets, as they are traded without the need for an intermediary. In closed blockchains, where an intermediary can record details of asset holders, it may be possible for the intermediary to record charges, although this process is manual and separate from the blockchain. Moreover, many cryptoassets provide anonymity to traders, making it practically impossible for a buyer to determine if a cryptoasset is subject to a charge or mortgage unless informed by the seller. Without knowledge of the lender's interest through other means (eg registration at Companies House), the buyer may acquire the cryptoasset without being aware of the existing security interest.[53]

4.59 To enforce security over a cryptoasset, the lender typically takes possession of the cryptoasset or the wallet held with a custodian. The lender may then sell the cryptoasset to recover the funds lent. In cases where a mortgage has been perfected concerning a bearer security token, the lender already holds

52 Hatfield and Kellner (n 40 above), 5.
53 *Ibid.*

possession of the token. Consequently, the lender can enforce its security by exercising its rights to sell the token. The specific enforcement rights available to the lender will depend on the provisions outlined in the security document or, in the absence of explicit provisions, will be governed by applicable statutes and common law. As with securing any asset, the lender should explicitly state in detail its desired enforcement rights in the security document when taking security over a cryptoasset.[54]

4.60 An advantage of taking security over cryptoassets is the possibility of establishing a smart contract that facilitates the automatic transfer of cryptoassets upon the occurrence of a specific event. This feature allows for enforcement without manual intervention. However, for this to work effectively, there must be a sufficient level of trust between the lender and the borrower that the cryptoassets will remain in the relevant wallet to enable the smart contract to operate as intended upon the specified event.[55]

Regulatory considerations for taking security

4.61 In situations where regulated firms are taking custody over regulated cryptoassets, FCA regulated firms must observe the Principles for Business[56] and Principle 10 requires a firm to arrange adequate protection for clients' assets[57] and follow the rules set out in the FCA's Client Assets Sourcebook (CASS)[58] when holding regulated assets in custody, as part of their business. Where cryptoassets are specified investments (ie security tokens), firms carrying out regulated activities involving custody of these assets are likely to be subject to the CASS regime. If firms have any questions about how the CASS rules may apply, they should speak to their relevant FCA supervisory contact.[59]

4.62 The regulatory landscape may impact how a cryptoasset can be dealt with and, consequently, affect the feasibility of taking security over it. Some crypto-asset tokens are regulated financial instruments and dealing with such tokens is subject to regulatory restrictions, such as compliance with custody rules and restrictions on trading.

4.63 FCARs constitute the UK's domestic implementation of the European Directive on Financial Collateral Arrangements (FCD).[60] The Law Commission concluded that unregulated cryptoassets (specifically, those denominated in their

54 *Ibid* 6.
55 *Ibid*.
56 FCA, *FCA Handbook* PRIN (Release 31, August 2023) www.handbook.fca.org.uk/handbook/PRIN.pdf [accessed 27 September 2023].
57 *Ibid* PRIN 2.1.1.
58 FCA, *FCA Handbook* CASS www.handbook.fca.org.uk/handbook/CASS/ [accessed 27 September 2023].
59 FCA, 'Notice to all FCA regulated firms with exposure to cryptoassets' (24 March 2022).
60 Directive 2002/47/EC of 6 June 2002 on financial collateral arrangements [2002] OJ L168/43.

own unit of account) typically do not fall under the jurisdiction of the FCARs regime. However, when it comes to other types of collateral that might involve cryptoassets or tokens that merely represent of CBDCs, stablecoins, equity and debt securities, and credit claims, for example, the situation could be different. There is a stronger argument that some of these might indeed fall within the scope of the FCARs regime; however, even if regulated cryptoassets fall within scope, the FCARs do not comprehensively provide a satisfactory regime because of the requirement that security-based financial collateral be in the 'possession or control' of the collateral taker and the problems that raises when applied to cryptoasset collateral arrangements.[61] The FCARs defines 'financial collateral' as: 'cash', 'financial instruments' and 'credit claims'. It is possible to argue that certain crypto tokens, cryptoassets (including CBDCs, stablecoins, equity and debt securities and credit claims) or mere record/register tokens might already fall within the definition of 'financial collateral' but this will have to be assessed on a case-by-case basis.[62]

4.64 The characterisation of assets that are linked to or stapled to crypto tokens under the FCARs should focus on the substantive nature of the underlying asset rather than its specific technological form if the underlying asset satisfies the definition of 'financial collateral'. In the Law Commission's view the financial collateral is not affected by the fact that an asset is recorded by a mere register/record token on the basis that paper-based bearer bonds are included within the FCARs regime. Their characterisation as 'financial collateral' occurs by reference to the substantive nature of the underlying asset rather than its (physical) form. On that basis tokenised financial collateral (including both financial instruments and credit claims) or financial collateral that is subject to a linking or stapling arrangement represents the current law but requires clarificatory statutory amendments.[63]

4.65 Taking security over certain cryptoassets, especially those representing shares in a regulated company, may have regulatory consequences. Lenders must be aware of any change in control notifications or regulatory applications that might be necessary when enforcing security over such tokens. The extent to which UK companies might use tokenised equity and other registered corporate securities is constrained by the need to comply with the requirements of the Companies Act 2006, namely statutory requirements relating to the maintenance of registers.[64]

Trusts

4.66 The question of whether cryptoassets can be held under on trust was considered in the case of *Wang v Darby*.[65] While the Court ruled that no trust

61 Law Commission, 'Digital Assets' (n 44 above) [8.55]-[8.56].
62 *Ibid* [8.57].
63 *Ibid* [8.76]–[8.77].
64 *Ibid* [8.78]–[8.85].
65 [2021] EWHC 3054 (Comm).

existed based on the specific circumstances of the case, it acknowledged that there could be scenarios where a trust might be established. The Court determined that the fundamental economic reciprocity of the transaction, involving the transfer and re-transfer of ownership, contradicted the essence of a trust. The Court argued that a beneficiary's interest in trust property pertains to the right to receive it, not the option to re-acquire it for value or repurchase it. While not explicitly stated in the judgment, the inference drawn from its reasoning is that there is no inherent reason why cryptoassets cannot be subject to trust arrangements like any other form of property.[66]

4.67 The Law Commission has indicated that provided the 'three certainties' are satisfied by a trust over cryptoassets it will be considered a valid trust.[67] The three certainties are:[68]

(i) **Certainty of intention**: to meet this requirement a clear substantive intention, based on an objective assessment, by the relevant party or parties for the holding intermediary to hold its title to specified crypto token entitlements on trust for one or more beneficiaries. Determining whether there is a clear intention to create a trust for crypto tokens should be based on the user-intermediary agreement. Courts are likely to take a purpose-based and commercially responsive approach in recognising trust intentions by crypto token holding intermediaries. A key factor is whether the intermediary is meant to have unrestricted use of the assets, which strongly indicates against recognising a trustee/beneficiary relationship.

(ii) **Certainty of objects**: To meet this requirement sufficient identification of the beneficiaries that are the objects of the trust must be made. The requirement for certainty of objects in a trust is generally easy to meet. This should not pose practical challenges when structuring book-entries or crypto-token issuances as equitable interests. Beneficiaries and their individual interests can be identified through accounting records maintained by holding intermediaries or through distributed ledgers and smart contracts for token-related claims.

(iii) **Certainty of subject matter**: To meet this requirement sufficient identification of the crypto token entitlements constituting the things that will be the subject matter of the trust. Certainty of subject matter can be achieved whether assets are segregated or held in commingled, unallocated holdings like omnibus accounts. When crypto tokens are held in commingled

66 See Steven Baker and Julia Bihary, 'From cryptic to (some) clarity: English law and policy rising to the challenge of cryptoassets', (2022) 37(9) JIBLR 311, 313–314; see New Zealand High Court Decision, *Ruscoe v Cryptopia Ltd (in Liquidation)* [2020] NZHC 728, in which it was determined that digital assets held by a crypto exchange for its customers constituted property and were held under express trust on behalf of those customers; See also *Quoine Pte Ltd v B2C2 Ltd* [2020] SGCA(I) 02 (Singapore); *Re GateCoin Ltd (In Liquidation)* [2023] HKCFI 914 (Hong Kong).

67 Law Commission, 'Digital Assets' (n 44 above), [7.42].

68 *Ibid* [7.43]–[7.52].

accounts, identifying specific assets may be challenging. However, two legal approaches address this:

(a) **Intangible asset exception**: property rights can arise in an unidentified portion of a specified quantity of indistinguishable intangible assets, as established in *Hunter v Moss*;[69] and

(b) **Equitable co-ownership**: *Hunter v Moss* characterises beneficiaries' interests as co-ownership rights in an equitable tenancy in common over the entire pool. Users' co-ownership rights represent proportional entitlements to the entire quantity of crypto-token entitlements identifiable by reference to specific network addresses or higher-tier intermediary accounts.

4.68 The Law Commission indicate that crypto tokens are held in commingled accounts would be best characterised as equitable co-ownership and this conclusion was supported by consultees and academic law experts.[70]

Insolvency shortfall rules

4.69 The Law Commission considered shortfall situations that arise when a custodian of cryptoassets does not have sufficient crypto tokens to meet the aggregate claims of its customers. It concluded that law reform is required to clarify the apportionment of shortfall losses arising out of commingled crypto-token holdings that are held on trust by an insolvent custodian. They indicated, on balance, they were in of a general pro rata shortfall allocation rule of relatively broad application on the basis that it is conceptually coherent and a sensible pragmatic intervention that addresses potential uncertainty as to the correct approach to shortfall allocation in this context. They indicated that shortfalls arising on custodial holding intermediary insolvency must be considered within wider regulatory and policy frameworks rather than by the application of a standalone rule of private law.[71] They noted that their HM Treasury 'Consultation and Call for Evidence: Future financial services regulatory regime for cryptoassets'[72] is currently in progress. Paragraph 8.7(1) and Table 8.A. 'Proposed Design Features for Cryptoasset Custody Regime' specifically call for input in relation to insolvency and resolution.[73]

69 [1994] 1 WLR 452.

70 *Ibid* [7.53].

71 *Ibid* [7.91].

72 HM Treasury, 'Consultation and call for Evidence: Future financial services regulatory regime for cryptoassets' (February 2023) [4.8] Table 4.A https://assets.publishing.service.gov.uk/government/uploads/system/uploads/attachment_data/file/1133404/TR_Privacy_edits_Future_financial_services_regulatory_regime_for_cryptoassets_vP.pdf [accessed 28 September 2023].

73 Law Commission, 'Digital Assets' (n 44 above), [7.92].

CONCLUSION

4.70 The BCBS SCO60 provides clarity as to how banks should manage cryptoasset exposure from a prudential regulatory perspective. Lending practice in relation to this novel asset class is developing and requires bespoke approaches from lawyers to make sure that security is perfected and enforceable. In the UK further initiatives in relation to DeFi are being considered by HM Treasury and HMRC which will bring further clarity on crypto lending arrangements. Lenders considering taking security over cryptoassets should keep in mind the following key considerations:[74]

(a) **Volatility**: cryptoassets, particularly decentralised ones lacking asset backing, are known for their high volatility. This poses risks for lenders since the value of crypto-assets can significantly fluctuate over time. Lenders must be cautious and may be hesitant to take security over cryptoassets, especially for long-term loans, as the asset's value may decline below the amount lent.

(b) **Trust in custodians**: if the cryptoassets are held with a custodian, the lender must trust the custodian to handle the assets appropriately. For enforcement purposes, lenders may prefer reputable custodians with a track record of reliability to mitigate the risk of assets being transferred out of the wallet before an event of default.

(c) **Custodian's perspective**: custodians holding cryptoassets may also seek to take security over the assets they hold. However, the regulatory position in relation to cryptassets is constantly evolving and many large custodians may be hesitant to enter the market until the legal landscape is more established and clients become institutional.

74 Hatfield and Kellner (n 40 above), 6–7.

Chapter 5

Taxation of Cryptocurrency in the UK

5.1 In the UK, cryptocurrencies are subject to taxation. The tax treatment of cryptocurrencies is a complex area and depends on the specific circumstances and activities involved. For individuals, capital gains tax may apply when disposing of cryptocurrencies, while businesses may be subject to corporation tax on their cryptocurrency-related activities.

5.2 HMRC guidance on cryptoasset transactions is currently based on existing tax rules rather than specific rules for cryptocurrencies. The guidance is outlined in HMRC's Cryptoassets Manual.[1]

5.3 It is important to note that HMRC may not always strictly adhere to their published guidance, but it can serve as a starting point when considering their approach to a case.[2] The views presented in the guidance may evolve over time as the cryptoasset space develops.

5.4 HMRC's specific stance on cryptoassets states that they are not considered money or currency.[3] Consequently, the tax rules that apply to traditional currencies do not extend to exchange tokens.[4] When determining the value of tokens, the standard method is to calculate it under Generally Accepted Accounting Principles (GAAP) unless a different valuation method is required.[5] Under GAAP, cryptocurrencies are not regarded as currency and are more likely to be considered intangible assets in most cases.

CLASSIFICATION OF CRYPTOCURRENCIES

5.5 In the UK, cryptocurrencies are treated as digital assets for tax purposes. The tax treatment of cryptocurrencies depends on their specific characteristics and the activities involving them. HMRC define cryptoassets as:[6]

1 HMRC internal manual: Cryptoassets Manual (30 March 2021, updated 21 August 2023) www.gov.uk/hmrc-internal-manuals/cryptoassets-manual [accessed 9 October 2023].

2 In the Court of Appeal case, *R (on the application of Aozora GMAC Investment Ltd) v HMRC* [2019] EWCA Civ 1643, the court indicated that HMRC's guidance can give rise to circumstances where a legitimate expectation may arise, but the ability to bring a successful claim for a breach of legitimate expectation are limited.

3 CRYPTO10100 and CRYPTO41050.

4 Non-applicability of currency-related rules.

5 CRYPTO40100.

6 CRYPTO10100.

> '… cryptographically secured digital representations of value or contractual rights that can be
>
> - transferred
> - stored
> - traded electronically
>
> While all cryptoassets use some form of …[DLT] not all applications of DLT involve cryptoassets.'

5.6 HMRC identify four main types of cryptoasset: (i) exchange tokens; (ii) utility tokens; (iii) security tokens; and (iv) stable coins.[7]

UTILITY TOKENS, SECURITY TOKENS AND STABLECOINS

5.7 The Cryptoassets Manual primarily focuses on exchange tokens and does not extensively cover the complexities of security and utility tokens and the general principles of taxation should be used. The guidance on exchange tokens can be applied to stablecoins where applicable.

SMART CONTRACTS

5.8 Entering into a smart contract can trigger tax liability similar to traditional contracts. The automatic performance of the contract does not seem to be relevant for tax purposes; what matters is the actual transactions that occur upon performance. Normal principles apply to determine liability, including the timing determined in accordance with s 28 of TCGA 1992. Smart contracts follow the principles of normal contract law for tax analysis.[8]

GAMBLING

5.9 Although there is an element of risk, HMRC do not classify buying and selling cryptoassets as gambling.[9]

DERIVATIVES AND EXCHANGE TRADED NOTES

5.10 HMRC's stance is that derivative contracts involving cryptoassets are not considered cryptoassets themselves, primarily due to the contractual rights

7 *Ibid.*
8 UKJT, 'Legal statement on cryptoassets and smart contracts' (November 2019), The LawTech Delivery Panel, [18] www.blockchain4europe.eu/wp-content/uploads/2021/05/6.6056_JO_Cryptocurrencies_Statement_FINAL_WEB_111119-1.pdf [accessed 26 September 2023],
9 CRYPTO10450.

and obligations between the parties involved. Instead, they are categorised as derivative contracts under the Corporation Tax Act 2009 (CTA), Pt 7.[10]

RESIDENCE AND UNDERLYING ASSET RULES

5.11 HMRC's approach focuses on clarifying the tax implications for non-UK domiciled and non-UK resident individuals who own cryptoassets. It is crucial for these individuals to determine the location of their cryptoassets for tax purposes in order to effectively utilise the remittance basis and engage in estate and inheritance tax (IHT) planning. It can also impact capital gains tax (CGT) if a non-domiciled individual realises a cryptoasset gain overseas.

5.12 Identifying the situs of cryptoassets can be complex due to the diverse nature and rules governing different tokens. DLT adds to the challenge as ownership records are scattered across multiple locations. Cryptoassets lack physical tokens, and private keys might not always be physically stored, making it difficult to pinpoint their exact location. The UKJT statement also highlights the possibility of separating legal and beneficial ownership.[11]

5.13 To determine the location of a token, HMRC classify cryptoassets into two categories:[12]

(a) **No underlying assets**: these tokens are distinct from any underlying asset.

(b) **Underlying assets**: these tokens are simply a digital representation of an underlying asset, ie real estate.

Different rules apply to CGT and IHT regarding the situs (location) of crypto-assets. The following rules described below specifically apply to CGT.[13]

5.14 Where the cryptoasset is simply a digital representation of an underlying asset then the location of the underlying asset will determine the location of the cryptoasset (eg certain stablecoins). These tokens are treated as transparent containers rather than standalone assets, limiting the scope for tax planning beyond what is typically possible. This rule primarily aims for simplicity and formal compliance.[14] While it may be reasonable to apply the underlying asset rule when the value and rights of a token primarily come from another asset, there is a wide range of tokenisation models, and not all stablecoins follow the same pattern. Therefore, it may be necessary to investigate the exact nature of the underlying asset.[15]

10 CRYPTO10150.
11 UKJT, Legal statement on cryptoassets (n 8 above), [58] and [133].
12 CRYPTO22600.
13 Lauren Rapeport, 'Digging for Gold: the situs of cryptoassets' (2021) 5 PCB 183, 184.
14 *Ibid* 186.
15 *Ibid*.

5.15 The rule mainly targets stablecoins; however, not all stablecoins will be subject to this rule, particularly if they are backed by cryptoassets that cannot be located by reference to an underlying asset. In such cases, the residence rule may apply, subject to the restriction on exchange tokens.[16]

5.16 When there is no underlying asset, HMRC use the statutory residence test (SRT)[17] to determine the location of an individual's cryptoassets for CGT purposes based on their tax residence. According to the manual, the location of the cryptoasset is determined by the residency of the beneficial owner. This means that if a person is a UK resident and conducts a transaction with their tokens that is subject to UK tax, they are liable to pay UK tax.[18]

5.17 This approach deviates from the typical situs rules in UK tax law and restricts remittance basis users from keeping their cryptoassets offshore unless they transfer them to a separate holding structure while non-UK resident. The residence rule simplifies the determination of the situs of an intangible asset and avoids complicated considerations related to storage methods and levels of control.[19] However, this rule may conflict with the practical usage of cryptoassets by taxpayers. For example, even if a UK resident keeps their private keys in cold storage offshore and does not access them, they will be treated as if they held the keys directly in the UK.[20]

5.18 For CGT, ss 275 and 275A of TCGA 1992, which determine asset location, do not generally apply to exchange tokens. The focus is on the beneficial owner of the exchange token. If the token is co-owned, s 275C of TGCA 1992 applies, treating each co-owner's beneficial interest separately and located based on the owner's residency.

5.19 For IHT, when no double taxation agreements determine the location, common law governs.[21]

5.20 Both Kessler and STEP have stated that HMRC's adoption of SRT as the relevant residence criterion is incorrect on the basis that situs is a concept in general law and therefore the correct indicator of residence should be the ordinary residence, not the SRT. Kessler points out that the SRT's determination of residence is tied to a specific tax year, making it unsuitable for situs considerations that require a particular moment's determination. He argues for limited instances where the SRT and common law tests for ordinary residence yield differing results, as the SRT was designed to codify existing common law residence tests at the time.[22]

16 *Ibid.*

17 HMRC, *RDR3: Statutory Residence Test (SRT) notes* (Guidance, 22 January 2020) www.gov.uk/government/publications/rdr3-statutory-residence-test-srt/guidance-note-for-statutory-residence-test-srt-rdr3 [accessed 8 October 2023].

18 Rapeport (n 13 above), 185.

19 *Ibid.*

20 *Ibid.*

21 Inheritance Tax Act 1984, s 158(1).

22 See **2.27–2.34**. See also Ethan (Ho-Ning) Yu, 'Locating the Ethereal: the situs of cryptoassets reexamined' (2022) 6 PCB, 220–226, 225.

INDIVIDUALS

Income tax

Earnings from employment

5.21 Cryptoassets received as employment income are considered 'money's worth' and are subject to income tax and National Insurance contributions based on their value. Cryptoassets are classified as readily convertible assets (RCAs) when there are existing or likely trading arrangements in accordance with Income Tax (Earnings and Pensions) Act 2003 (ITEPA 2003), s 702. For instance, exchange tokens like bitcoin can be easily exchanged for money on token exchanges, implying the presence or potential emergence of trading arrangements when cryptoassets are received as employment income.[23]

5.22 When cryptoassets are provided in the form of readily convertible assets, the employer must report and pay the corresponding tax and National Insurance contributions to HMRC, based on the best estimate of the asset's value.[24] Any disposal of the token received through employment may result in a chargeable gain for CGT.[25]

Mining[26]

5.23 Cryptocurrency mining activities are subject to income tax; the pound sterling value (at the time of receipt) of any tokens awarded will be taxable as income (miscellaneous income[27]) with any appropriate expenses reducing the amount chargeable. Whether such activity amounts to a taxable trade (with the tokens as trade receipts) depends on a range of factors such as: [28]

(a) degree of activity;

(b) organisation;

(c) risk; and

(d) commerciality.

23 CRYPTO21100.

24 For more details on employer obligations, refer to CRYPTO42050. Additional information about RCAs can be found in HMRC, Employment Income Manual (HMRC Internal Manual, 22 May 2014, updated 14 September 2023) EIM11900 www.gov.uk/hmrc-internal-manuals/employment-income-manual/eim11900 [accessed 28 September 2023].

25 CRYPTO21100.

26 See CRYPTO10300 for HMRC guidance on mining.

27 For more information on miscellaneous income, see HMRC, Business Income Manual (HMRC Internal Manual, 22 November 2013, updated 20 September 2023) BIM100000 www.gov.uk/hmrc-internal-manuals/business-income-manual/bim100000 [accessed 28 September 2023].

28 CRYPTO21150.

Staking[29]

5.24 If an individual is not participating in a trade and keeps the awarded assets earned from staking, the pound sterling value (at the time of receipt) of any tokens awarded will be taxable as income (miscellaneous income) with any appropriate expenses reducing the amount chargeable. They may have to pay CGT when they later dispose of them. [30]

Trading

5.25 Profits or gains derived from cryptocurrency trading are generally subject to income tax. The timing and frequency of trading activities are essential factors in determining whether the activity is considered trading or investment.

Airdrops

5.26 Income tax will not always apply to airdropped tokens received in a personal capacity. Income tax may not apply if they are received:

- without doing anything in return; and
- not as part of a trade or business involving cryptoasset exchange tokens or mining.

5.27 Airdrops that are provided in return for, or in expectation of, a service are subject to income tax either as:

- miscellaneous income; or
- receipts of an existing trade

5.28 The disposal of a token received through an airdrop may result in a chargeable gain for CGT, even if it is not chargeable to income tax when it is received. Where changes in value get brought into account as part of a computation of trade profits, income tax will take priority over CGT.[31]

Capital gains tax

5.29 CGT applies to gains on disposals of chargeable assets for individuals and trustees.[32] Tokens are digital and therefore intangible, but count as a 'chargeable asset' for CGT if they are:[33]

29 See CRYPTO10300 for HMRC guidance on proof of work and proof of stake.
30 CRYPTO21200.
31 CRYPTO21250.
32 TCGA 1992, s 1(1).
33 CRYPTO22050.

(a) capable of being owned; and

(b) have a value that can be realised.[34]

5.30 HMRC generally consider the buying and selling of tokens by an individual will normally amount to investment activity rather than a trade and thus they will normally have to pay CGT on realised gains.[35]

5.31 Individuals must calculate gains or losses when they dispose of tokens to determine if they owe CGT. A 'disposal' includes:[36]

(a) Selling tokens for money.

(b) Exchanging tokens for a different type of token.

(c) Using tokens to pay for goods or services.

(d) Giving tokens to someone else, except for gifts to a spouse or civil partner.

No disposal occurs if the individual retains beneficial ownership of the tokens during the transaction, such as moving tokens between wallets they control.[37]

5.32 Using a mixer or similar service to receive the same type of tokens is not a disposal, except when receiving a different token in return.[38]

5.33 When giving tokens to someone other than a spouse or civil partner, the individual must determine the pound sterling value of the gift. For CGT, they are treated as receiving that amount of pound sterling, even if they did not actually receive anything.[39]

5.34 If income tax was charged on the token's value, TCGA 1992, s 37 applies, reducing any consideration by the amount already subject to income tax.[40]

5.35 Donating tokens to charity is exempt from CGT, unless it is a 'tainted donation' or the tokens are sold to the charity for a profit.[41]

34 For more information on HMRC's treatment of chargeable assets see HMRC, Capital Gains Manual (HMRC Internal Manual, 12 March 2016, updated 5 October 2023) CG12010 www.gov.uk/hmrc-internal-manuals/capital-gains-manual [accessed 8 October 2023].

35 For further information see HMRC, 'Check if you need to pay tax when you sell cryptoassets' (Guidance, 19 December 2018) www.gov.uk/guidance/check-if-you-need-to-pay-tax-when-you-sell-cryptoassets [accessed 28 September 2023].

36 CRYPTO22100.

37 *Ibid.*

38 *Ibid.*

39 *Ibid.*

40 *Ibid.*

41 *Ibid.* For further details on CGT and charitable donations see CG66620P.

Transferring tokens between distributed ledgers

5.36 Tokens cannot be directly moved from one cryptoasset's distributed ledger to another's. For instance, you cannot move Bitcoin to the Ethereum blockchain. However, you can achieve a similar result using a smart contract and secure public addresses. Token holders use a smart contract to send tokens to an address they do not control. In return, an equivalent amount of tokens from the second cryptoasset is sent from a secure public address to an address controlled by the person. Whether this transaction triggers CGT depends on the specific circumstances.[42]

One-way transfers

5.37 Some transfers are irreversible and can only go in one direction. An example is transferring ether from the Ethereum mainnet to the Beacon Chain, which is permanent. HMRC view this as subject to TCGA 1992, s 43. The allowable costs of the first cryptoasset are fully attributed to the second cryptoasset. Any gain or loss occurs when the second cryptoasset is later disposed of.[43]

Allowable expenses

5.38 When calculating gains or losses from token disposal, not all costs can be deducted. TCGA 1992, s 38 outlines allowable deductions, including:[44]

(a) the original purchase price (in pounds) of the asset;

(b) transaction fees for ledger inclusion;

(c) advertising costs for buyers or sellers;

(d) professional fees for contract preparation;

(e) costs for valuations or apportionments for gain/loss calculation; and

(f) costs deducted against income tax profits are not deductible for CGT.

5.39 Regarding exchange fees, the treatment depends on the situation:[45]

(a) **Swapping sterling for non-sterling fiat**: deductible as acquiring non-sterling fiat (TCGA 1992, s 38(1)(a)).

(b) **Swapping non-sterling fiat for sterling**: deductible as an incidental cost (TCGA 1992, s 38(1)(c)).

(c) **Depositing sterling**: not deductible since sterling is not a CGT asset.

42 *Ibid.*
43 *Ibid.*
44 CRYPTO22150.
45 *Ibid.*

(d) **Depositing non-sterling fiat**: not deductible as there is no acquisition/disposal.

(e) **Using sterling to buy tokens**: deductible as token acquisition (TCGA 1992, s 38(1)(a)).

(f) **Using non-sterling fiat to buy tokens**: deductible as token acquisition (TCGA 1992, s 38(1)(a)).

(g) **Swapping token A for token B**: deductible for both disposals (TCGA 1992, s 38(1)(c) for A, TCGA 1992, s 38(1)(a) for B).

5.40 Mining costs (equipment and electricity) are not allowable as they do not solely acquire tokens (TCGA 1992, s 38(1)(a)). Some may be deductible for income tax. Equipment costs may be deductible when disposing of the equipment, subject to relevant provisions. For tokens mined in a trade, they form part of trading stock initially. When removed, use their value in trading accounts as an allowable cost.[46]

Pooling

5.41 Pooling under TCGA 1992, s 104 simplifies CGT for shares, securities, and certain assets that cannot be individually identified when bought or sold. For tokens dealt with similarly, a 'section 104 pool' is created. Owners have one pooled asset for CGT, changing with each acquisition or disposal. NFTs are treated individually because they cannot be pooled.[47]

Separate pools for different tokens

5.42 Each token type (eg Bitcoin, Ether, Litecoin) has its own pool, with a unique 'pooled allowable cost' that adjusts with token transactions.[48]

Record keeping

5.43 Individuals must track spending on each token type and their respective pooled allowable costs.[49]

Same-day rule (TCGA 1992, s 105)

5.44 If someone buys and sells the same type of tokens on the same day, this rule ensures a single CGT computation per calendar day. Tokens acquired and disposed of on the same day are treated as a single transaction, with excess

46 *Ibid*. For further information see CG69220.
47 CRYPTO22200.
48 *Ibid*.
49 *Ibid*.

tokens either entering the section 104 pool or being considered for the 30-day rule.[50]

Acquiring tokens within 30 days of selling (TCGA 1992, s 106A)

5.45 If tokens of the same type are sold and then repurchased within 30 days, the same-day rule applies first. Tokens acquired within the 30-day window are matched to the earlier disposals, starting with the earliest. Excess tokens go into the section 104 pool.[51]

5.46 Worked examples of the foregoing are set out at CRYPTO22250.

Fees satisfied in tokens

5.47 When conducting cryptoasset transactions, fees are often involved, and these fees are typically paid in tokens. It is important to consider these fees both as a part of the costs for disposing of tokens and as separate disposals themselves.[52]

5.48 These fees are given in exchange for services, commonly for order matching and ledger inclusion, among others. According to TCGA 1992, s 17(1)(b), if an asset is disposed of in consideration for services, its market value is used. This means the tokens given as fees are treated as disposed of at their market value, and allowable costs are calculated accordingly (eg using the same-day rule, 30-day rule, or relevant part of TCGA 1992, s 104 pooled allowable expenditure).[53]

5.49 Furthermore, these fees are paid for services related to acquiring or disposing of tokens. The price of the service is determined by the market value of the token. Therefore, when tokens are used as fees, the relevant capital gains computation includes:[54]

(a) consideration equal to the market value of the token given as a fee;

(b) allowable cost equal to the market value of the token given as a fee; and

(c) allowable cost, determined by applying the same-day rule, 30-day rule, or section 104 pool rules, as appropriate.

HMRC's examples of fees in token disposals are set out at CRYPTO22280.

50 *Ibid.*
51 *Ibid.* For more information see CG51560.
52 CRYPTO22280.
53 *Ibid.*
54 *Ibid.*

Forks and airdrops

5.50 In the cryptoassets ecosystem, some are decentralised, relying on community consensus rather than central control. When a significant portion of the community desires a change, they can initiate a 'fork' in the distributed ledger. There are two types: a soft fork and a hard fork.[55]

(a) **Soft fork**: this updates the protocol and aims for universal adoption. No new tokens or ledgers are created.

(b) **Hard fork**: this is different and can result in new tokens. Before the hard fork, there is a single ledger. After the hard fork, a new branch (and cryptoasset) is created.

5.51 The original and new cryptoassets share a history until the fork. Holders of the original cryptoasset typically have an equal number of tokens on both ledgers after the fork. The value of new tokens is derived from the original tokens, so s 43 of TCGA 1992 applies.[56]

5.52 After a fork, new tokens must be placed in their separate section 104 pool. Allowable costs in the original cryptoasset's section 104 pool are split between the two pools.[57]

5.53 If an individual holds tokens through an exchange, the exchange decides whether to recognise the new tokens created by the fork. Cost splitting should be just and reasonable under TCGA 1992, s 52(4), with no specific method prescribed. HMRC can investigate if they deem the method unjust.[58]

5.54 The disposal of new tokens is only possible if the exchange recognises them. If not, the individual can choose to allocate all allowable costs to the original tokens, but it should be considered just and reasonable. Alternatively, they can allocate costs and make a negligible value claim for the new tokens, provided all conditions are met. In complex cases, seek technical advice through the relevant process.[59]

5.55 An airdrop occurs when an individual receives tokens, often as part of a marketing or advertising campaign. The cryptoasset involved in the airdrop usually operates independently with its own infrastructure, like a smart contract, blockchain, or DLT.[60]

5.56 Airdropped tokens go into their own section 104 pool unless the recipient already holds tokens of that cryptoasset. In that case, the airdropped tokens join

55 CRYPTO22300.
56 *Ibid.*
57 *Ibid.*
58 *Ibid.*
59 *Ibid.*
60 CRYPTO22350.

the existing section 104 pool. Notably, the value of airdropped cryptoassets does not derive from existing tokens held by the individual, so TCGA 1992, s 43 does not apply.[61]

Losing private keys, being defrauded, s 24 and negligible value

5.57 When an individual loses their private key, such as by mistakenly discarding it, they lose access to their tokens. While the private key still technically exists within the cryptography, the owner no longer knows it. Simultaneously, the tokens remain on the distributed ledger. Importantly, misplacing the key does not constitute a disposal for CGT purposes.[62]

5.58 If there is no realistic chance of recovering the private key or accessing the tokens, a negligible value claim can be filed. If HMRC approve this claim, the individual is treated as if they disposed of and re-acquired the tokens they cannot access. This allows them to realise a loss for tax purposes.[63]

5.59 HMRC do not view theft as a disposal since the individual still owns the stolen asset and has the right to recover it. Therefore, victims of theft cannot claim a loss for CGT. Individuals who enter into contracts to acquire tokens but do not receive them may also face challenges in claiming a capital loss.[64]

5.60 Individuals who contract to acquire tokens and actually receive them can potentially make a negligible value claim to HMRC if the tokens become worthless. However, if the tokens were already worthless upon acquisition, a negligible value claim will not be permitted. This does not affect the individual's ability to dispose of the tokens in other ways to realise a capital loss.[65]

5.61 Just like with other assets, individuals can claim losses for tokens they still own if those tokens become worthless or have 'negligible value' while in their possession. A negligible value claim treats all the tokens in a section 104 pool as disposed of and immediately re-acquired at a specified amount in the claim. It is important to note that this claim applies to the entire pool, not individual tokens.[66]

5.62 To make a negligible value claim, you must provide:

(a) the asset in question;

(b) the specified amount for the disposal (which may be £nil); and

(c) the date when the asset should be considered disposed of and immediately reacquired.

61 *Ibid.*
62 CRYPTO22400. For further information see CG13155.
63 *Ibid.* Additional guidance on negligible value claims can be found at CRYPTO22500.
64 CRYPTO22450.
65 *Ibid.* Additional guidance can be found at CG13155.
66 CRYPTO22500.

This disposal generates a loss that should be reported to HMRC. You can make negligible value claims to HMRC while reporting the loss.[67]

Currency

5.63 HMRC do not classify cryptoassets as currency or money, aligning with the Cryptoasset Taskforce Report (CATF). Consequently, TCGA 1992, ss 252 and 269 do not apply.[68]

Determining the location of exchange tokens

5.64 Cryptoassets, being digital in nature, lack a physical location, yet their location (referred to as 'situs') is crucial for tax considerations, especially for:[69]

(a) UK residents and non-domiciled individuals computing CGT and IHT liabilities; and

(b) those assessing whether the RTC and offshore penalty regime apply.

5.65 To establish a cryptoasset's location, first check if there are any statutory rules, either for tax or general purposes, specifying the location. For CGT, TCGA 1992 outlines statutory location rules in ss 275 (for assets) and 275A (for certain intangible assets), supplemented by s 275B. For IHT, no statutory rules exist, relying on general principles applicable to private property.[70]

Underlying asset

5.66 If a cryptoasset represents an underlying asset, its location is determined by the location of that underlying asset.[71]

No underlying asset

5.67 When a cryptoasset is distinct from any underlying asset, HMRC's view is that none of the statutory rules in TCGA 1992 apply. Instead, HMRC considers that:[72]

(a) exchange tokens have economic value, as they can be used for transactions;

(b) they are a new type of intangible asset, different from shares or debentures; and

67 *Ibid*. For more information see CG13120P.
68 CRYPTO22550.
69 CRYPTO22600.
70 *Ibid*.
71 CRYPTO22600.
72 CRYPTO22600.

(c) the location of the cryptoasset is determined by the residency of the beneficial owner.

5.68 This means that the cryptoasset's location is where the beneficial owner resides, providing a clear, logical, and easily applicable rule. UK tax liability applies if a UK resident (determined by the statutory residence test) conducts a transaction with their tokens subject to UK tax.[73]

5.69 If exchange tokens are co-owned, each co-owner's interest follows their residency. If one or more co-owners are UK residents, it does not affect the location for non-UK resident co-owners.[74] HMRC has provided further guidance on determining the location of cryptoassets at CRYPTO100500.

5.70 For IHT, common law applies unless double taxation agreements dictate the location.[75]

Valuation

5.71 Many cryptoassets (such as bitcoin) are traded on exchanges which do not use pound sterling, so the value of any gain or loss must be converted into pound sterling on the self-assessment tax return.[76]

5.72 If the transaction does not have a pound sterling value (for example if bitcoin is exchanged for Ether) an appropriate exchange rate must be established in order to convert the transaction to pound sterling. Reasonable care should be taken to arrive at an appropriate valuation for the transaction using a consistent methodology. Details of the valuation methodology should be kept.[77] Further information on valuation can be found in the HMRC guidance 'Shares and Assets Valuations for Tax' (SAV),[78] where assistance is required in agreeing a value for tax purposes.[79]

Stamp taxes and land

Stamp duty

5.73 Stamp duty applies to instruments transferring stocks, marketable securities, and partnership interests with such assets.[80]

73 *Ibid.*
74 *Ibid.*
75 *Ibid.* See Inheritance Tax Act 1984, s 158.
76 CRYPTO23000.
77 *Ibid.*
78 HMRC, *Shares and assets valuations for tax* (Guidance, 7 May 2019) www.gov.uk/guidance/shares-and-assets-valuations-for-tax [accessed 27 September 2023].
79 CRYPTO23000.
80 CRYPTO24000.

Stamp duty reserve tax

5.74 Stamp duty reserve tax (SDRT) applies to agreements transferring chargeable securities. For cryptoasset transfers to be subject to stamp duty or SDRT, they must meet the definitions of 'stock or marketable securities' or 'chargeable securities.' This determination considers the cryptoasset's characteristics, not labels. HMRC generally does not consider existing exchange tokens to meet these definitions.[81]

Exchange tokens as consideration

5.75 Exchange tokens used as consideration for purchasing 'stock or marketable securities' or 'chargeable securities' are treated as 'money's worth' for SDRT, with tax based on their pound sterling value. However, for stamp duty, exchange tokens are not considered 'money' and typically not 'stock or marketable securities.' 'Debt' can be chargeable consideration for stamp duty in scenarios involving the release or assumption of debt in exchange for shares.[82]

Stamp duty land tax

5.76 Stamp Duty Land Tax (SDLT) applies to land and building acquisitions above a certain price in England and Northern Ireland.[83] It does not apply to land in Scotland or Wales.[84] Cryptoasset transfers are not considered land transactions, so SDLT does not apply. When exchange tokens are used as consideration for land transactions, they are treated as 'money's worth' and are subject to SDLT based on their market value on the transaction date.[85]

Inheritance tax

5.77 HMRC treat cryptoassets as property for IHT purposes, aligning with the UKJT and Law Commission statements.[86] HMRC categorise exchange tokens as property, making them potentially subject to IHT. Cryptocurrencies held as part of an individual's estate are subject to inheritance tax upon their death. The value of cryptocurrencies at the time of death is included in the calculation of the estate's total value, and IHT is levied accordingly.

81 *Ibid*. For further information, see HMRC, Stamp Taxes on Shares Manual (HMRC Internal Manual, 7 March 2016. updated 17 May 2022) www.gov.uk/hmrc-internal-manuals/stamp-taxes-shares-manual [accessed 8 October 2023].

82 *Ibid.*

83 Land Transaction Tax is payable on land purchased Wales on or after 1 April 2018.

84 Land and Buildings Transaction Tax is payable on land purchased in Scotland on or after 1 April 2015.

85 CRYPTO24000. For further information see HMRC, *Stamp Duty Land Tax Manual* (HMRC Internal Manual, 19 March 2016, updated 12 July 2023) www.gov.uk/hmrc-internal-manuals/stamp-duty-land-tax-manual [accessed 8 October 2023].

86 CRYPTO25000.

5.78 For UK-domiciled individuals, IHT applies to their worldwide estate. Non-UK domiciled individuals are subject to IHT only on their UK estate. Additionally, the location of cryptoassets should be considered, as the asset's situs affects the IHT liability.

Situs for inheritance tax purposes

5.79 Determining the location (situs) of assets may be necessary for non-UK domiciled taxpayers. For HMRC's stance on this, refer to CRYPTO22550.[87] The Cryptoassets Manual states that the rules for determining the situs of cryptoassets for IHT purposes will be the common law rules, unless a double tax treaty specifies otherwise.[88]

Will drafting

5.80 Cryptoassets require specific consideration in will drafting. Testators should determine if their will's definition of personal chattels or possessions encompasses cryptoassets. If the existing definition does not cover digital assets, it may be necessary to amend the will to include cryptoassets explicitly. Alternatively, testators can create a separate legacy for cryptocurrency, with a carefully constructed definition to ensure clarity. Including a specific power in the will for personal representatives to handle cryptassets is prudent and will drafters must be clear and explicit about including cryptocurrency in the estate plan to ensure its proper handling and distribution according to the testator's wishes. As it stands, the definition of 'personal chattels' under s 3 of the Inheritance and Trustees' Powers Act 2014 does not include cryptoassets.

Pension contributions

Registered pension schemes

5.81 Cryptoassets are not recognised as currency or money for tax-relieved pension contributions to a registered pension scheme (RPS).[89] If cryptoassets are placed into an RPS without any tax advantage, they become subject to RPS tax rules.[90]

87 CRYPTO25000

88 Inheritance Tax Act 1984, s 158(1).

89 For details on RPS contributions, refer to HMRC, Pensions Tax Manual (HMRC Internal Manual, 27 March 2015, updated 12 September 2023) PTM041000 www.gov.uk/hmrc-internal-manuals/pensions-tax-manual [accessed 28 September 2023].

90 CRYPTO26000. Further information on these rules can be found in the Pensions Tax Manual.

BUSINESSES

Trade

5.82 The Cryptoassets Manual focuses on buying and selling exchange tokens as part of a trade and is silent on utility tokens, security tokens, and stable coins.[91] Businesses engage in buying and selling exchange tokens as part of their trade. If they accept exchange tokens as payment for goods or services during their trading activities, the receipt of tokens is subject to income tax or corporation tax.[92] A trade in cryptoasset exchange tokens resembles trading in shares and other financial products, and similar criteria apply.[93] Whether the buying and selling of exchange tokens amounts to a trade depends on a range of factors including frequency, level of organisation, and intention.[94] The caselaw on this issue is discussed below.

5.83 Challenges lies in computing profits and determining the value of the receipt, which must be converted into pounds sterling for tax return purposes. Profits or gains (or losses) should be calculated by converting to pounds sterling using the appropriate rate at the time of each transaction. HMRC require consistent valuation methodology, with records retained for tax purposes.[95] Trading an exchange token on an exchange may facilitate this process.

5.84 Section 989 of the Income Tax Act 2007 (ITA 2007) defines 'trade' as any venture that resembles a trade. Tax liability can be triggered if cryptoassets are treated as part of trade (stock) and, for accounting purposes, are appropriated to fixed assets (or vice versa).[96] HMRC consider an individual to be trading in exceptional circumstances, taking into account the 'frequency, level of organisation and sophistication that the activity amounts to a financial trade in itself'.[97]

5.85 In the case of *Eclipse Film Partners No 35 LLP v Revenue and Customs Commissioners*,[98] it was noted that the Income Tax Acts have not further defined 'trade'. The determination of whether an activity qualifies as a trade is a matter of law. The evaluation of the activity depends on the factual circumstances and applicable legal principles, as determined by the fact-finding tribunal.

5.86 Essentially, the presence of a 'trade' is determined based on the specific facts and circumstances of each case. The authorities often refer to the 'badges

91 CRYPTO40150.
92 CRYPTO40050.
93 Information on HMRC's approach and case law for share transactions and financial traders can be found in BIM56800.
94 CRYPTO40150.
95 CRYPTO40100, Income Tax (Trading and Other Income) Act 2005, s 28A and Corporation Tax Act 2009, s 49A.
96 TCGA 1992, s 161.
97 CRYPTO20250.
98 [2015] EWCA Civ 95 at [112], [2015] STC 1429, 1449.

of trade' as indicators of whether a trade is being conducted. In *Eclipse Film Partners*, Sir Terence Etherton C mentioned that the list of badges of trade had been summarised in the judgment of Sir Nicholas Browne-Wilkinson V-C in *Marson v Morton*.[99] These badges, relevant to the sale of cryptocurrencies, can be summarised as follows:

(a) Is the transaction a one-off or repetitive? While a one-off transaction can still be considered an adventure in the nature of trade, the lack of repetition may suggest otherwise.

(b) Is the transaction related to the taxpayer's regular trade? For example, a one-off purchase of silver cutlery by a general dealer is more likely to be a trade transaction compared to a retired colonel making the same purchase.

(c) What is the nature of the subject matter of the transaction? Is it a commodity commonly associated with trade, such as toilet paper or whisky, or is it something primarily for personal enjoyment?

(d) What was the purchaser's intention regarding resale at the time of purchase? An intention to hold the object for a long time and make a capital profit indicates investment, while an intention to resell in the short term suggests a deal or trade.

It is important to note that the badges of trade listed by Sir Nicholas Browne-Wilkinson V-C are not an exhaustive list, and no single badge is determinative of whether a trade exists or not.

5.87 In relation to the 'intention' of a taxpayer and its relevance to whether the taxpayer is 'trading,' The Privy Council in *Iswera v CIR*[100] observed that:

> 'If, in order to get what he wants, the taxpayer has to embark on an adventure which has all the characteristics of trading, his purpose or object alone cannot prevail over what he in fact does. But if his acts are equivocal his purpose or object may be a very material factor when weighing the total effect of all the circumstances.'[101]

5.88 The determination of whether there is a 'trade' or not rests on the judgment of the tribunal of fact, considering the specific circumstances of each case. They base their decision on various factors, particularly the 'badges of trade'.

5.89 In essence, the tribunal of fact makes an 'impressionistic' judgment by examining all the facts and circumstances to determine if a 'trade' exists. This approach was supported by Sir Terence Etherton C in the *Eclipse* case: 'It is necessary to step back and consider the overall picture, taking into account what the taxpayer actually did, and ask whether it constituted a trade.'[102]

99 [1986] 1 WLR 1343, 1348–1349.

100 [1965] 1 WLR 663.

101 *Ibid* at 668.

102 *Eclipse Film Partners No 35 LLP v Revenue and Customs Commissioners* [2015] EWCA Civ 95, [111], [2015] STC 1429, 1449. This approach was also endorsed by Henderson LJ in *Samarkand Film Partnership No 3 v Revenue and Customs Commissioners* [2017] EWCA Civ 77, [59], [2017] STC 926, 946.

5.90 The fact-finding and decision-making of the First-tier Tax Tribunal regarding the existence of a 'trade' are crucial. The grounds for overturning the evaluative judgment of the tribunal of fact are limited. They can only be overturned if there is an error of law or if the only reasonable conclusion based on the found facts contradicts the tribunal's conclusion. In practice, it is rare for the finding of the first-tier tax tribunal regarding the existence or absence of a 'trade' to be overturned on appeal.[103]

5.91 Principles regarding the classification of the purchase and sale of marketable securities as a 'trade' can be derived from relevant cases:[104]

(a) Generally, buying and selling marketable securities are considered investment activities.[105]

(b) A higher frequency and volume of transactions, along with rapid turnover of securities, indicate a higher likelihood of engaging in a 'trade'.[106]

(c) If a series of transactions involving marketable securities is carried out as part of a deliberate profit-making scheme, it may be deemed a trade.[107]

(d) It is generally easier to classify a company's activities involving marketable securities as a 'trade' compared to those of an individual.[108]

(e) Some level of organisation is usually required, such as basic bookkeeping, capital, and possibly a business plan and trading strategy, particularly for individuals.[109]

5.92 In the recent case of *Dr K M A Manzur v HMRC*,[110] a retired surgeon conducted 240–300 share transactions using £160,000 through an online broker. However, the tribunal determined that his activities did not constitute a 'trade' because they lacked the characteristics of an established share trading business.

5.93 In contrast, in the case of *Ali v HMRC*,[111] the taxpayer successfully argued that his share trading activities qualified as a 'trade'. While running a successful pharmacy business, he dedicated himself full-time to share trading from an office above the pharmacy. Despite minimal formality and expense, without a written business plan but an articulated oral plan, he engaged in short-term trading with four to ten transactions daily. Relying mostly on broker research reports, the

103 Ben Symons, *Bloomsbury Professional Tax Insight – Cryptocurrency and Blockchain* (1st edn, Bloomsbury Professional, London, 2022), [4.3]–[4.4].

104 *Ibid* [4.5].

105 *Cooper (Inspector of Taxes) v C & J Clark Ltd* [1982] STC 335, Nourse J at 340.

106 *Lewis Emanuel & Son Ltd v White (H M Inspector of Taxes)* (1965) 42 TC 369 Penycuick J at 377; *Cooper (Inspector of Taxes) v C & J Clark Ltd* [1982] STC 335, Nourse J at 340.

107 *Cooper (Inspector of Taxes) v C & J Clark Ltd* [1982] STC 335, Nourse J at 340.

108 *Ibid.*

109 *Wannell v Rothwell (Inspector of Taxes)* [1996] STC 450, Walker J at 461.

110 [2010] UKFTT 580 (TC).

111 [2016] SFTD 335.

tribunal still recognised his activities as a 'trade', even considering his lack of sophistication.

5.94 Lastly, the case of *Thomson and others v HMRC*[112] exemplifies a situation where a taxpayer was deemed not to be conducting a 'trade' in CFDs due to their complete lack of sophistication in purchasing and selling. The court found the taxpayer's decision-making regarding which CFDs to buy and sell as 'amateurish and impressionistic'. The taxpayer relied heavily on information from the financial press and friends, leading the tribunal to conclude that their activities did not meet the criteria for a 'trade'.

5.95 Taxpayers who claim to have a 'trade' in cryptocurrency may need to demonstrate the following:[113]

(a) A deliberate and preferably sophisticated trading strategy. Examples include arbitraging on different exchanges or utilising a 'pairs' trading strategy. Less sophisticated strategies based on 'crypto broker' research or 'charting' could also qualify depending on the circumstances.

(b) Consistent execution of transactions aligned with the chosen strategy.

(c) Basic bookkeeping to maintain records of the cryptocurrency transactions.

(d) Ideally, a written business plan, although an oral plan presented at the first-tier tax tribunal, as shown in the *Ali v HMRC*[114] case, could be acceptable.

5.96 In reality, the outcome of arguing for cryptocurrency trading before the First-tier Tax Tribunal can be unpredictable. Different judges may reach varying conclusions despite similar circumstances, as seen in the share 'trading' cases mentioned above. Appellate courts generally grant the First-tier Tribunal significant discretion in determining whether a taxpayer is engaged in 'trading'. They can only overturn a decision based on an error of law, not by reevaluating the facts.[115]

5.97 While an unsophisticated strategy does not necessarily disqualify a taxpayer from being classified as 'trading', it does make it more challenging to establish such a classification, as demonstrated in the aforementioned share 'trading' cases.

Mining

5.98 Mining activity can be considered a trade. Whether mining amounts to trading depends on the specific circumstances and level of activity. A single

112 [2018] UKFTT 396 (TC).
113 Symons (n 104 above), [4.6].
114 [2016] SFTD 335.
115 Symons (n 104 above), [4.3]–[4.4].

computer engaged in mining passively is unlikely to be considered a trade, while using a large bank of computers dedicated to mining for profit may be classified as a trading activity.[116]

5.99 HMRC tax the profits from mining (ie the value of newly issued tokens) for individuals and businesses as either trading profits or under miscellaneous income provisions.[117] Mining costs are deductible following the applicable rules for that income type. The taxable amount is based on the sterling value of the tokens received at the time of receipt, which is especially significant considering the energy and equipment expenses involved in mining.[118] If miners retain the awarded assets, they may face CGT or corporation tax when they later dispose of them.[119]

5.100 Any fees or rewards received for mining, such as transaction confirmation, are also subject to income tax or corporation tax, based on the same criteria as mentioned earlier. Individuals are also liable to pay National Insurance Contributions (NICs) on income received from mining activities.

Staking

5.101 Staking is an alternative method of earning cryptoassets without the need for energy-intensive mining. Staking involves existing block holders locking in their tokens for a specific duration, and new tokens are distributed among them. HMRC treats staking in the same manner as mining.[120]

Business income paid in cryptoassets

5.102 Companies or businesses engaged in activities involving being paid in exchange tokens are subject to tax obligations. If exchange tokens are used within an existing trade, any profits derived from them must be incorporated into the trading profits. For instance, if a company involved in a trade accepts exchange tokens as payment from customers or uses them for supplier payments, these tokens must be included in the taxable trading profits.

5.103 HMRC assess cryptoassets based on the actions of the holder. If the holder is conducting a trade, income tax or corporation tax is applied to the trading profits.[121]

116 CRYPTO40200.
117 ITTOIA 2005, ss 687–689 and CTA 2009, ss 979– 981.
118 See BIM100155.
119 CRYPTO40200.
120 CRYPTO21200 and CRYPTO40250.
121 CRYPTO40350.

Corporation tax

5.104 Cryptocurrency activities conducted by companies fall within the scope of corporation tax. Companies are required to calculate taxable profits and gains using standard accounting principles and report them in their annual tax returns.[122] This includes cryptocurrency mining, trading, and any other commercial activities involving digital assets.

Loan relationships

5.105 The loan relationship rules (CTA 2009, Pt 5) are a separate regime applying to UK corporation tax-paying companies that are parties to certain loan relationships. These rules govern how corporation tax is charged on profits and deficits from these arrangements. Broadly, a loan relationship exists when a company is party to a money debt arising from a transaction involving lending money.[123]

Exchange tokens

5.106 HMRC does not consider exchange tokens as money, and since there is no counterparty enforcing a debt, a company acquiring or holding exchange tokens is not involved in a loan relationship. The extended loan relationship rules also do not apply to exchange tokens for the same reason.[124]

Security and utility tokens

5.107 Treatment of crypto-assets as debt depends on the token's terms, ecosystem, and the company-holder relationship. Some tokens may yield returns similar to interest, like ICO tokens granting rights within a project's ecosystem or STO tokens linked to underlying assets. The classification of tokens from a regulatory, legal, and taxation perspective is determined by the rights attached to them. Income and losses from transactions with these tokens may result in a loan relationship or taxation under disguised interest rules, as they are unlikely to be considered shares for the exemption in CTA 2009, s 303(4).

Acquiring exchange tokens

5.108 Acquiring exchange tokens generally does not create a loan relationship because there is no backing entity for the exchange token, meaning no money debt and, therefore, no loan relationship to apply the rules.[125]

122 CRYPTO41050.
123 CRYPTO41100.
124 CRYPTO41100.
125 *Ibid.*

Loans backed by exchange tokens as securities or collateral

5.109 Using exchange tokens as loan security does not change the nature of the loan relationship, a loan relationship exists and the ordinary loan relationship rules will apply (whether the company is the debtor or creditor).[126]

Loans of exchange tokens

5.110 Loaning exchange tokens is unlikely to constitute a loan relationship since such relationships are defined as 'money' debts.[127] As such there would not be a there would not be a money debt or a transaction for the lending of money.[128]

Intangible fixed assets

5.111 A UK corporation tax-paying company holding cryptoassets falling under the intangible fixed assets rules applies those rules to profits from the disposal of exchange tokens, prioritising them over chargeable gains (CG) rules.

5.112 Companies may be taxed under corporation tax rules for intangible fixed assets if the token is both:

(a) an intangible asset for accounting purposes[129] – if the company does not prepare GAAP-compliant accounts, the rules apply as if they had; and

(b) acquired or created by a company for continuous use, qualifying it as an intangible fixed asset.[130]

HMRC considers that exchange tokens merely held by a company, even in the course of its activities, do not meet the definition of an intangible fixed asset.

5.113 Specific exclusions to the intangibles rules, such as for financial assets,[131] assets held for non-commercial purposes or for mutual trading and for rights in a company, trust or partnership may apply to cryptoassets in some cases.[132]

5.114 HMRC do not consider cryptoassets as currency or money, and as a result, the following corporation tax rules do not apply:

(a) foreign currency rules,[133]

(b) exchange gains and losses,[134] and

(c) designated currency elections.[135]

126 *Ibid.*
127 CTA 2009, s 303.
128 CRYPTO41100.
129 CTA 2009. s 712(1).
130 CTA 2009, s 713.
131 CTA 2009, s 806.
132 CRYPTO41150.
133 CTA 2009, s 328.
134 Loan Relationships and Derivative Contracts (Disregard and Bringing into Account of Profits and Losses) Regulations 2004 (SI 2004/3256).
135 CTA 2010, s 9A. See CRYPTO10100 and CRYPTO41050.

Corporation tax on chargeable gains

5.115 Tax obligations for holding exchange tokens as investments vary depending on the type of entity:[136]

(a) If a company holds exchange tokens as an investment, they must pay corporation tax on any gains realised when they sell them.

(b) If a sole trader holds exchange tokens as an investment, they are responsible for paying CGT on any gains they make.

(c) For partnerships or limited liability partnerships holding exchange tokens as investments, the partners or members will be liable for corporation tax (if they are a company) or CGT (if they are an individual) on any gains they realise.

5.116 HMRC view cryptoassets as a 'chargeable asset' for CGT and corporation tax if they are both:[137]

(a) capable of being owned; and

(b) have a value that can be realised.

5.117 A 'disposal' is a broad concept and includes:[138]

(a) selling tokens for money;

(b) exchanging tokens for a different type of token;

(c) using tokens to pay for goods or services; or

(d) giving away tokens to another person.'

5.118 When a company gives away exchange tokens to another company not in the same group or to an individual or entity, the company making the transfer must determine the market value of the tokens given away. This value is used to calculate any chargeable gain (CG). The recipient is also treated as acquiring the cryptoassets at their market value at the time of the gift.[139]

5.119 No disposal occurs if the company maintains beneficial ownership of the tokens during the transaction, such as transferring tokens between public addresses it controls (commonly known as moving tokens between wallets).[140]

5.120 Using a mixer, tumbler, or similar service where the company receives the same type of tokens as they initially put into the transaction is not considered

136 CRYPTO41200.
137 *Ibid.*
138 CRYPTO41250.
139 CRYPTO41250.
140 *Ibid.*

a disposal. However, it becomes a disposal if the company puts token A into the transaction and receives token B in return.[141]

5.121 When a chargeable person donates exchange tokens to a charity, they are not required to pay corporation tax on any accrued gains.[142] However, this exemption does not apply if either:[143]

(a) they make a 'tainted donation', or

(b) the company disposes of the tokens to the charity for more than the acquisition cost, resulting in a gain.

Transferring tokens between distributed ledgers

5.122 Transferring tokens between different distributed ledgers is not a straightforward process. You cannot directly move a token from one blockchain to another, for instance, you cannot put a bitcoin on the Ethereum blockchain. However, you can achieve an effect similar to a 'swap' by using a smart contract and secure public addresses, in the following manner:

(a) the token holder initiates a smart contract to transfer their tokens to a public address they do not control; and

(b) simultaneously, an equivalent amount of tokens from the second cryptoasset are transferred from a secure public address to a public address controlled by the token holder.

Whether this type of transaction results in a disposal for CGT purposes depends on the specific circumstances and HMRC will determine it on the facts.[144]

5.123 There are also 'one-way' transfers where the transfer cannot be reversed or moved back in the future. For instance, with Ethereum, you can move ether from the Ethereum 'mainnet' to the 'Beacon Chain', but you can't transfer it back to the mainnet. In such cases, HMRC considers that TCGA 1992, s 43 applies. The allowable costs associated with the first cryptoasset are fully attributed to the second cryptoasset, and any gains or losses will occur upon the subsequent disposal of the second cryptoasset.[145]

Allowable costs

5.124 When calculating gains or losses from token disposal, not all costs can be deducted. TCGA 1992, s 38 outlines allowable deduction types, which, according to HMRC, include:

141 *Ibid.*
142 CG66620P.
143 CRYPTO41250.
144 CRYPTO41260.
145 *Ibid.*

(a) the consideration (in pound sterling) initially paid for the asset;

(b) transaction fees paid for ledger inclusion;

(c) advertising costs for finding buyers or sellers;

(d) professional costs for contract drafting in token acquisition or disposal; and

(e) costs for valuations or apportionments needed to compute gains or losses.

However, costs deducted against income for income tax[146] are not allowable deductions for CGT.

Exchange fees

5.125 It is common for people to use a crypto exchange to perform transactions and some fees charged by exchanges are allowable, but not all of them. HMRC has outlined common fees charged by exchanges and whether they satisfy TCGA 1992, s 38, such as:[147]

(a) **Swapping sterling for a non-sterling fiat currency**: deductible under TCGA 1992, s 38(1)(a) as a cost of acquiring non-sterling fiat.

(b) **Swapping non-sterling fiat for sterling**: deductible under TCGA 1992, s 38(1)(c) as an incidental cost of disposing of non-sterling fiat.

(c) **Depositing sterling**: not allowable, as sterling is not an asset for CGT.

(d) **Depositing non-sterling fiat**: not allowable, as the depositor retains ownership.

(e) **Purchasing tokens with sterling or non-sterling fiat**: deductible under TCGA 1992, s 38(1)(a) as a cost of acquiring tokens.

(f) **Swapping token A for token B**: the fee applies to both assets and is deductible under TCGA 1992, s 38(1)(c) for token A's disposal and TCGA 1992, s 38(1)(a) for token B's eventual disposal. For fees related to multiple assets, an equal 50/50 split is considered just and reasonable for apportionment unless the customer chooses otherwise.

Mining

5.126 Costs for mining activities (eg equipment and electricity) are not allowable costs for tokens since they do not exclusively acquire tokens as per TCGA 1992, s 38(1)(a). Some of these costs may be deductible against income tax or corporation tax. Equipment costs used for mining may be deductible when disposing of the equipment, subject to exemptions like chattels and wasting assets. If mining is considered a trade for tax purposes, tokens are part of trading

146 CG10260.
147 CRYPTO41300.

stock, and their value in trading accounts is used as an allowable cost when disposed of.[148]

Pooling

5.127 Pooling under TCGA 1992, s 104 simplifies CGT calculations. It applies to shares, securities, and assets that can be traded without specifying individual items.[149]

5.128 If the nature of tokens allows them to be traded without identifying specific tokens in transactions, they should be pooled under TCGA 1992, s 104(3)(ii),[150] often referred to as a 'section 104 pool.' Under this rule, the beneficial owner has a single pooled asset for CGT, its value changing with each token acquisition, part disposal, or disposal.[151]

5.129 Each type of token requires its own pool. For instance, if someone owns Bitcoin, Ether, and Litecoin, they have three separate pools, each with its own 'pooled allowable cost.' This cost changes as more tokens of that type are acquired or disposed of.[152]

5.130 Businesses must still track the amount spent on each type of exchange token and maintain records of the pooled allowable cost for each pool. It is important to note that there are slight differences in pooling rules for CGT and corporation tax purposes.[153]

5.131 There are two exceptions to the pooling rules for companies, allowing new exchange tokens and their acquisition costs to be kept separate from the main pool: [154]

(a) If a company acquires tokens on the same day it disposes of tokens of the same type (even if the disposal occurred first), the disposal is matched with the same-day acquisition, taking priority over any tokens in an existing pool.

(b) If a company acquires tokens that would otherwise create or add to a pool but then disposes of tokens of the same type within ten days, the disposal is matched with the acquisition from the previous nine days, again taking priority over existing pool tokens. If multiple acquisitions occurred within that period, the 'first in, first out' principle applies.

148 CRYPTO41300. For further information on trading accounts value disposals, see CG69220.
149 CRYPTO41350.
150 See CG11820.
151 CRYPTO41350.
152 *Ibid.*
153 For CGT see CRYPTO22200.
154 CRYPTO41350.

5.132 The gain or loss should be calculated using the costs of the new tokens, which are kept separate. If the number of tokens disposed of exceeds the number of new tokens acquired, the calculation of any gain or loss may also include a proportion of the pooled allowable cost.[155]

Losses

Capital losses

5.133 When a company sells exchange tokens for less than their allowable costs, it results in a loss. These losses, known as 'allowable losses', can be used to offset the overall gain for tax purposes. However, before applying these losses, they must be reported to HMRC. Special rules come into play when a company disposes of exchange tokens to a 'connected person'.[156]

Section 24 and negligible value

5.134 Businesses and companies, like with other assets, can recognise losses for exchange tokens they still own if these tokens become worthless or nearly worthless.

5.135 To do this, a 'negligible value claim' is filed, treating the exchange tokens as if they were disposed of and then re-acquired at a specified value mentioned in the claim. Since exchange tokens are typically pooled together, the claim pertains to the entire pool, not individual tokens. The claim should specify:

(a) the asset subject to the claim;

(b) the value at which the asset should be treated as disposed (which may be £nil, meaning zero); and

(c) the date when the asset should be considered disposed of.

This disposal results in a loss that must be reported to HMRC. Negligible value claims can be submitted to HMRC concurrently with reporting the loss.[157]

Losing private keys

5.136 Losing the private key, such as by accidentally discarding the printed copy, results in the inability to access tokens. Although the private key still exists within the cryptographic system, the owner no longer knows it though the tokens remain on the distributed ledger. Importantly, misplacing the key does not trigger a CGT disposal event.[158] However, if it becomes evident that there is no way to recover the private key or access the tokens, a 'negligible value claim' can be

155 *Ibid.*
156 CRYPTO41400.
157 CRYPTO41450. For more information on negligible value claims, refer to CG13120P.
158 For more details, see CG13155.

submitted. If HMRC accept this claim, it treats the situation as if the person disposed of and re-acquired the tokens they cannot access, allowing them to realise a loss for tax purposes.[159]

Being defrauded

5.137 HMRC do not view theft as a disposal since the owner still maintains ownership rights and the potential to recover the stolen asset. Consequently, victims of theft cannot claim a loss for CGT or corporation tax. For individuals who enter into token acquisition contracts but do not receive the tokens they paid for, their ability to claim a capital loss may be limited. However, individuals who contract to acquire tokens and actually receive them can potentially file a 'negligible value claim' with HMRC if these tokens become worthless over time. It is important to note that if the tokens were already worthless when acquired, a negligible value claim will not be permitted. This does not affect the person's ability to dispose of the tokens through other means to realise a capital loss.[160]

Forks and airdrops

Forks

5.138 In the paradigm of cryptoassets, some operate based on community consensus without a central authority. When a significant portion of the community wants to make a change, it can lead to a 'fork' in the distributed ledger, resulting in two types – soft forks and hard forks:

(a) **Soft fork**: this update is meant to be adopted by everyone and does not create new tokens or ledgers.

(b) **Hard fork**: a hard fork, on the other hand, can result in the creation of new tokens. It occurs when there is a split, and a new cryptoasset is born. Both the original and new cryptoassets share a history up to the fork, so if you held tokens in the original ledger, you will usually have an equal number of tokens in both ledgers after the fork.

5.139 The value of the new tokens is linked to the original tokens held by individuals, making TCGA 1992, s 43 applicable. After the fork, the new tokens must be placed into their own section 104 pool, and any allowable costs from the original cryptoassets are divided between the two pools for the original and new tokens.

5.140 For those who hold tokens through an exchange, the exchange decides whether to recognise the new tokens generated by the fork. Cost division should be done on a just and reasonable basis under TCGA 1992, s 52(4), and while HMRC does not prescribe a specific method, they can inquire into any method they find unjust or unreasonable.

159 CRYPTO41500.
160 CRYPTO41550. Additional details can be found in CG13155.

5.141 The ability to dispose of the new tokens depends on whether the exchange recognises them. If not, individuals may choose to allocate all allowable costs to the original tokens, provided it is just and reasonable. Alternatively, they can split the costs and attempt a negligible value claim for the new tokens, provided all conditions for such a claim are met.[161]

Airdrops

5.142 When airdropped tokens are received, they are placed into their own section 104 pool, unless the recipient already holds tokens of the same cryptoasset. In that case, the airdropped tokens join the existing section 104 pool. Importantly, the value of airdropped tokens is not derived from existing tokens held by the individual, so TCGA 1992, s 43 does not apply.[162]

5.143 The tax treatment of airdropped tokens depends on the context. In cases like advertising campaigns, receiving airdropped tokens may not trigger taxable income upon receipt. However, any gains realised upon their disposal could be subject to CGT or corporation tax. Airdropped tokens are distinguished from tokens received through a hard fork, as HMRC consider them as not deriving from already held tokens (hence TCGA 1992, s 43 does not apply).

Income

Paying employees in cryptoassets

5.144 When an employer provides an employee with a notional payment in the form of a RCA, they must determine whether this payment should be treated as employment income for both income tax purposes (according to ITEPA 2003, s 62) and NIC purposes (according to Social Security Contributions and Benefits Act 1992 (SSCBA 1992), s 3(1)(a)) defines earnings as any remuneration or profit derived from employment).[163] The cryptoassets are considered 'money's worth', and the charge is based on the value of the asset.[164]

5.145 The HMRC considers exchange tokens to be equivalent to 'money's worth' and therefore RCAs.[165] Consequently, they are treated as employment income and are subject to both income tax and National Insurance contributions (NICs) based on the value of the asset.[166] However, this may not apply to all exchange tokens, such as those not traded or lacking an exchange facility.

161 CRYPTO41600.
162 CRYPTO41650.
163 For further information see EIM11956.
164 ITEPA 2003, s 62(3).
165 EIM00530.
166 CRYPTO42050.

5.146 For RCAs, the employer must use their best estimate for valuation and deduct appropriate PAYE income tax and Class 1 NICs. The employee must then make good the deducted amounts, as the employer cannot withhold payment. Failure to do so within 90 days after the tax year's end will result in an additional income tax and NICs charge.

5.147 For non-RCAs, the employer is not required to apply PAYE income tax and Class 1 NICs deductions. Instead, the employee must declare the received amount and pay income tax through self-assessment. For NIC purposes, the employer should treat the payment as a benefit in kind and pay and report Class 1A NICs.

Exchange tokens provided in the form of readily convertible assets

5.148 The tax treatment of exchange tokens regarding income tax and NICs depends on whether they are RCAs. Exchange tokens are considered readily convertible assets if there are trading arrangements in place or likely to be established, enabling them to be easily converted into their monetary value.[167]

5.149 HMRC generally views exchange tokens as RCAs. When employers provide employees with employment income in the form of readily convertible assets, they must estimate the asset's value and deduct the appropriate PAYE income tax and Class 1 NICs. These deductions should be reported and remitted to HMRC in real-time.

5.150 Employers typically recover these taxes and NICs from the employee's future employment income payments. However, if they cannot recover these amounts, they are still responsible for paying the full tax and NICs to HMRC.

5.151 If the employer pays these amounts to HMRC but cannot recover them from the employee, the employee is required to reimburse the income tax and employee Class 1 NICs that the employer paid on their behalf. If the employee does not reimburse these amounts within 90 days after the end of the tax year in which the notional payment was made, additional charges for income tax and both primary and secondary Class 1 NICs will be imposed on the outstanding liabilities.[168]

National Insurance contributions

5.152 When cryptoassets are given as RCAs, HMRC views this as earnings subject to NICs under SSCBA 1992, s 3. As a result, the employer is required to

167 EIM11900.
168 CRYPTO42100.

report and pay the correct amount of primary and secondary Class 1 contributions to HMRC through PAYE/real time information for the relevant earnings period.[169]

Exchange tokens which are not RCAs

5.153 If the exchange token is not readily convertible, the employer does not need to deduct PAYE income tax or Class 1 NICs. However, the employee should report any received exchange tokens as income on their self assessment tax return and settle any income tax owed to HMRC through self assessment.

5.154 Regarding NICs, if the exchange token is not readily convertible, the employer should consider it a benefit in kind and pay and report any Class 1A NICs to HMRC.[170]

Employment income provided through third parties

5.155 Under Pt 7A of ITEPA 2003, if a third party provides exchange tokens to an employee, it may trigger an income tax charge under disguised remuneration rules. Employers are responsible for reporting and paying the income tax due to HMRC through PAYE when they provide exchange tokens as employment income. The amount of PAYE income subject to income tax is estimated to the best of their ability.[171]

5.156 Regarding NICs, if exchange tokens are supplied by a third party, the National Insurance contribution obligation remains, but in specific cases, the third party, rather than the employer, may be liable for paying Class 1A NICs.[172]

Contributions to registered pension schemes

5.157 HMRC does not classify exchange tokens as currency or money, so they are not eligible for deductions under the registered pension schemes (RPS) tax rules when employers contribute to these schemes. Employers cannot contribute to a RPS using exchange tokens, as HMRC does not view these assets as currency or money.[173]

169 CRYPTO42200.

170 CRYPTO42250. For guidance on Class 1A NICs see HMRC, National Insurance Manual (HMRC internal manual, 11 April 2016, updated 29 September 2023) NIM13000 www.gov.uk/hmrc-internal-manuals/national-insurance-manual/nim16350 [accessed 8 October 2023].

171 EIM45000.

172 CRYPTO42300. Further information can be found at NIM16350.

173 CRYPTO26000. For a discussion about HMRC's approach and Counsel's view on non-cash contributions to pensions, see Michael Furness QC, 'Comments from Counsel: To pay or not to pay? HMRC's approach to contributions in kind to pension schemes' *Practical Law Company* (18 May 2017).

5.158 However, if exchange tokens are somehow included in an RPS (even without tax benefits), they become subject to RPS tax rules as part of the scheme.[174] The specific implications can vary depending on the individual circumstances and these considerations will depend on the particular details of each case.[175]

Stamp taxes, land, and smart contracts

5.159 Stamp duty is charged on instruments transferring stocks, marketable securities, and interests in partnerships.[176] Stamp duty reserve tax (SDRT) applies to agreements to transfer chargeable securities.[177]

5.160 HMRC's view is that existing exchange tokens are unlikely to be considered stocks, marketable securities, or chargeable securities.[178] While other tokens' status is not addressed, certain security tokens may potentially meet the definition.

5.161 If stocks, securities, or shares are sold for token consideration, SDRT will be due based on the sterling value of the tokens at the charge's date. HMRC view exchange tokens as not typically constituting chargeable consideration for stamp duty purposes unless they are treated as debt. This distinction from the SDRT treatment may create challenges for intra-group share sales, affecting stamp duty group relief availability.[179]

5.162 Exchange tokens are not considered interests in land for stamp duty land tax (SDLT), land and buildings transaction tax (LBTT), or land transaction tax (LTT) purposes.[180] However, if exchange tokens are used as consideration for a land transaction, they fall within the definition of 'money or money's worth', potentially leading to an SDLT, LTT, or LBTT charge.[181]

5.163 Regarding smart contracts, a liability to SDRT, LTT, LBTT, or SDLT may arise when a contract is entered into but before it is completed.

VAT treatment of mining, exchanges and vouchers

5.164 HMRC's position is that exchange tokens received by miners during mining activities are generally outside the scope of VAT due to:[182]

174 CRYPTO43000.
175 Further information on the RPS tax rules can be found in the Pensions Tax Manual (n 90 above).
176 Finance Act 1999, s 13.
177 CRYPTO44050. See also Finance Act 1986, s 99(3).
178 CRYPTO24000.
179 CRYPTO44150.
180 CRYPTO44250.
181 CRYPTO44300.
182 CRYPTO45000.

(a) the lack of an economic activity for VAT purposes since there is insufficient link between services provided and consideration; and

(b) the absence of a customer for the mining service.

5.165 When exchange tokens are used for transactions to purchase goods and services, no VAT is due on the token itself, but VAT may apply to the goods and services being exchanged.[183]

5.166 Bitcoin exchanges were considered economic activities but exempt from VAT under the financial services exemption[184] in 2014,[185] and this was confirmed by the European Court of Justice (ECJ) in *Skatteverket v Hedqvist.*[186]

5.167 Charges made over the value of exchange tokens for arranging transactions may be VAT exempt under the VAT finance exemption, provided the service relates to an exempt financial transaction.[187]

5.168 Some tokens, particularly utility tokens representing the right to goods or services, may be considered vouchers for VAT purposes.[188] In such cases, the issuer may be required to account for VAT on the token issuance, based on the underlying supply if it is a single-purpose voucher for VAT purposes.

VAT in general

5.169 Cryptoassets are generally exempt from VAT in the UK. However, VAT may be applicable to certain cryptoasset-related activities, such as providing goods or services in exchange for cryptoassets or operating cryptoasset exchanges.[189] The VAT treatment may vary depending on the specific circumstances and the nature of the transaction.

5.170 Businesses that receive cryptoassets as consideration for the supply of goods and services are still liable to account for VAT to HMRC. The VAT liability is determined based on the value of the supply in accordance with s 19 of the Value Added Tax Act 1994 (VATA 1994).

5.171 According to VATA 1994, s 19(3), when consideration is provided in a non-monetary form, the value is the equivalent amount in money, including the VAT. Therefore, when cryptoassets are used as consideration, their sterling value at the time of the transaction is considered for VAT purposes.

183 See CRYPTO4500.
184 VATA 1994, Sch 9, Group 5, Item 1.
185 'Revenue and Customs Brief 9: Bitcoin and other cryptocurrencies' (HMRC, 2014).
186 (Case C-264/14) EU:C:2015:718.
187 VATA 1994, Sch 9, Group 5, Item 5.
188 VATA 1994. Sch 10B.
189 CRYPTO45000.

5.172 If the contract specifies the value of the non-monetary consideration, that value is generally accepted for VAT purposes. However, if the specified value appears to be unrealistic or abusive, the court may intervene. For valuing cryptoassets traded on an exchange, the exchange rate can be a good starting point, but it may not apply to security or utility tokens.

Venture capital schemes

5.173 When investing in new companies, investors may seek relief under a venture capital scheme such as the Enterprise Investment Scheme (EIS) or the Seed Enterprise Investment Scheme (SEIS), and companies may aim to promote the availability of such reliefs. The use of cryptocurrency by a company does not alter the standard rules for these schemes. For instance, the following will not stop a business meeting qualifying conditions:[190]

(a) target customers in the exchange tokens sector;

(b) accept exchange tokens as payment; and

(c) use DLT for recording or publishing information.

5.174 These actions are unlikely to affect the qualifying status of the investment, as long as the use of cryptoassets or DLT supports the core activity (the qualifying trade) that qualifies the investment for relief.

5.175 However, certain activities, such as dealing in exchange tokens on their own account, exchanging or brokering exchange token transactions, and mining exchange tokens, require further consideration. HMRC will assess whether the company is conducting a qualifying trade[191] and whether the activities fall under excluded activities.[192] For businesses uncertain about their eligibility for venture capital scheme relief, a non-statutory clearance can be obtained from HMRC. A range of tax reliefs are available if certain conditions are met regarding the activities of a particular individual or business including:[193]

(a) EIS and SEIS;

(b) venture capital trust scheme;

(c) reliefs for gifts of business assets; and

(d) business property relief.

Betting and gaming

5.176 The use of cryptoassets to participate in betting or gaming is treated in the same way as cash and excise duty is due from the bookmaker/gaming provider; the valuation provisions can be found in Finance Act 2014, s 191.[194]

190 CRYPTO46000.
191 ITA 2007, s 181.
192 ITA 2007, s 192.
193 CRYPTO46000.
194 CRYPTO47000.

Digital services tax and cryptoasset exchanges

5.177 Digital services tax (DST) is a 2% tax on revenues generated from UK users in specific digital activities, including 'online marketplace' services. To qualify as an online marketplace under DST, two conditions must be met:[195]

(a) The service must enable users to sell, advertise, or offer things for sale to other users.

(b) The primary or one of the main purposes of the service must be to facilitate the sale of these things.

5.178 Here, 'things' can refer to services, goods, or other property. So, an exchange that facilitates token sales, even if the sale does not occur directly on the exchange, qualifies as an online marketplace under DST. However, there is an exemption for online financial marketplaces. This exemption applies when over half of a marketplace's revenue comes from facilitating the trading of financial instruments, commodities, or foreign exchange. Regarding cryptoassets, HMRC's view is that they do not fall into these categories because they do not view them as:[196]

(a) financial instruments, in general, because they do not represent cash or a contract for cash or other financial instrument;

(b) commodities, so cryptoasset exchanges are not considered commodities exchanges; or

(c) currency or money, which means trading them is not considered foreign exchange.

Therefore, cryptoasset exchanges are unlikely to qualify for the exemption for online financial marketplaces under DST.

DECENTRALISED FINANCE

Introduction

5.179 There is no specific legislation or case law addressing the taxation of decentralised finance (DeFi) transactions, except for the investment manager's exemption.[197] Therefore, the tax treatment of DeFi transactions relies on applying general tax principles and the Cryptoassets Manual. DeFi is a developing area, and transactions that appear similar may have different tax implications based on their unique structures.

195 HMRC, Digital Services Tax Manual (HMRC internal manual, 19 March 2020, updated 24 May 2023) www.gov.uk/hmrc-internal-manuals/digital-services-tax/dst18100 [accessed 8 October 2023].

196 CRYPTO48000.

197 See **5.247–5.250**.

5.180 DeFi is a term used for offering financial services using DLT,[198] like Ethereum-based smart contracts. These services include decentralised exchanges, savings, lending, and derivatives, and they are accessible to anyone. Cryptoasset lending and borrowing has existed since the creation of Bitcoin in 2009. Initially, it was a risky activity due to anonymity and lack of regulation. Early agreements were often between parties that knew each other.[199]

5.181 DeFi lending platforms can provide services such as decentralised exchanges (DEXs), saving, lending and derivatives. DEXs enable lending between unrelated parties and lenders reduce their risk by lending to these platforms, spreading default risk across all lenders and using collateral. Lenders can earn returns on their loans, essentially generating income in addition to capital gains.[200]

5.182 In a typical lending transaction within DeFi, the lender transfers control of tokens to a borrower, which in this case is a platform. The specific terms of the transaction may vary between platforms, and platforms may offer different types of products. Once the platform receives the tokens, it either holds them in a liquidity pool or lends them. Lenders receive the right to reclaim their tokens, along with any agreed-upon returns, through a smart contract. Additionally, lenders may receive the following as part (or all) of the consideration:

(a) liquidity provider tokens or other cryptoassets; or

(b) an NFT that serves as a receipt and represents the right to receive the tokens back.

5.183 While some market participants call these returns 'interest,' HMRC do not consider returns as interest for tax purposes. Instead, it is the number of tokens received over the loan term exceeding the initial amount. Interest, for tax purposes, typically involves compensation for using or holding someone else's money, which does not apply to cryptoassets because HMRC do not see them as currency or money.[201]

Meaning of 'loan' and 'staking'

5.184 Lending and staking are popular DeFi activities, but it is important to clarify that these terms lack a specific legal definition in this context. The HMRC guidance on lending and staking[202] covers two types of transactions.[203]

198 CRYPTO10200.
199 CRYPTO61110.
200 *Ibid.*
201 *Ibid.*
202 CRYPTO61000.
203 CRYPTO61120.

Lending

5.185 In this scenario, a person (the 'lender') transfers tokens to another person (the 'borrower'). When this transfer happens, the lender gains the right to request the borrower to return an equivalent amount of tokens in the future to settle the loan.

Staking or providing liquidity

5.186 In this type of transaction, a person (the 'liquidity provider') transfers tokens to a DeFi lending platform. This is often referred to as 'staking' or 'providing liquidity.' When this transfer occurs, the DeFi lending platform gives the liquidity provider control over different tokens.

Income tax

Making a DeFi loan

5.187 The DeFi lending platform can then transfer these tokens, provided by the liquidity provider, to other individuals (the 'borrowers'). Typically, borrowers must return more tokens than they initially received to compensate the DeFi lending platform. A portion of this return serves as compensation for the liquidity provider, who supplied liquidity to the DeFi lending platform.[204]

5.188 Lending and staking in DeFi can take various forms, but it is essential to recognise that these terms lack a specific legal definition. The guidance[205] covers two primary transaction types:

(a) **Lending tokens directly to borrower**: In this setup, a person ('lender') transfers tokens to another person ('borrower') without involving a DeFi lending platform. It is a straightforward lending arrangement where tokens are directly exchanged between the lender and borrower.

(b) **Liquidity provider on DeFi lending platform**: This involves a person ('liquidity provider') transferring tokens to a DeFi lending platform. The DeFi platform pools these tokens into a liquidity pool. Another person ('borrower') can request a loan from the DeFi platform, and when approved, they receive control of the specified quantity of tokens for the loan term.

5.189 These transactions can result in the lender/liquidity provider receiving a reward for their lending/staking efforts, referred to as the 'return'. This return may be considered taxable income for income tax or corporation tax purposes.[206] How the return is calculated and rewarded depends on the specific transaction

204 CRYPTO61120.
205 CRYPTO61000.
206 See CRYPTO61200 or CRYPTO61400.

model, and there is not a one-size-fits-all DeFi lending platform operating model. Therefore, understanding the platform's terms and conditions is crucial to determine the tax implications.[207]

5.190 Here are common types of 'loan' transactions:[208]

(a) **Direct lender to borrower**: lender directly lends tokens to a borrower.

(b) **Liquidity provider on DeFi platform (no token received)**: liquidity provider transfers tokens to a DeFi lending platform, and the DeFi platform lends these tokens to borrowers without giving any tokens back to the liquidity provider.

(c) **Liquidity provider on DeFi platform (fixed ratio token received)**: liquidity provider transfers tokens to a DeFi lending platform, and the DeFi platform lends different tokens to borrowers, with a fixed ratio of these tokens given to the liquidity provider.

(d) **Liquidity provider on DeFi platform (liquidity tokens received)**: liquidity provider transfers tokens to a DeFi lending platform, and in return, they receive tokens representing their stake in the liquidity pool (commonly known as 'liquidity tokens'). The DeFi platform lends different tokens to borrowers.

(e) **Liquidity provider on DeFi platform (non-fungible token received)**: liquidity provider transfers tokens to a DeFi lending platform and, in return, receives a NFT that records the loan's terms. Borrowers can request loans, and if approved, they receive control of the specified tokens. The DeFi platform may also issue an NFT to the borrower, recording the loan's terms.

Taxing provisions

5.191 HMRC does not categorise the return[209] received by the lender/liquidity provider as interest for tax purposes.[210] Therefore, any tax provisions specifically related to interest do not apply to this return. How the return is taxed depends on whether it is considered capital or revenue in nature.[211]

Capital receipt

5.192 If the return is deemed capital in nature, it falls under CGT and is not subject to income tax.[212, 213]

207 CRYPTO61120.
208 *Ibid.*
209 CRYPTO61130.
210 CRYPTO61110.
211 CRYPTO61212. For further guidance, refer to CRYPTO61214.
212 CRYPTO61630.
213 CRYPTO61212.

Revenue receipt

5.193 If the return is considered income, it falls under income tax. Assuming the transactions are not part of a trade conducted by the customer, the receipt falls within the scope of miscellaneous income provisions.[214, 215]

5.194 Sections 687–689 of ITTOIA 2005, known as the 'sweep-up provisions,' tax income from any source not otherwise covered by ITTOIA 2005 or any other act.[216]

5.195 Previous cases have examined the scope of these provisions. In essence, the return is taxable under the miscellaneous income sweep-up provisions if it qualifies as income and arises from an understanding between both parties that the recipient will compensate the provider for services, even without a formal written contract.[217]

5.196 When a lender/liquidity provider lends/stakes tokens to a borrower/DeFi lending platform, an agreement exists between the borrower/DeFi platform and the lender/liquidity provider. This agreement, which may not always be a legally enforceable contract, outlines the terms of the loan/staking, including:[218]

(a) borrowing term (fixed or indefinite);

(b) principal of the loan/staking; and

(c) any return owed by the borrower/DeFi lending platform to the lender/liquidity provider.

The return's exact amount may be uncertain (eg due to fluctuating rates or an indefinite borrowing period). Still, the crucial factor is the borrower/DeFi lending platform's obligation to make the payment. Therefore, if the return qualifies as income, it is subject to income tax under the miscellaneous income sweep-up provisions[219].[220]

Amount chargeable to income tax

5.197 The miscellaneous income sweep-up provisions apply to the return[221] received by the lender/liquidity provider, not the repayment of the principal, which is treated as a capital transaction.[222]

214 ITTOIA 2005, Pt 5.
215 CRYPTO61212.
216 For general information on miscellaneous income sweep-up provisions, refer to BIM100000.
217 For more details on the role of contracts and arrangements, consult BIM100105.
218 CRYPTO61212.
219 ITTOIA 2005, s 687–689.
220 CRYPTO61212.
221 CRYPTO61130.
222 CRYPTO61213. See also CRYPTO61620.

5.198 The return received by the lender/liquidity provider is a non-cash receipt. It is valued for tax purposes based on its money's worth, which means the pound sterling value of the tokens received by the lender.[223]

5.199 In certain situations, the trading and miscellaneous income allowance might be relevant.[224]

Nature of the return

5.200 Lenders of cryptoassets typically receive a financial return similar to interest for lending tokens. The nature of this return for tax purposes depends on the terms of the loan. How the return[225] is taxed upon receipt by the lender/liquidity provider depends on whether it has the nature of capital or revenue (income). The nature of the return hinges on the transaction's structure, and DeFi lending/staking is continually evolving.[226]

5.201 If the return is capital, any CG will be subject to CGT. If it is considered income, any profit would be subject to income tax or corporation tax, but it would not be treated as interest.

5.202 You must determine whether the return has an income or capital nature in the hands of the lender/liquidity provider. This is influenced by whether the return results from providing a service to the borrower/DeFi lending platform or from capital asset growth owned by the lender/liquidity provider.[227]

5.203 Due to varying operating models, the answer may not always be clear. Consider the following factors:[228]

(a) If the return is known at the time of the agreement, it leans towards being a revenue receipt. If it is unknown and speculative, indicating a potential loss, it leans towards being a capital receipt.

(b) If the return results from the disposal of a capital asset, it is considered a capital receipt. If the borrower/DeFi lending platform pays the return, it's considered a revenue receipt.

(c) Whether the return is paid periodically or upon repayment of the principal. A one-off payment leans toward capital, while recurring payments lean toward income.

These factors, while important, are not exhaustive, and no single factor is decisive.[229]

223 CRYPTO61213. For more information, refer to BIM100150.
224 *Ibid*. For more information, refer to BIM86000.
225 See CRYPTO61130.
226 CRYPTO61214. For more general guidance on determining the nature of receipts or expenses, refer to BIM35000.
227 *Ibid*.
228 *Ibid*.
229 *Ibid*.

When the return might be considered income

5.204 In some cases, the return is received by the lender/liquidity provider in exchange for lending tokens or staking them with a DeFi lending platform. This resembles interest paid to a lender for the use of money. Therefore, it's expected that the return, despite not being paid in money or currency,[230] will have a similar nature to interest when it compensates the lender/liquidity provider for lending/staking tokens.[231]

5.205 *Ryall v Hoare*[232] considered the scope of miscellaneous income provisions, with Rowlatt, J stating that 'profits or gains' mean something akin to interest or fruit, as opposed to principal or tree. Applying this analogy, interest from lending money is the 'interest or fruit,' while the money lent is the 'principal or tree.' In cases where the return compensates the lender/liquidity provider for lending/staking tokens, it will have the same nature as interest and be considered an income (revenue) receipt.[233]

When the return might be considered capital

5.206 In some cases, the return received by the lender/liquidity provider may not resemble interest or a reward for a service but rather a capital return. This occurs when the lender/liquidity provider seeks to benefit from their activities through capital asset growth, and the return is not a reward from the borrower or DeFi platform for providing their services. For example, the lender realises their return by disposing of a capital asset representing their lending, and the disposal proceeds are uncertain and speculative. Depending on the specific facts, it may be deemed that the lender has realised their return from the capital asset's value growth, making it a capital receipt.[234]

5.207 However, if the disposal proceeds of the capital asset representing the tokens lent/staked are agreed when the tokens are advanced, the return may have an income rather than capital nature, as the lender/liquidity provider provides a service for an agreed reward. Thus, obtaining all transaction facts is essential before determining the return's nature.[235]

5.208 Please note that the above HMRC guidance is illustrative, and real-world situations may involve additional factors affecting the conclusion.[236]

5.209 If the return on lending is considered income, the next step is to determine whether this income is received as part of the lender's trade or not.

230 CRYPTO6110.
231 *Ibid.*
232 [1923] 8TC521.
233 CRYPTO61214.
234 *Ibid.*
235 *Ibid.*
236 *Ibid.* If you encounter difficulty determining the return's nature, refer the case to HMRC for advice following the guidance at CRYPTO100500.

Case law principles can help determine if the activity qualifies as trading.[237] HMRC's view is that individuals lending to DeFi platforms are unlikely to be engaged in trading.[238]

Corporate tax

Introduction

5.210 A lender/liquidity provider can earn a return from engaging in DeFi loans, which might be subject to corporation tax for customers within the regime. How the corporation tax treats this return depends on whether the customer's activities amount to a trade.[239]

5.211 When determining if an incorporated entity is engaged in a trade related to DeFi loans, similar considerations to those for determining a trade in shares, securities, and other financial products apply.[240]

Treatment when a trade is conducted

5.212 If a customer is deemed to conduct a trade related to DeFi loans, the activity falling within the scope of that trade becomes subject to Corporation Tax under s 35 of CTA 2009.[241]

5.213 In cases involving cryptoassets within a trade, these assets can potentially be held either as trading stock or as investment assets outside of the trade. It is essential to consider whether there have been any appropriations to or from trading stock.[242]

Treatment when a trade is not conducted

5.214 If a customer does not conduct a trade or the activity generating the return is outside the trade's scope, making a DeFi loan could trigger a disposal of a chargeable asset.[243] In such situations, there may be a chargeable gain subject to corporation tax under CTA 2009, s 2.[244]

237 See **5.82–5.97**.
238 HMRC, 'Consultation outcome: The taxation of Decentralised Finance involving the lending and staking of cryptoassets – call for evidence' (27 April 2023) www.gov.uk/government/consultations/call-for-evidence-the-taxation-of-decentralised-finance-involving-the-lending-and-staking-of-cryptoassets/the-taxation-of-decentralised-finance-involving-the-lending-and-staking-of-cryptoassets-call-for-evidence [accessed 28 September 2023].
239 CRYPTO61411.
240 *Ibid.* For detailed guidance, refer to CRYPTO40150 and BIM56800. See also **5.82–5.97**.
241 *Ibid.*
242 *Ibid.* Refer to BIM33630 for further guidance on appropriations to and from trading stock.
243 See CRYPTO61600.
244 CRYPTO61411.

5.215 However, the lender/liquidity provider may receive a return in exchange for making the DeFi loan. If this return is not part of the customer's trade, it may be chargeable as miscellaneous income under CTA 2009, s 979.[245]

Taxing provisions

5.216 HMRC does not classify the return[246] earned by the lender/liquidity provider as 'interest' for tax purposes.[247] Consequently, any provisions in the Tax Acts related to interest will not apply to this return. Additionally, HMRC does not anticipate that the lending/staking of tokens by a customer subject to corporation tax will be considered a loan relationship.[248] The taxation of the return depends on whether it has the characteristics of capital or revenue.[249]

Capital receipt

5.217 If the return is considered capital in nature, it will be subject to corporation tax as a chargeable gain.[250]

Revenue receipt

5.218 If the lender/liquidity provider is not engaged in a trade involving DeFi loans, and the receipt is income in nature, it falls within the scope of the miscellaneous income provisions.[251]

5.219 CTA 2009, ss 979–981 (known as the 'sweep-up provisions') impose corporation tax on income that is not otherwise taxable under the Corporation Tax Acts.[252]

5.220 Many cases have examined the scope of these provisions. Broadly, the reward is taxable under the miscellaneous income sweep-up provisions if it represents income and arises from an understanding between both parties that the recipient will compensate the provider for their services, such as a quid pro quo arrangement. The existence of a formal written contract is not necessary.[253]

245 *Ibid*. For detailed information on when the return may be chargeable as miscellaneous income, consult guidance pages CRYPTO61412–CRYPTO61414.
246 CRYPTO61130.
247 CRYPTO61110.
248 CRYPTO41100.
249 CRYPTO61212. Refer to CRYPTO61414 and CRYPTO61214 for guidance on determining the return's nature.
250 CRYPTO61212. See CRYPTO61620.
251 *Ibid*. CTA 2009, Pt 10.
252 *Ibid*. For general information about the miscellaneous income sweep-up provisions, refer to BIM100000.
253 *Ibid*. For further details on the relevance of contracts and arrangements, consult BIM100105.

5.221 When a lender/liquidity provider lends/stakes tokens to a borrower/DeFi lending platform, there is an agreement between the two parties, which might fall short of being considered an enforceable contract. This agreement outlines the loan terms, including:[254]

(a) borrowing term, which can be fixed or indefinite;

(b) principal amount of the loan; and

(c) any return payable by the borrower/DeFi lending platform to the lender/liquidity provider.

5.222 The specific amount to be paid does not matter (eg if the rate of return fluctuates or the borrowing/staking period is indefinite) as long as there is an obligation on the borrower/DeFi lending platform to make a payment. Consequently, if the return is of an income nature, it becomes subject to corporation tax under the miscellaneous income sweep-up provisions.[255]

Amount chargeable to corporation tax

5.223 The miscellaneous income sweep-up provisions apply solely to tax the return[256] received by the lender/liquidity provider and not the repayment of the principal under Corporation Tax. The repayment of the principal is considered a capital transaction.[257]

5.224 The return received by the lender/liquidity provider is in a non-cash form. The chargeable amount under CTA 2009, ss 979–981 is determined based on the value of the receipt in pounds sterling.[258]

Nature of the return

5.225 How the return[259] is taxed when received by the lender/liquidity provider depends on whether it has the characteristics of capital or revenue. The nature of the return is determined by how the transaction is structured. Since the lending/staking of tokens is an evolving field, it is not possible to cover all scenarios in which a lender/liquidity provider earns a return and its nature.[260]

5.226 The criteria for determining the nature of the return are consistent for both corporation tax and income tax.[261]

254 *Ibid.*
255 *Ibid.*
256 See CRYPTO61130.
257 CRYPTO61413. See CRYPTO61620.
258 CRYPTO61413. See BIM100150.
259 See CRYPTO61130.
260 CRYPTO61414.
261 CRYPTO61414. For more details, refer to CRYPTO61214.

Chargeable gains

DeFi lending and repos

5.227 A repo is essentially a financing arrangement where a person holding securities sells them to another person with an agreement to buy them back at a specified time and price, resulting in a profit for the buyer. Despite being structured as a sale and repurchase, repos are economically financing transactions.

5.228 From a tax perspective, there is an actual sale of securities, leading to a disposal for CG purposes. However, repos are treated as finance transactions, and any gains on the sale and repurchase are disregarded.[262] Instead, the return paid by the other party to the original owner is taxed as interest. Since cryptoassets are treated as assets (rather than currency), lending them and transferring beneficial ownership constitute disposals for CG purposes, unless the lender conducts lending as part of their trade. This principle applies to transfers made by both the lender and the borrower (with the platform, if applicable, more likely to be engaged in trading). The return earned from lending is considered income and subject to income tax.

5.229 Section 263A of TCGA 1992 applies to repos of securities. Section 263B of TCGA 1992 applies to the lending of securities. Both of these provisions rely on the definition of securities in TCGA 1992, s 263AA(8). This says that 'securities' for these purposes means:

> '(a) shares in a company wherever resident,
>
> (b) loan stock or other securities of—
>
> > (i) the government of the United Kingdom,
> >
> > (ii) a local authority in the United Kingdom,
> >
> > (iii) another public authority in the United Kingdom,
> >
> > (iv) a company resident in the United Kingdom or other body resident in the United Kingdom, or
>
> (c) shares, loan stock, stock or other securities issued by—
>
> > (i) a government, local authority or other public authority of a territory outside the United Kingdom, or
> >
> > (ii) another body of persons not resident in the United Kingdom.'

5.230 HMRC indicates that it will be a question of fact whether the tokens being loaned and borrowed or staked (as applicable) satisfy this definition to be securities for the purposes of TCGA 1992, ss 263A or 263B. Generally tokens will not qualify as securities for this purpose.[263] If in doubt a reference can be made to HMRC for clarification.[264]

262 TCGA 1992, s 263A(1).
263 CRYPTO61610.
264 CRYPTO100500.

Making a DeFi loan

5.231 To determine if the transfer of tokens to the platform (by the lender) or as collateral (by the borrower) falls within the CG regime (instead of being classified as trading), it is essential to establish whether there has been an actual disposal for CG purposes. This hinges on whether the donor's beneficial interest in the property has been transferred. Consider if the lender/liquidity provider truly transfers ownership of tokens to the borrower/ DeFi lending platform. This depends on the contract/terms and conditions and examining the terms and conditions of the arrangement is crucial. If the recipient can freely use the tokens, it suggests they have acquired beneficial ownership. Conversely, if there are restrictions on token use, it implies no beneficial ownership.[265] In many cases, if there is no transfer of beneficial ownership, simply transferring legal title to the platform (which might hold the tokens on bare trust for the beneficial owner) is unlikely to trigger a tax liability.

5.232 Transferring beneficial ownership of tokens to the borrower/DeFi lending platform during a loan/staking[266] triggers a disposal of the loaned/staked tokens. This happens when the lender/liquidity provider transfers beneficial ownership to the borrower/DeFi lending platform. The consideration the lender/ liquidity provider receives depends on circumstances. [267]

Lender transfers control of tokens to a borrower

5.233 The lender disposes of tokens for a right to receive future tokens. This right is deferred consideration. Tax treatment depends on whether the future token quantity is known. If known, TCGA 1992, s 48(1) applies. The lender values future tokens in sterling at loan inception. If no return is agreed,[268] TCGA 1992, s 48(1) always applies. For situations with known future token quantities but taxed as income due to return, TCGA 1992, s 37 applies. It excludes the income-taxed sterling amount from consideration to prevent double taxation.[269]

Lender holds a right to receive unascertainable deferred consideration

5.234 If the future token quantity is unknown, the lender has a right to receive unascertainable deferred consideration. It is an asset for CG purposes. The consideration is its market value at receipt.[270] It is rare for the total tokens to be unknown, as the loan is for a known token quantity (the principal). Only the return can be unknown. In this case, treat the principal as known under TCGA 1992, s 48(1). The right to the return represents a '*Marren v Ingles*[271]

265 CRYPTO61620.
266 CRYPTO61120.
267 CRYPTO61620.
268 CRYPTO61130.
269 CRYPTO61620.
270 For valuation guidance, see CG14950.
271 54 TC 76.

right' CG computation.[272] Section 37 of TCGA 1992 does not apply to exclude any *Marren v Ingles* right value from the CG computation.[273] No part of this right is subject to income tax. A loss may occur on the right's disposal when the loan is repaid, offsetting any gain from loan origination.[274]

Liquidity provider transfers token control to DeFi lending platform for one or more tokens

5.235 This is a token exchange. The consideration is the market value in sterling of tokens received from the DeFi lending platform. The acquisition price is the market value in sterling of tokens transferred to the DeFi lending platform. For multi-token transfers to receive one token, apportion the received token's value fairly among the disposals.[275]

5.236 Worked examples of CG scenarios are set out at CRYPTO61670. While the section is mostly on person-to-person lending examples rather than lending through platforms, the underlying principles remain unchanged. These examples assume that any income-like return does not result from trading.

Borrowing

5.237 When a person borrows tokens, it is considered an acquisition. In a loan agreement, the borrower promises to do something: transfer tokens to the lender later. In the High Court case *Chaney v Watkis*,[276] it was ruled that an obligation to do something had 'money's worth' and could be considered expenditure. Thus, the value of the borrower's obligation to transfer tokens to the lender in the future becomes the acquisition cost of the borrowed tokens.[277]

Collateral

5.238 Many DeFi lending platforms require borrowers to provide collateral. The collateral amount is often higher than the transferred tokens to account for price fluctuations. If the value of borrowed tokens declines, the collateral might be used to cover the loss, and the platform could sell it off through a smart contract process known as 'liquidation' of the collateral. Whether giving collateral constitutes a disposal depends on the DeFi lending platform's terms

272 CG14990.

273 CRYPTO61650.

274 CRYPTO61620. For further guidance on obtaining a valuation of a '*Marren v Ingles* right' see CG14950. For an example of a CG computation involving a '*Marren v Ingles* right', see CRYPTO61673. An election may allow this loss to offset the gain, detailed in CG15080 onwards.

275 CRYPTO61620. For a CG computation example involving token exchange for a liquidity token, refer to CRYPTO61674.

276 58 TC 707.

277 CRYPTO61630. For more details on allowable costs, refer to CRYPTO22150. For guidance on pooling tokens and their associated allowable costs, see CRYPTO22200.

and conditions. If the platform can deal with the collateral as it wishes, it likely acquires beneficial ownership, and the borrower disposes of it. Conversely, if the platform is restricted from dealing with the collateral, the borrower retains ownership and has not made a disposal. When a disposal occurs, the consideration is the market value in sterling of the tokens given, and gains or losses are computed normally. If collateral is withdrawn, it is an acquisition, and the cost is the market value in sterling of tokens received.[278]

5.239 Liquidation by the DeFi platform has no CG consequences because the borrower already disposed of the tokens when transferring them to the platform. If no disposal occurs, TCGA 1992, s 26 applies. When collateral is withdrawn, it has no CG consequences because the borrower retained ownership. In case of liquidation by the DeFi platform, TCGA 1992, s 26(2) treats the platform as a nominee for the borrower, and any gain or loss on token disposal is attributed to the borrower, with tokens deemed to be disposed of at their market value in sterling.[279]

5.240 Liquidation may involve third-party liquidators, and any tokens taken as a penalty will not satisfy TCGA 1992, s 38. This section allows deductions for specific expenditure categories, and tokens taken as a penalty do not fit these criteria.[280]

Satisfaction of a DeFi loan and withdrawal of a stake

5.241 When a loan or stake is settled, both the borrower and the lender or liquidity provider will face tax consequences. In this context, 'settlement' can mean either:[281]

(a) the borrower transferring tokens to the lender to fulfil their obligations under the loan agreement; or

(b) the liquidity provider withdrawing their staked tokens from a DeFi lending platform's liquidity pool.

Borrower's position

5.242 When the borrower settles the loan, they transfer ownership of tokens to the lender, effectively selling those tokens. To calculate the gain or loss from this sale for tax purposes, the market value of the tokens in sterling at the time of the transaction must be used. This includes any tokens given to the lender as interest on the loan. The borrower can deduct allowable costs when computing any gain or loss.[282]

278 CRYPTO61640.
279 CRYPTO61640.
280 *Ibid*. For a CG computation example involving collateral liquidation, see CRYPTO61675.
281 CRYPTO61650.
282 *Ibid*. For guidance on allowable cost see CRYPTO22150. For an example of this calculation, refer to CRYPTO61676.

Lender/liquidity provider's position

5.243 The outcome for the lender when the loan is settled depends on how the loan was initially treated for CGT purposes.[283] If the lender treated the future quantity of tokens to be received as ascertainable, they should have included the sterling value of the tokens at the time the loan was made in the CGT computation.[284] When the borrower settles the loan, the tokens received by the lender are considered a capital sum derived from that right, resulting in a disposal under TCGA 1992, s 22(1). This reflects any change in token value during the loan term, potentially leading to a gain or loss. If TCGA 1992, s 37(1) applied to the first CGT computation, then the sterling value of those tokens would be excluded in the second CGT computation.[285]

5.244 If the lender treated the future quantity of tokens to be received as unascertainable, they would have acquired a '*Marren v Ingles* right,' and its value should have been included in the CGT computation when the loan was made. When the borrower settles the loan, the tokens received by the lender are considered a capital sum derived from the *Marren v Ingles* right, resulting in a disposal under TCGA 1992, s 22(1). The acquisition price of the *Marren v Ingles* right is the value included in the CGT computation when the loan was made. If this disposal results in a loss, it may be possible to offset that loss against any gain from the loan's initial creation.[286]

5.245 In cases where a liquidity provider originally transferred tokens to a DeFi lending platform and wants to withdraw their staked tokens, they will be disposing of the tokens initially received from the DeFi lending platform in exchange for tokens from the platform. This exchange represents a disposal by the liquidity provider, and the consideration for this disposal is the market value in sterling of the tokens received from the DeFi lending platform.[287]

GIFTS OF CRYPTOASSETS TO CHARITIES

5.246 When a charity receives a gift of cryptoassets, the donor can claim relief against any chargeable gain, following standard principles. However, corporations cannot claim corporation tax relief for gifts of cryptoassets to charity[288] and individuals cannot benefit from gift aid, since cryptoassets are not considered money.[289]

283 See CRYPTO61620.

284 See CG14881. The lender should apply TCGA 1992, s 48(1).

285 CRYPTO61650. For examples, see CRYPTO61677 and CRYPTO61678.

286 CRYPTO61650. For more information about this election CG15080 onwards. For an example, see CRYPTO61679.

287 CRYPTO61650.

288 CTA 2010, s 191(2),

289 ITA 2007, s 416(2). For companies, see CRYPTO41250, and for individuals, see CRYPTO22100.

INCLUSION OF DIGITAL ASSETS IN INVESTMENT TRANSACTIONS LIST

5.247 To attract financial services and facilitate tax-efficient management of offshore funds by UK investment managers, certain digital asset transactions were added to the investment transactions list (ITL) under Investment Transactions (Tax) Regulations 2014, effective from 1 January 2023.

5.248 The IME (investment manager's exemption) allows UK investment managers to handle offshore funds without creating a UK tax liability. With the expansion of the ITL, transactions within it, including certain digital asset transactions, can now benefit from the IME. This applies to authorised investment funds, exempt unauthorised unit trusts, and investment trusts, and is relevant for calculating the reportable income of diversely owned offshore funds.

5.249 The regulations follow a consultation on extending the IME to cover cryptoasset transactions, which concluded with positive outcomes. Before these regulations, cryptoasset transactions were unlikely to fall within the ITL, and the IME was unavailable for such transactions.

5.250 The Investment Manager (Investment Transactions) (Cryptoassets) Regulations 2022, published by HMRC on 20 December 2022, define cryptoassets by reference to the 10 October 2022 version of the Crypto-Asset Reporting Framework (CARF) and updated Common Reporting Standards (CRS) by the Organization for Economic Cooperation and Development (OECD).[290] The extension to the ITL only applies to the IME and not to other fund tax regimes that use the definition.

REPORTING OBLIGATIONS AND COMPLIANCE

5.251 Taxpayers engaging in cryptocurrency-related activities are required to maintain accurate records of their transactions, including details of acquisitions, disposals, and any associated costs. Individuals should these retain records for at least 22 months, self-employed individuals for five years, and companies should retain records for at least six years from the date of filing their tax return. [291] Failure to comply with tax obligations can result in penalties and potential legal consequences.[292]

290 See **19.54–19.58**.

291 CRYPTO10400. See HMRC, 'A general guide to keeping records for your tax return' (HMRC guide, RK BK1, February 2013) https://assets.publishing.service.gov.uk/media/5a7dc00540f0b65d886342e1/rk-bk1.pdf [accessed 8 October 2023].

292 HMRC, Enquiry Manual (HMRC internal manual, 12 April 2016, updated 26 September 2023) www.gov.uk/hmrc-internal-manuals/enquiry-manual [accessed 8 October 2023].

CONCLUSION

5.252 The taxation of cryptocurrencies in the UK is governed by specific rules and guidance provided by HMRC. Individuals and companies engaged in cryptocurrency activities should carefully consider the tax implications and fulfil their reporting obligations to ensure compliance with the tax laws. It is advisable to consult with tax professionals who specialise in cryptocurrency.

Part III

Legal Challenges

Chapter 6

Contractual Issues and Smart Contracts

INTRODUCTION

6.1 With the advent of blockchain technology, smart contracts have emerged as a promising innovation in the field of contract law. In the UK, smart contracts are subject to existing contractual principles and legal frameworks.

DEFINITION AND FEATURES OF SMART CONTRACTS

6.2 The Law Commission defined smart contracts as 'a legally binding contract in which some or all of the contractual obligations are defined in and/or performed automatically by a computer program.'[1] Put simply smart contracts are self-executing agreements that are coded on a DLT platform.

6.3 In terms of the technology, Ethereum co-founder Vitalik Buterin has said he regrets using the term 'smart contracts' and indicated a more accurate description is 'persistent scripts.' In this context smart contracts are computer programs rather than contracts.[2]

6.4 Smart contracts automate the performance and enforcement of contract terms using computer code and are characterised by their decentralised nature, immutability, and reliance on cryptographic technology for security and verification. Smart contracts can be integrated into token designs, providing automated services to token holders when specific events/milestones occur, such as delivering goods upon blockchain-verified receipt of payment using technologies like DLT and consensus, ensuring compliance with their terms.

6.5 The International Swaps and Derivatives Association have noted that 'derivatives are fertile territory for the application of smart contracts and DLT because their main payments and deliveries are heavily dependent on conditional logic'.[3] More general areas include insurance, finance, decentralised finance, real

1 Law Commission, 'Smart legal contracts Advice to Government' (Law Com No 401, 2022), [1.2].
2 David G.W. Birch, 'They're Not Smart And They're Not Contracts' (4 September 2021) *Forbes* www.forbes.com/sites/davidbirch/2021/09/04/theyre-not-smart-and-theyre-not-contacts/ [accessed 4 October 2023].
3 Law Commission, 'Smart legal contracts' (n 1 above), [2.66].

estate, supply chain, peer to peer, and intellectual property (IP) use cases.[4] The benefits of smart contracts are efficiency, transparency and reduced enforcement costs.[5] The disadvantages include: costs involved in creating a smart contract, complications in enforcement, environmental costs.[6]

VALIDITY AND ENFORCEABILITY OF SMART CONTRACTS

6.6 In the UK, the validity and enforceability of smart contracts are determined by established contractual principles. For a smart contract to be legally binding, it must meet the essential elements of a contract, including offer, acceptance, consideration, and intention to create legal relations. The fact that a smart contract is executed through code does not diminish its legal effect.

6.7 The UKJT statement and Law Commission report acknowledge that smart contracts can hold contractual force, even though they do not follow traditional contractual forms. As valid contracts under English law, they should adhere to standard principles of contract law:[7] The Law Commission conclude that deeds are not capable of forming a smart contract under the current legislative framework.[8]

6.8 The Law Commission set out the elements of a binding legal contract that smart contracts must meet, as follows:[9]

(a) agreement;[10]

(b) consideration;[11]

(c) certainty and completeness;[12]

(d) intention to create legal relations;[13] and

(e) formality requirements.[14]

6.9 According to the UKJT, normal rules of contractual interpretation should be applied to smart contracts. In some cases, the entire contract may exist within the code, leaving no room for interpretation. However, it is more common

4 *Ibid* [2.86]. Specific industry examples of use cases and notional ones are given at [2.88]–[2.102].
5 *Ibid* [2.105]–[2.109].
6 *Ibid* [2.110]–[2.117].
7 UKJT, 'Legal statement on cryptoassets and smart contracts' (November 2019), The LawTech Delivery Panel, [18] www.blockchain4europe.eu/wp-content/uploads/2021/05/6.6056_JO_Cryptocurrencies_Statement_FINAL_WEB_111119-1.pdf [accessed 26 September 2023].
8 Law Commission, 'Smart legal contracts' (n 1 above), [3.133]-[3.139].
9 *Ibid* [3.2].
10 *Ibid* [3.4]–[3.38].
11 *Ibid* [3.39]–[3.43].
12 *Ibid* [3.44]–[3.45].
13 *Ibid* [3.63]–[3.75].
14 *Ibid* [3.76]–[3.139].

for the code to govern certain aspects while other elements of the contract rely on external evidence. Interpretation questions may arise, especially regarding the behaviour of the code under different circumstances, potentially requiring expert evidence.[15] The Law Commission has also indicated that the definition of 'writing' pursuant to Sch 1 of the Interpretation Act 1978 is defined as 'representing or reproducing words in a visible form' which encompasses source code.[16]

6.10 Regarding formal requirements, the UKJT believes that a private key is likely to fulfil statutory signature requirements, as electronic signatures intended to authenticate a document generally satisfy such requirements. [17] The Law Commission has also reached the same conclusion.

6.11 The UKJT suggests that even a statutory 'in writing' requirement can be met by code that can be displayed or printed out.[18] In practice, the terms of the actual agreement between the parties can be easily reduced to writing, and the role of the smart contract would be to govern the execution. This analysis helps overcome potential difficulties that may arise.[19]

PERFORMANCE AND EXECUTION OF SMART CONTRACTS

6.12 Smart contracts are designed to self-execute based on predefined conditions and criteria. The execution of a smart contract occurs automatically without the need for manual intervention once the specified conditions are met. However, challenges may arise when the performance of contractual obligations requires off-chain actions or interactions with the physical world.

6.13 The Law Commission sets out three forms of smart contracts:[20]

(i) **External contract**: a natural language contract in which some or all of the contractual obligations are performed automatically by the code of a computer program. The code itself does not define any contractual obligations, but is merely a tool employed by one or both of the parties to perform those obligations. The code falls outside the scope of the parties' legally binding agreement. These are most commonly used.[21]

(ii) **Hybrid contract**: contractual obligations are defined in natural language, and others are defined in the code of a computer program. Some or all of the

15 UKJT, 'Legal statement on cryptoassets' (n 7 above), [149]-[155].
16 Law Commission, 'Smart legal contracts' (n 1 above), [3.97].
17 UKJT, 'Legal statement on cryptoassets' (n 7 above), [158]–[160].
18 *Ibid* [164].
19 Dean Armstrong, Fergus McCombie, and Ceri Davis, *Cyber Litigation: The Legal Principles* (1st edn, Bloomsbury Professional, 2021), [3.34].
20 Law Commission, 'Smart legal contracts' (n 1 above), [2.51].
21 *Ibid* [2.64].

contractual obligations are performed automatically by the code. The level of natural language versus code will vary on a spectrum.

(iii) **Code contract**: a contract in which all of the contractual terms are defined in, and performed automatically by, the code of a computer program. No natural language version of the agreement exists.

6.14 The Law Commission indicates the classification of a smart legal contract, or indeed of the individual obligations within the contract (while helpful for the purposes of the legal analysis) should not be approached too rigidly or prescriptively.

6.15 In designing a smart contract the Law Commission outlined the following questions that should be asked:[22]

(a) What obligations do the parties wish to automate, and what is the relationship between those obligations and any non-coded terms?

(b) What is the translation process involved in coding a natural language obligation?

(c) If some terms are defined in natural language and some in code, what hierarchy applies in the event of a conflict?

(d) Where does liability lie if the code fails, there is a security breach or data is comprised?

(e) What is the dispute resolution process, bearing in mind cross-border elements and local laws?

(f) The LawTech Sounding Board indicated parties 'conduct a rigorous planning phase' involving collaboration between the lawyers and coders and parties should be clear as to what the goals and business requirements are.[23]

6.16 It is worth noting that while in some cases a smart legal contract will be negotiated and agreed upon between two or more parties, this may not always be the case. For example, one party could develop a smart legal contract and deploy it on a platform (such as Ethereum) for other participants to interact with in which case there will not be negotiation between the parties.

LEGAL REMEDIES AND DISPUTE RESOLUTION

6.17 In case of a breach or dispute concerning a smart contract, the parties may seek legal remedies through traditional legal channels. The UK legal system provides mechanisms for enforcing smart contracts and resolving disputes, including through negotiation, arbitration, or court proceedings. The

22 *Ibid* [2.56].
23 *Ibid* [2.57].

enforceability of smart contracts may depend on the specific circumstances and the legal interpretation of the contractual terms.

6.18 In April 2021, the UKJT published the first version of its Digital Dispute Resolution Rules[24] ('UKJT Rules'). The UKJT Rules are to be 'used for and incorporated into on-chain digital relationships and smart contracts,' with a view to 'facilitate the rapid and cost-effective resolution of commercial disputes' involving novel technologies.[25] The UKJT Rules can be incorporated into smart contract by reference, or parties may agree to adopt them after a dispute arises.

6.19 In brief, the UKJT Rules aim to expedite dispute resolution. Initially, they establish that outcomes from automatic dispute resolution are binding. Disputes not covered by this process go to arbitration. Experts settle expert matters. These rules also accelerate the dispute timeline. For instance, upon getting a claim notice, respondents have three days to respond. The 'appointment body' must promptly select the tribunal. The tribunal should strive to deliver a verdict within 30 days of appointment, unless the parties agree otherwise. The tribunal holds full control over procedure, evidence, and submissions. Where the 16 broadly framed rules are silent, parties can use the Arbitration Act 1996 to access 'sensible defaults'. Under the UKJT Rules, there is also no right of appeal on a point of law, and the only other challenges permitted are those available under the Arbitration Act 1996. The UKJT Rules are governed by the law of England and Wales.[26]

OTHER CHALLENGES AND UNCERTAINTIES

6.20 The use of smart contracts poses certain legal challenges and uncertainties within the UK legal framework. For example, issues related to data protection, privacy, IP rights, and jurisdiction may arise. As smart contract technology evolves, legal frameworks may need to adapt to address these challenges and provide clarity in specific areas.

6.21 The Law Commission identified issues in the processing of the consumer's personal data, especially in how traders would comply with their data protection and processing obligations in the context of consumer smart contracts.[27]

6.22 While smart contracts themselves are not subject to specific regulatory frameworks in the UK, the underlying activities or industries they relate to may have regulatory implications. It is important to consider any relevant regulations,

24 UKJT, 'Digital Dispute Resolution Rules' (Version 1.0, 2021) UKJT https://27221500.fs1.hubspotusercontent-eu1.net/hubfs/27221500/UKJT%20work/Digital%20Dispute%20resolution%20rules.pdf [accessed 8 October 2023].
25 *Ibid* [3].
26 *Ibid* [4]–[8].
27 Law Commission, 'Smart legal contracts' (n 1 above), [6.22]–[6.24].

such as financial, consumer protection, or data protection laws, when deploying smart contracts in specific industries or sectors.

CONCLUSION

6.23 Smart contracts offer potential benefits in terms of efficiency, transparency, and automation of contractual relationships. In the UK, the legal validity and enforceability of smart contracts are determined by existing contractual principles. However, as smart contract technology continues to evolve, it is crucial to closely monitor legal developments and ensure compliance with applicable laws and regulations.

Chapter 7

Intellectual Property Issues regarding Cryptocurrencies

INTRODUCTION

7.1 Cryptocurrencies have raised several IP issues in the UK due to their technological and decentralised nature. This chapter explores key IP considerations related to cryptocurrencies within the UK legal framework.

COPYRIGHT

7.2 The underlying technology behind cryptocurrencies, known as DLT, involves the creation and storage of digital records. Copyright protection may apply to the code and software components of DLT systems, subject to meeting the requirements of originality and authorship.

7.3 White papers and technical documentation associated with cryptocurrencies may be protected by copyright. For instance, in *Wright v Persons Unknown,*[1] a High Court Chancery Division Court Order by default was obtained to have the Bitcoin white paper removed from a website for copyright infringement. It is important for creators to consider copyright ownership and licensing when publishing such materials.

Overview of UK copyright

7.4 From a legal perspective in the UK, the term 'computer program' and its definition is somewhat ambiguous. The Copyright, Designs, and Patents Act 1988 (CDPA 1988), which governs intellectual property rights (IPRs), does not provide a specific definition for what qualifies as a 'computer program.'

7.5 The definition of a 'computer program' is outlined in the Software Directive 2009,[2] which replaced the previous Software Directive 1991.[3] The

1 [2021] 12 WLUK 212. Dr Craig Wright, who claims to be Satoshi Nakamoto, obtained an order by default to have the Bitcoin white paper, 'Bitcoin: a Peer-to-Peer Electronic Cash System', removed from Bitcoin.org. The Bitcoin white paper is still available online: see Satoshi Nakamoto, 'Bitcoin: A Peer-to-Peer Electronic Cash System' (2008) Sathoshi Nakamoto Institute https://nakamotoinstitute.org/bitcoin/ [accessed 8 October 2023].

2 Council Directive 2009/24/EC on the legal protection of computer programs [2009] OJ L111/16.

3 Council Directive 91/250/EEC on the legal protection of computer programs [1991] OJ L122/42.

Software Directive's implementation in the UK is reflected in the Copyright (Computer Programs) Regulations 1992 (CCPR 1992) [4] which amended the CDPA states that:[5]

> 'Protection in accordance with this Directive shall apply to the expression in any form of a computer program. Ideas and principles which underlie any element of a computer program, including those which underlie its interfaces, are not protected by copyright under this Directive.'

7.6 According to recital 7 of the Software Directive 2009 which is reflected in s 3 of the Computer Program Regulations, the term 'computer program' includes:

> '... programs in any form, including those which are incorporated into hardware [and] ... preparatory design work leading to the development of a computer program provided that the nature of the preparatory work is such that a computer program can result from it at a later stage.'

7.7 The Software Directive therefore defines a 'computer program' as including programs in any form, even those integrated into hardware, and preparatory design work that leads to the development of a computer program if it can eventually result in one.

7.8 The Intellectual Property (Copyright and Related Rights) (Amendment) (EU Exit) Regulations 2019 (Brexit Database Regulations 2019), passed under the powers of the European Union (Withdrawal) Act 2018 (EUWA 2018), came into force on 1 January 2021. These regulations removed or corrected references to the EU, EEA, or Member States in UK copyright legislation and preserved the effect of UK law where possible. Many of the changes that EU legislation and ECJ caselaw made to UK copyright law over the years of UK membership of the EU will persist for the foreseeable future after Brexit as part of the 'retained EU law' that is now embodied in UK law; however, the UK courts may depart from that case law, subject to certain limitations set out in EUWA 2018, s 6.

7.9 For a clearer understanding, the Model Provisions on the Protection of Computer Software (Model Provisions), dated January 1978 and prepared by the World Intellectual Property Organization offers an insightful definition:

> '[a] set of instructions capable, when incorporated in a machine readable medium, of causing a machine having information processing capabilities to indicate, perform or achieve a particular function, task or result.'[6]

7.10 This definition suggests that a computer program consists of both its source code (human-readable form) and its object code (machine-readable form). This interpretation seems to align with Article 10(1) of the Agreement on Trade-Related Aspects of Intellectual Property Rights 1994 (TRIPS Agreement), which

4 Regulation 3.
5 Article 1(2).
6 Section 1(i).

considers both source code and object code as literary works protected under the Berne Convention:

> 'Computer programs, whether expressed in source code or in object code, will be protected as literary works pursuant to the Berne Convention [(Paris Act of 24 July 1971), as amended on 28 September 1979].'

7.11 The ECJ's judgment in *Bezpečnostní softwarová asociace – Svaz softwarové ochrany v Ministerstvo kultury*[7] (BSA) also supports the notion that a computer program is the expression of the program in any form, encompassing both source and object code.

7.12 To understand the term 'computer program' in a technical sense, we can see it as a set of instructions that guide a computer to perform specific tasks or functions, such as displaying text or images on a screen. This is distinct from hardware, which refers to tangible computer equipment like servers, terminals, keyboards, or printers. Computer programs can be supplied in different forms, such as on a disk, in hardware form (firmware), or printed on paper.[8]

7.13 The instructions used by a computer program can be explained as follows:[9]

(a) **Object code**: when feeding instructions into a computer to make it perform tasks, the code takes the form of binary code, consisting of 0s and 1s. This binary code is known as the object code, which is typically what is provided to licensed users of the software.

(b) **Source code**: however, writing instructions directly in binary code is not practical for humans. Instead, programmers use a higher-level language or code called the source code, which is then translated into object code by a program called a compiler. There are numerous high-level programming languages like Python, Java, JavaScript, C++ or HTML. The source code often includes a mix of keywords and equations, and it may also contain comments from the programmer, providing insights into various aspects of the code, like the location of crucial elements and the rationale for certain coding decisions. The source code is crucial for fully understanding the program, fixing errors or bugs, and enabling it to interact with other programs (interface). Consequently, logically structured, clearly defined, and well-commented source code holds significant commercial value and is typically closely guarded by software developers. Documentation related to the software's development is also essential for understanding, modifying, and advancing the program.

7.14 A computer program is primarily protected as a copyright work under the CDPA 1988. The CDPA 1988 defines an original literary work, which includes

7 Case C-393/09.

8 Practical Law IP&IT, 'Legal protection of software' *Practical Law UK* (Practice Note 7-202-4703, 2023), 6.

9 *Ibid* 6–7.

a 'computer program' and its 'preparatory design material'.[10] However, the CDPA 1988 does not specifically define what constitutes a computer program, but it implements the Software Directive 2009's provisions,[11] which protect 'computer programs' and their preparatory design material as literary works.

7.15 Software differs significantly from traditional copyright works like books or paintings, leading to some complexities in its application to software: it serves both as a record of information and as a functional work creating effects like screen displays or sounds, and may require ongoing support or maintenance. This dual nature raises challenges in providing legal protection through copyright because copyright protects expressions of ideas, not the ideas or schemes themselves.

7.16 Furthermore, the term 'computer program' seems to be interpreted as pertaining only to the source code and object code, which can create difficulties when determining the extent of copyright protection for a software package that includes more than just the code.[12]

Requirements for copyright protection

7.17 In order for copyright to subsist under UK law:

(a) a work must fall into one of the categories of work protected by copyright under UK law;

(b) a work must qualify for protection under UK law (this usually depends on the nationality of the author or place of first publication); and

(c) the term of copyright must not have expired.

7.18 The works protected by copyright are original literary, dramatic, musical or artistic works which, in the case of literary, dramatic or musical works are recorded in some way.[13] A literary work includes:[14]

(a) a table or compilation other than a database;

(b) a computer program and preparatory design material for a computer program;

(c) a database which meets a specific originality test;

(d) sound recordings, films or broadcasts; and

(e) typographical arrangements of published editions.

10 CDPA 1988, s 3(1) as amended by CCPR, 1992 reg 3.
11 Software Directive 2009, Art 1(1),
12 Practical Law IP&IT, Legal protection of software (n 8 above), 8.
13 CDPA 1988, s 3(2).
14 CDPA 1988, s 1(1).

7.19 Under UK law, to meet the originality requirement under the CDPA 1988, a work does not need to have artistic or literary merit. It simply means that the author must have created the work using their own skill, judgement, and individual effort, without copying it from other works.

7.20 In the case of *Infopaq International A/S v Danske Dagblades Forening*,[15] the ECJ ruled that storing and printing 11-word extracts from newspaper articles can be considered a reproduction of a copyright work under the Copyright Directive 2001[16] if the elements reproduced represent the author's intellectual creation. Following this case, the ECJ has further clarified the 'author's intellectual creation' standard in subsequent cases. The key test, as refined in *Cofemel – Sociedade de Vestuário SA v G-Star Raw CV*,[17] has two cumulative conditions for subject matter to be considered a work within Article 2(a) of the Copyright Directive 2001:[18]

(a) **Originality requirement**: the subject matter must be original, meaning it reflects the author's personality and involves their free and creative choices. If the realisation of the subject matter was dictated purely by technical constraints, rules, or other limitations, lacking creative freedom, it cannot be considered a work.

(b) **Identifiability requirement**: in order to classify subject matter as a 'work' within the scope of the Copyright Directive 2001, it must be identifiable with sufficient precision and objectivity.

Originality

7.21 The impact of *Infopaq* on the originality test applied by UK courts remains somewhat uncertain. The Court of Appeal in *The Newspaper Licensing Agency Ltd and others v Meltwater*[19] concluded that *Infopaq* did not alter the originality test. However, in *SAS Institute Inc v World Programming Ltd,*[20] the Court of Appeal acknowledged that the *Infopaq* test 'may not be quite the same as the traditional test under English law'.[21]

7.22 Significantly, the Software Directive 2009 also stipulates this higher test for the originality of software. Article 1(3) of the Software Directive 2009 provides that:

> 'A computer program shall be protected if it is original in the sense that it is the author's own intellectual creation. No other criteria shall be applied to determine its eligibility for protection.'

15 Case C-5/08.
16 Council Directive 2001/29/EC on the harmonisation of certain aspects of copyright and related rights in the information society [2001] OJ L167.
17 Case C-683/17.
18 *Ibid* [30]–[32].
19 [2011] EWCA Civ 890.
20 [2013] EWCA Civ 1482.
21 *Ibid* [36].

7.23 Since the CDPA does not include this requirement there is a question mark over whether it has correctly implemented the Software Directive. However, in *Infopaq* the ECJ held that, in establishing a harmonised framework for copyright, the Copyright Directive applied the standard of originality of 'author's own intellectual creation' to literary and artistic works.[22] For an example of the test of originality not being met see *Bezpečnostní softwarová asociace – Svaz softwarové ochrany v Ministerstvo kultury*[23] which held in relation to graphical user interfaces that the methods of implementing the idea and expression were so limited as to be indissociable.

Fixation

7.24 Copyright cannot subsist in a literary, dramatic or musical work unless and until it is recorded, in writing or otherwise.[24] This requirement may lead to challenges in certain cases, especially when it is claimed that elements of a program's user interface have been copied, but these specific elements are not explicitly recorded as such in the source code.[25]

7.25 In *Wright and ors v BTC Core and ors*,[26] regarding fixation, Mellor J highlighted the following points made in *World Programming Ltd*,[27] namely that:[28]

(a) It may be important to distinguish between the putative work on the one hand and any particular fixation of the work on the other hand.

(b) The fixation must not be confused with the work. For instance, a printed book is a fixation that may encompass various distinct works, possibly created by different authors and subject to separate copyright terms. For example, a printed book could include a literary work (the text) and a series of artistic works (illustrations).

(c) The fact that one can identify a fixation is a necessary, but not sufficient, condition for the subsistence of copyright.

7.26 In *Wright*, Mellor J examined the question of whether copyright existed for a File Format employed in the Bitcoin system. The judge determined that the File Format was not eligible for copyright protection. One of the reasons for this decision was that the claimant failed to demonstrate when and how the supposed literary work within the Bitcoin File Format was initially recorded, whether in writing or any other form.[29]

22 *Infopaq* [34]–[37].
23 Case C-393/09.
24 CDPA 1988, s 3(2).
25 See *Navitaire Inc v Easyjet Airline Company (1) and Bulletproof Inc (2)* [2004] EWHC 1725 (Ch).
26 [2023] EWHC 222 (Ch).
27 *World Programming Ltd*, (n 20 above).
28 *Wright*, (n 1 above) [27].
29 *Ibid* [61].

7.27 According to the claimants' evidence, blocks were written to file in the Bitcoin File Format, adhering to the structure specified in Schedule 2 of the Particulars of Claim. However, the judge pointed out that this did not resolve the matter of fixation, meaning where this structure was precisely recorded in a tangible form.[30]

7.28 Mellor J acknowledged that the first claimant, Dr Wright, demonstrated considerable skill and judgement in developing the Bitcoin File Format. Nonetheless, the judge disagreed with the claimants' assertion that the requirement for fixation or sufficient identifiability was automatically met when the program was executed. The reason for this was twofold:[31]

(a) The claimants failed to identify any pertinent 'work' that contained content defining the structure of the Bitcoin File Format.

(b) The claimants did not specify which parts of the Bitcoin File Format, as presented in each block, constituted content rather than just structure.

There was no evidence demonstrating that the Bitcoin File Format was explicitly laid out in any section of the software or early blocks written to the Bitcoin Blockchain.[32]

Duration

7.29 Copyright in a computer program lasts for 70 years from the end of the calendar year in which its author died.[33] However, if the work is 'computer-generated', that is generated by a computer in circumstances such that there is no human author of the work,[34] copyright expires 50 years from the end of the calendar year in which the work was made.[35]

7.30 A work is not considered computer-generated merely because it is performed using a computer. It can only be classified as computer-generated if the computer mechanically creates it based on a pre-entered program that a human being has merely activated.[36] In other words, the work must be a product of the computer's autonomous mechanical process, rather than just a human-guided operation on the computer.

30 *Ibid* [8].
31 *Ibid* [54]–[55].
32 *Ibid* [58].
33 CDPA 1988, s12(2).
34 CDPA 1988, s 178.
35 CDPA 1988, s 12(7).
36 Practical Law IP&IT, Legal protection of software (n 8 above), 15.

Databases

7.31 UK citizens, residents, and businesses are no longer eligible to receive protection in the EEA for newly created databases, although their databases already protected in the EEA at the end of 2020 will continue to have protection in the EEA for the rest of their standard duration. Under Article 58 of the Withdrawal Agreement, database rights that existed in the UK or EEA before 1 January 2021 will continue to exist in both territories for their duration under the Withdrawal Agreement.[37] UK undertakings are not eligible to hold or receive database rights in the EEA in respect of databases created on or after 1 January 2021. The government legislated to create a new UK database right to protect databases created after the end of the transition period by amending the Copyright and Rights in Databases Regulations 1997 (Database Regulations) so that they refer to the UK rather than to the EEA.[38] The amending regulations are the Brexit Database Regulations 2018. The new right gives the same rights in the UK as the EU database right gives in the EEA, for the same duration, but it will provide protection only within the UK.

7.32 UK businesses that also have establishments in the EU may be able to rely upon them for EU database right protection for databases created after the end of 2020. It may also be possible to rely upon copyright protection for databases where relevant originality can be shown.

7.33 Databases are defined as a collection of independent works, data or other materials which are arranged in a systematic or methodical way, and are individually accessible by electronic or other means.[39] They are subject to a higher originality test. Databases may only be protected by copyright (as opposed to database right) if they are 'original' in the sense that 'by reason of the selection or arrangement of the contents of the database the database constitutes the author's own intellectual creation'.[40] Tables and compilations of data or other materials are also subject to this higher test if they fall within the statutory definition of a database.[41]

7.34 The duration of a database right is 15 years, counted from the conclusion of the calendar year when the database creation was finalised. Alternatively, if the database becomes accessible to the public before this period's end, the 15-year duration starts from the conclusion of the calendar year when the database was initially accessible to the public.[42] This protection period is notably shorter compared to copyright, which persists for 70 years following the demise of

37 Agreement on the withdrawal of the United Kingdom of Great Britain and Northern Ireland from the European Union and the European Atomic Energy Community [2019] OJ C 384 I/1. See also Brexit Database Regulations 2018, reg 38.

38 Brexit Database Regulations 2018, reg 28.

39 CDPA 1988, s 3A.

40 CDPA 1988, s 3A(2).

41 Practical Law IP&IT, Legal protection of software (n 8 above), 10.

42 Copyright and Rights in Databases Regulations 1997, reg 17.

the database's author. If, however, a 'substantial change' is introduced to the database's contents, resulting in it being viewed as a 'substantial new investment,' the modified database becomes eligible for a fresh 15-year term of protection.[43] Essentially, this implies that databases that undergo continuous updates can potentially enjoy an ongoing, indefinite protection period.

TRADEMARKS

7.35 Trademarks can be used to protect the names, logos, and branding associated with cryptocurrencies. Registering a trademark with the Intellectual Property Office (ITPO) provides exclusive rights to use and protect the registered mark, preventing third parties from using similar marks that may cause confusion.

7.36 Trade mark law does not directly protect computer programs, but it is worth noting that brands or logos used in connection with a computer program may receive protection as registered trade marks or under the law of passing off.[44] A January 2020 decision by ECJ from a reference from the English High Court, *Sky plc and others v Skykick UK Limited and another,*[45] clarified that an application for a trade mark will not be invalid due to public policy or bad faith solely because it is filed for a broad category like 'computer software'. Nevertheless, trade mark owners should still consider the ECJ's guidance on what constitutes 'bad faith' when applying for trade mark. In *Lidl Great Britain Limited and another v Tesco Stores Limited and another*,[46] drawing on the Court of Appeal's decision in *Sky v Skykick*, Mrs Justice Joanna Smith DBE reminded that bad faith as a ground for invalidity requires the trade mark system be used in a manner inconsistent with 'honest practices or acceptable commercial behaviour'. The burden lies with the party alleging bad faith and a presumption of good faith exists unless the contrary is proved.

7.37 After the Brexit transition period, significant changes to UK trade mark law occurred, resulting in a new UK mark (known as comparable marks) automatically arising for each registered EU trade mark and international mark (EU).[47] The legal stance on exhaustion of rights also underwent changes.[48]

7.38 Unregistered marks or elements of 'get-up' used in association with software may be protected under the common law action of passing off, provided they meet the necessary requirements. When transferring an unregistered mark,

43 *Ibid*, reg 17(3).

44 *Microsoft Corporation v William Ling & Ors* [2006] EWHC 1619.

45 (Case 371/18) ECLI:EU:C:2020:45, 29 January 2020.

46 [2022] EWHC 1434 (Ch).

47 ITPO, 'EU trade mark protection and comparable UK trade marks' (Guidance, 20 January 2020) www.gov.uk/guidance/eu-trade-mark-protection-and-comparable-uk-trade-marks [accessed 29 September 2023].

48 ITPO, 'Exhaustion of IP rights and parallel trade' (Guidance, 30 January 2020) www.gov.uk/guidance/exhaustion-of-ip-rights-and-parallel-trade [accessed 29 September 2023].

the goodwill connected to the mark must be included in the assignment to enable the assignee to initiate proceedings against third parties for passing off.[49]

PATENTS

7.39 Specific technological innovations related to blockchain systems, such as consensus algorithms, cryptographic protocols, and DApps, may be eligible for patent protection in the UK. Patents provide exclusive rights to the inventor, allowing them to prevent others from using, making, or selling the patented invention.

7.40 Innovations in the business methods and processes surrounding cryptocurrencies, such as payment systems or token issuance methods, may also be eligible for patent protection, subject to meeting the patentability criteria. The UK has proven a popular destination for DLT patent filings.[50]

7.41 Brexit has had relatively limited impact on patents since there is little harmonisation of substantive patent law at the EU level. The application processes and registration systems for UK domestic patents, administered by the ITPO, and European patents designating the UK, managed by the European Patent Office (EPO) – a non-EU institution – remain unaffected. Additionally, the UK's membership in the Patent Cooperation Treaty[51] and the European Patent Convention (EPC)[52] remains intact.

7.42 In the UK, patents can be obtained for inventions that are new, involve an inventive step, have industrial or technical applicability, and do not fall under any exclusions.[53] However, s 1(2) of the Patents Act 1977 excludes the grant of patents for 'a program for a computer' to the extent that the patent relates to the program 'as such,' aligning with Article 52 of the EPC.

7.43 Despite the EPC's provision that computer programs are not patentable 'as such,' it is recognised that the application of a computer program may still be patentable if it possesses a technical character. However, determining what qualifies as the necessary technical character to overcome the exclusion is challenging. It should be noted that there is inconsistency and uncertainty across Europe concerning software patenting, with different national courts and patent offices adopting varying approaches.[54] Nevertheless, both the EPO and national

49 Practical Law IP&IT, Legal protection of software (n 8 above), 34.

50 Andrew Snowden, 'UK ranked fourth in the world for number of blockchain patents filed, but is falling behind for AI patents' (*UHY Hacker Young*, 21 January 2019) www.uhy-uk.com/insights/uk-ranked-fourth-world-number-blockchain-patents-filed-falling-behind-ai-patents [accessed 29 August 2023].

51 (19 June 1970) www.wipo.int/wipolex/en/text/288637 [accessed 29 August 2023].

52 Agreed in 1973 and revised in 2000, OJ EPO 2001, Special edition No 4, p 55.

53 Patents Act 1977, s 1(1).

54 Practical Law IP&IT, Legal protection of software (n 8 above) 33-34.

patent offices, including the UK ITPO, have been granting patent claims related to computer programs for many years.

TRADE SECRETS AND CONFIDENTIALITY

7.44 Trade secrets play a significant role in the protection of valuable information related to cryptocurrencies. Businesses involved in developing or operating cryptocurrency systems may rely on trade secrets to safeguard proprietary algorithms, codebases, or data structures. Implementing appropriate confidentiality measures and non-disclosure agreements helps protect trade secrets from unauthorised disclosure or use.

7.45 For software protection, copyright is the primary form of safeguarding given its long duration. However, most proprietary software companies also treat their source code as a trade secret, disclosing it only under secrecy agreements when necessary, such as to related software producers. The source code is vital for understanding how the software functions and is essential for maintenance, development, and error correction.

7.46 To be considered confidential under UK law, information must have the necessary quality of confidence and be disclosed under circumstances that impose an obligation of confidence.[55] The owner of confidential information can take action for breach of confidence to prevent unauthorised disclosure and seek damages for such disclosures.

7.47 The term 'know-how' typically refers to commercial confidential information of a practical or technical nature. Know-how covers all forms of information, knowledge and skill, technical or otherwise, for example a procedure, a process, an identifiable knowledgeable way of doing something, and has value. Know-how can be associated with any or all IPR but may not be protectable in itself. It might encompass material which could go on to be protected by IP, such as a copyrightable or patentable innovation. It might be something related to, but not part of, IPR, such as specialist knowledge required to operate a machine. Know-how might also be something entirely separate from IP rights, such as the competitive advantage inherent in having a more efficient business model than a competitor. The only way you to protect valuable know-how is through confidentiality.[56] Contracts are a key tool in protecting know-how, particularly non-disclosure clauses and agreements.[57] Relationships

55 *Coco v A N Clark* [1969] RPC 41, *Attorney-General v Guardian Newspapers (No 2)* [1990] 1 AC 109.

56 Government Office for Technology Transfer, 'Guide to Managing Intellectual Property and Confidentiality' (Guidance, April 2023) 16 https://assets.publishing.service.gov.uk/government/uploads/system/uploads/attachment_data/file/1162954/Guide_to_Managing_Intellectual_Property_and_Confidentiality.pdf [accessed 30 September 2023].

57 *Ibid* 21–24.

with employees, consultants and contractors should be governed by contractual provisions protecting know-how. Ensuring valuable technical information remains confidential is an effective means of protection, even when other IPRs like copyright may apply. The practicalities of identifying copying, meeting the burden of proof, and enforcement can be difficult and costly.

7.48 Confidential information itself is a chose in action and can be transferred through equitable or statutory assignment under Law of Property Act 1925, s 136. Practically, owners usually disclose the secret to the proposed transferee along with supporting documentation and materials, while simultaneously agreeing not to use or disclose the information to third parties. They must give notice to the other contracting party and agree to lend their name to any proceedings brought by the transferee. It is advisable to also include provisions that provides for the transferor not to compete with the transferee, such non-compete provision should be limited in duration and scope.

7.49 In May 2016, the EU formally adopted the Trade Secrets Directive[58] to harmonise the civil law on trade secrets and enforcement across the EU. The Directive came into force on 5 July 2016. The UK implemented its provisions through the Trade Secrets (Enforcement, etc) Regulations 2018 (TSR 2018), which took effect on 9 June 2018.

7.50 The TSR 2018 'trade secret' is information which:[59]

(a) is secret in the sense that it is not, as a body or in the precise configuration and assembly of its components, generally known among, or readily accessible to, persons within the circles that normally deal with the kind of information in question;

(b) has commercial value because it is secret; and

(c) has been subject to reasonable steps under the circumstances, by the person lawfully in control of the information, to keep it secret.

7.51 This definition is sufficiently broad to encompass the common law and equity position regarded as confidential information as well as trade secrets. Recent case law from the High Court suggests that the common law principles are unaffected.[60] The national nature of the legal protection for trade secrets in the UK means that Brexit does not impact trade secrets protection in the UK. As a signatory to the Hague Convention on Choice of Court Agreements, the UK courts will continue to recognise and give effect to exclusive jurisdiction clauses, including those conferring jurisdiction on the courts in the UK in respect of trade secrets. As there has been no agreement on the Brussels and

58 Council Directive (EU) 2016/943 of 8 June 2016 on the protection of undisclosed know-how and business information (trade secrets) against their unlawful acquisition, use and disclosure [2016] OJ L 157/1.

59 TSR 2018, reg 2.

60 *Trailfinders v TCL* [2020] EWHC 591 (IPEC); *Shenzhen Senior v Celgard* [2020] EWCA Civ 1293.

Lugano regimes on jurisdiction and enforcement of judgments in the EU and the EEA,[61] the common law governs such issues from 1 January 2021. The common law already governs such issues as between the courts in the UK and the courts in the US and Canada. The transition presents some opportunities for well-informed potential litigants.

OPEN-SOURCE SOFTWARE AND LICENSING

7.52 Cryptocurrency projects often rely on open-source software (OSS) to foster community collaboration and innovation. Developers must comply with the licensing terms associated with OSS, such as the General Public License[62] or the MIT License,[63] when distributing or modifying open-source code. Understanding and adhering to the obligations and restrictions of OSS licences is crucial to avoid potential legal issues. OSS licences commonly impose strict requirements on developers and users who copy, distribute, or modify the OSS code. For instance, nearly all OSS licences mandate users to mention the name of the author whenever they distribute the work or integrate it into a commercial product. Additionally, some OSS licences may stipulate that the resulting software must be made freely available as OSS under certain circumstances.[64]

ENFORCEMENT AND CHALLENGES

7.53 Enforcing IPR in the cryptocurrency ecosystem can be challenging due to the decentralised and borderless nature of the technology. Tracking infringers, identifying jurisdiction, and meeting the burden of proof of infringement can be complex. Ensuring proper structuring and implementing legal protections from the inception is essential to avoid ensuing difficulties.

7.54 As the cryptocurrency landscape evolves, new IP issues may arise. These may include IP-related disputes among cryptocurrency projects, the intersection of IP and DeFi, and the emergence of NFTs as IP assets. Ongoing legal developments and regulatory initiatives will shape the IP landscape in the sector.

61 European Parliament, 'The United Kingdom's possible re-joining of the 2007 Lugano Convention' (Briefing, 2021) www.europarl.europa.eu/RegData/etudes/BRIE/2021/698797/EPRS_BRI(2021)698797_EN.pdf [accessed 30 September 2023].

62 GNU General Public License (Version 3, 29 June 2007) Free Software Foundation www.gnu.org/licenses/gpl-3.0.en.html [accessed 30 September 2023].

63 'The MIT License' Open Source Initiative https://opensource.org/license/mit/ [accessed 30 September 2023].

64 Practical Law IP&IT, Legal protection of software (n 8 above), 35.

CONCLUSION

7.55 IP considerations are integral to the development, protection, and commercialisation of cryptocurrencies within the UK. Copyright, trademarks, patents, trade secrets, and open-source licensing all play important roles in safeguarding innovation and creating value in the cryptocurrency ecosystem. Businesses and individuals involved in cryptocurrencies should seek legal advice and establish proper IP strategies to protect their creations and rights effectively from inception.

Chapter 8

Cryptocurrency Fraud and Theft

8.1 The rise of cryptocurrencies has led to an increase in fraud and theft-related activities in the digital asset space. The UK has seen its share of cryptocurrency fraud and theft cases, prompting the need for robust legal frameworks to address these issues effectively.

TYPES OF CRYPTOCURRENCY FRAUD AND THEFT

8.2 There are myriad of cryptocurrency fraudulent schemes and scams currently in use globally, set out below are some of the most common ones identified by TRM Labs in use at the time of writing.[1]

(a) **Investment fraud**: investment fraud centres on the solicitation of funds for fraudulent investments or projects. In the cryptocurrency space, these often involve fake ICOs, unregistered securities or fraudulent investment platforms. Pyramid and Ponzi schemes form a major part of this ecosystem and rely on the constant recruitment of new investors or investments to generate returns for earlier investors. These schemes often collapse when it becomes impossible to recruit enough new investors or investments to maintain payouts. 'Pig butchering' scams rely on psychological manipulation and social engineering to wipe out a victim's life savings on the promise of making large returns on their investment.

(b) **Deceptive smart contracts**: deceptive smart contracts are intentionally designed to trick users into transferring funds or granting permissions to them. The most notable example of this is 'drainware': smart contracts that, upon interaction, grant the attacker permission to move funds from the victim's crypto wallet. These are also referred to as 'drainers', 'sweepers' and 'wallet drainers.' Drainware attacks operate by draining cryptocurrency and NFTs directly from a user's wallet after they unknowingly sign a transaction to purchase and mint an NFT or interact with a phishing website. Spoof tokens are crypto tokens – whether new coins or NFTs – set up by scammers who manipulate the token to make it look like they have been sent from addresses associated with celebrities, high-profile influencers, companies, or specific projects. To manufacture spoof tokens, scammers create a new token smart contract and give it a name related to what they are spoofing. They may also modify the smart contract code to enable the

1 TRM Labs, 'Illicit Crypto Ecosystem Report' (June 2023) www.trmlabs.com/report#Cybercrime-Services [accessed 8 October 2023].

scammer to send the token on behalf of other addresses, making it appear that those addresses initiated the transfer.

(c) **Exit scams**: exit scams, also known as 'rugpulls', occur when the operators of a project – one often related to investments or a new token – stop developing the project and withdraw user funds for themselves. They can either happen abruptly where project developers and funds suddenly disappear, or they can occur more slowly, where money is siphoned off a bit at a time and developers get less and less active, this is more difficult to outright label as fraud. They often target DeFi projects.

(d) **Phishing**: phishing involves the use of fraudulent emails, websites, or messages to trick users into revealing sensitive information, such as private keys or login credentials to digital wallets or exchanges in order to steal funds.

(e) **Impersonation scams**: related to phishing, impersonation scams involve criminals posing as well-known individuals or organisations to deceive victims into sending funds or revealing sensitive information. Criminals often pretend to be representatives of exchanges, wallet providers or celebrities to trick users into sending cryptocurrencies to fraudulent addresses or divulging sensitive information. Scammers can create fake websites or social media accounts that resemble legitimate crypto exchanges or wallet providers. They often impersonate customer support agents and reach out to unsuspecting users, offering assistance with technical issues or account problems. The users are persuaded to share their login credentials, private keys, or sensitive information, allowing the scammers to steal their funds. Similarly, they often use these tactics to impersonate legitimate crypto projects to convince unsuspecting users send their cryptocurrency and disappear with the funds.

(f) **Business email compromise (BEC)**: BEC is a type of scam where criminals impersonate a legitimate business or organisation to trick employees or partners into transferring funds or revealing sensitive information. BEC scams may involve the compromise of email accounts belonging to employees of legitimate businesses or organisations, leading to the theft of funds or sensitive data.

(g) **Illicit commerce scams (ICS)**: For almost every type of illicit commerce or activity in the crypto space, there is a scam version of it, sometimes found on the dark web. TRM Labs has identified the following ICS: money laundering services, carding shops, drug vendors, murder-for-hire providers, weapons dealers, child sexual abuse material sellers, hacking services, market manipulation services, scam-as-a-service providers and ransomware sellers.

(h) **Blackmail scams**: blackmail scams typically involve the scammer sending threatening emails to random recipients, claiming knowledge and/or evidence of infidelity, pornography use or other potentially embarrassing personal details that will be released publicly unless a cryptocurrency payment is made (usually Bitcoin). In many cases, the scammer does not in fact have the information or material in question.

(i) **Misappropriation of funds**: misappropriation of funds often occurs as part of many of the other frauds and scams mentioned above, though it can also occur independently. Misappropriation of funds frequently accompanies investment fraud schemes, where, instead of investing customer funds as promised, the operator of the scheme instead diverts them either for personal use or for other business purposes.

(j) **Extortion**: crypto extortion can take many forms. At its most basic, it involves individuals threatening their victims and demanding payment in cryptocurrency or malicious software known as ransomware. Other variations of extortion begin with the scammer using phishing techniques to take control of the victim's Instagram profile. The criminals then force the victims into filming videos instructing their followers to participate in fraudulent get-rich-quick Bitcoin schemes. By far the biggest driver of crypto extortion is ransomware, which has also increasingly been adopted by groups targeting countries' national security infrastructure. Ransomware is a type of malicious software that encrypts a victim's files or data, rendering them inaccessible. The attacker then demands a ransom, usually in cryptocurrency, in exchange for the decryption key. Ransomware has become a significant threat to individuals, businesses, and even governments, with high-profile attacks making headlines. In March 2023 FATF published a report on Countering Ransomware Financing.[2]

(k) **Market manipulation**: market manipulation in the cryptocurrency space can involve various schemes designed to artificially influence the price of a crypto token, these schemes can include pump and dump schemes, scalping, touting, and front-running. Prominent recent examples include Mango Markets and FTX's FTT token. Pump and dump schemes involve the coordinated buying of a crypto token to inflate its price artificially, followed by a coordinated sell-off once the price has reached a certain level resulting in a price crash leaving investors with significant losses. These schemes are often organised through online forums or social media groups and can involve the use of misleading or false information to entice new investors. Thousands of online chat rooms in the deep and dark web as well as public chat channels on Telegram are dedicated to pump and dump schemes.[3] Several celebrities have been sanctioned by the SEC for

2 FATF, 'Countering Ransomware Financing' (Paris, March 2023) www.fatf-gafi.org/content/dam/fatf-gafi/reports/Countering-Ransomware-Financing.pdf.coredownload.pdf [accessed 8 October 2023].

3 The phenomenon is widespread. See J T Hamrick, Farhang Rouhi, Arghya Mukherjee, Amir Feder, Neil Gandal, Tyler Moore and Marie Vasek, 'An examination of the cryptocurrency pump-and-dump ecosystem' (2021) 58(4) Information Processing & Management 102506, www.sciencedirect.com/science/article/abs/pii/S0306457321000169?via%3Dihub [accessed 30 August 2023].

violating US touting laws when promoting ICOs.[4] Front-running involves individuals or groups exploiting their access to information or trading systems to profit from upcoming trades. This can involve using privileged access to exchange order books or exploiting the latency of decentralised exchanges to execute trades before other users and then selling them the asset at an inflated price.

(l) **Insider trading**: crypto insider trading entails the use of non-public information to purchase cryptocurrency or other digital assets ahead of exchange listing announcements and profiting from the price surge that follows an announcement. In August 2023, a former employee of an NFT marketplace, OpenSea, became the first individual to be sentenced to prison for insider trading, wire fraud and money laundering in connection with a scheme to use confidential information about what NFTs were going to be featured on the exchange's homepage to front run.[5]

(m) **Tax evasion**: high net worth individuals may shift taxable assets into the crypto economy to avoid tax, as governments may not be able to trace crypto income or transactions if they go unreported by exchanges, businesses and other third parties. HMRC have contacted crypto exchanges and requested transaction information on their customers to assess whether they have reported tax correctly.[6]

(n) **Other scams**: scammers are creative and can make a scam version out of nearly any activity. As such, there are many other types of scams than those mentioned above. They include asset recovery scams, overpayment scams, giveaway scams, fake job listing scams, romance scams, money mule scams, different variations of the advance-fee scam, and the basic scam of simply not giving the buyer what they purchased.

4 For example, Kimberly Kardashian, Cease and Desist Order, Securities and Exchange Commission, Release No 11116 / October 3, 2022 (SEC) www.sec.gov/files/litigation/admin/2022/33-11116.pdf [accessed 30 September 2023]; SEC, 'SEC Charges Crypto Entrepreneur Justin Sun and His Companies for Fraud and Other Securities Law Violations' (22 March 2023) www.sec.gov/news/press-release/2023-59 [accessed 30 September 2023]; Jake Joseph Paul, Cease and Desist Order, Securities and Exchange Commissions, Release No 11171 / March 22, 2023 (SEC) www.sec.gov/files/litigation/admin/2023/33-11171.pdf [accessed 30 August 2023]; and Lindsay Dee Lohan, Cease and Desist Order, Securities and Exchange Commission, Release No 11173 / March 22, 2023 (SEC) www.sec.gov/files/litigation/admin/2023/33-11173.pdf [accessed 30 September 2023].

5 US Attorney's Office Southern District of New York, 'Former Employee Of NFT Marketplace Sentenced To Prison In First-Ever Digital Asset Insider Trading Scheme' (22 August 2023) www.justice.gov/usao-sdny/pr/former-employee-nft-marketplace-sentenced-prison-first-ever-digital-asset-insider [accessed 30 August 2023].

6 Ian Allison, 'British Authorities Seek Data from Crypto Exchanges in Search of Tax Evaders' (6 August 2019, updated 23 May 2023) *CoinDesk* www.coindesk.com/business/2019/08/06/british-authorities-seek-data-from-crypto-exchanges-in-search-of-tax-evaders/ [accessed 8 October 2023].

LEGAL FRAMEWORK AND ENFORCEMENT

Introduction

8.3 Cryptocurrency fraud and theft cases can be prosecuted under existing criminal laws in the UK, such as the Fraud Act 2006, Computer Misuse Act 1990, or Theft Act 1968. These laws encompass various offences related to fraudulent activities, hacking, and theft.

Fraud and theft offences

8.4 In relation to s 4 of the Theft Act 1968 cryptoassets fall under the charge of theft of 'other intangible property'. 'Other intangible property' was considered in *AG of Hong Kong v Nai-Keung*[7], which concerned the theft of a transferable export quota. The quota itself did not confer the right to export goods but entitled the holder to apply for a formal licence to do so. Nevertheless, it was considered intangible property.

8.5 The offences of blackmail and extortion[8] are statutory offences under s 21(1) of the Theft Act 1968. The offence has the following four elements:

(a) a demand;

(b) made with menaces;

(c) the menaces are unwarranted; and

(d) the menaces are made with a view to gain for himself or another or with intent to cause loss to another.

8.6 In this regard 'gain' and 'loss' are to be construed as extending only to gain or loss in money or other property, but as extending to any such gain or loss whether temporary or permanent: and 'gain' includes a gain by keeping what one has, as well as a gain by getting what one has not; and 'loss' includes a loss by not getting what one might get, as well as a loss by parting with what one has.[9]

8.7 Under s 5(2) of the Fraud Act 2006, to demonstrate the defendant made a gain for himself or another person or to inflict a loss, cryptoassets fall under 'gain or loss in money or other property'. Property for these purposes 'means any property, whether real or personal (including things in action and other intangible property)'. For these purposes, cryptoassets would be intangible property.

7 [1987] 1 WLR 1339.

8 The crime of blackmail seems to have been coextensive with robbery and attempted robbery, but over the years the definition has been extended to more subtle methods of extortion encapsulated in s 21 of the Theft Act 1968. See *Smith, Hogan & Ormerod's Criminal Law* (16th edn, Oxford University Press, 2022), [24.1].

9 Theft Act 1968, s 32(2)(a).

Computer misuse and terrorism

8.8 Pursuant to the Computer Misuse Act 1990, offences in relation to hacking, malware and ransomware are encapsulated in ss 1–3, 3ZA and 3A.

8.9 The sections outline deal with the following offences respectively:

(a) section 1 – unauthorised access to computer material;

(b) section 2 – unauthorised access with intent to commit or facilitate further offences;

(c) section 3 – unauthorised acts with intent to impair or recklessness as to impairment of a computer;

(d) section 3ZA – impairing a computer such as to cause serious damage; and

(e) section 3A – making, supplying or obtaining articles for use in offences under ss 1, 3 or 3ZA.

8.10 In relation to terrorism, s 1(2)(e) defines an act of terrorism to include actions 'designed seriously to interfere with or seriously disrupt an electronic system'. To be an offence under the Terrorism Act 2000 as opposed to s 3 of the Computer Misuse Act 1990, other constituent elements for an 'act of terrorism' would have to be present:[10]

(a) the 'use or threat is designed to influence the government or an international governmental organisation or to intimidate the public or a section of the public'; and

(b) the use or threat is 'for the purpose of advancing a political, religious, racial or ideological cause'.

Proceeds of Crime Act 2002

8.11 The recovery and seizure of assets are regulated by the Proceeds of Crime Act 2002 (POCA 2002), legislation crafted long before the inception of cryptocurrencies like Bitcoin. It enables the confiscation of assets acquired through criminal activities, including cryptocurrency proceeds obtained through fraud or theft.

8.12 The core offences under POCA 2002 are:

(a) concealing criminal property;[11]

(b) arrangements for the acquisition or use of criminal property;[12] and

10 Terrorism Act 2000 s 1(1)(b) and (c) respectively, as amended by the Terrorism Act 2006 s 34 and Counter-Terrorism Act 2008 s 75(1)(2)(a).
11 POCA 2002, s 327.
12 POCA 2002, s 328.

(c) acquiring, using, or possessing criminal property.[13]

Cryptoassets fall under 'other intangible or incorporeal property'.[14]

8.13 HMRC's seizure of NFTs serves as an example of a government agency confiscating assets believed to have been acquired through criminal proceeds, in this case, stored in the form of NFTs, a novel asset class.[15]

FCA Regulations

8.14 The Financial Conduct Authority (FCA), as the UK's financial regulatory body, plays a role in combating cryptocurrency fraud by enforcing regulations on cryptocurrency-related activities, including anti-money laundering (AML) and counter-terrorist financing (CTF) requirements for cryptocurrency businesses.

8.15 In circumstances where organisations or individuals are dealing with crypto assets and fall within ss 21 (Restrictions on Financial Promotions) and 22 (Regulated Activities) of FSMA 2000 as amended by s 69 of FSMA 2023 they must register and be authorised by the FCA.[16]

8.16 Although cryptoassets can, in theory, be transferred anonymously in a peer-to-peer manner, in practice, most individuals rely on centralised intermediaries for certain key functions:

(a) initially converting their fiat cash into cryptoassets;

(b) exchanging one type of cryptoasset for another; and

(c) storing their cryptoassets with centralised custodians.

8.17 These intermediaries and custodians become focal points for law enforcement to concentrate their efforts and regulatory entities to impose regulations. Regulation is crucial for investigations of transactions through these intermediaries and locating cryptoassets stored by custodians. Similar to traditional financial intermediaries, these entities are responsible for AML/CTF reporting and record-keeping requirements, and they may be required to provide information relevant to illicit funds investigations.

8.18 The FCA recognises the importance of cryptoasset businesses adhering to the same principles of financial crime regulation as traditional markets, such as performing KYC checks, record keeping, transaction monitoring techniques

13 POCA 2002, s 329.
14 POCA 2002, s 326(9).
15 Tax Journal, 'HMRC seizure of NFTs' (Issue 1564, 16 February 2022) www.taxjournal.com/articles/hmrc-seizure-of-nfts [accessed 8 October 2023].
16 For further information see **3.2–3.53**.

to prevent handling the proceeds of crime, and proactively monitor users for suspicious activity.[17]

REPORTING AND SEEKING LEGAL REMEDIES

Reporting to authorities

8.19 Victims of cryptocurrency fraud or theft should report the incidents to their local police and relevant authorities, providing as much information and evidence as possible to aid in the investigation.[18] Action Fraud is the UK's national reporting centre for fraud and cybercrime for reporting fraud, scams and cybercrime in England, Wales and Northern Ireland.[19] CyberScotland is Scotland's relevant reporting centre.[20]

Consumer protection and compensation schemes

8.20 In the UK, cryptoassets are generally not eligible for compensation through the Financial Services Compensation Scheme (FSCS). [21] Cryptoassets fall outside the remit of the Financial Ombudsman Service (FOS)[22] but it has ordered regulated financial institutions to compensate customers for crypto-related fraud and scams where they have not intervened in relation to suspicious transactions.[23]

Civil litigation

8.21 Victims may pursue civil remedies against fraudsters by initiating legal action to recover stolen funds or seek compensation for damages caused.

17 FCA, speech by Therese Chambers, Director of Retail and Regulatory Investigations, 'Unstable coins: cryptoassets, financial regulation and preventing financial crime in the emerging market for digital assets' (6 March 2020) www.fca.org.uk/news/speeches/unstable-coins [accessed 30 September 2023].

18 Metropolitan Police, 'Cyber-crime' www.met.police.uk/advice/advice-and-information/fa/fraud/online-fraud/cyber-crime-fraud/ [accessed 30 September 2023].

19 www.actionfraud.police.uk/ [accessed 30 September 2023].

20 www.cyberscotland.com/report-an-incident/ [accessed 30 September 2023].

21 FSCS, 'Five things to consider about cryptoassets' (11 May 2023) www.fscs.org.uk/news/protection/cryptocurrencies-risk-cover/ [accessed 30 September 2023]; See also FSCS, 'FSCS Investment protection checker' www.fscs.org.uk/check/investment-types/ [accessed 30 September 2023].

22 FCA, FCA Handbook DISP 2.1 www.handbook.fca.org.uk/handbook/DISP/2/?view=chapter [accessed 29 August 2023].

23 FOS, 'Consumer contacts us to complain after a cryptocurrency investment scam' www.financial-ombudsman.org.uk/decisions-case-studies/case-studies/consumer-contacts-us-complain-cryptocurrency-investment-scam [accessed 29 August 2023].

ECONOMIC CRIME AND CORPORATE TRANSPARENCY ACT 2023

8.22 Broadly speaking there are two categories of asset recovery powers under POCA 2002: criminal regime and civil regime. POCA 2002 is structured as follows:

(a) criminal powers, or 'in personam' powers, which are used to impose a debt against any person convicted of a crime, who is found to have benefited from their crime(s) — these powers are contained in the criminal regime in Pts 2, 3 and 4 of POCA 2002 (for England and Wales, Scotland and Northern Ireland respectively); and

(b) civil powers, or 'in rem' powers, which order the direct possession of identifiable assets deemed to have been obtained through unlawful conduct or which are intended for use in unlawful conduct. These are contained in Pt 5 of POCA 2002.

8.23 The reforms in the Economic Crime and Corporate Transparency Act 2023 (ECCTA 2023) amend both the criminal and civil regimes to facilitate the recovery of cryptoassets. ECCTA 2023 includes measures to amend the supplementary investigatory powers in Pt 8 of POCA 2002, which may be used to gather information in support of a criminal or civil asset recovery investigation. Changes to the criminal powers in POCA 2002 will also apply to those parts which cover Scotland and Northern Ireland.

8.24 Given the rapidly evolving nature of crypto technology, ECCTA 2023 includes provisions to adapt to future developments and changes in terminology. It introduces delegated powers to amend key terms like 'cryptoasset', 'crypto wallet', 'cryptoasset service provider', 'cryptoasset exchange provider' and 'custodian wallet provider' ensuring that unforeseen technological advancements can be accommodated.[24]

8.25 The amendments in ECCTA 2023 are designed to grant law enforcement additional powers, enabling them to more efficiently seize and recover

24 ECCTA 2023, Sch 8, para 12 inserts POCA 2002, s 67ZB(5) (meaning of 'UK-connected cryptoasset service provider') in relation to England and Wales; ECCTA 2023, Sch 8, para18 inserts POCA 2002, s 84A(5) (Cryptoassets etc) in relation to England and Wales; ECCTA 2023, Sch 8, para 29 inserts POCA 2002, s 131ZC(5) (Meaning of 'UK-connected cryptoasset service provider') in relation to Scotland; ECCTA 2023, Sch 8, para 36 inserts POCA 2002, s 150(A)(5) (Cryptoassets etc) in relation to Scotland; ECCTA 2023, Sch 8, para 48 inserts POCA 2002, s 215ZB(5) (Meaning of 'UK-connected cryptoasset service provider') in relation to Northern Ireland; ECCTA 2023, Sch 8, para 54 inserts POCA 2002, s 232A(5) (Cryptoassets etc) in relation to Northern Ireland; ECCTA 2023, Sch 9, para 1 inserts POCA 2002, ss 303Z20(2) (Recovery of cryptoassets: searches, seizure and detention, Definitions) and 303Z35(4) (Recovery of crypto assets: Freezing Orders, Definitions); ECCTA 2023, Sch 10, para 2 inserts ACSA 2001, ss 10Z7A(2) (Seizure and Detention Terrorist Cryptoassets, Interpretation) and 10Z7B(3) (Terrorist cryptoassets: crypto wallet freezing orders, Interpretation); ECCTA 2023, Sch 10, para 7 inserts the Terrorism Act 2000, s 6(1AF).

cryptoassets linked to economic crime or terrorism. By modifying both criminal confiscation powers and civil recovery powers under POCA 2002 and the Anti-terrorism, Crime and Security Act 2001 (ACSA 2001) and the Terrorism Act 2000, ECCTA 2023 aims to enhance enforcement agencies' ability to combat criminal use of cryptoassets.

8.26 At a high level, the measures proposed in the ECCTA 2023 concentrate on:

(a) addressing price volatility;

(b) overcoming practical challenges in the seizure and recovery of cryptoassets; and

(c) addressing practical considerations related to storing and destroying seized cryptoassets.

Criminal regime

8.27 There are four key powers:

(a) In certain circumstances, there is no requirement for a person to have been arrested before seizure powers can be used earlier in the process, so that those assets can be more easily confiscated at a later date.[25] These powers are now expanded to cryptoassets.[26]

(b) Specific provision for officers to recover cryptoassets (intangible items) in a broadly similar way provided for tangible property. This involves making it clear that officers have authority to 'recreate' cryptoasset wallets and transfer assets into a law enforcement-controlled wallet under search, seizure, and detention powers.[27]

(c) Provide the magistrates' court (as the authority responsible for enforcement of confiscation orders) with the powers to authorise the sale of any cryptoassets, in the same way magistrates can already with cash, funds in bank accounts, and other types of personal seized property.[28]

25 POCA 2002, s 47B(1).

26 ECCTA 2023, Sch 8 para 3 inserts sub-s 5A into POCA 2002, s 47C (power to seize property) in England and Wales; ECCTA 2023, Sch 8 para 21 inserts sub-s 5A into POCA 2002, s 127C (power to seize property) in Scotland; ECCTA 2023, Sch 8 para 39 inserts sub-s 5A into POCA 2002, s 195C (power to seize property) in Northern Ireland; ECCTA 2023, Sch 10 para 2 inserts ACSA 2001, s 10Z7AA(1) (Seizure of cryptoasset-related items).

27 ECCTA 2023, Sch 8 para 3 inserts sub-s 5C into POCA 2002, s47C (power to seize property) in England and Wales; ECCTA 2023, Sch 8 para 21 inserts sub-s 5C into POCA 2002, s127C (power to seize property) in Scotland; ECCTA 2023, Sch 8 para 39 inserts sub-s 5C into POCA 2002, s195C (power to seize property) in Northern Ireland; ECCTA 2023, Sch 10 para 2 inserts ACSA 2001, s 10Z7AD(2) (Seizure of cryptoassets).

28 ECCTA 2023, Sch 8 para 12 inserting POCA 2002, s 67ZA(3) (Cryptoassets) in England and Wales; ECCT, Sch 8 para 48 inserting POCA 2002, s 131ZB(3) (Cryptoassets) in Scotland; ECCT, Sch 8 para 48 inserting POCA 2002, s 215ZA(3) (Cryptoassets) for confiscation in Northern Ireland.

(d) Provide for the destruction of cryptoassets in exceptional circumstances:

  (i) where it is not reasonably practicable to realise the cryptoassets; or

  (ii) there are reasonable grounds to believe that the realisation of the cryptoassets would be contrary to the public interest, having regard to how likely it is that the entry of the cryptoassets into general circulation would facilitate criminal conduct.[29]

8.28 ECCTA 2023 introduces early seizure powers in investigations, even before an arrest occurs, which is particularly beneficial when dealing with easily transferable cryptoassets. This allows law enforcement to seize assets earlier, preventing their dissipation. However, challenges arise when encountering cryptoassets stored in offline wallets, such as USB sticks or circuit boards, during a search. The physical item containing the cryptoassets can be seized, but transferring the assets might be more complicated. To address this, ECCTA 2023 allows law enforcement to transfer the assets into a law enforcement controlled wallet, ensuring secure storage and transfer.

8.29 Accessing an online wallet, secured by a private key or complex authentication, poses another challenge. Unlike traditional bank accounts with centralised intermediaries, there is no entity to provide account access under compulsion. Under ECCTA 2023, law enforcement could potentially use existing powers, like those of the Serious Fraud Office (SFO), to compel an individual to provide the key and unlock the wallet, facilitating the seizure of the contents.[30]

8.30 The prices of cryptoassets have shown significant volatility in the market. With investigations potentially lasting for years, this could lead to a significant decrease or increase in the value of the seized assets. High-profile seizures of specific types of cryptoassets, especially in cases involving investor fraud allegations, may cause the price of those cryptoassets to collapse due to a 'run' on the market. To address this, ECCTA 2023 allows for early seizures of cryptoassets during investigations before arrest. While the power to sell comes later, after involvement with the magistrates' court, law enforcement could potentially have insider knowledge for a period, requiring careful management of the publicity aspect in such cases. As cryptoassets are not currently traded on

29 ECCTA 2023, Sch 8, para 10(4) inserts sub-s 9A into POCA 2002, s 51 (powers of enforcement receiver) in England and Wales; ECCTA 2023, Sch 8 para 13 inserts POCA 2002, s 67AA(2) (destruction of seized cryptoassets) in England and Wales; ECCTA 2023, Sch 8 para 17 inserts sub-s 2A into POCA 2002, s 69 (powers of court and receiver etc) in England and Wales; ECCT, Sch 8 para 27 inserts sub-s 13A into POCA 2002, s 128 (enforcement administrators) in Scotland; ECCT, Sch 8 para 30 inserts POCA 2002, s 131AA (destruction of seized cryptoassets) in Scotland; ECCT, Sch 8 para 46 inserts sub-s 9A into POCA 2002, s 199 (powers of enforcement receiver) in Northern Ireland; ECCT, Sch 8 para 49 inserts POCA 2002, s 215AA(2) (destruction of seized cryptoassets) in Northern Ireland; ECCT, Sch 8 para 53 inserts sub-s (2A) into POCA 2002, s 217 (powers of court and receiver etc) in Northern Ireland.

30 ECCTA 2023, Pt 5, s 211 amending s 2A of Criminal Justice Act 1987 and omitting para 2 Sch 1 of the Bribery Act 2010.

regulated markets insider trading rules do not apply; nevertheless, individuals on the inside who attempt to gain from such scenarios could face potential liability under the Fraud Act 2006, s 3.[31]

8.31 Cryptoassets feature in a small but increasing number of terrorist investigations. This includes fundraising through the use of social media platforms using cryptocurrency as a method of payment.[32] ECCTA 2023 amends key pieces of counter-terrorism legislation. Specifically, they update the ACSA 2001 and the Terrorism Act 2000 to ensure that civil forfeiture and seizure powers are available to cryptoassets.[33]

Civil regime

8.32 ECCTA 2023 introduced a new subset of 'forfeiture powers' so that cryptoassets (and related items, such as physical wallets) can be recovered swiftly in the magistrates' court by more agencies.[34] These powers are modelled on account freezing and forfeiture powers (introduced under the Criminal Finances Act 2017).

8.33 There are five key provisions, which:

(a) enable law enforcement agencies to take control of and recover cryptoassets discovered when executing a search warrant. These powers will be used in circumstances where cryptoassets are 'unhosted' and not in the custody of a third-party, such as a cryptoasset exchange. Assets may be recovered where the magistrates court is satisfied – on the balance of probabilities – that they are recoverable property or are intended for unlawful conduct,[35] or, in the case of a terrorist investigation, they are property that has been earmarked as terrorist property;[36]

(b) enable law enforcement to recover cryptoassets direct from cryptoasset exchange providers and custodian wallet providers. Assets may be recovered where the magistrates court is satisfied they are recoverable property or are intended for use in unlawful conduct;[37]

31 Department for Business & Trade and Others, 'Economic Crime and Corporate Transparency Bill 2022, Factsheet: cryptoassets – legislation'.

32 *Ibid.*

33 ECCTA 2023, Sch 10.

34 ECCTA 2023, Sch 9, para 1 inserts POCA 2002, ss 303Z41 (Forfeiture of cryptoassets following detention or freezing order, Forfeiture order), 303Z42 (Forfeiture order: supplementary) and 303Z60 (Forfeiture order).

35 *Ibid.*

36 ECCTA 2023, Sch 10, para 2 inserts ASCA 2001, s 10Z7DG.

37 ECCTA 2023, Sch 9, para 1 inserting POCA 2002, s 303Z36 (Application for crypto wallet freezing order); ECCTA 2023, Sch9, para 1 inserting POCA 2002, s 303Z43 (Forfeiture order: Supplemental).

(c) enable detained cryptoassets, or those that have been frozen in a wallet, to be converted to cash pending the outcome of a final forfeiture hearing. This is to safeguard against market volatility;[38]

(d) provide for the destruction of cryptoassets (for example privacy coins, more often than not to launder funds) in exceptional circumstances – where the financial gain for the sale of those assets would be outweighed by the loss to the public of allowing the circulation of funds to continue to be used in potentially criminal ways;[39] and

(e) replicate provision for detained or frozen cryptoassets and related items to be released to victims at any stage of proceedings, ameliorating the negative impacts of fraud.[40]

8.34 As far as possible, to futureproof both the criminal and civil regimes, ECCTA 2023 introduces a series of delegated powers to ensure that any defined terms such as 'cryptoasset', 'crypto wallet', 'crypto exchange provider', 'custodian wallet provider' and 'cryptoasset service provider' can be amended by affirmative order as required.[41]

8.35 The proposed amendments to the civil regime aim to expedite the recovery of cryptoassets (and related items like physical wallets) through appropriate court orders. For illicit cryptoassets traceable on centralised exchanges, the ECCA enables direct recovery from both cryptoasset exchange providers and custodian wallet providers, similar to current account freezing order powers. The recovery conditions require demonstrating on a balance of probabilities that the cryptoassets are recoverable property or intended for unlawful conduct.[42]

8.36 In the scenario of offline wallets discovered during a search (as mentioned in the criminal regime), the enhanced civil powers allow law enforcement to take control and recover the cryptoassets found in an un-hosted wallet (not in a centralised exchange).[43] This recovery can occur when executing a search, and

38 ECCTA 2023 Sch 9, para 1 inserts POCA 2002, s 303Z54 (Detained cryptoassets: conversion); ECCTA 2023 Sch 9, para 1 inserts POCA 2002, s 303Z55 (Frozen crypto wallet: conversion).

39 ECCTA 2023, Sch 9 para 1 inserting POCA 2002, s 303Z48 (Realisation or destruction of forfeited cryptoassets etc).

40 ECCTA 2023, Sch 9, para 1 inserting POCA 2002, ss 303Z50 (Victims and other owners: detained cryptoassets), 303Z51 (Victims and other owners: crypto wallet freezing orders), 303Z63 (Victims and other owners) and 303Z17A (Victims and other owners); ECCTA 2023, Sch 9 para 6(5) inserts POCA 2002, s 303Z17A (Victims and other owners).

41 ECCTA 2023, Sch 9, para 1 inserts POCA 2002, ss 303Z20(2) (Recovery of cryptoassets: searches, seizure and detention, Definitions) and 303Z35(4) (Recovery of cryptoassets: Freezing order, Definitions).

42 ECCTA 2023, Sch 9 para 1 inserting POCA 2002, ss 303Z36 (Application for crypto wallet freezing order), 303Z37 (Making of a crypto wallet freezing order), 303Z41 (Forfeiture order), 303Z42 (Forfeiture order: supplementary).

43 ECCTA 2023, Sch 9 para 1 inserting POCA 2002, ss 303Z21 (Searches), 303Z22 (Searches: supplemental provision) and 303Z26 (Seizure of cryptoasset-related items).

the assets may be further detained once the magistrates' court confirms they are recoverable property.[44]

FREEZING CRYPTOASSETS

8.37 An injunction is a court order by which a party to an action is required to do, or refrain from doing, a particular thing and may be granted as an interim (interlocutory), or a final remedy, and may be either prohibitory or mandatory.

8.38 A freezing order or injunction is a type of interim prohibitory injunction intended to prevent the dissipation of assets outside of the ordinary course of business rendering any future judgment unenforceable. A freezing order operates directly on the person against whom the injunction is made, and does not produce proprietary rights in respect of the assets themselves.

8.39 A proprietary injunction (also a type of interim prohibitory injunction) prevents a defendant from dealing with, or disposing of, assets in respect of which a proprietary claim has been made. A freezing injunction restricts a defendant from dealing with their own assets, whereas a proprietary injunction (at least in part) restrains a defendant from dealing with assets to which the claimant asserts title.[45]

8.40 When dealing with freezing orders over cryptoassets as a form of property subject to interim remedies, litigators should consider the unique challenges it presents, such as its interaction with the standard form freezing order and the obligations of freezing order applicants. To effectively apply for freezing orders, practitioners should seek specific details from respondents regarding their cryptoassets. These details may include:

(a) public addresses of cryptoassets wallets held by the respondent;

(b) information on whether the wallets are held through formal exchanges;

(c) the technical form of the wallet, whether custodial or non-custodial, impacting the user's ability to operate it without exchange oversight;

(d) access to the wallet's private key by other parties; and

(e) existence of any contractual or legal rights over the cryptoassets, along with the terms of those rights.

8.41 Given cryptoassets' volatility, practitioners must carefully advise clients on the potential exposure and scope of compensation required under the freezing order. The usual undertaking in damages, compensating respondents for losses caused by an improperly granted freezing order, may pose challenges due to cryptoassets' price fluctuations. In the case of *Toma v Murray*,[46] the High Court

44 ECCTA 2023, Sch 9 para 1 inserting POCA 2002, ss 303Z29 (Seizure of cryptoassets) and 303Z32 (Further detention of seized cryptoassets).

45 Law Commission, 'Digital Assets: Final report' (Law Com No 412, 2023), [9.84]–[9.85].

46 [2020] EWHC 2295.

found that Bitcoin's extreme volatility created a significant barrier to granting a freezing injunction over allegedly fraudulently obtained Bitcoins.

8.42 *Toma* serves to demonstrate the difficulty of incorporating Bitcoin into the traditional freezing order regime. The inability of the applicants in that case to compensate for material damages suffered by the respondent highlights the need for creative approaches to mitigate risks.

INVESTIGATIONS

8.43 When dealing with asset freezes and tracing undisclosed assets, litigators and asset-tracing professionals rely on established methods for traditional assets. However, handling cryptoassets requires new approaches due to their decentralised nature and the lack of traditional institutional infrastructure typically used for asset tracing. In theory, it is possible to trace most cryptoassets from their current location back to their original source and all the addresses they passed through; however, specialised assistance would be needed to achieve this level of tracing.

8.44 Cryptoasset users aware of the traceability may employ advanced techniques like 'mixers' to obscure transaction tracing by processing multiple transactions simultaneously. To counter this, asset tracers can seek assistance from specialist crypto-recovery professionals who use advanced analytics to follow transactions, identify transaction patterns, and find connected wallets that may belong to the same owner. This analysis has the potential to reveal undisclosed addresses and uncover complex networks of transactions.

8.45 Part 5 of ECCTA 2023 contains a range of provisions relating to investigating different aspects of economic crime. These include:

(a) **Defence against money laundering disclosures**: it would amend POCA 2002 to introduce exemptions from the principal money laundering offences where a business in the regulated sector ends a business relationship with a client or customer and for that purpose hands over property worth less than £1,000, and where a business in the regulated sector is dealing with property for a client or customer and keeps hold of property worth at least as much as the part of that property to which the knowledge or suspicion relates. This is intended to decrease disruption and hardship to affected customers and businesses.[47]

47 ECCTA 2023, Pt 5, s 182 (Money laundering: exiting and paying away exemptions) inserts sub-ss 2D and 2E into POCA 2002, s 327 (concealing etc), inserts sub-ss 6 and 7 into POCA 2002, s 328 (arrangements), inserts sub-ss 2D and 2E into POCA 2002, s 329 (acquisition, use and possession), inserts sub-s 6A into POCA 2002, s 339A (threshold amounts), sub-s 17 into POCA 2002, s 340 (Interpretation of Part 7), and inserts sub-ss 4(azaa) and 6ZBA into POCA 2002, s 459 (orders and regulations).

(b) **Information orders (IOs)**: ECCTA 2023 allows NCA officers to proactively gather intelligence without reliance on a suspicious activity report, increasing the UK's ability to support foreign partner financial intelligence unit requests.[48]

(c) **Disclosures to prevent, detect, or investigate economic crime**: these sections provide that businesses that disclose information about customers to prevent, detect, and investigate economic crime would not face civil liability for breach of confidence.[49]

(d) **Regulatory and investigatory powers**: ECCTA 2023 amends the powers of regulatory bodies in the legal services profession to strengthen their position on enforcing economic crime rules. This includes removing the Solicitor Regulation Authority's fine cap (currently set at £25,000) where a solicitor or law firm is in breach of economic crime rules.[50] It also extends the SFO's pre-investigation powers so that they are no longer restricted to cases involving international bribery and corruption and may be used in all potential SFO cases at the pre-investigative stage.[51]

(e) **Enhanced due diligence**: the high-risk third countries list sets out those countries identified as having 'strategic deficiencies' in their anti-money laundering, counter-terrorism financing, and proliferation financing regimes, 'thus posing a high risk to the UK and places from which all customers and transactions must undergo enhanced checks by the UK's regulated businesses'.[52] ECCTA 2023 provides for the imposition of requirements relating to enhanced customer due diligence measures by reference to prescribed high-risk countries; in particular this may include the list of countries published by the FATF.[53]

48 ECCTA 2023, Pt 5, s 185 amends POCA 2002, s 339ZH (further information orders) and inserts POCA 2002, s 339ZL (Code of practice about certain information orders); ECCTA 2023, Pt 5, s 186 amends Terrorism Act 2000, s 22B (further information orders) and inserts Terrorism Act 2000, s 22F (Code of practice about certain information orders).

49 ECCTA 2023, Pt 5, ss 188–193.

50 ECCTA 2023, Pt 5, s 207 inserts sub-ss 2A-2C into Solicitors Act 1974, s 44D (disciplinary powers of Law Society), inserts sub-ss 2A-2C into Administration of Justice Act 1985, Sch 2, para. 14B (disciplinary powers of Law Society); ECCTA 2023, Pt 5, s 208 amending Solicitors (Scotland) Act 1980, s 53 (powers of tribunal).

51 ECCTA 2023, Pt 5 s 211 amending Criminal Justice Act 1987, s 2A (Director's pre-investigation powers in relation to bribery and corruption: foreign officers etc) and omitting Bribery Act 2010, Sch 1 para. 2.

52 Explanatory Notes, Economic Crime and Corporate Transparency Bill at [41]. See Sch 3ZA of the Money Laundering, Terrorist Financing and Transfer of Funds (Information on the Payer) Regulations 2017.

53 ECCTA 2023, Pt 5, s 187 amends Sanctions and Anti-Money Laundering Act 2018, Sch 2 (money laundering and terrorist financing etc).

INFORMATION GATHERING, PRESERVATION AND ENFORCEMENT

8.46 The decentralised nature of DLT means that traditional financial institutions are not necessary for its functioning. However, institutions similar to traditional financial entities have emerged, these exchanges provide access to wallets, transaction services, and user-friendly interfaces, often accessible through mobile apps resembling retail investment or banking apps. Another type of institution is 'mining pools,' where sophisticated Bitcoin miners combine their computing power and share mining proceeds. Depending on local regulations, these institutions may hold substantial user information and even exercise some control over users' Bitcoin.

8.47 In practice, legal practitioners can leverage these institutions for information gathering and implementing asset freezes or other remedies. This may involve:

(a) seeking client due diligence documents from cryptocurrency exchanges or mining pools, either through voluntary cooperation or court orders under the court's equitable jurisdiction; or

(b) notifying exchanges about the existence of a freezing order. The status of a respondent's Bitcoin wallet is crucial in this regard. Many retail exchanges operate custodial wallets, wherein they retain significant control over the user's Bitcoin, akin to a bank account. However this may be more challenging for non-custodial wallets, where users maintain higher independence.

Creative approaches may be necessary to seek relief in foreign jurisdictions given many exchanges and mining pools operate overseas.

8.48 A successful claimant may take steps to enforce that court order or judgment using the many available methods of enforcement which may include:[54]

(a) the appointment of a receiver;

(b) third party debt orders;

(c) charging orders; and/or

(d) an attachment of earnings.

CONCLUSION

8.49 This chapter highlights the pervasive challenges of cryptocurrency fraud and theft, emphasising the need for a robust legal framework. It covers a range of fraudulent activities, showcasing criminals' adaptability in exploiting the decentralised nature of digital assets. Regarding legal measures, the UK employs existing criminal laws and POCA 2002 to address cryptocurrency offences,

54 Law Commission, 'Digital Assets' (n 45 above), [9.88].

demonstrating adaptability to the evolving nature of digital assets. The FCA plays a key role in regulating crypto-related activities, emphasising AML and CTF requirements.

8.50 The section on reporting and seeking legal remedies emphasises diverse options for victims, including reporting to local authorities and pursuing civil litigation. In a civil litigation context, freezing cryptoassets presents challenges, especially given their volatility, as seen in cases like *Toma v Murray*.

8.51 ECCTA 2023 stands out for introducing comprehensive reforms, addressing challenges in asset recovery under both criminal and civil regimes. Under ECCTA 2023, law enforcement has been granted enhanced investigatory powers, early seizure powers, as well as addressing complexities associated with offline wallets. The Act introduces forfeiture powers for swift recovery, covers assets held by crypto exchanges, allows conversion of detained cryptoassets to cash, and in exceptional circumstances their destruction.

8.52 The chapter underscores the need for innovative approaches in investigating and recovering cryptoassets. The decentralisation of DLT institutions provides opportunities for information gathering and enforcement. The collaborative effort of legal, regulatory, and law enforcement entities is crucial in adapting to the dynamic crypto landscape and ensuring a secure environment.

Chapter 9

International Legal Challenges

INTRODUCTION

9.1 Cryptocurrencies operate in a global and decentralised environment, which presents unique legal challenges for countries, including the UK. This chapter explores the international legal challenges that the UK faces concerning cryptocurrencies and the implications for regulatory frameworks and cross-border transactions.

JURISDICTIONAL ISSUES

9.2 Cryptocurrencies transcend national borders, making it difficult to establish jurisdiction and enforce regulations. Determining which jurisdiction has authority over a particular cryptocurrency-related activity, such as an exchange or an ICO, can be complex.

9.3 After Brexit, the UK and the EU no longer have a clear and comprehensive framework for recognising and enforcing civil court judgments between them. However, there are indications that this uncertainty might be resolved.

9.4 The EU regulations Rome I[1] and Rome II[2] were retained under the European Union (Withdrawal) Act 2018, and have been amended to function as domestic legislation by the Law Applicable to Contractual and Non-Contractual Obligations (Amendment etc) (EU Exit) Regulations 2019. The Rome Convention (which determines the law applicable to contracts entered into between 1 April 1991 and 16 December 2009) is also preserved in domestic law by the Contracts (Applicable Law) Act 1990, as amended by the Jurisdiction, Judgments and Applicable Law (Amendment) (EU Exit) Regulations 2020.

9.5 Rome I applies to contractual obligations in civil and commercial matters, where the parties have a choice of law or where no choice is made and certain criteria are met. Under Article 3(1) a 'contract shall be governed by the law chosen by the parties' and that choice 'shall be made expressly or clearly demonstrated by the terms of the contract or the circumstances of the case'.

1 Council Regulation (EC) No 593/2008 of 17 June 2008 on the law applicable to contractual obligations (Rome I) [2008] OJ L177.

2 Council Regulation (EC) No 864/2007 of 11 July 2007on the law applicable to non-contractual obligations (Rome II) [2007] OJ L199/40.

9.6 Article 4 of the Rome I Regulation sets out the criteria for the applicable law in the absence of choice. For the purposes of cryptoassets, Article 4(4) is likely to be the most relied upon provision: 'the contract shall be governed by the law of the country with which it is most closely connected.' The Law Commission has indicated that in its view the Rome I Regulation, and the choice of law rules contained therein, apply to the binding contractual obligations that arise from or are performed by smart contracts.[3]

9.7 Rome II deals with deals with the choice of law in cross-border tort (civil wrongs) and non-contractual disputes. The general rule is that the law applicable to a non-contractual obligation arising out of a tort/delict situation is the law of the country where the damage occurs, regardless of the country in which the event giving rise to the damage occurred.[4] Similar rules apply to unjust enrichment.[5] Non-contractual obligations arising from an infringement of an IP right shall be the law of the country where protection is claimed.[6]

9.8 The Hague Convention of 2005 on Choice of Court Agreements[7] deals with choice of court agreements in international commercial contracts. A choice of court agreement is a provision in a contract where the parties agree to resolve any disputes in a specific court or jurisdiction. The primary purpose of the Convention is to provide predictability and enforceability to choice of court agreements across different jurisdictions. The Hague Convention facilitates the recognition and enforcement of judgments rendered by the chosen court in the contracting jurisdiction agreed upon by the parties. The Hague Convention covers exclusive choice of court agreements in civil or commercial matters. It does not cover consumer or employment contracts.

9.9 On 28 September 2020, the UK deposited an instrument of accession to the Hague Convention in its own right, as a result of which it entered into force for the UK on 31 December 2020 at 11pm, the moment at which the UK ceased to be bound pursuant to EU membership. The Hague Convention has the force of law in the UK by virtue of a new s 3D in the Civil Jurisdiction and Judgments Act 1982 introduced by the Private International Law (Implementation of Agreements) Act 2020 (PIL Act 2020).

9.10 The 2019 Hague Convention on the Recognition and Enforcement of Foreign Judgments in Civil and Commercial Matters (2019 Hague Judgments

3 Law Commission, 'Smart legal contracts Advice to Government' (Law Com No 401, 2022), [7.142].
4 Rome II Regulation, Art 4.
5 *Ibid* Art 10.
6 *Ibid* Art 8.
7 https://assets.hcch.net/docs/510bc238-7318-47ed-9ed5-e0972510d98b.pdf [accessed 30 September 2023].

Convention)[8] offers a comprehensive structure for recognising and enforcing civil and commercial judgments among countries that are part of the convention.

9.11 Starting from 1 September 2023, the 2019 Hague Judgments Convention will be in effect between the EU (excluding Denmark) and Ukraine. At present, it has been signed (but not yet ratified) by Costa Rica, Israel, Montenegro, North Macedonia, Russia, the United States, and Uruguay.

9.12 If the UK decides to join (which is expected), the convention will apply between the EU and the UK. This would bring more certainty to this aspect than what is currently in place. Article 4 of the 2019 Hague Convention provides for automatic recognition of judgments from a contracting state. Article 5 lists criteria for eligibility of recognition.

9.13 The common law rules for determining jurisdiction in relation to contractual disputes are, broadly speaking, that the court asks itself two questions in order to establish that it has jurisdiction to adjudicate a contractual dispute:[9]

(a) Is there a jurisdictional basis for the court to adjudicate upon the dispute?

(b) If so, is the UK the proper place for the claim to be brought?

9.14 As to the first question, and in the absence of a jurisdiction agreement between the parties, a UK court may have jurisdiction to adjudicate upon a contractual dispute if:[10]

(a) the defendant was served with the claim form whilst physically present in the jurisdiction;

(b) the court grants permission to serve the claim form on a defendant who is not physically present in the jurisdiction, because there is a good arguable case that the claim falls within one or more of the jurisdictional gateways set out in para 3.1 of Practice Direction 6B – Service out of the Jurisdiction in the Civil Procedure Rules, and there is a serious issue to be tried; or

(c) the defendant submits to the jurisdiction of the court.

9.15 As to the second question, the exercise of the court's discretion to refuse to hear a dispute is referred to as the principle of *forum (non) conveniens*. If a basis for jurisdiction is made out, the court will have jurisdiction to hear the case only if it is satisfied that England and Wales is clearly the appropriate forum to adjudicate the dispute. The 'fundamental principle' is that the court has 'to identify the forum in which the case can be suitably tried for the interests of all the parties and for the ends of justice.'[11]

8 https://assets.hcch.net/docs/806e290e-bbd8-413d-b15e-8e3e1bf1496d.pdf [accessed 30 September 2023].
9 Law Commission, Smart Legal Contracts (n 3 above), [7.9].
10 *Ibid* [7.10].
11 *Ibid* [7.11].

9.16 The criteria for asserting jurisdiction over defendants who are domiciled in Scotland and Northern Ireland are outlined in Sch 4 of the Civil Jurisdiction and Judgments Act 1982. This schedule sets forth the rules for allowing legal action against a person who is domiciled in one part of the UK (England and Wales, Scotland, or Northern Ireland) in another part of the UK. Additionally, it includes rules within the UK that assign exclusive jurisdiction to a court in a specific part of the UK for certain matters. For instance, this applies to cases concerning rights in property over land (as described in para 11(a)), irrespective of the defendant's domicile.

9.17 The Law Commission identified two broad issues as problematic for cryptoassets:[12]

(a) determining the location of digital assets; and

(b) determining the location of particular actions, such as the place of performance or the place of breach, when those actions 'take place' on a distributed ledger.

9.18 Overall, the most significant issue is the difficulty of ascribing real-world locations to digital actions and digital objects.[13]

REGULATORY COORDINATION

9.19 The global nature of cryptocurrencies requires close coordination among countries to establish consistent and effective regulatory frameworks. The UK faces the challenge of aligning its regulations with international standards while ensuring the security of its financial system and protecting investors. Collaborative efforts are currently being made, such as sharing best practices and information exchange, and are crucial to address regulatory challenges.[14]

ANTI-MONEY LAUNDERING (AML) AND COUNTER-TERRORIST FINANCING (CTF) COMPLIANCE

9.20 Cryptocurrencies have been associated with potential money laundering and terrorist financing risks. The UK, along with other countries, has implemented AML and CTF regulations to mitigate these risks.[15] However, enforcing AML and CTF compliance on a global scale poses challenges, as different jurisdictions may have varying regulatory requirements and levels of enforcement.[16]

12 *Ibid* [7.144].
13 *Ibid* [7.145].
14 See **19.22–19.73**.
15 See **3.26–3.33.**
16 See **19.67**.

CROSS-BORDER TRANSACTIONS AND TAXATION

9.21 Cryptocurrency transactions occur across borders, challenging traditional tax frameworks. The UK faces difficulties in tracking and taxing cross-border cryptocurrency transactions effectively. The OECD is working on the harmonisation of tax regulations and international cooperation to prevent tax evasion and ensure a fair taxation system.[17]

DATA PROTECTION AND PRIVACY

9.22 The use of cryptocurrencies involves the processing and transfer of personal data, raising concerns about data protection and privacy. The UK, in line with GDPR, must address the challenges of safeguarding personal data in cryptocurrency transactions, particularly when data is stored on decentralised blockchains.[18]

INTERNATIONAL TRANSFERS AND REMITTANCES

9.23 Cryptocurrencies have the potential to revolutionise international money transfers and remittances. However, regulatory challenges arise when reconciling existing financial regulations with the borderless nature of cryptocurrencies. Under MLR the UK has adopted the 'Travel Rule' requiring reporting of cross-border cryptoasset transfers.[19] The UK aims to facilitate efficient and secure cross-border transactions while ensuring compliance with international standards and further development in this area is likely.

INTERNATIONAL DISPUTE RESOLUTION

Domestic and international initiatives

9.24 Cryptocurrency transactions can give rise to cross-border disputes, posing challenges for traditional legal systems. The Business and Property Courts of England & Wales have dealt with a range of disputes dealing with digital assets domestically and internationally.[20] In October 2022, the Law Commission launched a project on digital assets entitled 'Digital assets: which law, which court?' which will set out the current rules on private international law and digital assets and make recommendations for reform if necessary.[21]

17 See **19.54–19.58** and **19.67**.

18 See **10.2–10.48**.

19 See **3.26–3.33**.

20 Courts and Tribunals Judiciary, 'Digital Disputes' www.judiciary.uk/courts-and-tribunals/business-and-property-courts/commercial-court/the-work-of-the-commercial-court/digital-disputes/ [accessed 1 October 2023].

21 Law Commission, 'Digital assets: which law, which court?' https://lawcom.gov.uk/project/digital-assets-which-court-which-law/ [accessed 15 November 2023].

9.25 The risk of divergence between jurisdictions has prompted harmonisation initiatives. The International Institute for the Unification of Private Law (UNIDROIT) also launched a consultation on its Draft Principles and Commentary on Digital Assets and Private Law, which addressed conflicts of laws in one of its modules.[22]

9.26 The UK will likely develop mechanisms for international dispute resolution, such as market dominant arbitration rules or specialised digital asset courts, to address conflicts arising from global cryptocurrency activities.

Arbitration

9.27 Smart legal contracts can incorporate arbitration agreements, raising complex issues. These agreements may exist as natural language text within the contract's code or in accompanying notes. It remains uncertain whether such agreements are legally binding under English law, as the Law Commission expressed doubts regarding choice-of-law agreements within code but did not address arbitration agreements.[23] It is also unclear if these agreements meet the criteria of a written arbitration agreement under Article II(1) of the New York Convention.[24]

9.28 An alternative approach involves creating a 'smart' arbitration agreement within the code. This agreement would trigger arbitration proceedings when specific dispute conditions arise or upon a party's request. It might also include a feature to temporarily halt contract performance to maintain the current state. The smart contract could generate arbitration requests based on established institutional rules. Furthermore, it could facilitate disputes being referred to new arbitration institutions specialised in blockchain conflicts, with provisions for on-chain arbitrator enforcement of awards, including transaction reversals, completions, or even smart contract modifications.[25]

9.29 In practice, resolving cryptoasset-related disputes often requires separate bilateral written arbitration agreements. Common examples of contracts containing such agreements include agreements for cryptoasset transfers,[26] user agreements for online service providers like crypto exchanges, and terms associated with ICOs typically hosted on issuer-related websites.[27]

22 UNIDROIT, 'Draft Principles and Commentary on Digital Assets and Private Law' (2023 Study LXXXII – PC, January 2023) www.unidroit.org/wp-content/uploads/2023/01/Draft-Principles-and-Commentary-Public-Consultation.pdf [accessed 8 October 2023].

23 Law Commission, Smart Legal Contracts (n 3 above), [7.74].

24 Sam Brown, 'Arbitration of cryptoasset and smart contract disputes: arbitration unchained?' *Practical Law UK* (19 July 2023), 2 www.cliffordchance.com/content/dam/cliffordchance/briefings/2023/07/arbitration-of-cryptoasset.pdf [accessed 13 September 2023].

25 *Ibid*.

26 For example, token sale agreements or Simple Agreement for Future Tokens (SAFTs).

27 Brown, Arbitration of cryptoasset and smart contract disputes (n 24 above), 3.

9.30 In England and Wales, the Arbitration Act 1996,[28] in conjunction with delegated legislation, deems agreements automatically unfair (under the Consumer Rights Act 2015)[29] when the claim is less than £5,000.

9.31 Additionally, the presence of an arbitration agreement in a crypto exchange's user agreement does not necessarily prevent English courts from hearing claims by English consumers against the exchange. For example, a UK-based NFT collector initiated proceedings against a marketplace in breach of a JAMS arbitration agreement, the English Court of Appeal refused to stay the proceedings and ordered the High Court to decide on the arbitration agreement's validity, despite ongoing arbitration in New York.[30] In a related case, the English commercial court declined to enforce an award from a California-seated tribunal, citing the arbitrator's refusal to consider English law and stating that enforcement would contradict public policy.[31] This decision clarified that while UK consumers might accept arbitration under English law, they would not likely agree to arbitration in California, under JAMS Rules and subject to the US Federal Arbitration Act.

9.32 In the crypto sector, arbitration agreements typically utilise existing institutional arbitration rules rather than creating specialised or custom rules. For online user agreements, there is a trend toward adopting rules from US institutions, adapted for consumer arbitration, such as the American Arbitration Association (AAA) and JAMS. Companies in the Asia Pacific region often prefer the Singapore International Arbitration Centre (SIAC) and the Hong Kong International Arbitration Centre (HKIAC). Notable cryptoasset-related arbitrations have occurred under the AAA and JAMS rules in the US, while a prominent case involved Binance users launching arbitration proceedings under HKIAC rules to recover losses caused by a platform outage.[32]

9.33 Regarding arbitral seats, the choice varies widely. While traditional arbitration centres are common, lesser-known and less-established jurisdictions are also used, sometimes with motives ranging from seeking a perceived 'home' advantage to discouraging claims through jurisdictional complexities. Anecdotally, Seychelles appears to be a preferred seat among crypto businesses, although it is not widely recognised in international commercial arbitration.[33]

Arbitration Rules

9.34 Efforts have been made to establish dedicated arbitration rules:[34]

28 Section 91.

29 Paragraph 20 of Sch 2. This amount is currently set at £5,000 in the Unfair Arbitration Agreements (Specified Amount) Order 1999. It is possible that this amount may change from time to time.

30 *Soleymani v Nifty Gateway LLC* [2022] EWCA Civ 1297.

31 *Payward Inc and Others v Chechetkin* [2023] EWHC 1780 (Comm).

32 Brown, Arbitration of cryptoasset and smart contract disputes (n 24 above), 4–5.

33 *Ibid* at 5.

34 *Ibid*.

(a) **JAMS**: in 2018, JAMS introduced specialised rules for smart contract disputes.[35] These rules streamline the process by limiting discovery to expert witness depositions on code interpretation and the arbitrator's review of evidence to code, wrapper contracts, and witness statements. Code takes precedence, with translation into natural language considered only in cases of ambiguity or logic contradictions. The process is fast, with a 30-day deadline for issuing an award.

(b) **Digital Dispute Resolution Rules (DDRR)**: in 2021, the UK Jurisdiction Taskforce of LawtechUK introduced DDRR for digital disputes.[36] Key features include a straightforward procedure with room for customisation, a default 30-day process, the potential for 'on chain' arbitration with an appeals process, the option for parties to remain anonymous, and the arbitrator's authority to modify digital assets (subject to parties providing the necessary tools).

(c) **EOSIO**: when EOSIO blockchain launched in 2018, it included an arbitration process, though the constitution's status remains contentious. Under this process, disputes were resolved using the Rules of Dispute Resolution of the EOS Core Arbitration Forum (ECAF), with arbitral awards enforced 'on chain' by the blockchain's validators. In the short time it operated, the system produced reasoned awards and emergency orders to freeze suspected on-chain fraud accounts, with arbitrators potentially being volunteers from the crypto community, but their legal qualifications remain unclear.[37]

'On-chain' arbitration

9.35 'On-chain' arbitration encompasses various procedures and concepts within the blockchain space. These can range from enhancing traditional 'off-chain' dispute resolution processes by using blockchains for communication and document storage, to more innovative approaches departing from traditional dispute resolution methods. Some examples of 'on-chain' arbitration procedures include:[38]

(a) **Oracles**: while not strictly arbitration, smart contracts can define a limited set of potential disputes resolved by referencing external data sources (oracles). For instance, a dispute about undelivered goods can be settled by checking a courier company's database.

35 JAMS, 'JAMS Smart Contract Clause and Rules (DRAFT)' www.jamsadr.com/rules-smart-contracts [accessed 1 October 2023].

36 UKJT, 'Digital Dispute Resolution Rules' (Version 1.0, 2021) UKJT https://27221500.fs1.hubspotusercontent-eu1.net/hubfs/27221500/UKJT%20work/Digital%20Dispute%20resolution%20rules.pdf [accessed 8 October 2023].

37 'ECAF orders' (EOS Authority) https://eosauthority.com/ecaf-orders [accessed 13 September 2023].

38 Brown, Arbitration of cryptoasset and smart contract disputes (n 24 above), 6.

(b) **Multi-signature transactions**: these are commonly used for cryptoasset payments, where a transfer typically requires two out of three keys to authorise it. In case of a dispute, a neutral third party uses their key to determine whether the transfer should proceed.

(c) **'On-chain' arbitration systems and apps**: some projects attempt to bring traditional arbitral processes onto the blockchain and integrate them with smart contracts. Examples include Datarella's Codelegit project, Kleros, and Aragon's Aragon Network Jurisdiction.[39]

(d) **DLT with arbitration 'modules' or 'layers'**: certain platforms allow the integration of custom arbitration modules or layers into DLT. Examples include Hedera Hashgraph, Jur, and COTI.

Enforcing arbitration awards

9.36 Enforcing arbitral awards related to cryptoassets is a relatively new challenge due to the nascent nature of the cryptocurrency sector. Issues can arise in jurisdictions, where they may refuse to recognise awards involving cryptocurrencies due to public policy or legal defects in the decision:[40]

(a) The Shenzhen Intermediate People's Court in China set aside an award ordering Bitcoin payment, citing public policy concerns.[41]

(b) A Greek court refused to enforce an award related to a Bitcoin loan, arguing that cryptocurrencies pose risks like tax evasion and fraud.[42]

(c) The English commercial court refused to enforce an arbitral award because the arbitrator did not consider English law, which was relevant to the dispute.[43]

(d) The Amsterdam Court of Appeal refused to enforce an award from an online dispute resolution service due to onerous terms in the arbitration agreement.[44]

9.37 Regarding 'on-chain' enforcement, several arbitration rules aim to facilitate it. This addresses the challenge of rectifying or reversing transactions on immutable blockchains during ownership disputes, fraud cases, contract breaches, or mistakes. 'On-chain' enforcement options vary from granting arbitrators direct control over smart contracts to establishing independent

39 Note that information about these projects' current status may be limited.

40 Brown, Arbitration of cryptoasset and smart contract disputes (n 24 above), 7.

41 *Gao Zheyu v Shenzhen Yunsilu Innovation Development Fund Enterprise (LP) and Li Bin* (2018) Yue 03 Min Te No. 719.

42 Court of Appeal of Western Central Greece, No 88/2021 (unreported).

43 *Payward Inc and Others v Chechetkin* [2023] EWHC 1780 (Comm).

44 Amsterdam Court of Appeal, 29 January 2019 (ECLI:NL:GHAMS:2019:192).

enforcement mechanisms, potentially enhancing efficiency but also raising concerns about arbitrator oversight.[45]

CONCLUSION

9.38 The international legal challenges for cryptocurrencies present complex issues for the UK. Balancing the need for regulatory oversight and consumer protection while fostering innovation and maintaining competitiveness is a delicate task. The UK should actively engage with international counterparts, participate in global discussions, and adapt its regulatory frameworks to address these challenges effectively.

45 Brown, Arbitration of cryptoasset and smart contract disputes (n 24 above), 7–8.

Chapter 10

Data Privacy and Cybersecurity

DATA PRIVACY

10.1 The use of cryptocurrencies involves the processing and transfer of sensitive data, raising significant concerns regarding data privacy and cybersecurity. This chapter explores the data privacy and cybersecurity considerations specific to the UK in the context of cryptocurrencies.

Data protection laws and cryptocurrencies

10.2 The UK data protection regime comprises the General Data Protection Regulation (that is, the retained EU law version of the General Data Protection Regulation) (EU GPDR),[1] along with the Data Protection Act 2018 (DPA 2018) and the Privacy and Electronic Communications (EC Directive) Regulations 2003 (PECR). Post-Brexit, the GDPR is retained in domestic law as the UK GDPR by s 3 of the European Union (Withdrawal) Act 2018 (EUWA 2018) and as amended by Sch 1 to the Data Protection, Privacy and Electronic Communications (Amendments etc) (EU Exit) Regulations 2019. It is defined in s 3(10) of the DPA 2018, supplemented by s 205(4). The UK has the independence to keep the framework under review. The UK GDPR sits alongside an amended version of the DPA 2018 and both need to be considered in data privacy contexts.

10.3 The EU GDPR has extraterritorial effect,[2] meaning it may apply to UK controllers or processors under certain conditions. If a UK-based organisation has an establishment in the European Union/European Economic Area (EU/EEA), offers goods or services to EU/EEA data subjects, or monitors their behaviour within the EU/EEA, it may fall under the scope of the EU GDPR. In such cases, these organisations could be subject to both the UK GDPR and the EU GDPR, leading to dual data protection regulatory regimes.

10.4 When dealing with a blockchain, which involves multiple participants and data stored in various locations, it is essential to carefully consider the applicability of data protection laws like the UK GDPR and the DPA 2018. Additionally, if the blockchain extends to other countries outside the EU/EEA,

1 Council Regulation (EU) 2016/679 of 27 April 2016 on the protection of natural persons with regard to the processing of personal data and on the free movement of such data, and repealing Directive 95/46/EC [2016] OJ L119/1.

2 EU GDPR, Art 3.

relevant privacy legislations from those countries should also be taken into account.

10.5 Even if some participants are not directly subject to the UK GDPR while others are, it may still be advantageous to ensure compliance for the entire blockchain network as a whole. This approach helps maintain consistency and robust data protection measures throughout the entire chain, benefiting all participants and users involved.[3]

10.6 The UK GDPR and DPA 2018, set forth stringent requirements for the protection of personal data requiring compliance with lawful processing, data minimisation, security measures, and user consent when handling personal data.

Personal data

10.7 Personal data refers to information that can identify a specific natural person, such as a name, image, identification number, or online identifier. In the context of a blockchain, it is essential to determine if personal data can be fully anonymised. When personal data is irreversibly anonymised, it falls outside the scope of data protection requirements, as it no longer relates to an identifiable individual, as stated in Recital 26 of the UK GDPR:

> '… the principles of data protection should therefore not apply to anonymous information, namely information which does not relate to an identified or identifiable natural person or to personal data rendered anonymous in such a manner that the data subject is not or no longer identifiable.'

10.8 However, personal data that has been pseudonymised, meaning it can still be linked to an individual with additional information, retains its classification as personal data. Organisations developing blockchain solutions should carefully consider whether the techniques used provide true anonymisation or only pseudonymisation. [4]

10.9 It is essential for organisations to determine the nature of the data to be stored on the blockchain from the beginning since the immutability of the blockchain makes it challenging to modify data. Even if personal data used for identification purposes is kept off-chain, other personal data may still be present on the chain within transactions, contracts, or deeds. Thus, a comprehensive approach to data protection and privacy, like data protection by design and

3 Rob Sumroy, Duncan Mykura and Ian Ranson, 'Blockchain and data protection (UK)' *Practical Law UK* (Practice Note w-020-5436), 7.

4 Encryption and hashing techniques have been considered pseudonymisation by the Article 29 Working Party which was set up by the European Parliament and Council, though this classification may undergo updates. See Article 29 Data Protection Working Party, 'Opinion 05/2014 on Anonymisation Techniques' (0829/14/EN WP216, 10 April 2014) https://ec.europa.eu/justice/article-29/documentation/opinion-recommendation/files/2014/wp216_en.pdf [accessed 1 October 2023].

by default[5] and Data Protection Impact Assessments[6] (DPIAs), should be implemented from the outset.

10.10 According to Article 4(2) of the UK GDPR, processing refers to:

> '... any operation or set of operations which is performed on personal data or on sets of personal data, whether or not by automated means, such as collection, recording, organisation, structuring, storage, adaptation or alteration, retrieval, consultation, use, disclosure by transmission, dissemination or otherwise making available, alignment or combination, restriction, erasure or destruction.'

10.11 As a result of this broad definition, any personal data that is stored in or transmitted through a blockchain will be considered as being processed. Furthermore, even if personal data is held off-chain in connection with a blockchain, it will also be considered as being processed.[7]

10.12 According to Article 4(7) of the UK GDPR, a controller means 'the natural or legal person, public authority, agency or other body which, alone or jointly with others, determines the purposes and means of the processing of personal data', while a processor under Article 4(8) of the UK GDPR is a 'natural or legal person, public authority, agency or other body which processes personal data on behalf of the controller'. Article 28(3) of the UK GDPR requires that the relationship between controller and processor be governed by a contract.

10.13 Identifying whether an organisation is a controller or a processor in the context of a blockchain is crucial for ensuring UK GDPR compliance, structuring the relationship, and assigning risk and responsibility.[8] However, in practice, determining the boundary between controller and processor can be unclear, particularly in the context of a DLT. Each participant transmitting personal data may potentially be considered a controller, depending on their involvement in determining the purposes and means of processing. Designers of DLT architecture could also fall into either category, based on their interaction with personal data, and miners validating transactions could be regarded as processors. Joint controllership may apply when multiple participants collaborate to establish a blockchain for a common purpose.[9]

5 ICO, 'Data protection by design and default' https://ico.org.uk/for-organisations/uk-gdpr-guidance-and-resources/accountability-and-governance/guide-to-accountability-and-governance/accountability-and-governance/data-protection-by-design-and-default/ [accessed 1 October 2023].

6 ICO, 'Data protection impact assessments' https://ico.org.uk/for-organisations/uk-gdpr-guidance-and-resources/accountability-and-governance/guide-to-accountability-and-governance/accountability-and-governance/data-protection-impact-assessments/ [accessed 1 October 2023].

7 Sumroy, Mykura and Ranson, (n 3 above), 8.

8 ICO, 'Controllers and processors' https://ico.org.uk/for-organisations/uk-gdpr-guidance-and-resources/controllers-and-processors/controllers-and-processors/ [accessed 1 October 2023].

9 ICO, 'Response of the Information Commissioner's Office to the Treasury Select Committee inquiry into the cryptoasset industry', 2 https://ico.org.uk/media/about-the-ico/consultation-responses/4022678/treasury-select-committee-inquiry-into-cyrpto-assets-ico-response.pdf [accessed 8 October 2023].

10.14 It is vital to ascertain the status of each party to properly structure the governance of DLT, including risk allocation and responsibility. Participants may consider establishing a separate legal entity to act as the controller. The terms governing the blockchain should be clear on the roles and responsibilities of the parties, although these roles are questions of fact and cannot be artificially construed.[10]

10.15 In the context of a blockchain, determining the roles of the parties as controllers or processors becomes crucial. Based on their roles, they must then determine what information needs to be given to data subjects, in what format, and most importantly, by whom. Although the primary responsibility to provide information rests with controllers, processors may also be involved in providing the required information on behalf of their controllers. All parties involved in the blockchain should ensure the accuracy and practical enforceability of the information provided.

10.16 Guidance from the European Data Protection Board (EDPB) entitled 'the concepts of controller and processor in the GDPR' provides insights into controllers and processors' roles within a blockchain environment.[11] The European Parliament conducted a comprehensive analysis of the interplay between blockchain and the GDPR in its research paper titled 'Blockchain and the General Data Protection Regulation: Can distributed ledgers be squared with European data protection law?' dated July 2019. [12] The paper asserts that crypto wallet addresses are likely considered personal data when held by a single individual. A similar standpoint is also endorsed by the French regulatory body, the Commission Nationale Informatique et Libertés (CNIL).[13] Although the CNIL paper lacks an extensive examination of this aspect, the European Parliament's paper clarifies that even when public blockchain keys are hashed into wallet addresses, they fall under the category of identifiers described in Recital 30 of the GDPR and the personal data definition in Article 4(1). In the ICO's response to the Treasury Select Committee into the cryptoasset industry, the ICO indicated:

> 'While blockchain transactions may not involve certain personal data such as an individual's name, that does not itself eliminate the possibility that individuals could be identified. This is because information recorded as part of blockchain transactions may be pseudonymised data (and therefore still personal data) rather

10 Sumroy, Mykura and Ranson, 'Blockchain and data protection (UK)' (n 3 above), 8.

11 European Data Protection Board, 'Guidelines 07/2020 on the concepts of controller and processor in the GDPR' (Version 2.1, 7 July 2021) https://edpb.europa.eu/our-work-tools/our-documents/guidelines/guidelines-072020-concepts-controller-and-processor-gdpr_en [accessed 8 October 2023].

12 Panel for the Future of Science and Technology European Parliament (PFSTEP), 'Block Chain and General Data Protection Regulation: Can distributed ledgers be squared with European data protection law?' (Study, PE 634.445, European Parliament, July 2019) www.europarl.europa.eu/RegData/etudes/STUD/2019/634445/EPRS_STU(2019)634445_EN.pdf [accessed 1 October 2023].

13 CNIL, 'Blockchain and the GDPR: Solutions for a responsible use of the blockchain in the context of personal data' (1 October 2018) www.cnil.fr/sites/cnil/files/atoms/files/blockchain_en.pdf [accessed 1 October 2023].

than anonymous information. Pseudonymised data does not directly identify individuals, but the identity of the person can be determined by using additional information.

For example, information about the transactions of an user may be stored on the blockchain in hashed form (i.e. the result of converting plaintext to ciphertext). This means it is not immediately attributable to a named individual. However, the individual may still be identifiable if cryptographic protections were undermined or if they were singled out in the context of these transactions.

If it is reasonably likely that a link can be established between the information processed by a blockchain system and an identified or identifiable individual (even if the information does not enable the "real world identity" of that individual to be determined) then this information is personal data and falls under UK data protection law.'[14]

10.17 Participants should consider these guidelines and questions when determining their status and structuring the blockchain arrangement.

10.18 One counter-argument to the above points out that a significant portion of the supplementary information necessary to pinpoint an individual based on a wallet address is not generally accessible. For instance, even transaction data, available to the public on certain blockchains via the blockchain ledger, would often require extensive analysis to link back to a specific individual. Consequently, it can be argued that in most cases, while the potential for re-identifying individuals from wallet addresses exists, many entities in control and third parties lack the 'means reasonably likely to be used' (as defined in Recital 26 of the UK GDPR) to connect a wallet address to a specific individual. In essence, the wallet address can be considered effectively anonymised. This aligns with the nature of blockchain technology, which inherently includes elements of anonymisation, albeit not with the intention of evading the scope of the UK GDPR.[15] Recital 26 states:

"The principles of data protection should apply to any information concerning an identified or identifiable natural person. Personal data which have undergone pseudonymisation, which could be attributed to a natural person by the use of additional information should be considered to be information on an identifiable natural person. To determine whether a natural person is identifiable, account should be taken of all the means reasonably likely to be used, such as singling out, either by the controller or by another person to identify the natural person directly or indirectly. To ascertain whether means are reasonably likely to be used to identify the natural person, account should be taken of all objective factors, such as the costs of and the amount of time required for identification, taking into consideration the available technology at the time of the processing and technological developments. The principles of data protection should therefore not apply to anonymous information, namely information which does not relate to an identified or identifiable natural person or to personal data rendered anonymous in

14 ICO, 'Response of the Information Commissioner's Office to the Treasury Select Committee inquiry into the cryptoasset industry' (n 9 above).

15 Daniel Owen, 'Are crypto wallet addresses personal data?' (2023) 23(5) P & DP 9, 10.

such a manner that the data subject is not or no longer identifiable. This Regulation does not therefore concern the processing of such anonymous information, including for statistical or research purposes.'

10.19 Under the UK GDPR, controllers are required to conduct a DPIA for processing operations that present specific risks to individuals due to the nature or scope of the operation.[16] A DPIA is specifically required in the following cases:

(a) When there is a systematic and extensive evaluation of personal aspects based on automated processing, including profiling, that leads to decisions with legal effects or significantly affects the individual.[17]

(b) When processing involves large-scale use of special categories of personal data[18] or personal data related to criminal convictions and offences.[19]

(c) When there is systematic monitoring of a publicly accessible area on a large scale, such as through CCTV.[20]

10.20 The DPIA should include a systematic description of the envisaged processing operations and their purposes, including the legitimate interests pursued by the controller.[21]

10.21 If the assessments indicate a high risk in the absence of risk-mitigating measures, controllers must consult the ICO before commencing processing.[22]

10.22 The concepts of privacy by design and by default[23] are also crucial in the context of blockchain solutions, as they emphasise the importance of considering data protection from the outset of developing new technologies and data processes.

10.23 Controllers, developers, designers, and processors involved in blockchain solutions need to carefully consider the DPIA requirements and integrate privacy considerations into the design from the start. While Article 25 of the UK GDPR applies specifically to controllers, Recital 78 of the UK GDPR states that producers of products, services, and applications based on personal data processing are to consider data protection rights in design and ensure that controllers and processors can fulfil their data protection obligations, with respect to the state of the art.

16 UK GDPR, Art 35(1).
17 UK GDPR, Art 35(3)(a).
18 UK GDPR, Art 35(3)(b).
19 UK GDPR, Art 35(3)(c).
20 UK GDPR, Art 35(3)(d).
21 UK GDPR, Art 35(7).
22 UK GDPR, Art 36(1).
23 UK GDPR, Art 25.

10.24 Under Article 5(1) of UK GDPR there are six personal data processing principles:

(a) lawfulness, fairness, and transparency;

(b) purpose limitation;

(c) data minimisation;

(d) accuracy;

(e) storage limitation; and

(f) integrity and confidentiality.

10.25 Article 5(2) of the UK GDPR requires the controller to be responsible for complying with the six principles mentioned in Article 5(1) of the UK GDPR and to demonstrate such compliance. Therefore, it is crucial for controllers to maintain records of DPIAs, privacy notices, and other compliance mechanisms to ensure compliance with the UK GDPR.

10.26 Controllers and processors engaging in any DLT solution must implement suitable technical and organisational measures to ensure an appropriate level of security based on the associated risks. This entails considering the latest technological advancements, the implementation costs, the nature of data processing, and employing measures like anonymisation and encryption, maintaining confidentiality, ensuring data integrity, availability, and resilience of the system and services, and having the capability to restore data in case of any incidents. Regular testing of security measures is also necessary.[24]

10.27 Controllers and processors involved in a blockchain project should be content with the security measures in place. This includes measures to mitigate potential blockchain failures, governance around software changes, and access permissions. Furthermore, the UK GDPR has introduced requirements for security breach notifications. In the event of a personal data breach, controllers may be obligated to report such incidents to the Information Commissioner.[25]

10.28 Lawfulness, fairness and transparency are essential requirements under the UK GDPR for processing personal data.[26] This includes the responsibility to provide data subjects with specific information, typically in the form of a privacy notice, both when collecting data directly from individuals and when collecting it through third parties.[27]

10.29 The UK GDPR requires that processing of personal data must be based on one of the lawful bases listed in the UK GDPR, Article 6. Special categories

24 UK GDPR, Art 32.
25 UK GDPR, Art 33.
26 UK GDPR, Art 5(1)(a).
27 UK GDPR, Arts 13 and 14.

of personal data and data related to criminal convictions and offences[28] require an additional lawful basis under the Data Protection Act 2018, which are typically more limited.

10.30 Pursuant to Article 4(11) of the UK GDPR, when relying on consent as a lawful basis for processing, the consent obtained must meet a high threshold: 'freely given, specific, informed and unambiguous indication of the data subject's wishes by which he or she, by a statement or by a clear affirmative action, signifies agreement to the processing of personal data relating to him or her'. However, obtaining and managing consent on an immutable blockchain can be challenging, as consent must also be capable of being withdrawn.[29]

10.31 An alternative to consent is to rely on the legitimate interests of the controller or a third party, unless they are overridden by the interests or fundamental rights and freedoms of the data subject.[30] The ICO has provided specific guidance on legitimate interest.[31] When relying on this lawful basis, the controller must provide information about the legitimate interests pursed in the privacy notice to data subjects.[32]

10.32 Another potential ground for processing personal data in the context of a blockchain is contractual necessity.[33] However, relying on this basis can be difficult in practice, as it requires an objective assessment of whether there are less intrusive alternatives and must be necessary in the context of a specific, valid contract. Additionally, this basis only applies when there is a contract in place with the affected data subject, which may not always be the case in commercial blockchain solutions.

10.33 The storage limitation principle is a significant topic of discussion when it comes to the relationship between blockchain and data subjects' rights under the UK GDPR. According to this principle,[34] personal data should not be kept in an identifiable form for longer than necessary for the purposes for which it is processed.

10.34 To comply with this principle, organisations should define data retention periods for personal data. These retention periods should be included in the information provided to individuals under Articles 13 and 14 of the UK GDPR, as well as in the register of processing required under Article 30 of the UK GDPR.

28 UK GDPR, Arts 9 and 10.
29 UK GDPR, Art 7(3).
30 UK GDPR, Art 6(1)(f).
31 ICO, 'Guide to the General Data Protection Regulation (GDPR): Legitimate interests' https://ico.org.uk/for-organisations/uk-gdpr-guidance-and-resources/lawful-basis/a-guide-to-lawful-basis/lawful-basis-for-processing/legitimate-interests/ [accessed 1 October 2023].
32 UK GDPR, Arts 13 and 14.
33 UK GDPR, Art 6(1)(b).
34 UK GDPR, Art 5(1)(e).

10.35 However, blockchain poses a challenge because personal data stored on-chain cannot be deleted. Therefore, it is essential to consider which personal data can be stored off-chain. For any personal data stored on-chain, organisations must explore technical methods for anonymisation and justify the need for retaining any remaining personal data throughout the blockchain's duration. This involves considering privacy by design and default concepts and conducting a DPIA.

10.36 CNIL has issued guidance regarding identifiers of participants and miners in a blockchain.[35] They suggest that as these identifiers are crucial for the blockchain's functioning, their retention periods could be permissible for the duration of the blockchain's existence.[36]

10.37 Potential options to address this issue include 'pruning', where participants agree to delete historical blocks that pre-date a specific point in time (eg a retention period required by law or regulation),[37] and 'forking,' where participants agree to update the blockchain with new rules that remove personal data.[38] Encryption is also an option, although it is subject to other considerations.[39] Editable blockchains may also be considered, but this contradicts the advantages of immutability that blockchains provide.[40] Addition of 'noise' to the data is also an option.[41]

Data subject rights

10.38 Data subject rights are a crucial aspect of the UK GDPR, as it grants specific rights to individuals regarding their personal data. These rights, such as the right to erasure, right to rectification, and right to access, require particular attention when developing a blockchain solution. This is due to the potential conflict between the functioning of distributed ledger technology and the rights individuals possess under the UK GDPR.

(a) **Right to rectification**: individuals have the right to have inaccurate or incomplete personal data rectified.[42] In the context of a blockchain, for incomplete data, a supplementary statement or statement of correction could be kept. However, for correcting inaccurate information, deletion via encryption might be considered.

(b) **Right to erasure (right to be forgotten)**: individuals have the right to have their personal data erased.[43] However, this right is applicable only under certain circumstances, such as when the data is no longer necessary for

35 CNIL, Blockchain and the GDPR (n 13 above).
36 *Ibid* 7.
37 PFSTEP, 'Block Chain and General Data Protection Regulation (n 12 above), [3.58].
38 *Ibid* [7.2].
39 *Ibid* [3.5.3].
40 *Ibid* [3.5.6].
41 *Ibid* [3.5.5].
42 UK GDPR, Art 16.
43 UK GDPR, Art 17.

its initial purpose or if the data subject withdraws consent. It can also be exercised when the controller relies on legitimate interests, but no overriding legitimate ground exists. This right can pose challenges for a blockchain that cannot alter or remove data, and solutions like pruning and encryption may not fully address this issue. The CNIL guidance suggests that making the data practically inaccessible 'moves closer to the effects of data erasure,' even if it does not technically equate to erasure.[44]

(c) **Right of access**: individual have a right of access to their personal data.[45] Organisations need to consider how to comply with data subject access rights in the context of a blockchain. They must develop approaches to search and retrieve appropriate information.

(d) **Other rights**: besides the three rights listed above, there are other essential rights granted to individuals under the UK GDPR, which must all be considered in the context of blockchain. These rights include the right to information,[46] the right of data portability,[47] the right to object to processing,[48] and the right to restrict processing.[49]

Data protection contractual framework

10.39 To comply with the key obligations of the UK GDPR, any deployment of a commercial DLT solution requires a well-defined contractual framework that binds all participants. There are three specific aspects that need to be addressed:

(a) **Processor contracts**: if a processor handles personal data on behalf of a controller within the DLT network, they must have a written contract that includes provisions as outlined in Article 28 of the UK GDPR. The contract must ensure that the processor only processes the personal data based on documented instructions from the controller. This contractual framework should cover the subject-matter and duration of processing, the nature and purpose of processing, the type of personal data involved, and the categories of data subjects impacted by the DLT's data processing. To ensure compliance with these key obligations, a robust contractual framework is essential for any commercial DLT deployment, considering the specific requirements and roles of processors and joint controllers in the network.

(b) **Joint controller arrangements**:[50] in the context of DLT, joint controllership should be carefully considered when multiple controllers collectively determine the purposes and means of processing personal data within

44 CNIL, Blockchain and the GDPR (n 13 above), 8.
45 UK GDPR, Art 15.
46 UK GDPR, Arts 13 and 14.
47 UK GDPR, Art 20.
48 UK GDPR. Art 21.
49 UK GDPR, Art 18.
50 UK GDPR, Art 26.

the network. This is common in many DLT solutions. Joint controllers must establish transparent arrangements to determine their respective compliance responsibilities, especially regarding providing information to individuals and handling data subject rights. An arrangement should be in place, reflecting each joint controller's roles and responsibilities towards data subjects, including the designation of a contact point. The essence of this arrangement must be made available to data subjects.

(c) **International data transfers:**[51] if the DLT involves the international transfer of personal data, adequate safeguards must be in place, and standard contractual clauses can be incorporated to fulfil this requirement. International data transfers under the UK GDPR require additional data protection measures such as when data is hosted or accessed by support or maintenance providers located outside the UK. To comply with the restrictions on international data transfers, the controller must assess whether the importing country ensures an adequate level of protection for the personal data, considering the specific circumstances of the transfer. The UK data protection legislation allows transfers to the EU and continues to recognise the adequacy of data protection regimes in non-EU countries with adequacy findings from the EU. Some examples include Guernsey, Japan, Jersey, Isle of Man, Canada (for certain data), Argentina, and Switzerland. However, for transfers to other countries, controllers or processors must find another legitimate basis for the transfer.[52]

10.40 For DLT solutions with global implications, compliance with UK GDPR transfer provisions becomes crucial. While obtaining data subject consent is an option, it may not always be practical due to the possibility of consent withdrawal and inaccessibility of some data subjects. A better alternative could be incorporating the European Commission's standard contractual clauses (the 'model clauses') for international data transfers under the previous Data Protection Directive (95/46/EC) into the contractual governance arrangements,[53] as these clauses continue to be acceptable in the UK.[54]

10.41 While other means of lawful international transfers exist, such as binding corporate rules, they may not be widely applicable outside a group of corporate entities. Certification mechanisms and binding corporate rules between non-affiliate organisations may develop in the future, but at present, they do not provide viable alternatives to standard contractual clauses.[55]

51 UK GDPR, Chapter V.
52 Sumroy, Mykura and Ranson, 'Blockchain and data protection (UK)' (n 3 above), 13.
53 European Commission, 'Standard Contractual Clauses' (4 June 2021) https://commission.europa.eu/law/law-topic/data-protection/international-dimension-data-protection/standard-contractual-clauses-scc_en [accessed 2 September 2023].
54 ICO, 'International data transfer agreement and guidance' https://ico.org.uk/for-organisations/uk-gdpr-guidance-and-resources/international-transfers/international-data-transfer-agreement-and-guidance/ [accessed 2 September 2023].
55 Sumroy, Mykura and Ranson, 'Blockchain and data protection (UK)' (n 3 above), 14.

10.42 Blockchain technology presents challenges for UK GDPR compliance, as certain principles within the GDPR may conflict with the immutability of the blockchain. Some of these conflicting principles include:

(a) the right to be forgotten;

(b) data subject rights; and

(c) accuracy and data retention.

10.43 In terms of designing a new privacy compliant DLT, the following principles should be borne in mind.[56]

(a) **Opt for a private, permissioned blockchain**

In a private, permissioned blockchain networks require participants to obtain authorisation before joining, viewing data, or engaging with the network. To approve new participants, various processes are employed, and part of this process involves ensuring that new participants agree to a set of rules or terms and conditions governing their network usage.

(b) **Minimisation of personal data storage on DLT if possible**

While achieving a completely personal data-free DLT is challenging, efforts can be made to keep personal data off-chain as much as possible. For instance, one approach is to store an encrypted and fully anonymous hash of the personal data on-chain, while keeping the identifiable personal data off-chain. Minimising free-form data can also help. The expanded definition of personal data under the UK GDPR means it is essential to consider the data environment as a whole, not just information that is clearly identifiable as personal data. Indirectly identifiable information, when combined with other data, can build a profile of an identifiable individual. Additionally, despite efforts to avoid storing personal data on the blockchain, there may be instances where personal data is accidentally or maliciously added to the ledger. To prevent personal data from being added to the network, specifically designed blockchain middleware applications can be used. These applications, acting on top of underlying DLT networks, can avoid including specific data fields for personal data (eg names, phone numbers, email addresses). Moreover, advanced techniques, such as AI or machine-learning-based tools, can be employed by these applications to recognise and remove personal data from information before submitting it to the blockchain network.

(c) **Establish a comprehensive governance framework**

For a UK GDPR-compliant commercial blockchain solution, it's crucial to have a detailed and legally binding governance framework that clearly outlines the rights and responsibilities of all participants. This framework is essential due to the following reasons:

56 *Ibid* 4-6.

(i) **Ensuring adequate protection of personal data**

The governance framework should address how personal data will be adequately protected on the blockchain.

(ii) **Meeting UK GDPR requirements for contractual relationships**

The UK GDPR mandates the establishment of contractual relationships between parties involved in the processing of personal data.

(iii) **Fulfilling legal obligations**

Controllers must provide privacy notices to individuals, uphold data subjects' rights, responding to subject access requests.

(iv) **Enabling lawful data transfers**

Established contractual mechanisms are needed to facilitate the lawful transfer of personal data across international borders.

When developing and documenting the governance framework, participants must carefully consider the following aspects:

(i) **Contractual terms**

Establish clear contractual terms between controllers and processors involved in the blockchain solution.

(ii) **Joint controllers arrangements**

Define roles and responsibilities in documented arrangements when multiple controllers are involved.

(iii) **Data sharing arrangements**

Determine data sharing arrangements between independent controllers.

(iv) **Liability**

Address liability issues both among the parties and towards data subjects.

(v) **International data transfers**

Include mechanisms for lawful international data transfers.

(vi) **Points of contact**

Agree on designated points of contact for communication and coordination.

(vii) **Privacy notices**

Determine agreed forms of privacy notices for individuals and how these notices will be delivered to relevant individuals.

(viii) **Data subject rights**

Establish agreed processes for handling data subject rights, such as access requests and corrections.

(ix) **Security measures**

Define agreed technical and organisational security measures to ensure data protection.

(x) **Change control**

Include provisions for managing changes and updates to the governance framework.

(d) **Embrace innovative solutions for data protection challenges**

The immutability of DLT data presents a significant challenge when it comes to complying with the UK GDPR, especially concerning the right to erasure and rectification. However, by adopting innovative approaches, it is possible to align with the spirit and intent of data protection laws, if not yet fully with the specific requirements. One such solution involves employing advanced irreversible encryption as a form of data deletion. While it may be technically complex and costly to remove historical data blocks ('pruning') or restructure the blockchain ('forking') to delete personal data, irreversible encryption offers an alternative. With this approach, personal data stored on the blockchain can be 'deleted' by encrypting it in a way that makes it impossible to decrypt without the corresponding keys. In essence, the encrypted data remains on the blockchain, but the actual personal data is effectively rendered inaccessible. By embracing such innovative strategies, blockchain technology can be better aligned with data protection principles, offering improved compliance and privacy safeguards for users.

Data ethics

10.44 Data ethics is a critical consideration for organisations developing blockchain solutions to foster trust and compliance within their networks. While not unique to blockchain technology, data ethics has become increasingly important to regulators, governments, and private organisations.

10.45 Regulators, like the ICO, have highlighted the growing significance of ethical principles in data use. For example, in 2017, the ICO noted the need for explicit ethical policies due to public awareness and suspicions about data sharing. Similarly, the private sector is driven by a commercial imperative to mitigate risk.[57] To address data ethics, various entities are developing ethical frameworks. The ICO has suggested approaches such as establishing an ethics board, setting industry standards, and considering discriminatory impacts.[58]

57 ICO, 'Big data, artificial intelligence, machine learning and data protection' (21 March 2017) https://ico.org.uk/media/for-organisations/documents/2013559/big-data-ai-ml-and-data-protection.pdf [accessed 2 September 2023].

58 Sumroy, Mykura and Ranson, 'Blockchain and data protection (UK)' (n 3 above), 17.

10.46 The UK Government launched the Centre for Data Ethics and Innovation in 2018 to handle ethical issues posed by new technologies and establish best practices for using personal data. The Centre aims to build to enable trustworthy innovation using data and artificial intelligence in line with the National Data Strategy.[59] The Central Digital and Data Office published its Data Ethics Framework on 16 September 2020 and is designed for anyone working directly or indirectly with data in the public sector but provides useful general guidance to private sector operators.[60] The framework can be used throughout the process of planning, implementing, and evaluating a new project and is designed to be regularly revisited throughout the project, especially when any changes are made to data collection, storage, analysis or sharing processes. Its overarching principles are:

(a) transparency;

(b) accountability; and

(c) fairness.

The methodology contains a scoring of 0–5. If any principle obtains a score less than 3 the project should be checked and potentially changed. The specific actions contained in the framework are:

(a) define and understand public benefit and user need;

(b) involve diverse expertise;

(c) comply with the law;

(d) review the quality and limitations of data; and

(e) evaluate and consider wider policy implications.

10.47 The European Data Protection Supervisor (EDPS) has also shown interest in data ethics and privacy standards for businesses. In its 2020–2024 Strategy, the EDPS sets out a number of commitments to ensure that personal data is processed in compliance with European values and rules to ensure a human-centric data economy where individuals remain in control of their data.[61]

10.48 In summary, while data ethics is not specific to DLT, it is crucial and beneficial for organisations developing solutions to prioritise ethics to promote

59 Department for Science, Innovation and Technology, 'About us' (Centre for Data Ethics and Innovation) www.gov.uk/government/organisations/centre-for-data-ethics-and-innovation/about#overview [accessed 1 October 2023]. See also Department for Digital, Culture and Sport, 'Centre for Data Ethics and Innovation Consultation' (Consultation Outcome, 20 November 2018) www.gov.uk/government/consultations/consultation-on-the-centre-for-data-ethics-and-innovation/centre-for-data-ethics-and-innovation-consultation [accessed 2 October 2023].

60 Central Digital and Data Office, 'Data Ethics Framework' (Guidance, 16 September 2020) www.gov.uk/government/publications/data-ethics-framework/data-ethics-framework-2020 [accessed 1 October 2023].

61 CNIL, 'The EDPS Strategy: 2020–2024' (PDF/Vol_01, EDPS), 8 and 16 www.cnil.fr/sites/cnil/files/atoms/files/blockchain_en.pdf [accessed 1 October 2023].

trust and compliance in their networks. Regulators, governments, and private organisations are increasingly emphasising ethical design in data use in the age of advanced technologies which is expected to lead to heightened regulatory requirements and industry standards.

CYBERSECURITY

Blockchain consensus mechanisms

10.49 Blockchain participants that maintain a copy of the ledger are generally known as nodes. Each node maintains one or more current copies of the ledger on its system. Each node receives an identical copy of the updated ledger as participants add validated data.[62]

10.50 Every blockchain application establishes rules for adding new data blocks to the ledger. These rules encompass the following:[63]

(a) **Validation procedures**: procedures are put in place to ensure the integrity of new data blocks before they are added to the ledger.

(b) **Network participation**: these rules apply to all nodes that participate in the blockchain, collectively forming the network.

(c) **Consensus mechanisms**: consensus mechanisms are validation procedures that enable participants to reach agreement on new data blocks. These agreements are implemented in code through algorithms that align with the blockchain application's governance structure.

(d) **Agreement criteria**: consensus mechanisms typically require a majority or a predetermined number of nodes to agree on two critical aspects:

   (i) the validity and appropriateness of adding a new data block to the shared ledger; and

   (ii) the correctness of the entire ledger's history, ensuring compliance with the network's rules.

10.51 By following these consensus mechanisms, blockchain applications ensure the security and integrity of their data while maintaining trust and agreement among network participants. Consensus mechanisms in a blockchain provide continuous checks on the integrity of new data blocks and past ledger transactions. They ensure the accuracy and security of the blockchain's information.

62 Jared R Butcher, 'Cybersecurity Tech Basics: Blockchain Technology Cyber Risks and Issues: Overview' (*Practical Law,* Resource ID: w-017-1916), 2 www.steptoe.com/a/web/189187/Cybersecurity-Tech-Basics-Blockchain-Technology-Cyber-Risks-and.pdf [accessed 13 September 2023].

63 *Ibid.*

10.52 In public blockchains, consensus mechanisms like PoW and PoS are commonly used. PoW requires users to compete to solve complex puzzles, and those who succeed get the right to publish the next block and earn rewards. For example, cryptocurrency miners invest in powerful computing resources to solve these puzzles and gain rewards.

10.53 On the other hand, PoS determines the right to publish new blocks based on a user's current known investment in the blockchain application. This means users with more stakes in the network have higher chances of being selected to create new blocks.

10.54 In private blockchains, consensus mechanisms are generally less complex and computationally intensive. Examples include:[64]

(a) proof of authority (PoA), which verifies the identity of a node before allowing it to publish new blocks;

(b) simple delegation of authority, where certain trusted nodes are responsible for approving new blocks; and

(c) allowing participating nodes to publish new blocks at will or on a rotating basis, subject to verification.

10.55 These consensus mechanisms play a crucial role in maintaining the integrity and security of data within the blockchain network, ensuring that all participants agree on the validity of new transactions and blocks.

10.56 Blockchain technology provides significant cybersecurity benefits but is not invulnerable to cyberattacks. While it secures networked ledgers effectively, it does not ensure individual participants' security or replace the need for other cybersecurity best practices. When evaluating cyber risks, organisations must differentiate between the technology itself and the surrounding environment where it operates. The points of interaction between the blockchain and users or connected systems represent potential opportunities for cyberattacks.

10.57 When considering the use of blockchain technology, it is important to understand the following key cybersecurity risks and issues:[65]

(a) **Blockchain transaction security**: assess how the technology safeguards transaction data.

(b) **Blockchain network governance**: analyse transaction validation risks and potential attacks on the blockchain's integrity.

(c) **External data dependencies and the oracle problem**: determine whether the blockchain application relies on external data or resources susceptible to risks.

64 *Ibid* 3.
65 See **10.61–10.71** below.

(d) **Blockchain cyber vulnerabilities**: identify possible cyber vulnerabilities in the blockchain application's implementing code, weaknesses in the environment where the blockchain technology operates, and the cyber vulnerabilities that may exist in end-user environments interacting with the blockchain.

10.58 By understanding and addressing these cybersecurity risks, organisations can enhance the overall security of their blockchain implementations. It is essential to complement blockchain technology with comprehensive cybersecurity measures to protect the entire system effectively.

10.59 Issues may arise regarding laws and regulations that may apply, according to how a particular ledger is geographically distributed. Some jurisdictions' data localisation and data protection laws and regulations may limit whether and where organisations store certain kinds of transaction data. Participants in public blockchains typically can only control their own nodes' locations. However, organisations considering private blockchain projects may have some influence over most or all of the nodes and wish to build location requirements into the application's administrative governance structure.[66]

10.60 Blockchain applications can address these data protection issues by implementing measures such as limiting the use of personal data, storing it separately from the transaction register, supporting data processing agreements in private blockchains, or using enhanced encryption techniques that allow for data deletion when needed.[67]

Blockchain transaction security

10.61 Blockchain technology offers a more robust approach than traditional centralised computing services for securing networked transaction ledgers. Here are some key points:[68]

(a) **Cyber resiliency**: unlike centralised databases, where a single breach can disrupt the entire system, DLTs provide increased cyber resiliency. There is no single point of failure, as each node holds an identical copy of the ledger. This means that even if one or a few participants are attacked, other nodes can maintain the integrity and availability of the ledger, ensuring transactions can continue between unaffected participants.

(b) **Enhanced transparency**: distributed ledgers provide enhanced transparency, making it challenging for cyber attackers to corrupt blockchains using malware or manipulative actions. Since each participant has an identical copy of the ledger, any attempt to corrupt or modify historical transaction records

66 Jared R Butcher, 'Cybersecurity Tech Basics: Blockchain Technology Cyber Risks and Issues: Overview' (n 62 above), 2.

67 *Ibid* 4. See **10.2–10.6** and **10.39–10.43**.

68 *Ibid* 3.

can be quickly detected. The encryption technologies used in blockchain applications further safeguard individual transactions and the entire ledger.

(c) **Consensus mechanisms**: consensus mechanisms play a crucial role in protecting new data blocks. These mechanisms require network participants to validate and continually compare new blocks with past transactions. This process mitigates the risk of cyber attackers or rogue organisations inappropriately manipulating new ledger blocks, ensuring the integrity of the blockchain.

10.62 Blockchain security measures are specific to each application, but they commonly include:[69]

(a) **Public-private key encryption**: this method is used to manage participant access to the blockchain, ensuring secure interactions.[70]

(b) **Transaction data integrity protection**: blocks within the blockchain are protected using cryptographic hashes, which ensure the integrity of the data. Any attempt to alter the data within a block changes the hash values, making tampering easily detectable by other participants. This feature also provides the widely known immutability principle, making transactions recorded on the blockchain highly secure.[71]

10.63 It is important to note that different blockchain applications may use additional security measures, impacting the level of risk involved. Potential users must thoroughly investigate and understand the specific security measures employed by a blockchain application to avoid unexpected vulnerabilities. Private blockchains require particular scrutiny since they may not have a robust network of users, making it essential to prevent attempts to introduce erroneous data mistakenly or intentionally.[72] Cryptocurrency transactions must be conducted securely to prevent unauthorised interception or alteration. Users should verify the authenticity of wallet addresses and adopt secure communication channels to mitigate the risk of data breaches during the transfer process. Blockchain explorers can also be used to verify the authenticity of wallet addresses.[73]

Blockchain network governance

10.64 The integrity of a blockchain is determined by its network governance model and the methods used to validate transactions. Different blockchain

69 *Ibid* 2.

70 Sagar Joshi, 'How Public Key Encryption Ensures Data Integrity' (*G2*, 30 July 2021) https://learn.g2.com/public-key-encryption [accessed 13 September 2023].

71 World Economic Forum (WEF), 'Module: Data Integrity' https://widgets.weforum.org/blockchain-toolkit/data-integrity/index.html#the-importance-of-data-integrity-and-key-requirements [accessed 9 October 2023].

72 Butcher, 'Cybersecurity Tech Basics' (n 62 above), 2.

73 Doubloin, 'How To Check If A Crypto Wallet Address Is Valid?' (*Doubloin*, 29 May 2023) www.doubloin.com/learn/crypto-wallet-address-valid [accessed 13 September 2023].

applications utilise various mechanisms for this purpose. However, some potential integrity attacks have been identified, including:[74]

(a) **Centralisation of miners or the 51 per cent attack**: blockchain networks relying on majority consensus are vulnerable if attackers gain control over a large group of nodes. For example, bad actors may compromise a public blockchain by acquiring or controlling at least 51 per cent of its mining and consensus power. While this is unlikely in robust networks with many users, small private blockchains may be more susceptible. Private blockchain applications typically vet participants and implement authentication and controls to mitigate this risk.

(b) **Selfish miners**: researchers have suggested scenarios where self-interested miners may deceive others into wasting time and computing power on already validated transactions. This could reduce the number of miners performing real mining work and potentially facilitate manipulation.

(c) **The eclipse attack**: disrupting node communications or disseminating false information to confirm fake transactions may compromise the blockchain network's integrity.

10.65 It is important for organisations considering private blockchain applications to:[75]

(a) understand the chosen network governance model, consensus mechanisms, and associated risks of the specific blockchain application; and

(b) implement risk management strategies, including thorough upfront due diligence, negotiating contractual protections with other participants, continuous monitoring for security incidents, and obtaining appropriate cyber insurance if available.

By being aware of these potential risks and employing proactive risk management measures, organisations can enhance the security and integrity of their blockchain implementations.[76]

External data dependencies and the oracle problem

10.66 Blockchains rely on real-world information to function properly. For instance, a payment transaction needs accurate details about the payor and the payee. More complex applications, like supply chain management or cross-border transactions, require even more external data. However, using external data sources introduces certain risks that participants must address, such as:[77]

74 Butcher, 'Cybersecurity Tech Basics' (n 62 above), 3–4.
75 *Ibid.*
76 *Ibid* 4.
77 *Ibid.*

(a) **Oracles**: these are trusted data sources that provide reference points for blockchain applications, such as pricing data for smart contracts. Oracles typically operate outside the blockchain's network consensus validation mechanisms.

(b) **Data reliability**: blockchain networks and participants must ensure that the data from external sources is reliable and trustworthy. Since oracles may be more vulnerable to tampering or malicious actions, hackers could compromise a blockchain's integrity by breaching an oracle or feeding it false information.

To mitigate these risks, blockchain participants need to monitor external data sources carefully and implement measures to verify the data's accuracy and authenticity. By doing so, they can strengthen the overall security and reliability of their blockchain applications.[78]

Blockchain cyber vulnerabilities

Code vulnerabilities

10.67 Like any computer system, blockchain applications are susceptible to coding errors that can introduce cyber risks. Unusual or novel functionalities in network protocols may increase the likelihood of potential vulnerabilities.[79] For example, the DAO hack in 2016 exploited a coding defect in the Ethereum blockchain's smart contracts, resulting in the theft of Ethereum tokens worth approximately $60 million necessitating a fork to remedy the error.[80]

Blockchain platform vulnerabilities

10.68 Blockchain applications often run on general-purpose operating systems and platforms, which are subject to known hardware and software vulnerabilities. Special-purpose blockchain platforms may also still depend on general-purpose hardware and software. Organisations should treat these environments as critical computing resources and follow standard cybersecurity practices, including identifying and managing known vulnerabilities.[81] Cryptocurrency organisations should prioritise robust cybersecurity measures to protect user data and funds including employing encryption, multi-factor authentication, and regular security audits to identify and address vulnerabilities.

78 *Ibid.*
79 *Ibid.*
80 David Z Morris, 'CoinDesk Turns 10: 2016 – How The DAO Hack Changed Ethereum and Crypto' (CoinDesk, 9 May 2023, updated 15 May 2023) www.coindesk.com/consensus-magazine/2023/05/09/coindesk-turns-10-how-the-dao-hack-changed-ethereum-and-crypto/ [accessed 9 October 2023].
81 Butcher, 'Cybersecurity Tech Basics' (n 62 above), 4.

End-user vulnerabilities

10.69 The edge of any blockchain, where users interact with the system, is a gateway for cyberattacks. Cryptocurrency thefts often involve exploiting vulnerabilities in connected systems rather than attacking the blockchain itself. Specific end-user vulnerabilities to address include:[82]

(a) **Private key management**: The integrity of blockchain networks depends on encryption algorithms, and most cyberattacks target stolen private keys rather than the blockchain itself. Users must understand and protect their private keys stored on their systems or other media.

(b) **Wallet controls**: Service providers, like digital wallet providers, offer key management services to minimise risks, but they depend on passwords, device authentication, or other user authentication controls that can be vulnerable if not handled with care. Cryptocurrency users must prioritise the security of their digital wallets, which store private keys needed to access and transfer funds. Implementing robust security measures, such as two-factor authentication, encryption, and hardware wallets, helps protect against unauthorised access and theft.[83]

(c) **Impersonation, phishing, malware, and other end-user attacks**: General end-user attacks can gather user credentials and infiltrate blockchain applications, especially damaging to private blockchains with less robust consensus mechanisms. Cryptocurrency users are vulnerable to phishing attempts and social engineering attacks, where fraudsters deceive individuals into disclosing sensitive information. Education and awareness campaigns are crucial to help users recognise and avoid such threats.[84] Malicious software can compromise cryptocurrency wallets and systems, leading to theft or ransom demands. Regular software updates, strong antivirus protection, and cautious browsing habits can help mitigate these risks.[85]

Further examples of cybersecurity risks in the cryptocurrency ecosystem are outlined in Chapter 8 (Types of Cryptocurrency Fraud and Theft).[86]

10.70 To enhance cybersecurity, organisations considering blockchain applications should be aware of these vulnerabilities and implement measures

82 *Ibid.*

83 Samantha Avotch, 'The Safest Crypto Wallet: What You Need to Know' (Coin Wallet, 1 September 2023) https://coin.space/the-safest-crypto-wallet-what-you-need-to-know/ [accessed 9 October 2023].

84 Cryptopedia, 'Common Social Engineering Techniques' (Gemini, 10 March 2022) www.gemini.com/cryptopedia/social-engineering-definition-attack-examples#section-quid-pro-quo-social-engineering-attack [accessed 9 October 2023].

85 National Cyber Security Centre, 'Guidance: Mitigating malware and ransomware attacks' (Version 3.0, 13 February 2020, reviewed 9 September 2021) www.ncsc.gov.uk/guidance/mitigating-malware-and-ransomware-attacks [accessed 9 October 2023].

86 See **8.2**.

to mitigate risks, including proper private key management, wallet controls, and protection against general end-user attacks.

10.71 Cryptocurrency transactions offer numerous benefits, but security remains a paramount concern. Participants in the cryptocurrency ecosystem should take proactive measures to protect their assets and stay informed about evolving security threats. Additionally, compliance with relevant laws and regulations is essential to ensure a secure and lawful experience when engaging in cryptocurrency transactions.

Regulatory oversight and compliance

10.72 The Financial Conduct Authority (FCA) in the UK plays a vital role in regulating cryptoasset-related activities, including data privacy and cybersecurity. Cryptoasset businesses operating in the UK must adhere to the FCA's requirements, such as AML and CTF regulations and cyber resilience standards.

10.73 The FCA has established key principles and rules related to cyber resilience, including:[87]

(a) **Principle 3**: firms must responsibly and effectively organise and control their affairs with adequate risk management systems.

(b) **Principle 11**: firms must cooperate openly with regulators and disclose relevant information promptly.

(c) **SYSC 3.1.1**: firms must establish and maintain appropriate systems and controls for their business.

(d) **SYSC 3.2.6**: firms must have effective systems and controls to comply with regulatory requirements and combat the risk of being used for financial crime.

(e) **SUP 15.3.1**: firms must immediately notify the FCA when they become aware of certain conditions, reputation risks, customer service disruptions, or potential threats to the financial system.

10.74 Regarding cyber events, the FCA emphasises reporting material cyber events, which:[88]

(a) results in significant loss of data;

(b) results in the unavailability or control of its IT systems;

87 Norton Rose Fullbright, 'Cybersecurity: Not just an IT issue, but a regulatory one too' (Publication, August 2020) www.nortonrosefulbright.com/en/knowledge/publications/b8178be8/cybersecurity-not-just-an-it-issue-but-a-regulatory-one-too [accessed 13 September 2023].

88 FCA, 'Operational Resilience' (17 May 2017, updated 10 February 2023 www.fca.org.uk/firms/operational-resilience [accessed 2 October 2023].

(c) impacts a large number of victims; and

(d) results in unauthorised access to its information and communication systems.

10.75 The Prudential Regulation Authority (PRA) has eight Fundamental Rules that are similar to the FCA's Principles for Businesses. In particular:[89]

(a) **Fundamental Rule 2**: a firm must conduct its business with due skill, care and diligence.

(b) **Fundamental Rule 5**: a firm must have effective risk strategies and risk management systems.

(c) **Fundamental Rule 6**: a firm must organise and control its affairs responsibly.

(d) **Fundamental Rule 7**: a firm must deal with its regulators in an open and cooperative way and must disclose to the PRA appropriately anything relating to the firm of which the PRA would reasonably expect notice.

10.76 In the cyber-resilience context, the Fundamental Rules are further supplemented by the risk control part of the PRA Rulebook. The BoE and PRA/FCA have created a framework for regulators to work with firms voluntarily using a simulated cyber attack called CBEST and a questionnaire, CQUEST, which consists of multiple-choice questions covering all aspects of cyber-resilience. The answers provide a snapshot of a firm's cyber-resilience capability and build adequate resilience capabilities to prepare for, and respond to, cyber events and incidents that could cause operational disruption. [90]

10.77 On 20 November 2022, the UK published a consultation setting out how it proposes to reform the Network and Information Systems Regulations 2018[91] (NIS Regulations) in order to address the security and resilience of important digital services in the UK.[92] This follows the EU's implementation of its NIS 2 Directive.[93]

10.78 The NIS Regulations were introduced in the UK in 2018 and had the effect of transposing the EU's Network and Information Security Directive[94] (NIS 1

89 Norton Rose Fullbright, 'Cybersecurity: Not just an IT issue' (n 87 above).

90 BoE, 'Operational resilience of the financial sector' www.bankofengland.co.uk/financial-stability/operational-resilience-of-the-financial-sector [accessed 2 October 2023].

91 SI 2018/506.

92 Department for Digital, Media, Culture and Sport, 'Proposal for legislation to improve the UK's cyber resilience' (Consultation Outcome, 30 November 2022) www.gov.uk/government/consultations/proposal-for-legislation-to-improve-the-uks-cyber-resilience/proposal-for-legislation-to-improve-the-uks-cyber-resilience [accessed 2 October 2023].

93 Council Directive (EU) 2022/2555 of 14 December 2022 on measures for a high common level of cybersecurity across the Union, amending Regulation (EU) No 910/2014 and Directive (EU) 2018/1972, and repealing Directive (EU) 2016/1148 (NIS 2 Directive) [2022] OJ L333/80.

94 Council Directive (EU) 2016/1148 of 6 July 2016 concerning measures for a high common level of security of network and information systems across the Union [2016] OJ L194/1.

Directive) into UK law. The NIS Regulations currently apply to organisations that provide 'essential services' (eg healthcare, energy and transportation) and digital service providers (such as online marketplaces and search engines)[95] and impose certain requirements on those organisations to ensure appropriate security measures to manage cybersecurity risks faced by their systems and certain reporting obligations in the case of security incidents.[96] The finance and banking sectors were excluded from the UK transposition of the NIS 1 Directive on the basis that they are already heavily regulated, with a strong focus on cyber security and therefore inclusion in the NIS Framework was not required.[97]

10.79 In a 2022 Review of Cyber Security Incentives and Regulation, the UK Government identified the growing threat of ransomware attacks due to increased digital reliance and interconnected supply chains.[98] The proposed reforms are part of the UK's National Cyber Strategy, which aims to enhance security across all sectors, especially those crucial to the economy, like managed service providers. To address these challenges, the government is taking a proactive approach. Reforms are divided into two pillars:[99]

(a) **Pillar I – expanding Digital Service Provider Regulations**

- (i) Expanding NIS Regulations' scope from 'digital service providers' to include 'managed service providers' offering IT outsourcing, security monitoring, and network management.
- (ii) Abandoning a two-tier regulatory system and opting for a flexible risk-based assessment approach, regulated by the Information Commissioner.

(b) **Pillar II – future-proofing NIS Regulations**:

- (i) Granting the government the power to update NIS Regulations through secondary legislation.
- (ii) Allowing the government to expand the regulations to include new sectors to address evolving cyber threats.
- (iii) Extending the scope to cover critical suppliers and services that essential and digital services rely on.

95 NIS Regulations, reg 8 and Sch 2. The thresholds for the digital infrastructure subsector are set out at Sch 2, reg 10.

96 NIS Regulations, regs 10 and 11.

97 Department for Digital, Culture, Media & Sport and Department for Science, Innovation & Technology, 'Second Post-Implementation Review of the Network and Information Systems Regulations 2018' (27 July 2022) www.gov.uk/government/publications/second-post-implementation-review-of-the-network-and-information-systems-regulations-2018/second-post-implementation-review-of-the-network-and-information-systems-regulations-2018 [accessed 2 October 2023].

98 *Ibid.*

99 Department for Digital, Media, Culture and Sport, Proposal for legislation to improve the UK's cyber resilience (n 92).

(iv) Expanding incident reporting requirements to cover incidents posing significant risks to security and resilience.

(v) Working on a fairer cost recovery system for NIS functions in consultation with regulators.

The government has indicated their policy approach will also consider options to avoid regulatory overburdening in relation to finance and banking which are already covered by legislation aimed at protecting networks and information systems. The government intends to proceed with these reforms in 2024, pending the identification of a suitable legislative vehicle.[100]

10.80 The EU has since further strengthened the digital operational resilience in EU financial sectors. While the NIS 1 Directive aimed to enhance cybersecurity resilience but applied only to specific financial entities in Member States, the EU Commission has decided to impose a common information and communication technology (ICT) and security risk management principles since EU financial legislation lacked explicit provisions in this regard. The DORA Regulation[101] and DORA Directive[102] entered into force on 16 January 2023 and will apply in Member States on 17 January 2025 (collectively 'DORA'). DORA is designed to consolidate and upgrade ICT risk requirements throughout the financial sector to ensure that all financial system participants comply with a common set of standards to mitigate ICT risks for their operations and ensure the smooth functioning of the internal market. It aims to bring legal clarity on the applicable ICT risk provisions (especially in the case of cross-border financial entities), reduce regulatory complexity and lower the financial and administrative burdens resulting from diverse rules that apply across the EU, and draw rules addressing ICT risk in finance together into one single regime.

10.81 DORA covers a broad range of financial entities, including credit institutions, payment institutions, investment funds and cryptoasset service providers,[103] to ensure that ICT risks are managed in a homogenous and coherent way. It requires in-scope financial entities to put in place:

(a) dedicated ICT risk management capabilities;[104]

100 Department for Digital, Culture, Media & Sport, 'Consultation Outcome: Proposal for legislation to improve the UK's cyber resilience' (Detail of Outcome, 19 January 2022, updated 30 November 2022) www.gov.uk/government/consultations/proposal-for-legislation-to-improve-the-uks-cyber-resilience [accessed 3 October 2023].

101 Council Regulation (EU) 2022/2554 of 14 December 2022 on digital operational resilience for the financial sector and amending Regulations (EC) No 1060/2009, (EU) No 648/2012, (EU) No 600/2014, (EU) No 909/2014 and (EU) 2016/1011 [2022] OJ L333/1.

102 Council Directive (EU) 2022/2556 of 14 December 2022 amending Directives 2009/65/EC, 2009/138/EC, 2011/61/EU, 2013/36/EU, 2014/59/EU, 2014/65/EU, (EU) 2015/2366 and (EU) 2016/2341 as regards digital operational resilience for the financial sector [2022] OJ L333/153.

103 DORA Regulation, Art 2(1).

104 DORA Regulation, Ch II.

(b) introduce processes for ICT-related incident management, classification and reporting;[105]

(c) carry out digital operational resilience testing;[106]

(d) manage ICT third-party risk;[107]

(e) introduces a new oversight framework for critical ICT third-party service providers that provide services to financial entities;[108] and

(f) share information between themselves.[109]

The NIS 2 Directive applies to certain financial entities such as credit institutions, financial venue operators and central counterparties.[110] However, to avoid any overlaps with DORA, it provides that DORA will be considered as *lex specialis*,[111] which means that DORA's more specific provisions will prevail over the NIS 2 Directive's more general provisions in the event of conflict.

10.82 In relation to the DORA regime, the PRA and FCA published a discussion paper entitled 'Operational resilience: Critical third parties to the UK financial sector' on 21 July 2022.[112] They note that the then current financial regulatory and supervisory framework has very limited tools to manage failure or disruption of certain third parties simultaneously impacted the provision of services to:

(a) one or more systemically significant firms or financial market infrastructures (FMIs); or

(b) multiple firms and FMIs.

The PRA and FCA therefore considered that additional legislative and regulatory measures were needed and welcomed the proposed critical third parties (CTPs) measures in the Financial Services and Markets Bill to allow the authorities to monitor and manage the risks. Section 18 of FSMA 2023 inserted a new s 312L into FSMA 2000 giving FCA, PRA and BoE powers to regulate designated CTPs, FMI entities and relevant services providers. FMI entities and relevant services providers include investment exchanges, electronic money institutions, authorised payment institutions and payment service providers.[113]

105 DORA Regulation, Ch III.
106 DORA Regulation, Ch IV.
107 DORA Regulation, Ch V.
108 DORA Regulation, Ch V, Section II.
109 DORA Regulation, Ch VI.
110 NIS 2 Directive, Annex I.
111 DORA Regulation, Recital 16.
112 (PRA Discussion Paper 3/22, FCA Discussion Paper 22/3, BoE, 21 July 2022) www.bankofengland.co.uk/prudential-regulation/publication/2022/july/operational-resilience-critical-third-parties-uk-financial-sector [accessed 3 October 2023].
113 FSMA 2023, s 18.

10.83 In terms of international regulators, the Committee on Payments and Market Infrastructures and the Board of IOSC have published their cyber-guidance identifying, describing and comparing the range of observed cyber-resilience practices across jurisdictions.[114] The FSB is also working on aspects of resilience and recovery.[115] It has published reports on cyber incident reporting,[116] effective practices for cyber incident response and recovery,[117] a cyber lexicon,[118] and a cyber stocktake on cybersecurity regulation, guidance and supervisory practice.[119] Supplementing this work, there are a number of best practice cyber-resilience frameworks available, including ISO27000 and the NIST framework.[120]

Incident response and data breach notification

10.84 Cryptocurrency businesses should develop comprehensive incident response plans to address cybersecurity incidents promptly and effectively. These plans outline the steps to be taken in the event of a data breach, including containment, investigation, and mitigation measures.

10.85 Under DPA 2018, cryptocurrency businesses must notify affected individuals and ICO in the event of a data breach that poses a risk to individuals' rights and freedoms.[121] They may also need to notify the FCA if they are a regulated firm.[122] Timely and transparent communication is essential to mitigate the potential impact on affected users.

10.86 It is worth nothing that when cyber-attacks do happen, firms can face exposure to numerous regulators. For example, where there has been a personal data breach the ICO may become involved. The FCA and ICO have a Memorandum of Understanding in place which includes provisions in relation

114 Committee on Payment Infrastructures and Board of the IOSC, 'Guidance on cyber resilience for financial market infrastructures' (BIS and IOSC, June 2016) www.bis.org/cpmi/publ/d146.pdf accessed 2 October 2023.

115 FSB, 'Cyber Resilience' FSB https://www.fsb.org/work-of-the-fsb/financial-innovation-and-structural-change/cyber-resilience/ [accessed 2 October 2023].

116 FSB, 'Cyber Incident Reporting: Existing Approaches and Next Steps for Broader Convergence' (19 October 2021) www.fsb.org/wp-content/uploads/P191021.pdf [accessed 2 October 2023].

117 FSB, 'Effective Practices for Cyber Incident Response and Recovery' (Final Report, 19 October 2020) www.fsb.org/wp-content/uploads/P191020-1.pdf [accessed 2 October 2023].

118 FSB, 'Cyber Lexicon' (12 November 2018, updated 13 April 2023) www.fsb.org/wp-content/uploads/P121118-1.pdf [accessed 2 October 2023].

119 FSB, 'Summary Report on Financial Sector Cybersecurity Regulations, Guidance and Supervisory Practices' (13 October 2017) www.fsb.org/wp-content/uploads/P131017-1.pdf [accessed 2 October 2023].

120 Norton Rose Fullbright, 'Cybersecurity: Not just an IT issue' (n 87 above).

121 ICO, 'UK GDPR data breach reporting (DPA 2018)' https://ico.org.uk/for-organisations/report-a-breach/personal-data-breach/ [accessed 13 September 2023].

122 FCA, Operational Resilience (n 86 above).

to the coordination of investigations.[123] Under the DPA 2018, fines are up to a maximum of £17.5 million or four per cent of a company's worldwide annual turnover, whichever is higher. The Financial Ombudsman Service has also taken on cases in relation to cyber incidents in the past.[124]

CONCLUSION

10.87 Data privacy and cybersecurity are critical considerations for the UK's cryptocurrency ecosystem. By adhering to robust data privacy regulations and standards, implementing strong cybersecurity measures, and promoting user education, the UK can foster a secure and trusted environment for cryptocurrency transactions while safeguarding individual rights.

123 Memorandum of Understanding between the Information Commissioner and the FCA dated 18 February 2019 https://ico.org.uk/media/about-the-ico/documents/2614342/financial-conduct-authority-ico-mou.pdf [accessed 13 September 2023].

124 Norton Rose Fullbright, 'Cybersecurity: Not just an IT issue' (n 87 above).

Part IV

Legal Landscape for Specific Cryptocurrencies, Tokens, Sectors, and Organisations

Chapter 11

Bitcoin

INTRODUCTION

11.1 Bitcoin, as the pioneering cryptocurrency, has gained significant popularity and adoption worldwide. It operates as the secure and immutable base layer for the cryptocurrency ecosystem and therefore is the token that market participants follow closely.[1]

REGULATORY FRAMEWORK

11.2 The Financial Conduct Authority (FCA) is the primary regulatory authority overseeing cryptocurrency-related activities in the UK. While Bitcoin itself is classed as an unregulated cryptoasset and not directly regulated by the FCA, certain activities involving Bitcoin, such as operating cryptocurrency exchanges, providing cryptocurrency-related financial services and financial promotions will fall under FCA's regulatory purview. Businesses operating Bitcoin wallets or providing services that involve the issuance, storage, or transfer of Bitcoin into fiat or e-money tokens will need to comply with relevant e-money regulations.

11.3 The UK has implemented anti-money laundering (AML) and counter-terrorist financing (CTF) regulations, requiring cryptocurrency businesses, including Bitcoin exchanges, to comply with strict customer identification and due diligence requirements to prevent money laundering and terrorist financing.[2]

LEGAL STATUS

11.4 Bitcoin is not considered legal tender in the UK, meaning it is not recognised as an official form of payment for debts and obligations. However, parties can agree to accept Bitcoin as a means of payment if they willingly enter into such an arrangement.[3] The legal categorisation of Bitcoin within the UK

1 Jeff Boortz, 'Bitcoin's Layered Design: The Key To Greater Utility' (13 September 2023) *Forbes* www.forbes.com/sites/digital-assets/2023/09/13/bitcoins-layered-design-the-key-to-greater-utility/ [accessed 9 October 2023].

2 See **3.2–3.39, 3.48–3.53**.

3 See **2.3**.

remains a topic of debate. The courts in the UK have recognised Bitcoin as property, granting it certain legal protections.[4]

11.5 Bitcoin transactions and contracts executed with Bitcoin as the underlying asset are generally considered legally binding in the UK, provided they meet the requirements for a valid contract, such as offer, acceptance, and consideration.[5]

TAXATION

11.6 In the UK, Bitcoin is subject to taxation. Profits generated from Bitcoin mining, trading, or investments may be subject to income tax, CGT or corporation tax, depending on the specific circumstances and the individual or business's tax status. Tax obligations arise when Bitcoin is converted into fiat currency or used to purchase goods and services.[6]

11.7 The sale of Bitcoin itself is exempt from VAT in the UK. However, VAT may apply to goods or services purchased using Bitcoin, based on the regular VAT rules applicable to those goods or services.[7]

CONSUMER PROTECTION AND INVESTOR SAFEGUARDS

11.8 The UK takes consumer protection seriously, and individuals engaging in fraudulent activities involving Bitcoin can be subject to criminal prosecution. Consumers should exercise caution and conduct due diligence when dealing with Bitcoin-related investments or offers that appear too good to be true.[8]

11.9 Consumers and small businesses who encounter disputes with Bitcoin-related FCA authorised financial services may have recourse to the Financial Ombudsman Service (FOS), which provides an avenue for resolving complaints and seeking compensation.[9]

INTERNATIONAL COOPERATION AND REGULATIONS

11.10 The UK actively participates in international discussions and collaborations to establish global standards and regulatory frameworks for cryptocurrencies, including Bitcoin. Cooperation with international counterparts

4 See **2.7–2.26**.
5 See **6.6-6.11**.
6 See **5.21–5.178**.
7 See **5.164–5.172**.
8 See **8.2**.
9 See **3.37**.

is ongoing to address cross-border challenges and promote consistent regulatory approaches.[10]

FUTURE DEVELOPMENTS AND CHALLENGES

11.11 The legal landscape surrounding Bitcoin and cryptocurrencies is continually evolving. The UK may introduce new regulations or refine existing ones to adapt to technological advancements and changing market dynamics.[11] Regulating Bitcoin poses challenges due to its decentralised nature, cross-border transactions, and the evolving nature of blockchain technology.

CONCLUSION

11.12 The legal landscape surrounding Bitcoin in the UK is evolving as authorities seek to strike a balance between regulation, consumer protection, and fostering innovation. Businesses and individuals involved in Bitcoin-related activities should stay informed about regulatory developments and ensure compliance with applicable laws to navigate the legal landscape effectively.

10 See **19.21–19.72**.
11 See **19.1–19.20**.

Chapter 12

Ethereum

INTRODUCTION

12.1 Ethereum, a prominent DLT platform, has gained significant attention for its smart contract capabilities and DApps. Ethereum is a public DLT platform that supports smart contracts. Smart contracts are computer protocols that automate the execution of contract terms. It operates on a decentralised virtual machine and uses a cryptocurrency called Ether (ETH).

12.2 It uses PoS validation. In terms of Ethereum, staking is the act of depositing 32 ETH to activate validator software. Validators are responsible for storing data, processing transactions, and adding new blocks to the blockchain. In return they earn new ETH in the process at a current rate of 3.9% APR.[1]

12.3 The Ethereum platform has proven extremely important in the innovations in the crypto ecosystem:

(a) The vast majority of all stablecoins are issued on it.[2]

(b) Many of the initial DeFi applications were built on Ethereum, and the majority of the ecosystem's total value remains concentrated there.[3]

(c) It is the dominant blockchain for DAO projects.[4]

(d) Approximately three quarters of all NFT transactions take place on it.[5]

REGULATORY FRAMEWORK

12.4 The Financial Conduct Authority (FCA) is the primary regulatory authority overseeing cryptocurrency-related activities in the UK. While Ethereum

1 Ethereum.org, 'Staking with Ethereum' https://ethereum.org/en/staking/ [accessed 3 October 2023].

2 James Beck and Tom Hay, 'DeFi Report: An analysis of Ethereum's decentralized finance ecosystem in Q4 2020.' (*Consensys Codefi*, 19 January 2021) https://f.hubspotusercontent10.net/hubfs/4795067/consensys-q4-defi-report.pdf [accessed 3 October 2023].

3 Cointelegraph, 'What is DeFi? A beginner's guide to decentralized finance' https://cointelegraph.com/learn/defi-a-comprehensive-guide-to-decentralized-finance [accessed 25 September 2023].

4 Brian Newar, 'Is Ethereum really the best blockchain to form a DAO?' (*Cointelegraph,* 4 April 2022) https://cointelegraph.com/news/is-ethereum-really-the-best-blockchain-to-form-a-dao [accessed 3 October 2023].

5 Leeor Shimron, 'Ethereum's Major Upgrade Creates Big Questions, Complications For NFTs' (*Forbes*, 17 September 2022) www.forbes.com/sites/leeorshimron/2022/09/17/ethereums-major-upgrade-creates-big-questions-complications-for-nfts/ accessed 3 October 2023.

itself is not directly regulated by the FCA, certain activities involving Ethereum, such as operating decentralised exchanges or offering financial services based on Ethereum, may fall under the FCA's regulatory purview. However, the issuance of tokens or digital assets on the Ethereum blockchain through ICOs or STOs may trigger regulations if they meet the legal definition of securities, e-money, payment services, or stablecoins.[6]

12.5 Ethereum's native cryptocurrency, Ether (ETH), is an unregulated token.

LEGAL STATUS

12.6 The UK acknowledges the significance and potential of blockchain technology, including the Ethereum blockchain. While no specific legislation addresses Ethereum, courts recognise the legality and enforceability of smart contracts executed on the Ethereum platform.[7]

12.7 Ethereum is not classified as legal tender, but it is generally considered property under UK law. Similar to Bitcoin, Ethereum benefits from certain legal protections as a recognised form of property.[8]

SMART CONTRACTS AND CONTRACTUAL IMPLICATIONS

12.8 Smart contracts executed on the Ethereum blockchain are generally considered legally binding, provided they meet the essential elements of a valid contract, such as offer, acceptance, and consideration. However, contractual disputes involving smart contracts may present unique challenges for traditional legal systems.

12.9 The interpretation of smart contracts and their enforceability may require legal expertise in both contract law and blockchain technology. Courts in the UK will need to develop a nuanced understanding of Ethereum's smart contract capabilities to resolve disputes effectively.[9]

TAXATION

12.10 Profits generated from Ethereum staking, trading, or investments may be subject to income tax, CGT, or corporation tax in the UK, depending on the specific circumstances and the individual or business's tax status. Tax obligations

6 See **3.2–3.53**.
7 See **6.1–6.23**.
8 See **2.3, 2.7–2.26**.
9 See **3.48–3.53, 6.1–6.23**.

arise when Ethereum is converted into fiat currency or used to purchase goods and services.[10]

12.11 The sale or exchange of Ethereum itself is generally exempt from VAT in the UK. However, VAT may apply to goods or services purchased using Ethereum, based on the regular VAT rules applicable to those goods or services.[11]

CONSUMER PROTECTION AND INVESTOR SAFEGUARDS

12.12 Consumers participating in Ethereum-related activities, such as ICOs or DApps, should exercise caution to avoid fraudulent schemes and scams. Regulators in the UK take consumer protection seriously, and individuals engaging in fraudulent activities involving Ethereum can be subject to criminal prosecution.[12]

12.13 The UK authorities, including the FCA, strive to ensure that Ethereum-based projects comply with relevant regulations and consumer protection measures.[13] Investors should conduct thorough due diligence before participating in Ethereum-related ventures.[14]

12.14 Consumers who encounter disputes with Ethereum-related FCA authorised financial services may have recourse to the Financial Ombudsman Service (FOS), which provides an avenue for resolving complaints and seeking compensation.[15]

INTERNATIONAL COOPERATION AND REGULATIONS

12.15 The UK actively participates in international discussions and collaborations to establish global standards and regulatory frameworks for blockchain technology and cryptocurrencies. Collaboration with international counterparts is crucial to address cross-border challenges and promote consistent regulatory approaches.[16]

FUTURE DEVELOPMENTS AND CHALLENGES

12.16 The legal landscape surrounding Ethereum and blockchain technology is continuously evolving. Regulators in the UK may introduce new regulations

10 See **5.21–5.178**.
11 See **5.164–5.172**.
12 See Chapter 8 'Cryptocurrency Theft and Fraud'.
13 See **3.40–3.47**.
14 See **8.2**.
15 See **3.37**.
16 See **19.31–19.80**.

or refine existing ones to adapt to technological advancements and changing market dynamics.[17] Regulating Ethereum platforms poses challenges due to its decentralised nature, cross-border transactions, and the evolving nature of blockchain technology requiring international coordination.[18]

12.17 The emergence of smart contracts on Ethereum introduces novel legal challenges, such as determining liability and resolving disputes within the context of self-executing code. The UK legal system may need to develop specialised expertise to address these unique challenges effectively.[19]

CONCLUSION

12.18 The legal landscape surrounding Ethereum in the UK is still developing, with regulatory frameworks and legal interpretations gradually evolving to accommodate the complexities of smart contracts. Stakeholders engaging in Ethereum-related activities should stay informed about regulatory developments and ensure compliance with applicable laws to navigate the legal landscape effectively.

17 See **19.1–19.20**.
18 See **19.21–19.72**.
19 See **6.1–6.23, 9.24–9.37**.

Chapter 13

Ripple

INTRODUCTION

13.1 Ripple, a digital payment protocol and cryptocurrency, has garnered attention for its potential to revolutionise cross-border payments. Launched in 2012, Ripple is a decentralised system that utilises XRP, a pre-minted cryptocurrency, issued through a distributed protocol. Unlike Bitcoin, Ripple does not rely on mining or computing power for transaction validation. Instead, changes to the ledger are agreed upon through a consensus process among computers connected to the Ripple protocol. The Ripple protocol is currency-agnostic, so that its distributed ledger can be used for carrying out payment in other digital currencies as well as fiat currency.[1]

13.2 In 2020 the SEC issued proceedings against Ripple Labs, inc., its Chief Executive Officer and Chief Operations Officer alleging that their ICO breached securities laws.[2] The SEC claimed that XRP constituted an 'investment contract' which is a type of security as defined by the Securities Act of 1933.[3] The relevant test for investment contract constituting a security is *SEC v W J Howey Co*, wherein the Supreme Court held that under the Securities Act, an investment contract is:

> '… a contract, transaction[,] or scheme whereby a person [(1)] invests his money [(2)] in a common enterprise and [(3)] is led to expect profits solely from the efforts of the promoter or a third party.'[4]

13.3 The Court found that reasonable investors, situated in the position of the institutional buyers, would have purchased XRP with the expectation that they would derive profits from Ripple's efforts.[5] However, sales to the public through exchanges were to be considered speculative investment. Whereas the institutional buyers reasonably expected that Ripple would use the capital it received from its sales to improve the XRP ecosystem and thereby increase the price of XRP, public investors through exchanges could not reasonably expect the

1 Benjamin Geva, 'Disintermediating electronic payments: digital cash and virtual currencies', (2016) 31(12) 661, 671–672.

2 *Securities and Exchange Commission v Ripple Labs, inc*, Case 1:20-cv-10832-AT-SN, 13 July 2023 www.nysd.uscourts.gov/sites/default/files/2023-07/SEC%20vs%20Ripple%207-13-23.pdf [accessed 10 September 2023].

3 15 USC § 77b(a)(1).

4 328 US at 298–99.

5 *SEC v Ripple* (n 2 above), 19.

same as they did not know the funds were going to Ripple Labs.[6] Distributions to employees as compensation and to third parties to develop applications also did not meet investment contract requirements.[7]

13.4 The SEC have indicated they will appeal the judgment.[8] Ripple Labs has recently applied for to be registered as a cryptoassets firm with the Financial Conduct Authority (FCA) on foot of this judgment.[9]

REGULATORY FRAMEWORK

13.5 The FCA serves as the primary regulatory authority overseeing cryptocurrency-related activities in the UK. While Ripple itself is not directly regulated by the FCA, certain activities involving Ripple, such as operating cryptocurrency exchanges or providing financial services based on Ripple, may fall under the FCA's regulatory purview.[10] The FCA has previously indicated that XRP has similar features to Ethereum.[11] Ripple Labs has recently applied for to be registered as a cryptoassets firm with the FCA which may bring clarification.[12]

Security regulations

13.6 The regulatory classification of Ripple's native cryptocurrency, XRP, has been a subject of debate in various jurisdictions, including the UK. In the UK, the legal status of XRP is yet to be definitively determined, and its classification as a security would subject it to additional regulations. In the US, the Courts have decided that Ripple is a security when sold to institutional investors but not when sold to retail investors.[13]

LEGAL STATUS

13.7 The UK recognises the significance of blockchain technology, including Ripple's payment protocol. While no specific legislation addresses Ripple, courts

6 *Ibid* 23.
7 *Ibid* 26.
8 Nikhilesh De, 'SEC Will Appeal XRP Ruling in Case Against Ripple' (*CoinDesk*, 9 August 2023, updated 10 August 2023) www.coindesk.com/policy/2023/08/09/sec-will-appeal-xrp-ruling-in-case-against-ripple-regulator-says/ [accessed 10 September 2023]
9 Ana Paula Pereira, 'Ripple applies for crypto license in the United Kingdom' (*Cointelegraph*, 22 July 2023) https://cointelegraph.com/news/ripple-applies-for-crypto-license-united-kingdom [accessed 10 September 2023].
10 See **3.2–3.53**.
11 FCA, 'Prohibiting the sale to retail clients of investment products that reference cryptoassets' (Consultation Paper, CP19/22, July 2019) [2.7] www.fca.org.uk/publication/consultation/cp19-22.pdf [accessed 10 September 2023].
12 Pereira, Ripple applies for crypto license (n 9 above).
13 *SEC v Ripple Labs, inc.*, (n 2 above).

in the UK generally recognise and enforce transactions executed on Ripple's blockchain.[14]

13.8 The legal status of XRP in the UK is currently uncertain. Regulators and courts will likely evaluate the characteristics of XRP to determine if it falls under existing regulatory frameworks, such as securities or e-money regulations.

TAXATION

13.9 Profits generated from Ripple-related activities, such as trading or investments, may be subject to income tax, CGT, and corporation tax in the UK, depending on the specific circumstances and the individual or business's tax status. Tax obligations arise when XRP is converted into fiat currency or used to purchase goods and services.[15]

13.10 The sale or exchange of XRP itself is generally exempt from VAT in the UK. However, VAT may apply to goods or services purchased using XRP, based on the regular VAT rules applicable to those goods or services.[16]

CONSUMER PROTECTION AND INVESTOR SAFEGUARDS

13.11 The UK authorities, including the FCA, are committed to ensuring that Ripple-based projects and services comply with relevant regulations and consumer protection measures. Regulators in the UK actively pursue individuals engaged in fraudulent activities involving crytocurrencies.[17] Investors should conduct thorough due diligence before engaging with Ripple-related ventures.[18]

13.12 Consumers who encounter disputes with Ripple-related authorised financial services may have recourse to the Financial Ombudsman Service (FOS), which provides an avenue for resolving complaints and seeking compensation.[19]

INTERNATIONAL COOPERATION AND REGULATIONS

13.13 The UK actively participates in international discussions and collaborations to establish global standards and regulatory frameworks for blockchain technology and cryptocurrencies. Cooperation with international

14 See **2.22–2.26, 6.1–6.23**.
15 See **5.21–5.178**.
16 See **5.164–5.172.**
17 See **3.2–3.53**.
18 See **8.2**.
19 See **3.37**.

counterparts is essential to address cross-border challenges and promote consistent regulatory approaches.[20]

FUTURE DEVELOPMENTS AND CHALLENGES

13.14 The legal landscape surrounding Ripple and cryptocurrencies, in general, is continuously evolving. Regulators in the UK may introduce new regulations or refine existing ones to adapt to technological advancements and changing market dynamics.[21]

13.15 The classification of XRP as a security, e-money or another regulated asset may have significant implications for its treatment and regulatory oversight. Clarity from regulators or legal rulings in the UK would provide more certainty to market participants.

CONCLUSION

13.16 The legal landscape surrounding Ripple in the UK is evolving as regulators strive to strike a balance between fostering innovation and protecting consumers and investors. Stakeholders engaging in Ripple-related activities should stay informed about regulatory developments and ensure compliance with applicable laws to navigate the legal landscape effectively.

20 See **19.21–19.72**.
21 See **19.1–19.20**.

Chapter 14

Stablecoins

INTRODUCTION

14.1 The Financial Stability Board (FSB) defines 'stablecoins' as 'cryptoasset that aims to maintain a stable value relative to a specified asset, or a pool or basket of assets.'[1] Stablecoins have emerged as a prominent category of cryptocurrencies designed to maintain a stable value by pegging them to a reserve asset, such as a fiat currency or a commodity. Early examples of stablecoins include Tether (2014), Circle Internet Financial, Inc.'s USD Coin or USDC (2018), JPM Coin (2019), MUFG Coin and Sbercoin (2020).[2]

14.2 The rise of stablecoins is closely connected to the expansion in cryptocurrency markets and creation of DeFi. Stablecoins serve as the fundamental 'currency' within the realm of DeFi, enabling the functioning of various associated services. DeFi's primary goal is to offer financial services without relying on centralised financial institutions, even though different levels of centralisation might still be present. This system operates on open and permissionless blockchains, where financial transactions occur automatically based on predefined conditions set by programmed smart contracts.[3]

14.3 Stability is a crucial aspect of stablecoins, and developers use various methods to achieve it. Centralised Stablecoins are issued and managed by a centralised entity issuing stablecoins in exchange for consideration equal to their trading value. The received consideration is then invested in low-volatility and highly liquid assets like fiat currencies, commodities, and government bonds, creating a reserve or collateral. This reserve aims to preserve the coin's value and fulfil redemption requests from holders.

14.4 Tether is a virtual cryptocurrency that represents a claim-check to fiat currency. It converts cash and bank money into digital currency, anchoring its value to national currencies like the US dollar, euro, and yen. Tether is considered

1 FSB, 'Assessment of Risks to Financial Stability from Crypto-assets' (February 2022), 25 www.fsb.org/wp-content/uploads/P160222.pdf [accessed 3 October 2023].

2 Christian Perez, 'Institutional adoption of disruptive technologies' (*Foreign Policy*, 12 October 2021) https://foreignpolicy.com/2021/10/12/future-of-money-cbdc-digital-currency-dlt-libra-diem-tether-stablecoins-finance-regulation/ [accessed 20 August 2023].

3 Parma Bains, Arif Ismail, Fabiana Melo, and Nobuyasu Sugimoto, 'Regulating the Crypto Ecosystem: The Case of Stablecoins and Arrangements' (FinTech Notes No 2022/008, September 2022) IMF, 12 www.imf.org/en/Publications/fintech-notes/Issues/2022/09/26/Regulating-the-Crypto-Ecosystem-The-Case-of-Stablecoins-and-Arrangements-523724 [accessed 3 October 2023].

a stable currency as it is fully backed by traditional currency held in reserves, maintaining a 1-to-1 ratio. Tether is widely integrated as a digital-to-fiat currency through exchanges and is accessible on the Bitcoin blockchain using the Omni Protocol, an open-source software facilitating the issuance and redemption of 'tethers'.[4] Tether provides daily published reserve holdings.[5] Tether has however faced criticism for providing 'attestations' rather than third party audits of its reserves.[6]

14.5 Algorithmic stablecoins monitor the coin's trading value and adjust the supply by releasing or withdrawing coins from the market to maintain price stability based on demand and supply. Terra (LUNA) and Ampleforth (AMPL) are examples of algorithmic stablecoins.

14.6 Another key distinction lies in the hosting of stablecoins on public or private blockchains. Public blockchains, such as Ethereum, make stablecoins widely accessible, while private blockchains like R3 limit access to permitted participants. Decentralised stablecoins operate on blockchain platforms and algorithms to maintain price stability without direct backing. DAI, a stablecoin on the Ethereum platform, falls under this category. Private blockchains may offer enhanced security and better regulatory compliance for managing financial crime risks, even though they might be less scalable.

14.7 Recently, stablecoins have gained public attention and regulatory scrutiny,[7] especially when some coins have 'de-pegged,' or broken their fixed value to fiat currencies, during periods of economic volatility.[8]

14.8 The primary characteristic of stablecoins is their value stability, and developers have employed different methods to achieve this goal. The wide-ranging 'stablecoin' definition suggests that stablecoins could be supported by various types of assets, such as the dollar, euro, gold, or a mix of currencies. For a stablecoin to hold its value and be redeemable at its intended rate, it must maintain a consistent value against the underlying asset. The success of

4 Benjamin Geva, 'Disintermediating electronic payments: digital cash and virtual currencies', (2016) 31(12) JIBLR 661, 672.

5 https://tether.to/en/transparency/#usdt [accessed 20 August 2023].

6 'Tether Pushes Back Timeline on Audit: Report' (*Blockworks*, 29 August 2022) https://blockworks.co/news/tether-pushes-back-timeline-on-audit-report [accessed 20 August 2023].

7 For example, Tether was required to pay a civil monetary penalty of $41 million and to cease and desist from any further violations of the Commodity Exchange Act (CEA) and CFTC regulations, see CFTC, 'CFTC Orders Tether and Bitfinex to Pay Fines Totaling $42.5 Million' (Release Number 8450-21, 15 October 2021) www.cftc.gov/PressRoom/PressReleases/8450-21 [accessed 3 October 2023]; Tether was also banned from carrying on activities in New York and agreed to pay a fine, see New York State Attorney General, 'Consumer Alert: Attorney General James Ends Virtual Currency Trading Platform Bitfinex's Illegal Activities in New York' (23 February 2021) https://ag.ny.gov/press-release/2021/attorney-general-james-ends-virtual-currency-trading-platform-bitfinexs-illegal [accessed 3 October 2023].

8 'USDT selling sets off alarm bells as Curve, Uniswap pools flooded with tethers' (*Blockworks*, 15 June 2023) https://blockworks.co/news/usdt-selloff-alarm-bells-tether [accessed 20 August 2023].

this relies on how well the methods to stabilise it work and whether the issuer of the stablecoin can meet redemption demands. Some stablecoins may be far from stable in operation. Therefore, the use of the term 'stablecoins' follows a common naming convention; it does not imply actual stability.[9] Stablecoins have evolved to address the volatility issues of traditional cryptocurrencies and have garnered attention from regulators due to their potential impact on the financial system.[10]

14.9 Stablecoins offer several potential benefits, including:

(a) direct transfers between end users using DLT systems, leading to faster and cheaper cross-border transfers;

(b) instant or near-instant execution of transfers between counterparties, reducing credit risk exposure;

(c) increased market liquidity, as stablecoins contribute to the monetary supply of fiat currencies; and

(d) enhanced financial inclusion through accessible public blockchains, providing banking-style services to those with limited access to traditional banking.

14.10 However, stablecoins also raise regulatory concerns:

(a) They create a monetary supply outside central bank control, potentially posing systemic risks to the global financial system.

(b) Choices of fiat currencies for collateralising stablecoins may impact the stability of reserve currencies.

(c) Stablecoins may be volatile compared to certain fiat currencies, exposing coinholders to currency fluctuations.

(d) Financial crime risks could be inadequately managed due to the anonymity of transactions on public blockchains.

(e) Some stablecoins may not be fully collateralised or may lack secure maintenance of collateral, leading to market confidence issues and difficulties in redeeming coins for their full value.

14.11 The rise of potentially widespread stablecoins, circulating beyond the traditional financial system and outside of central bank control, has led to various regulatory responses from international organisations, governments and central banks.[11]

9 Bains and others, 'Regulating the Crypto Ecosystem' (n 3 above), 10.

10 See **19.4**, **19.21–19.47**, **19.58–19.72**.

11 *Ibid*. See also President's Working Group on Financial Markets, 'Report on Stablecoins' (November 2021) US Department of the Treasury [accessed 3 October 2023].

14.12 In August 2022, the Digital FMI Consortium, a group of private-sector companies, said it plans to test cross-border payments and provide recommendations to the BOE using its own sterling-backed stablecoin, dSterling.[12]

REGULATORY FRAMEWORK

Financial Conduct Authority (FCA)

14.13 The FCA serves as the primary regulatory authority overseeing cryptocurrency-related activities in the UK. While stablecoins themselves are not directly regulated by the FCA, certain activities involving stablecoins, such as operating stablecoin exchanges or offering financial services based on stablecoins, fall under the FCA's regulatory purview and require authorisation.[13]

HM Treasury and the Bank of England

14.14 In March 2023, the BoE began work on developing its regulatory framework for stablecoins. FSMA 2023 provides powers for the BoE to regulate stablecoins used in systemic payment systems in the UK, this brings activities relating to cryptoassets within existing regulatory frameworks. Section 22 of, and Sch 6 to the FSMA 2023 extends the BoE's supervisory reach, under the Banking Act 2009, to payment systems using Digital Settlement Assets[14] and DSA service providers. FSMA 2023, s 23 grants HM Treasury very wide powers to effect regulation of payments which include DSAs. HM Treasury has indicated that it intends to bring 'systemic stablecoins' with the DSA regulatory regime.[15]

E-money Regulations

14.15 Depending on the design and features of stablecoins, they may be subject to e-money regulations in the UK. Stablecoins that meet the legal definition of

12 Oliver Knight, 'UK Group to Test Stablecoin Payments, Provide Data to Bank of England' (*CoinDesk*, 17 August 2022) /www.coindesk.com/business/2022/08/17/uk-group-to-test-stablecoin-payments-provide-data-to-bank-of-england/ [accessed 20 August 2022]. See also **18.22–18.31**.

13 See **3.2–3.53**.

14 FSMA 2023, Sch 6, para 4(4) amends the Banking Act 2009, s 182 inserting 4A to define 'digital settlement asset' as 'a digital representation of value or rights, whether or not cryptographically secured, that— (a) can be used for the settlement of payment obligations, (b) can be transferred, stored or traded electronically, and (c) uses technology supporting the recording or storage of data (which may include distributed ledger technology).'

15 HM Treasury, 'Payments Regulation and the Systemic Perimeter' (Consultation Paper, August 2023), [2.60] https://assets.publishing.service.gov.uk/government/uploads/system/uploads/attachment_data/file/1176540/Payments_Regulation_and_the_Systemic_Perimeter_-_Consultation_Response.pdf [accessed 3 October 2023].

e-money need to comply with relevant EMRs, including licensing requirements and consumer protection measures.[16] In the EU and UK, a stablecoin could be classified as e-money, a deposit, or even an investment instrument, based on the nature of its reserve or collateral and the rights of coinholders against the issuer or reserve. In the US, stablecoins might be treated as securities or deposits, and they may also fall under money transmission regimes. The applicability of a specific regime depends on the location of the issuer, intermediaries, or end users. Stablecoins may be subject to regulation in the US, EU, and UK, depending on their specific structures.

Payment Services Regulations

14.16 Stablecoins involved in payment activities may need to comply with the Payment Services Regulations 2017 (PSR 2017) and obtain relevant licences.[17]

Financial institutions

14.17 Banks and financial institutions engaging with stablecoins must consider regulatory obligations, risk management, and potential impacts on their operations.[18]

Securities and Investment Regulations

14.18 Depending on the specific features of a stablecoin, it could be classified as a security or investment product, triggering obligations under UK securities laws.[19]

AML/CTF Regulations and consumer protection

14.19 Stablecoin issuers and service providers are likely subject to consumer protection and AML regulations, ensuring customer due diligence and reporting suspicious transactions.[20]

LEGAL STATUS

14.20 Stablecoins in the UK do not have a specific legal classification. The legal treatment of stablecoins would depend on their characteristics, including

16 See **3.2–3.53**.
17 *Ibid.*
18 See **4.1-4.30**.
19 See **3.2-3.12**.
20 See **3.26-3.33**.

the pegging mechanism, governance, and underlying assets. Stablecoins may be subject to existing financial regulations, such as DSA, e-money, or payment service regulations, or require a bespoke regulatory framework.

TAXATION

14.21 Profits generated from stablecoin-related activities, such as trading or investments, may be subject to income tax or capital gains tax in the UK, depending on the specific circumstances and the individual or business's tax status. Tax obligations arise when stablecoins are converted into fiat currency or used for transactions.[21]

14.22 The treatment of stablecoins for VAT purposes depends on their specific use cases and the underlying goods or services involved. VAT may apply to goods or services purchased using stablecoins, based on the regular VAT rules applicable to those goods or services.[22]

CONSUMER PROTECTION AND INVESTOR SAFEGUARDS

14.23 The UK authorities, including the FCA, aim to ensure that stablecoin projects and services comply with relevant regulations and consumer protection measures. Clear disclosure of the stability mechanisms, reserve assets, and risk factors is essential to protect consumers and investors. Stablecoin issuers and operators must comply with consumer protection regulations to ensure transparency, fair practices, and safeguarding customer funds. Stablecoin issuers should provide comprehensive and accurate information about the reserve assets, governance mechanisms, and risks associated with their stablecoins.[23]

INTERNATIONAL COOPERATION AND STANDARDS

14.24 The UK actively participates in international discussions and collaborations to establish global standards and regulatory frameworks for stablecoins in order to address cross-border challenges and promote consistent regulatory approaches.[24]

14.25 As private sector initiatives unfold, central banks are compelled to respond swiftly to potential threats posed by certain stablecoins, especially those with substantial issuance. The global mobilisation of central banks underscores their commitment to counter potential challenges to their own

21 See **5.21–5.178**.
22 See **5.164–5.172**.
23 See **3.2–3.53**.
24 See **19.21–19.47**, **19.58–19.72**.

sovereign currencies. This collective action illustrates the determination of states and regions, like Europe, to address the ongoing digital transformation within the financial system and safeguard their respective monetary sovereignties. The prevention of oligopolies or systemic players in the realm of currency has become a prominent goal on central banks' agendas. Numerous instances illustrate this competition, including the Bank of England's digital pound, the Banque de France's experimentation, the European Central Bank's discussions about a digital euro, and similar initiatives in China (People's Bank of China's digital currency electronic payment), Sweden (Swedish Riksbank's e-krona), and Canada (Central Bank of Canada's CBDC contingency plan).[25]

The European Regulation for Markets in Crypto-assets (MiCA)[26]

14.26 MiCA entered into force on 29 June 2023 and has solidified the EU's stance in the global landscape of stablecoins. MiCA offers a stablecoin framework for the EU, although it does not encompass all stablecoins under a global definition. Instead, it establishes specific guidelines for e-money tokens and tokens linked to assets.

14.27 Briefly, e-money tokens are defined as cryptoassets meant for exchange, designed to maintain a stable value based on legal tender. Asset referenced tokens are defined as cryptoassets maintaining a stable value by referencing legal tender currencies, commodities, other cryptoassets, or combinations thereof.

14.28 The European Commission has focused on regulating stablecoin categories tied to other assets, distinguishing between e-money tokens and ARTs based on underlying assets and their diversity. MiCA, however, does not directly target stablecoins using alternative stabilisation methods, like algorithms, which will likely fall under other regulatory categories.[27]

CONCLUSION

14.29 The widespread use of stablecoins could potentially impact traditional monetary policy, as well as central banks' ability to manage currency supply and interest rates. The potential for market manipulation, particularly in the case of centralised or algorithmic stablecoins, raises concerns over market integrity and investor protection. Stablecoins often operate across borders, raising challenges related to jurisdiction, regulatory harmonisation, and international coordination. Collaboration among regulators globally is necessary to establish consistent regulatory standards.

25 See **1.18–1.21** and **18.1–18.41**.

26 Council Regulation (EU) 2023/1114 of 31 May 2023 on markets in crypto-assets, and amending Regulations (EU) No 1093/2010 and (EU) No 1095/2010 and Directives 2013/36/EU and (EU) 2019/1937 [2023] OJ L150/40.

27 For a more detailed overview of MiCA, see **19.36–19.55**.

14.30 The legal landscape surrounding stablecoins is continuously evolving, with regulators seeking to balance innovation, financial stability, and consumer protection. As the adoption of stablecoins continues to grow, the UK regulatory framework is likely to evolve to address the unique features and associated risks.

14.31 Stakeholders involved in stablecoin-related activities should stay informed about regulatory developments and ensure compliance with applicable laws to navigate the legal landscape effectively.

Chapter 15

Non-Fungible Tokens

INTRODUCTION

15.1 The Cambridge Dictionary defines an NFT as 'a unique unit of data (the only one existing of its type) that links to a particular piece of digital art, music, video etc and that can be bought and sold.' [1]

15.2 NFTs are unique cryptographic tokens that leverage blockchain technology, making them immutable. Unlike fungible tokens, such as identical coins, each NFT is distinct and cannot be exchanged for another identical token. NFTs can be bought and sold, and their ownership and authenticity are evidenced through blockchain. NFTs serve as unique and unalterable digital authenticity certificates of ownership for virtual or physical assets such as art, collectibles, and gaming.[2] They can also be linked to physical assets, such as paintings or property.

15.3 Although the underlying technology in NFT crypto tokens may be similar (utilising technical standards), the legal structures within each NFT can vary. Rights holders can utilise this flexibility to impose legal terms governing the use and subsequent sale of the NFT. For example, these terms may clarify copyright ownership, convey specific licence rights, or establish a royalty payment for each subsequent sale of the NFT.

REGULATORY FRAMEWORK

15.4 From a financial regulatory perspective in the UK, NFTs do not fall within the scope of financial services regulation as there is no standardised regulatory framework for them. However, certain NFTs that exhibit characteristics similar to security tokens or e-money tokens may fall under the regulatory perimeter of the FCA.[3]

1 Cambridge University Press, 'NFT' (Cambridge Advanced Learner's Dictionary & Thesaurus) https://dictionary.cambridge.org/dictionary/english/non-fungible-token [accessed 11 September 2023].

2 ITPO, 'PAN 2/23: The classification of non-fungible tokens (NFTs), virtual goods, and services provided in the metaverse' (Statutory guidance, 3 April 2023) www.gov.uk/government/publications/practice-amendment-notice-223/pan-223-the-classification-of-non-fungible-tokens-nfts-virtual-goods-and-services-provided-in-the-metaverse [accessed 11 September 2023].

3 See **3.2–3.53**.

15.5 Depending on their features, some NFTs may be classified as securities, triggering compliance with securities regulations and potentially requiring FCA registration and authorisation. NFTs classified as security tokens are subject to the RAO as a 'specified investment.' These tokens offer rights and obligations akin to specified investments like shares or debt instruments, including ownership rights or entitlement to future profits. They may also be considered transferable securities or other financial instruments under MiFID II.[4]

15.6 NFTs classified as e-money tokens are regulated under the EMRs. Certain activities related to e-money tokens may require authorisation from the FCA. An NFT is considered an e-money token if it meets the definition of 'e-money,' involving monetary value stored electronically, issued against received funds, used for payment transactions, accepted as a means of payment by third parties, and not excluded by the EMRs. Exclusions may apply in cases where monetary value is used in a limited way or for specific payment transactions from electronic communications network providers.[5]

15.7 The government has introduced legislation to bring qualifying cryptoassets into the scope of the UK's financial promotion regime as controlled investments under FSMA 2000, s 21; however, NFTs, being non-fungible, would not fall within the definition. NFTs could be a qualifying cryptocurrency if:

(a) they have fractionalisation features that would cause them to become fungible; or

(b) they possess financial product features covered by the Financial Promotions Order.

15.8 NFT marketplaces may be subject to the AML/CTF obligations and will need to register and be authorised by the FCA if they are offering exchange services or custodian wallet services as part of their business.[6]

LEGAL STATUS

15.9 On 27 June 2023, the Law Commission published its Final Report on Digital Assets,[7] proposing law reform to recognise and protect digital assets, including the creation of a new category of 'data objects.' These 'data objects', such as NFTs, would fall into a third category of intangible property which would have the attributes of:[8]

(a) composed of data represented in an electronic medium, including in the form of computer code, electronic, digital, or analogue signals;

4 *Ibid.*
5 *Ibid.*
6 See **3.26-3.33**.
7 Law Commission, 'Digital Assets: Final report' (Law Com No 412, 2023).
8 *Ibid* [2.57].

(b) existing independently of persons and exists independently of the legal system; and

(c) being rivalrous.

15.10 Judicial treatment of NFTs categorises them as property in line with other cryptoasset case law.[9]

SPECIFIC ISSUES

Minting, sale and distribution

15.11 Minting refers to creating an NFT by linking it to the underlying asset through a smart contract. The digital asset underlying the NFT is often stored separately off-chain, either on a private server or a decentralised storage system. After minting, NFTs can be sold on various online marketplaces, each with different rules and curation processes.[10] NFT's can also be airdropped to crypto wallets. The FCA has indicated that such airdrops are banned if they form part of a promotion to encourage investing in cryptoassets.[11]

Intellectual property implications

15.12 NFTs often involve the creation and distribution of digital content. Legal questions often arise regarding copyright ownership, licensing, and the extent to which NFTs transfer rights to the underlying digital content. Issues that arise include:[12]

(a) **Copyright ownership**: the sale of an NFT does not necessarily imply a transfer of copyright ownership of the underlying digital content. Creators and purchasers should understand the rights they hold in relation to the NFT and the digital asset.

(b) **Trademark and patent rights**: trade marks are signs used by companies to differentiate goods or services. In the UK, the system operates on a 'first-to-file' basis, and early filing is recommended, such as during NFT development. For NFTs linked to digital files, the appropriate Nice Class is class 9 virtual goods, including 'downloadable digital files authenticated by

9 *Ibid* [3.39]. See also *Osbourne v Ozone Networks Inc and others* [2022] EWHC 1021 (Comm).

10 Stuart D Levi, Eve-Christie Vermynck, Jonathan Stephenson and Alistair Ho, 'An NFT Journey: Merits and Misconceptions' (*PLC Magazine,* October 2022), 5 www.skadden.com/-/media/files/publications/2022/10/an_nft_journey_merits_and_misconceptions.pdf?rev=0d1a02f0cb8b4803 91afb25644285d08 [accessed 11 September 2023].

11 Camomile Shumba, 'Free Promotional NFTs, Crypto Airdrops Would Be Banned Under New UK Rules, Official Says' (*CoinDesk,* 9 June 2023) www.coindesk.com/policy/2023/06/09/free-promotional-nfts-crypto-airdrops-would-be-banned-under-new-uk-rules-official-says/ [accessed 4 October 2023].

12 Levi and others, 'An NFT Journey' (n 10 above), 3.

non-fungible tokens.'[13] Patent protection may apply to the manner in which NFTs are used if the process is new, inventive, and industrially applicable.

(c) **Licensing and terms of use**: creators often establish licensing terms for NFTs, specifying how purchasers can use and display the digital content. Ensuring clarity in licensing terms is crucial to avoid disputes.

(d) **Attribution and moral rights**: moral rights, a part of copyright, protect the author's non-economic interests in their work, like attribution and preventing derogatory treatment. They apply regardless of the author's ownership, except for specific exceptions, and last as long as economic rights. Creators and purchasers must be mindful of the legal implications of altering or misattributing the digital content.

(e) **Other issues**: NFTs might sometimes incorporate images or names of celebrities or public figures without permission. While the UK lacks specific image rights, protection may rely on various rights, including contractual rights, trade marks, goodwill, copyright, passing off, defamation, misuse of private information, breach of confidence, and trade mark infringement.

Ownership of the intellectual property rights

15.13 When creating an underlying asset for an NFT, it is crucial to determine the rights of the potential issuer to mint the NFT of that asset. The ownership of intellectual property rights (IPR) in the underlying asset of an NFT typically rests with the author of the work. When buying an NFT, the owner usually receives a licence to the underlying asset's IPRs rather than full ownership. The scope of these rights varies depending on the NFT project and may include personal use or the ability to commercialise and create derivative works. Some NFT projects may release the underlying asset into the public domain under a creative commons license.[14] For clarity, explicit licensing or assignment of IPRs is essential as overbidding for NFTs has occurred due to misunderstandings about the acquired IPRs.[15]

15.14 In cases where employees create IPR during their employment, the employer generally owns those rights. However, for consultants or contractors engaged to create deliverables, they retain ownership of the IPR they contribute. Therefore, when using works created by a consultant or contractor to mint NFTs, obtaining an assignment of those rights is crucial.

15.15 If the consultant or contractor does not wish to assign the IPR, a broad and irrevocable licence for the NFT project becomes essential, along with restrictions on using the work in other NFT projects.

13 ITPO, 'The classification of non-fungible tokens (NFTs)' (n 2 above).
14 See **7.52**.
15 Levi and others, 'An NFT Journey' (n 10 above), 6.

15.16 Without an assignment or licence, a company hiring a consultant may have only a narrow implied licence to use the IPR for the purposes envisioned at the agreement's effective date. For NFT contracts involving the creation of IPR, it is vital to include provisions that vest, assign, or license the IPR in the underlying asset to the contracting party.

15.17 IPR in the underlying asset may involve contributions from multiple parties, either as co-developers with distinct IP contributions or joint developers with indivisible contributions. Co-developers maintain ownership of their respective contributions, while joint developers jointly own the IPR in the underlying asset. To ensure clarity in ownership and usage of contributed or created IPR, and to allocate risks and responsibilities for protection and enforcement, co-development, or joint development agreements should be established.[16]

Services and distribution agreements

15.18 Many NFT issuers use third-party providers for the minting and issuance process. Agreements should define the roles of each party, grant licences to use the licensed IP, outline approval processes for derivative works and promotional materials, and specify fees and royalties. Cybersecurity and storage arrangements should also be addressed in these agreements.[17] Controversy has arisen in relation to the enforceability of artists' royalties and NFT marketplaces making them optional on secondary sales.[18]

Data privacy considerations

15.19 NFTs may be associated with assets containing personal data. Under data protection laws, wallet addressed and token identifiers can also be considered 'personal data' if they can be identified with an individual. Entities handling such data must ensure that they comply with applicable legal requirements.

15.20 When NFTs involve personal data, issuers should adopt a privacy by design or default approach, addressing data protection at every stage of the NFT project's lifecycle, and consider whether a DPIA is required before processing.[19]

16 *Ibid* 3–4.

17 *Ibid* 6.

18 Megan DeMatteo, 'Artists Weigh In on the Battle Over NFT Creator Royalties' (*CoinDesk*, 30 January 2023) www.coindesk.com/web3/2023/01/30/artists-weigh-in-on-the-battle-over-nft-creator-royalties/ [accessed 4 October 2023]; Sander Lutz, 'OpenSea Will Make Creator Royalties Optional for NFT Trades' (*Decrypt*, 18 August 2023) https://decrypt.co/152878/opensea-make-creator-royalties-optional-nft-trades [accessed 4 October 2023].

19 See **10.1–10.48**.

Remedies

15.21 As of now, UK case law has not produced a comprehensive position on remedies for infringement of NFTs. However, there are some noteworthy cases that provide precedents for obtaining injunctions, including Bankers Trust disclosure orders compelling marketplaces to disclose user identities.

15.22 In the case of *Osbourne v Ozone Networks Inc and others*,[20] the High Court recognised two stolen NFTs as legal property separate from the digital portraits they represented and granted an injunction to freeze the NFTs during the proceedings to prevent further dissipation. Additionally, it compelled Ozone Networks Inc to disclose the contact information of the individuals controlling the traced NFT wallets, known as a Bankers Trust disclosure order.

15.23 Similarly, in *Janesh s/o Rajkumar v Unknown Person*[21] the Singaporean High Court granted a worldwide proprietary injunction to freeze the sale and ownership of a Bored Ape Yacht Club NFT listed on OpenSea, in a dispute related to a commercial finance arrangement.

TAXATION

15.24 The UK lacks specific tax guidance for NFTs, but they are generally treated like chargeable assets. According to PWC, in the absence of guidance early trends are to treat NFT sales as a service (not goods), meaning electronically supplied services rules are likely to apply. There are currently no applicable VAT exemptions.[22]

15.25 Stamp duty may not apply unless the NFT is linked to marketable securities or similar assets.[23]

15.26 Those incorporating images into NFTs should be aware of potential tax implications in relation to the use of image rights. Income from image rights exploitation may be categorised as employment income if they are not transferred to a corporate vehicle.[24] HMRC have also outlined parameters for moving image rights into a special purpose vehicle or image rights company as part of a hive-down of assets to be taxed on profits other than under the employment code.[25] Given this interaction between HMRC and taxpayers, careful drafting

20 [2022] EWHC 1021 (Comm).
21 HC/OC 41/2022.
22 PWC, 'Non Fungible Tokens: Significant and Emerging VAT Issues' www.pwc.co.uk/services/tax/indirect-taxes/non-fungible-tokens-significant-and-emerging-vat-issues.html [accessed 4 October 2023].
23 See **5.73–5.76**.
24 Kevin Offer, Taxation of Image Rights (*Tax Journal*, 21 March 2018) www.taxjournal.com/articles/taxation-image-rights-21032018 [accessed 11 September 2023].
25 EIM00732.

and negotiation of image rights contracts in NFTs are crucial to avoid default employment taxation.

CONSUMER PROTECTION AND INVESTOR SAFEGUARDS

15.27 Given NFTs relatively low minting costs, concerns about fraudulent or misrepresented NFT sales raise issues of consumer protection laws and regulations. Unregulated individuals and business marketing NFTs to the public will have to comply with Advertising Standards Authority (ASA) standards. The ASA has indicated that NFTs fall within its definition of cryptoassets and must comply with their marketing standards.[26]

CONCLUSION

15.28 NFTs represent a novel intersection of technology and law, offering new possibilities for digital ownership and creativity. The legal implications surrounding NFTs span various areas, from intellectual property to regulatory compliance. As the NFT landscape matures, legal clarity and innovative solutions are likely to emerge contributing to a mature ecosystem.

26 ASA, 'Financial products and services: Cryptoassets' (3 October 2022) www.asa.org.uk/advice-online/financial-products-and-services-cryptoassets.html [accessed 4 October 2023]. For further detail see **3.38–3.39**.

Chapter 16

Decentralised finance

INTRODUCTION

16.1 DeFi is a movement that leverages distributed ledger technology (DLT) to recreate traditional financial services in a decentralised and permissionless manner. The system uses cryptoassets, DLT, and smart contracts to automate financial products and services like lending, exchanges, and derivatives. It aims to replace traditional finance systems with lower fees, faster transactions, and increased accessibility for people without banking access.

16.2 The Law Commission in its Final Report on Digital Assets defined DeFi as:[1]

> '… an alternative model, which has emerged as market participants increasingly use the technological capabilities of cryptotoken systems to create collateral facilities, businesses and platforms that differ from those typically used in conventional financial contexts. DeFi arrangements rely on the functionalities of crypto-token systems themselves to automate certain processes that mimic or replicate the substantive economic effect of collateralised loans. "DeFi" is a general term for automated or deterministic and purportedly decentralised and/or disintermediated applications which provide financial services (or similar functional results as traditional financial services) on a (generally decentralised and often blockchain-based) settlement layer, including payments, lending, trading, investments, insurance, and asset management.'

16.3 A decentralised exchange (DEX) is software that allows direct, peer-to-peer cryptocurrency transactions without involving a central authority. DeFi projects may also offer margin trading, crypto derivatives trading, and other financial activities. In practice, many DeFi platforms may be considered trading entities subject to corporation tax on their revenue profits. Some of these platforms are organised as decentralised automated organisations (DAOs), whose legal and tax status can be challenging to determine.

16.4 DeFi's popularity stems from its ability to facilitate borrower-lender interactions without the involvement of traditional financial institutions. The use of anonymous tokens can discourage direct lending to third parties due to enforcement challenges. Instead, lenders often prefer lending to DeFi platforms, which they perceive as lower risk.

1 Law Commission, 'Digital Assets: Final report' (Law Com No 412, 2023), [8.14(2)].

16.5 DeFi also allows for pooling of assets in liquidity pools, where holders of cryptoassets contribute tokens for making loans. This pooling reduces the lender's risk by distributing it among other lenders in the pool, and it is essential for staking to hold a larger amount of proof of stake (PoS) tokens for obtaining rewards.

16.6 Although DeFi aims to move away from official oversight, the UK Government and the Financial Conduct Authority (FCA) have introduced regulatory requirements.[2] The government plans to establish clear tax and regulatory treatment for cryptoassets.

CENTRALISED FINANCE

16.7 The Law Commission in its Final Report on Digital Assets defined centralised finance (CeFi) as including:[3]

> '... arrangements made between identifiable persons that directly manage the establishment of credit facilities, the creation and servicing of loans and/or the intermediated holding of collateral using conventional operational processes. These arrangements bear many similarities to those used currently by intermediaries in mainstream financial markets and by traditional credit institutions such as banks when extending loans secured by investment securities, bank account cash balances and real world assets. In crypto-token and cryptoasset markets, this form of lending is often referred to as "CeFi" or "Centralised Finance", highlighting the dependence of such facilities on traditional intermediaries as direct providers of credit and/or intermediated holding arrangements for the underlying collateral.'

16.8 Some cryptoasset holders prefer CeFi for lending and staking due to its simplicity and accessibility through centralised exchanges like Binance or Coinbase.

DEFI LENDING AND BORROWING

16.9 Lenders in DeFi platforms expect financial returns and potential growth in the value of lent cryptoassets. Borrowers seek access to cryptoassets for their own transactions. To manage the volatility in cryptoasset markets, platforms may require borrowers to provide collateral in the form of other cryptoassets.

16.10 Lenders receive liquidity provider tokens representing their interest in a token pool, which can be transferred back to the platform when the transaction ends. The amount received back may exceed the original loan amount, acting as a 'return'. HMRC does not consider the return received by the lender to be 'interest' because cryptoassets are not money. The return earned by the lender can be determined as the number of tokens received over the course of the loan in excess of the principal advanced.[4]

2 See **3.2–3.53**.
3 Law Commission, Digital Assets: Final report (n 1 above), [8.14(1)].
4 CRYPTO61130.

16.11 According to HMRC's guidance, in this context 'lending' involves transferring tokens to a borrower and the lender acquires a right to demand that the borrower transfers to the lender the control of an equivalent quantity of tokens at a time in the future to satisfy the loan.[5]

LIQUIDITY POOLS

16.12 Liquidity pools are essential components of the DeFi ecosystem, operating through smart contracts. To make loans, platforms need a pool of tokens provided by lenders (liquidity providers). The platform uses this pool to lend to borrowers or for staking purposes.

16.13 Liquidity providers receive tokens representing their contribution to the pool (liquidity provider tokens or LP tokens). These tokens act as receipts and can be withdrawn, allowing lenders to retrieve their lent tokens. At the end of the loan, lenders may exchange their LP tokens for tokens from the pool, potentially receiving more than they originally lent.

16.14 Lenders may also receive additional tokens as a return for their lending (liquidity mining). Alternatively, the platform may provide a non-fungible token (NFT) as evidence of the loan.[6]

16.15 The specific terms of arrangements may vary, including whether the token owner transfers beneficial ownership to the platform, which is crucial for tax analysis.

DEFI STAKING

16.16 Certain cryptoasset holders can earn passive income through PoS, where they are rewarded with additional tokens based on the tokens they hold. DeFi allows smaller investors to pool their holdings to earn income. This typically involves depositing cryptoassets with the DeFi platform, but it may not involve transfers of beneficial ownership.[7]

REGULATORY LANDSCAPE

16.17 The regulatory landscape for DeFi is evolving in response to the rapid growth and innovation in the sector. Particular concerns have been expressed regulators in the UK and internationally about DeFI's use of stablecoins.[8]

5 CRYPTO61120.
6 CRYPTO61130.
7 CRYPTO61120.
8 See **13.29–13.35**, **19.4**, **19.17–19.52**, and **19.58–19.72**.

16.18 DeFi firms that intend to or are currently carrying on a regulated activity involving cryptoassets as defined under FSMA 2023, s 69(4), such as operating an exchange or custodian wallet services, will need to register with the FCA and comply with the Financial Promotions Restrictions.[9]

SECURITY AND RISKS

16.19 Despite their benefits, smart contracts can be susceptible to vulnerabilities, leading to hacks, breaches, and financial losses.[10]

16.20 Smart contracts are a cornerstone of DeFi, executing predefined actions when specific conditions are met. However, legal enforceability of smart contracts, dispute resolution mechanisms, and the potential for coding errors raise significant legal challenges. User lack of experience and mistakes in dealing with their own funds can lead to irreversible mistakes.[11]

16.21 Decentralised platforms can still be targets for market manipulation, and the absence of regulation does not necessarily prevent malicious actors from exploiting DeFi protocols. In HM Treasury's Consultation and Call for Evidence of February 2023, 'Future financial services regulatory regime for cryptoassets', they set out a proposed regulatory regime to cover market abuse on crypto trading platforms which, pending feedback, is likely to become legislation in the future.[12]

16.22 The lack of privacy features in some DeFi applications raises concerns about data protection.[13]

TAXATION

16.23 HMRC's Cryptoassets Manual provides guidance on DeFi taxation but it primarily focuses on the position of lenders and borrowers in DeFi. Understanding the position of DeFi platforms will depend on the particularities of their operations which can be complex.[14]

CONCLUSION

16.24 DeFi finance holds immense potential to transform how financial services are accessed and managed. However, its rapid growth also presents a complex array of legal and regulatory challenges. Balancing innovation with legal compliance, investor protection, and risk mitigation is crucial to realising the full potential of DeFi while ensuring a safe financial landscape for all participants.

9 See **3.2–3.53**.

10 See **10.49–10.71**.

11 See **6.1–6.23**.

12 HM Treasury, 'Consultation and call for Evidence: Future financial services regulatory regime for cryptoassets' (February 2023), [9.16] Table 9A.

13 See **10.1–10.48**.

14 See **5.179–5.245**.

Chapter 17

Decentralised Autonomous Organisations

INTRODUCTION

17.1 A decentralised autonomous organisation (DAO) is a 'novel type of technology mediated structure or organisation of participants made up of several composite elements.'[1] DAOs represent a novel paradigm in governance and decision-making, enabled by blockchain technology. DAOs are organisations that operate based on pre-defined smart contracts and code, executing decisions through decentralised consensus mechanisms. They enable stakeholders to participate directly in decision-making, fund allocation, and project governance, often without a traditional hierarchical structure.

17.2 DAOs pose challenges in terms of definition and legal classification. On 16 November 2022, the Law Commission initiated a Call for Evidence to explore how DAOs can be classified and function under existing laws.[2]

17.3 One key aspect of DAOs is their lack of central authority, relying on collective governance and user-driven decisions through smart contracts. This enables diverse membership and asset management without traditional leadership. Some of the most successful DAOs use cases include:[3]

(a) cryptocurrency exchanges;

(b) metaverse platforms governed by DAOs;

(c) software development communities;

(d) NFT art collectives – collaborating on NFT drops; and

(e) decentralised investment funds, which enable anyone to buy a stake in Web3 and DeFi start-ups and initiatives.[4]

1 Law Commission, 'Digital Assets: Final report' (Law Com No 412, 2023), [1.22].

2 Law Commission, 'Call for evidence: Decentralised autonomous organisations (DAOs)' (November 2022) https://s3-eu-west-2.amazonaws.com/lawcom-prod-storage-11jsxou24uy7q/uploads/2022/11/DAOs-Call-for-Evidence-LC.pdf [accessed 5 October 2023].

3 EY Global, 'How to navigate tax and legal complexity associated with DAOs' (2 August 2023) www.ey.com/en_gl/tax/how-to-navigate-tax-and-legal-complexity-associated-with-daos [accessed 9 October 2023].

4 Decentralised investment funds allow token holders to vote on how capital is spread across projects supported by the fund.

17.4 From a tax perspective, understanding the nature of a DAO is crucial to determine the tax implications of owning and disposing of digital assets. For example, some DAOs may be considered partnerships under English law, resulting in transparency for tax purposes. However, various DAOs have distinct structures, leading to different tax regimes. Additionally, in a decentralised setup, multiple jurisdictions may seek to impose taxation. Certain jurisdictions have introduced laws granting legal status to DAOs, like the US states of Tennessee,[5] Vermont,[6] and Wyoming.[7] The Marshall Islands introduced specific legislation to allow DAOs to register as a non-profit limited liability companies.[8]

REGULATORY LANDSCAPE

Lack of legal personality

17.5 The decentralised nature of DAOs poses challenges in assigning legal liability and accountability to a non-physical entity. The legal structure of DAOs can vary widely. Some may incorporate legal forms such as partnerships or companies, while others emphasise operational decentralisation through technological solutions. The term 'DAO' does not imply a specific structure. DAOs operate based on voting and consensus mechanisms, but determining how to resolve disputes or enforce decisions can be complex in a decentralised environment. The absence of legal personhood for DAOs complicates issues of liability, as well as their ability to enter into legal contracts. The Law Commission in its Call for Evidence[9] indicated that DAOs could potentially use the following legal structures:[10]

(a) private companies limited by shares;

(b) private companies limited by guarantee;

(c) public companies limited by shares;

(d) unlimited companies;

(e) community interest companies;

5 Tennessee Public Chapter No 852/Senate Bill No 2854/House Bill No 264, https://publications.tnsosfiles.com/acts/112/pub/pc0852.pdf [accessed 11 September 2023].

6 Vermont, An Act relating to Blockchain Business Development, 2018, No 205, https://legislature.vermont.gov/bill/status/2018/S.269 [accessed 11 September 2023].

7 Wyoming Decentralized Autonomous Organization Supplement, SF0038, No 73, www.wyoleg.gov/Legislation/2021/SF0038 (amended in 2022 by Decentralized Autonomous Organizations – Amendments, SF0068, No 16, www.wyoleg.gov/Legislation/2022/SF0068) [accessed 11 September 2023].

8 Decentralized Autonomous Organizations Act 2022, BILL No:75ND2P.L.2022 – 50 https://rmicourts.org/wp-content/uploads/2022/12/PL-2022-50-Decentralized-Autonomous.pdf [accessed 12 September 2023].

9 Law Commission, Decentralised Autonomous Organisations (DAOs) (n 2 above).

10 *Ibid* [4.2]. See also [4.10]–[4.34].

(f) limited partnerships;

(g) private fund limited partnerships;

(h) limited liability partnerships;

(i) charitable incorporated organisations; and

(j) registered societies (co-operative societies and community benefit societies).

17.6 Issues arise for unincorporated DAOs in terms of legal liability as in a litigation dispute the members may end up being sued personally for the actions of the DAO. An unincorporated DAO would likely be treated as a general partnership under the Partnership Act 1890, s 45.[11] The partnership does not have separate legal identity in and of itself. The rights and liabilities of the partnership are in actuality the rights and liabilities of the partners either against third parties or each other. Actions can be brought by or against partners in the name of the partnership. A partner is both a principal and an agent of their co-partners. As a principle, a partner is personally liable to meet the debts and/or liabilities of the partnership, whether or not they can be met out of the partnership assets.[12] In situations where the DAO does not have a profit motive, it may instead be considered an unincorporated association.[13]

Securities regulation

17.7 Depending on the nature of activities and fundraising mechanisms, DAO tokens might be classified as securities, subjecting them to securities regulations. DAOs often issue their native tokens to members, similar to shares, representing ownership and voting rights. Members may acquire tokens in exchange for currency, and DAOs may hold assets, the value of which is shared among token holders.[14]

Financial Conduct Authority

17.8 DAOs' activities can conflict with financial promotions restrictions, the Regulated Activities Order, and anti-money laundering/counter-terrorism financing requirements, raising regulatory concerns. Generally, the applicable regime in the UK focuses on certain activities and certain types of cryptoasset. These regulations will require analysis by any DAO wishing to operate in the UK.[15]

11 *Ibid* [3.17]–[3.24].
12 *Ibid* at [3.20].
13 *Ibid* at [3.21].
14 See **3.2–3.53**.
15 *Ibid*.

LEGAL CHALLENGES AND OPPORTUNITIES

Challenges

Cross-border considerations

17.9 DAOs can operate globally with no legal formalisation and often with anonymous/pseudonymous members which raises questions about jurisdiction, international cooperation, and harmonisation of legal standards.

Privacy and data protection

17.10 DAOs interact with personal data, necessitating considerations of data protection laws and user privacy.[16]

Smart contract audits

17.11 Smart contract vulnerabilities can lead to unforeseen outcomes or unintended consequences, raising questions about accountability and liability. Regular audits of DAO smart contracts can help mitigate risks and ensure the accuracy and security of their operations.[17]

Opportunities

Clarity and classification

17.12 Regulatory agencies are grappling with how to classify and regulate DAOs, often seeking to encourage innovation while balancing investor protection. Establishing and robust legal framework may make the UK attractive to the international crypto industry as a hub.

Regulatory sandbox

17.13 The FCA has a regulatory sandbox to allow experimentation while ensuring regulatory compliance which should be considered by a DAO seeking to do business in the UK.[18]

Adaptation of existing laws

17.14 There is an opportunity for the UK to adapt the existing legal framework to facilitate and attract DAOs, although challenges in interpretation and

16 See **10.49–10.71**.
17 See **10.1–10.48**.
18 See **3.52–3.53**.

enforcement may arise. The Final Report from the Law Commission will enable the UK Government to consider DAO-specific legal amendments.

TAXATION

17.15 DAO taxation is dependent on the legal structure used for its operations. Identifying key taxable events in DAO's activities will be useful in identifying tax liability and choice of legal structure. These events can include:[19]

(a) **Initial token transfer**: commercial DAOs often start with tokens transferred from a traditional corporate entity.

(b) **Token sales**: a DAO may sell its native governance tokens to fund community development or hedge against volatility.

(c) **Income from activities**: depending on the DAO type, it may generate income from various activities like portfolio gains (investment DAOs), asset appreciation (collector DAOs), or income from staking.

(d) **Grant programmes**: some DAOs establish grant programmes to fund protocol infrastructure, which can affect tax liability.

17.16 Each situation requires individual analysis due to the complexity of DAO activities and tax implications.

CONCLUSION

17.17 As DAOs continue to evolve, legal frameworks will adapt to accommodate their unique features and challenges. Collaborative efforts between blockchain developers, legal experts, regulators, and stakeholders will play a pivotal role in shaping the legal landscape for DAOs. Stakeholders should therefore engage with the FCA's regulatory sandbox, particularly in relation to regulation, liability issues, and operational risks. A balanced approach that encourages innovation while safeguarding participants' rights and interests would contribute to a thriving DAO ecosystem.

19 EY Global, 'How to navigate tax and legal complexity associated with DAOs' (2 August 2023) www.ey.com/en_gl/tax/how-to-navigate-tax-and-legal-complexity-associated-with-daos [accessed 9 October 2023].

Chapter 18

Central Bank Digital Currency

INTRODUCTION

18.1 Central Bank Digital currencies (CBDCs) have emerged as a significant development in the world of finance, with potential implications for monetary policy, financial stability, and payment systems. CBDCs are digital cash issued by central banks, functioning as liabilities on their balance sheets like physical cash.[1]

18.2 Globally, the concept of CBDCs is gaining momentum: the BIS reports that 93 per cent of countries are engaged in some form of CBDC work, with almost a quarter of central banks piloting a retail CBDC.[2] Central banks globally have been coordinating projects to allow interoperability of CBDCs. The wholesale CBDC experiments were Projects Jura, Dunbar, mBridge and Mariana and one retail experiment known as Project Icebreaker.[3] The Federal Reserve and the European Central Bank (ECB) are considering the development of their own digital currencies. Countries like the Bahamas, China, Eastern Caribbean Currency Union, Jamaica, Nigeria have already introduced their own central bank digital currencies.[4]

18.3 On 19 April 2021, the Bank of England (BoE) and HM Treasury announced the establishment of a joint taskforce to explore the potential of introducing a UK CBDC, the digital pound, colloquially known as 'Britcoin'.[5] In February 2023 the BOE and HM Treasury issued a consultation paper.[6] They are currently targeting 2025 for the launch of pilot tests.[7] Unlike cryptocurrencies, this digital currency would be issued by the BoE and coexist with physical cash

1 BIS, 'III. CBDCs: an opportunity for the monetary system' (BIS Annual Economic Report, 23 June 2021), 65 www.bis.org/publ/arpdf/ar2021e3.htm [accessed 12 September 2023].

2 BIS Innovation Hub, 'Lessons learnt on CBDCs Report submitted to the G20 Finance Ministers and Central Bank Governors' (July 2023), 12 www.bis.org/publ/othp73.pdf [accessed 19 August 2023].

3 *Ibid* 16–21 and 25–30.

4 See **1.18–1.21**.

5 BoE, 'Bank of England statement on Central Bank Digital Currency' (19 April 2021) www.bankofengland.co.uk/news/2021/april/bank-of-england-statement-on-central-bank-digital-currency [accessed 5 October 2023].

6 BoE and HM Treasury, 'The digital pound: a new form of money for households and businesses?' (Consultation Paper, February 2022) www.bankofengland.co.uk/-/media/boe/files/paper/2023/the-digital-pound-consultation-working-paper.pdf [accessed 19 August 2023].

7 *Ibid* 17.

and bank deposits instead of replacing them.[8] As a result, HMRC would likely treat this digital currency as a form of fiat currency for tax purposes.

18.4 The introduction of CBDCs would reshape the digital payments landscape and influence the adoption and usage of other cryptocurrencies. States are considering implementing CBDCs for several reasons:[9]

(a) **Payment system resilience**: faster, more secure, and more efficient transfer of funds compared to traditional fiat currency.

(b) **Quicker cross-border payments**: with CBDCs, money can be transferred globally in minutes, without the need for intermediaries like banks, and with minimal fees. CBDCs not only digitise money but also incorporate identification features, allowing national central banks to rely on common data standards and digital identification infrastructure. This is expected to facilitate faster and smoother cross-border transfers and assist in combating money laundering by enabling transaction tracing. While CBDCs share similarities with cryptocurrencies, they differ in terms of issuance, transaction verification, and valuation methods.[10]

(c) **Financial inclusion**: CBDCs will not require an individual to hold a bank account. For instance, private sector payment interface providers (PIPs) in the digital pound ecosystem would be able to provide innovative services in retail payments to end users.[11]

(d) **Direct transmission of monetary policy**: improved efficiency in monetary policy changes and enhancing the central banks' responsiveness to economic challenges. transmit monetary policy changes, such as adjustments to the central bank base rate, more directly to consumers and businesses, enabling better responses to economic challenges.

18.5 Central banks launching CBDCs have various policy objectives, as identified by the International Monetary Fund (IMF) research. Some aim to address underdeveloped financial or payment systems, with substantial activity in foreign currencies instead of the national currency, or to improve access to banking services for a significant portion of the population.[12]

8 For more information see, BoE, 'The digital pound' www.bankofengland.co.uk/the-digital-pound [accessed 5 October 2023].

9 BoE and HM Treasury, The digital pound (n 6 above), 24–25.

10 Santiago E Rodriguez Senior, 'May central bank digital currencies become a tool for hostile states to avoid investor-state arbitration?' (2019) 85(1) Arbitration 24, 27.

11 BoE and HM Treasury, The digital pound (n 6 above), 7–12.

12 IMF, 'How Should Central Banks Explore Central Bank Digital Currency?' (Fintech Notes, No 2023/008, 8 September 2023), 8–12 www.imf.org/en/Publications/fintech-notes/Issues/2023/09/08/How-Should-Central-Banks-Explore-Central-Bank-Digital-Currency-538504 [accessed 12 September 2023].

18.6 The World Bank has reported that approximately 1.7 billion individuals are unbanked, meaning they lack participation in the traditional banking system.[13] In the UK, it is approximately 1.2 million people.[14] CBDCs are expected to offer access to government-backed payment systems, even for those without bank accounts, as long as they have a mobile phone and internet access.

18.7 CBDCs may also give rise to other challenges. One notable concern is that CBDCs held directly on a central bank ledger could reduce funds held as bank deposits. This shift from bank deposits might be more significant if central banks offer interest or other returns on CBDCs, potentially leading banks to seek alternative sources of funding, with potential market impacts.[15]

18.8 Introducing CBDCs also raises various issues related to different areas of law, including tax law, property law, contract law, payment systems and settlement finality law, bankruptcy law, privacy and data privacy law, and international law. CBDC issuance is a potentially contentious central bank activity, and concerns have been expressed regarding the following:

(a) **Data collection and privacy concerns**: as CBDCs would require national governments to manage and secure vast amounts of personal data, as well as potentially providing a governmental window into individual spending habits, breaching privacy.[16]

(c) **Lack of scrutiny**: CBDCs increase in central bank power without sufficient scrutiny.[17]

(d) **Politicisation of the monetary system**: CBDCs being used as a mechanism to control, incentivise, or de-incentivise certain public spending behaviours.[18]

(e) **Financial instability**: During times of economic stress depositors may convert bank deposits to CBDC causing financial instability during periods of economic stress.[19]

13 Asli Demirgüç-Kunt, Leora Klapper, Dorothe Singer, Saniya Ansar, Jake Hess, 'The Global Findex Database 2017, Measuring Financial Inclusion and the Fintech Revolution' (Washington DC, 2018) World Bank 5 https://documents1.worldbank.org/curated/en/332881525873182837/pdf/126033-PUB-PUBLIC-pubdate-4-19-2018.pdf [accessed 12 September 2024].

14 BoE and HM Treasury, The digital pound (n 6 above), 10.

15 BIS, Lessons learnt on CBDCs (n 2 above), 12.

16 James Goddard, 'Central bank digital currencies: Lords Economic Affairs Committee report' (30 January 2023) House of Lords Library https://lordslibrary.parliament.uk/central-bank-digital-currencies-lords-economic-affairs-committee-report/ [accessed 12 September 2023].

17 *Ibid.*

18 Office of Governor Ron DeSantis, 'Governor Ron DeSantis Announces Legislation to Protect Floridians from a Federally Controlled Central Bank Digital Currency and Surveillance State' (20 March 2023) www.flgov.com/2023/03/20/governor-ron-desantis-announces-legislation-to-protect-floridians-from-a-federally-controlled-central-bank-digital-currency-and-surveillance-state/ [accessed 13 September 2023].

19 Goddard, Lords Economic Affairs Committee report (n 16 above).

(f) **Interoperability** interoperability of CBDCs with existing payment systems and the establishment of common standards pose significant technical challenges between various central banks.[20]

(g) **Cybersecurity Risks**: The digitised nature of the CBDC means that it could be a single point of failure for a cyber-attack,[21] and also the serious risk of a malfunction. For instance, in January 2022, the Eastern Caribbean CBDC DCash went offline for two months because of technological issues.[22]

18.9 The US state of Florida has banned the use of CBDCs in the jurisdiction citing concerns in relation to privacy, lack of scrutiny, and politicisation of the monetary system.[23]

18.10 While BIS suggests CBDC's would be present the possibility of a '*clean slate*' for central banks allowing them to unburden from legacy arrangements,[24] due to many design features being undecided and global cooperation lacking, the introduction of CBDCs has proven complicated.

UNDERSTANDING CBDCS

18.11 CBDCs will be issued by central banks or government agencies to regulate inflation. They will likely be pre-mined and centrally created but decentralised in their use. CBDCs may incorporate ledgers and blockchain technology, enabling governments to track their usage.[25] Users may create accounts through government agencies or use mobile applications with minimal requirements. CBDCs will validate transactions themselves, preventing double-spending. Central banks may collaborate with banks or exchanges for trading CBDCs. Their price will be pegged to the country's fiat currency or another stable currency/commodity. CBDCs can serve as an opportunity for developing countries to stabilise their economies or peg their value to trusted assets. CBDCs may operate as tokens on existing blockchain platforms like Ethereum, utilising smart contracts for automatic execution. Weaker economies may peg their CBDCs to foreign currencies or commodities to maintain stability.[26]

20 BIS, IMF and World Bank, 'International Report on CBDC Interoperability' (BIS, July 2022), 12 www.bis.org/publ/othp52.pdf [accessed 20 August 2023].

21 Goddard, Lords Economic Affairs Committee report (n 16 above).

22 Jim Wyss,, 'A Bold Caribbean Experiment in E-Cash Hits a Major Obstacle' (Bloomberg, 21 February 2022) www.bloomberg.com/news/articles/2022-02-21/eastern-caribbean-dcash-outage-is-test-for-central-bank-digital-currencies [accessed 20 November 2023].

23 An act relating to central bank digital currency, CHAPTER 2023-80 Senate Bill No 7054 https://laws.flrules.org/2023/80 [accessed 13 September 2023]. See also n 18 above.

24 BIS, 'CBDCs: an opportunity for the monetary system' (n 1 above), 87.

25 Rodriguez Senior, 'May central bank digital currencies become a tool for hostile states to avoid investor-state arbitration? (n 10 above), 27.

26 *Ibid* 28.

18.12 The characteristics and operational aspects of CBDCs vary across proposals. For instance, the BoE intends its CBDC to differ from cryptocurrencies based on distributed DLT, while Sweden's E-krona digital currency is based on DLT. Decisions on developing and hosting the core technology for a specific CBDC system, whether by a central bank or third parties, remain uncertain. Some central banks, like the BoE, may involve third parties to offer additional services on top of the CBDC platform, such as digital wallets or AML services.

18.13 An alternative proposal is the synthetic CBDC, issued by a private entity, backed by a reserve of fiat currency deposited with a central bank, and representing a contractual claim on that party. This type of instrument combines the characteristics of stablecoins and CBDCs, providing a higher level of assurance in maintaining the reserve safely. Providing that the regulatory framework ensures that these firms' liabilities were always fully backed by funds at the central bank, these liabilities could share many of the characteristics of a CBDC that is directly issued by the central bank. However, these liabilities would not be central bank money, as holders would not hold a direct claim on the central bank.[27]

18.14 Another distinction is between wholesale and retail CBDCs. Wholesale CBDCs (wCBDC) are used for settlement between financial institutions, while retail CBDCs (rCBDC) are issued to the general public for use in everyday transactions.

18.15 When creating a wholesale wCBDC, central banks must determine whether and how foreign payment service providers (PSPs) can utilise the system. The options are as follows:[28]

(a) **Closed access** – only domestic PSPs can access and use the wCBDC. Central banks issue and redeem wCBDCs to/from participants using their traditional settlement accounts or collateral. Foreign PSPs are not directly involved in the system but could use the wCBDC in cross-border scenarios through interoperability arrangements.

(b) **Indirect access** – foreign PSPs access the wCBDC through intermediaries. They might rely on a domestic participant for payment instructions, clearing, and settlement. Alternatively, foreign PSPs could hold wCBDCs directly and submit transactions while relying on a domestic participant for onboarding and possibly transaction processing. (eg Project Dunbar Phase I).

(c) **Direct access** – foreign PSPs can directly hold and transact wCBDCs issued by a central bank without intermediaries. They need to meet certain

27 BoE, 'Discussion Paper Central Bank Digital Currency Opportunities, challenges and design' (March 2020), 31, Box 3 www.bankofengland.co.uk/-/media/boe/files/paper/2020/central-bank-digital-currency-opportunities-challenges-and-design.pdf [accessed 12 September 2023].

28 BIS, IMF and World Bank, International Report on CBDC Interoperability (n 20 above), 12.

access criteria, and central banks would rely on home supervisors' oversight for these entities. (eg Helvetia Phase II, mBridge, Jura projects).

18.16 These options impact how foreign PSPs can interact with the wCBDC system and determine the degree of involvement and reliance on intermediaries or direct central bank access.

18.17 Access to non-residents and the role of PSPs in relation to rCBDC involves two key questions:

(a) **Who can hold and transfer rCBDCs and under what terms?**

Options range from allowing access to tourists and business travellers to broader inclusion of refugees, foreign entrepreneurs, resident branches of foreign companies, and expatriates for remittances and cross-border transfers. The terms for holding and using rCBDCs could be controlled through limits or fees.

(b) **How can non-residents access rCBDCs?**

Non-residents need the means to open and maintain rCBDC accounts either when visiting the issuing country or abroad. This requires an ecosystem where non-residents can acquire rCBDCs through transfers or currency exchange. The setup could be directly managed by the central bank (one-tier model) or facilitated by private sector intermediaries (two-tier model). The choice between these architectures affects various criteria and implementation complexities.

18.18 In scenarios where non-residents cannot hold rCBDCs, they might transact using intermediaries that possess rCBDC access, creating a claim on the intermediary rather than the central bank. Alternatively, interconnected CBDC systems could enable cross-system payments through intermediary PSPs performing CBDC conversions. Similar to wholesale CBDC access models, foreign PSPs could access rCBDC indirectly or directly.[29]

18.19 The introduction of a CBDC does not necessarily mean the exclusion or decline of other cryptocurrencies. Both CBDCs and cryptocurrencies may coexist, serving different purposes and meeting diverse user preferences.

18.20 Before enhancing money and payment services, several critical aspects must be addressed:[30]

(a) Legal considerations surrounding the authority of central banks to issue a CBDC and establish its status as legal tender.

29 *Ibid* 13–14.

30 Dr Matthew Barnes, 'Central bank digital currency: what is it and why now?' (2021) 36(9) JIBLR 390, 394.

(b) Measures need to be implemented to combat anti-money laundering/counter-terrorism financing (AML/CTF). The current technology behind cryptocurrencies allows for anonymity, which poses concerns regarding potential criminal activities. It has been indicated that large CBDC transfers would be require monitoring and reporting.

(c) Ensuring cybersecurity is paramount, especially given the challenges associated with managing it in the context of a mainstream CBDC. Threats like cyber-attacks, fraud, and electronic money transfers have posed issues for years and must be addressed comprehensively.

(d) The foundational technology supporting the evolution of money and payment services requires development, as the existing infrastructure is outdated and needs alignment with the digital era. Although distributed ledger technology (DLT) and its positive aspects enable the operation of digital currencies, thorough testing within the formal sphere of central banks remains essential. Enabling smooth cross-border transactions, regardless of the chosen payment method, hinges on the interoperability between CBDC systems and non-CBDC systems like fast payment systems or real-time gross settlement systems. For instance, in the case of wCBDC systems, connections might be established with non-CBDC systems in various jurisdictions to facilitate cross-border transfers. wCBDC systems could also serve as settlement platforms for local retail payment systems linked to them. Additionally, situations may arise where a payer aims to use a CBDC to send funds to a country without its own CBDC.[31]

18.21 The IMF have indicated that they intend to publish a CBDC Handbook in stages beginning in 2023.[32]

THE DIGITAL POUND

Functionality of the digital pound

18.22 The BoE has specific objectives for CBDCs, which include:[33]

(a) enhancing payment system resilience;

(b) mitigating the risks associated with private money creation;

(c) supporting competition, efficiency and innovation in payments;

31 BIS, IMF and World Bank, International Report on CBDC Interoperability (n 20 above), 18.

32 IMF, 'IMF approach to Central Bank Digital Currency Capacity Development' (Policy Paper No 2023/016, 11 April 2023), [19], [27]–[50] www.imf.org/en/Publications/Policy-Papers/Issues/2023/04/12/IMF-Approach-to-Central-Bank-Digital-Currency-Capacity-Development-532177 [accessed 19 August 2023].

33 Bank of England, Discussion Paper Central Bank Digital Currency Opportunities, challenges and design (March 2020), at [2.1] www.bankofengland.co.uk/-/media/boe/files/paper/2020/central-bank-digital-currency-opportunities-challenges-and-design.pdf [accessed 12 September 2023].

(d) meeting future payment needs in the digital economy;

(e) improving the availability and usability of central bank money;

(f) dealing with the decline in cash usage; and

(g) enabling better cross-border payments systems.

18.23 The primary focus pertains to the retail sector and the digital pound's applicability for households and businesses, as opposed to the wholesale sector. The BoE would issue the digital pound, backed by a direct claim on the BoE and supported by the central infrastructure, including the 'core ledger,' designed and operated by the BoE.[34]

18.24 The core ledger would hold the digital pounds of individual members of the public. Instead of directly interacting with the BoE, the public would engage indirectly through regulated private entities known as payment interface providers (PIPs) and external service interface providers (ESIPs). PIPs would provide 'pass-through wallets' to enable to them to access their digital pounds. ESIPs might provide non-payment, value-add services, such as business analytics, budgeting tools and fraud monitoring.[35] These wallets simply convey user instructions to the central core ledger, enabling actions like bill payments. PIPs and ESIPs manage 'user-facing interactions' through application programming interfaces (APIs) designed to facilitate user access to the digital pound. This layer accommodates external parties in developing innovative services for end users.[36] Depending on controls and user permissions, ESIPs might gain 'read' access to specific data on the digital pound ledger in order to provider services.[37] This aspect is in a preliminary stage, with the Bank completing the first phase of Project Rosalind at the BIS Innovation Hub London Centre.[38] Details of the second phase are pending.

Payment interface providers

18.25 Due to the financial risk-free nature of the digital pound and the fact that wallets do not hold user funds, extensive regulation for PIPs is not required.[39] As the digital pound eliminates market, credit, and liquidity risks, customers should be able to register on the digital pound ledger, open wallets, make payments, convert digital pounds to cash, view activity, and switch between wallets or close them.[40] While the BoE manages the payment system, it does not access personal data, but rather anonymised transaction data and aggregated system-wide data.[41]

34 BoE and HM Treasury, The digital pound (n 6 above), 11.
35 *Ibid* 14–16.
36 *Ibid* 53.
37 *Ibid* 56.
38 BIS Innovation Hub and BOE, 'Project Rosalind: Building API prototypes for retail CBDC ecosystem innovation' (16 June 2023) www.bis.org/publ/othp69.pdf [accessed 5 October 2023].
39 BoE and HM Treasury, The digital pound (n 6 above), 55.
40 *Ibid* 56.
41 *Ibid* 53.

18.26 The consultation does not specify the number or nature of PIPs. They could encompass existing banks, non-banking institutions, charities, or even civil society groups providing wallet services to vulnerable groups. Both PIPs and ESIPs must undergo robust regulation to ensure operational resilience, continuity, and customer protection, with regulatory measures aligned with their activities and proportional to the risks they pose to themselves and the broader financial system. All non-bank PIP providers would need extensive training in AML and CTF, as well as the security protocols necessary for privacy protection. These entities likely lack understanding or experience in addressing money laundering and terrorist financing.[42]

18.27 The BOE and HM Treasury have indicated that PIPs would confirm and validate users. However, before sharing this information with the BoE, they would remove any personal details to keep the data anonymous. This means that only the PIP would know the users' identities. Neither the government nor the BOE would be able to access the personal information of digital pound users, unless required by law enforcement agencies in specific situations outlined in the law. This approach would be similar to how personal data is treated in other digital payments and bank accounts.[43]

Limits on digital pound holdings

18.28 A consideration is the maximum amount individuals can hold in their wallets. The BoE proposes implementing 'some limits on digital pounds, at least initially.' The suggested individual limits are £10,000 and £20,000. The latter limit would permit 95 per cent of UK income earners to receive their salaries (or state pensions) in digital pound wallets without frequently exceeding their limits. This threshold could change after the transitional period. When it comes to corporations of varying sizes, the BoE lacks proposals for suitable limits or technological approaches to manage relatively higher limits, such as channelling excess holdings to designated bank accounts. Notably, no limits are set for corporations, and the BoE does not envision how to establish such limits. Consequently, corporations could potentially place all their income resources into digital pounds, challenging commercial banks.[44]

Considering disintermediation risks

18.29 The implications of disintermediation effects on commercial banks are a crucial aspect for the BoE's considerations. The BoE acknowledges potential consequences, referencing an illustrative scenario suggesting that, under certain assumptions, the impact of significant deposit disintermediation on credit

42 *Ibid* 52–62.
43 *Ibid* 12.
44 *Ibid* 80–82.

conditions may be modest in a steady-state economy. However, real-world economies are not in a steady state, rendering models based on this concept irrelevant.[45]

18.30 It remains uncertain how the introduction of the digital pound will affect individuals and corporations. Given the uncertainties outlined by the BoE, including a prolonged transition period, deposit outflows, replacing deposits with wholesale funding, and their impact on credit availability, any estimates can only be speculative. The complexity of these factors highlights the challenges, particularly the potential disintermediation effects on the banking sector and the broader economy.[46] Additionally, the suggested platform model involving a wide array of entities raises concerns about the security of personal and financial data.

18.31 The BoE's Technology Working Paper[47] underscores important design considerations like privacy, security, resilience, and performance. However, the paper primarily offers aspirational goals, guiding the BoE in creating a UK CBDC. The Technology Working Paper indicates that:[48]

(a) The digital pound would be subject to some limits on individuals' holdings, at least during its introductory period. The technology design should support the implementation of these limits, including, if needed, the ability to change either the design or the level of any limit. A limit of £10,000–£20,000 has been suggested.[49]

(b) There may also need to be restrictions on corporates' holdings of the digital pound. Given that corporates vary significantly in size, transaction volume and the activity they undertake, the design of corporate limits will be subject to further research. Technology solutions, such as balance sweeping, might have applications with respect to limits on corporate holdings by allowing corporates to freely receive digital pound payments, but preventing them from storing value in digital pounds in a way that might be detrimental to financial stability by disintermediating critical money markets.[50]

REGULATORY AND LEGAL CONSIDERATIONS FOR CENTRAL BANKS

18.32 Several legal considerations regarding the issuance of CBDCs remain unresolved. While the legal framework for a specific CBDC will depend on its design, there are some general patterns. Currently, most central bank rules do

45 *Ibid* 40–41.

46 *Ibid*.

47 BoE, 'The digital pound: Technology Working Paper' (February 2023) www.bankofengland.co.uk/-/media/boe/files/paper/2023/the-digital-pound-technology-working-paper.pdf [accessed 19 August 2023].

48 *Ibid* 17.

49 BoE and HM Treasury, The digital pound (n 6 above), 80–82.

50 *Ibid* 83.

not allow CBDCs to be issued to the general population.[51] However, this can be addressed with straightforward legislation.[52] Yet, CBDCs face significant challenges concerning monetary policy.

18.33 The issuance of CBDC involves central banks exercising their legal powers within the framework of their legislative tasks and authority. If there is no explicit mandate for a central bank to issue CBDC, questions may arise about the legality of issuing this liability (debt). Unauthorised issuance of debt by a central bank could lead to serious legal, financial, and reputational consequences, making it impossible in major global financial jurisdictions. Determining the legal status of CBDCs, particularly in comparison to physical cash and existing electronic payment methods, is a crucial legal consideration.[53]

18.34 A lack of a clear legal foundation for token-based[54] or account-based[55] CBDC issuance can be addressed through targeted central bank legislative amendments. The IMF's Working Paper No 2020/254 proposes draft legislation to address this issue.[56]

18.35 For central banks, three crucial functions of CBDCs are currency issuance, payment systems and current accounts:

(a) **Currency issuance**: a central bank's primary function is to issue currency into the economy. However, issues may arise if the current function only permits the issuance of certain forms of currency, such as banknotes and coins, but not all forms.[57]

(b) **Payment system**: central banks traditionally oversee and operate payment systems. The design of CBDC must include a means of transferring money between economic agents, effectively making it a payment system. Retail account-based CBDC, for instance, creates a public payment system, raising questions about whether the central bank has the legal authority to provide public access to this payment system.[58]

(c) **Current accounts**: essential powers related to CBDC issuance include the central bank's ability to create accounts in its records.[59]

51 IMF, 'Legal Aspects of Central Bank Digital Currencies: Central Bank and Monetary Law Considerations' (WP/20/254, November 2020) [95] www.imf.org/en/Publications/WP/Issues/2020/11/20/Legal-Aspects-of-Central-Bank-Digital-Currency-Central-Bank-and-Monetary-Law-Considerations-49827 [accessed 5 October 2023].
52 *Ibid* [49].
53 *Ibid* [23].
54 *Ibid* [28]–[38].
55 *Ibid* [40]–[44].
56 *Ibid* Annex I: Draft Central Bank Law Provisions Related To CBDC.
57 *Ibid* [42]–[44].
58 *Ibid* [46]–[48].
59 *Ibid* [42]–[45].

18.36 According to data from the IMF, out of the 171 central banks surveyed, 61 per cent have statutes that limit currency issuance to traditional banknotes and coins. Only 23 per cent of central banks' legislation explicitly allows for the direct issuance of cash in digital format. In 16 per cent of cases, it remains unclear whether the creation of a digital form of central bank currency is permitted.[60]

18.37 Further legal issues that need to be addressed are as follows:

(a) **Data privacy and security**: CBDCs involve the collection and management of personal and financial data, raising concerns about data protection, cybersecurity and overreach of the State institutions.[61]

(b) **AML and CTF**: CBDCs require robust AML and CTF measures to prevent illicit activities and ensure compliance with international standards.[62]

(c) **Negotiable instruments and counterfeiting**: officially sanctioned payment instruments that benefit from private law privileges such as cheques, bills of exchange will need to be examined. States also protect officially sanctioned means of payment by imposing criminal law sanctions on those who counterfeit, damage, or destroy those instruments which will need to be looked at in the context of CBDCs.[63]

18.38 Regulatory and policy issues that need to be addressed are as follows:

(a) **Implications for monetary policy**: CBDCs can influence the effectiveness of monetary policy tools, such as interest rates and money supply management and may have unintended consequences.[64]

(b) **Financial stability**: the introduction of CBDCs may impact financial intermediation, bank funding, and liquidity management, necessitating careful consideration of potential regulatory risks, known and unknown. [65]

(c) **Foreign exchange considerations**: the potential impact of CBDCs on foreign exchange markets and exchange rate stability requires attention in regulatory discussions.[66]

60 *Ibid* [39].

61 BoE and HM Treasury, The digital pound (n 6 above), 67–74.

62 *Ibid*.

63 Gabriel Soderberg, John Kiff, Herve Tourpe, Marianne Bechara, Stephanie Forte, Kathleen Kao, Ashley Lannquist, Tao Sun, and Akihiro Yoshinaga, 'How Should Central Banks Explore Central Bank Digital Currency?' (IMF, Fintech Notes No 2023/008, 8 September 2023) www.imf.org/en/Publications/fintech-notes/Issues/2023/09/08/How-Should-Central-Banks-Explore-Central-Bank-Digital-Currency-538504 [accessed 5 October 2023].

64 *Ibid* 41–49.

65 *Ibid* 38–41.

66 *Ibid* 34–35.

(d) **Technological infrastructure**: developing and maintaining the necessary technological infrastructure for CBDCs presents technical and legal challenges, particularly in relation to interoperability.[67]

(e) **Financial inclusion**: ensuring that CBDCs do not exacerbate existing inequalities in access to financial services.[68]

(f) **Implementation and adoption**: the successful introduction and adoption of CBDCs require collaboration between central banks, financial institutions, regulators, the private sector, and the public.

RECENT SELECTED CBDC REPORTS AND INITIATIVES

18.39 CBDCs raise questions about cross-border interoperability, standards, and cooperation between central banks and regulatory authorities. Below are listed reports and initiatives for further reading.

(a) BIS Innovation Hub, 'Lessons learnt on CBDCs Report submitted to the G20 Finance Ministers and Central Bank Governors' (BIS, July 2023).[69]

(b) ECB, 'Progress on the investigation phase of a digital euro – fourth report' (July 2023).[70]

(c) Federal Reserve Board, 'Report on US CBDC' (20 January 2022).[71]

(d) Working Group on E-CNY Research and Development of the People's Bank of China, 'Progress of Research & Development of E-CNY in China' (People's Bank of China, July 2021).[72]

CONCLUSION

18.40 The characteristics and operation of CBDCs vary, with some central banks, like the BoE, indicating their CBDC proposals would not be based on DLT like cryptocurrencies. Uncertainty remains about who will develop and host the core CBDC technology, with possibilities of involving private third parties to provide overlay services such as digital wallets or AML/CTF functions.

67 BOE, 'The digital pound: Technology Working Paper '(n 47 above).

68 BoE and HM Treasury, 'The digital pound' (n 6 above), 85–88.

69 See n 2 above.

70 www.ecb.europa.eu/paym/digital_euro/investigation/governance/shared/files/ecb.degov230713-fourth-progress-report-digital-euro-investigation-phase.en.pdf?704b0eee4c20eee4dbe4970f5091a96a [accessed 20 August 2023].

71 www.federalreserve.gov/publications/files/money-and-payments-20220120.pdf [accessed 20 August 2022].

72 Working Group on E-CNY Research and Development of the People's Bank of China, 'Progress of Research & Development of E-CNY in China' (July 2021) *People's Bank of China 13-14* www.pbc.gov.cn/en/3688110/3688172/4157443/4293696/2021071614584691871.pdf [accessed 25 September 2023].

18.41 CDBCs have the potential to reshape the global financial landscape. The legal considerations surrounding CBDCs are intricate, ranging from fundamental issues around whether it can be legal tender, data privacy overreach to financial and monetary stability implications. A thoughtful approach to regulatory frameworks, international cooperation, and technological implementation will be pivotal in realising the benefits of CBDCs while managing potential risks and concerns.

Part V

Future of Cryptocurrency

Chapter 19

Legal and Regulatory Outlook

19.1 The legal and regulatory landscape surrounding cryptocurrencies and DLT in the UK and internationally is constantly evolving. This chapter provides an overview of the current legal and regulatory outlook, discussing key developments, ongoing initiatives, and potential future directions.

UK REGULATORY DEVELOPMENTS

Financial Conduct Authority

19.2 The Financial Conduct Authority (FCA) has been at the forefront of regulating cryptocurrencies and related activities in the UK. It has introduced measures to combat money laundering and enhance consumer protection, including implementing anti-money laundering (AML) and counter-terrorism financing (CTF) regulatory requirements for cryptocurrency businesses. The new Financial Services and Markets Act 2023 (FSMA 2023) regime has given the FCA new powers to regulate cryptoassets involved in investment activities and financial promotions. The implementation of the 'Travel Rule' has also given the FCA powers regarding recording and monitoring cryptoasset transfers under the AML rules. Further powers are likely to be granted to the FCA at the conclusion of the HM Treasury Consultation and Call for Evidence: 'Future financial services regulatory regime for cryptoassets'.[1]

Bank of England

19.3 The UK brought in reforms to regulation in the wake of the 2008 global financial crisis in the form of the Financial Services Act 2012. The Bank of England (BoE) subsidiary, the Prudential Regulation Authority (PRA), is the prudential regulator in relation to supervising financial market infrastructure providers.

19.4 The UK Government has expressed its commitment to regulating stablecoins to address potential risks to financial stability and consumer protection. FSMA 2023 provides powers for the BoE to regulate stablecoins used in systemic

1 HM Treasury, 'Consultation and call for Evidence: Future financial services regulatory regime for cryptoassets' (February 2023) https://assets.publishing.service.gov.uk/government/uploads/system/uploads/attachment_data/file/1133404/TR_Privacy_edits_Future_financial_services_regulatory_regime_for_cryptoassets_vP.pdf [accessed 28 September 2023]. See also **19.9–19.11**.

payment systems in the UK. The PRA Business Plan 2023/24 indicates that work has begun to develop its regulatory framework for stablecoins.[2]

19.5 The BoE is actively exploring the potential issuance of central bank digital currency (CBDC) in the UK. This initiative aims to harness the benefits of digital currencies while ensuring monetary stability and maintaining trust in the financial system. The development of a CBDC may have implications for the broader regulatory landscape.[3]

19.6 On 24 March 2022 Sam Woods, CEO of the PRA, issued a 'Dear CEO' letter discussing the regulator's approach to existing or planned exposure to cryptoassets in the context of increasing growth and innovation in the industry.[4] The letter was intended to outline the PRA's expectations around risk management and measurement against the existing prudential framework until the BCBS cryptoasset banking supervision standards were announced. The BCBS SCO60 supervision standards were published on 16 December 2022 and the UK will implement SCO60 by 1 January 2025 and will become a new chapter of the consolidated Basel Framework for banks.[5]

19.7 In tandem, the Bank of England published its response to new forms of digital money[6] along with its Financial Policy Committee (FPC) report on cryptoassets and decentralised finance.[7]

Economic Crime and Corporate Transparency Act 2023

19.8 The Economic Crime and Corporate Transparency Act 2023 (ECCTA 2023) encompasses a range of provisions aimed at enhancing transparency at Companies House, preventing abuse of limited partnerships, and empowering law enforcement to seize and recover cryptoassets linked to criminal activities. ECCTA 2023 grants law enforcement augmented authority to seize and recover cryptoassets linked to criminal proceeds, money laundering, fraud, and ransomware attacks. Revisions to criminal confiscation and civil recovery powers within POCA 2002 enable a more effective response to the criminal use of cryptoassets.[8]

2 PRA, 'Prudential Regulation Authority Business Plan 2023/24' (BoE, 2 May 2023), 18 and 20 www.bankofengland.co.uk/prudential-regulation/publication/2023/may/pra-business-plan-2023-24 [accessed 5 October 2023]. For further detail, see **13.29–13.35**.

3 See **18.22–18.38**.

4 PRA, 'Dear CEO, Existing or planned exposure to cryptoassets' (24 March 2023) www.bankofengland.co.uk/-/media/boe/files/prudential-regulation/letter/2022/march/existing-or-planned-exposure-to-cryptoassets.pdf [accessed 27 September 2023].

5 See **4.1–4.30**.

6 BoE, Responses to the Bank of England's Discussion Paper (n 1 above).

7 FPC, 'Financial Policy Committee, Financial Stability in Focus: Cryptoassets and decentralised finance' (March 2022) www.bankofengland.co.uk/-/media/boe/files/financial-stability-in-focus/ 2022/cryptoassets-and-decentralised-finance.pdf [accessed 27 September 2023].

8 See **8.22–8.40**.

HM Treasury

19.9 On 1 February 2023, HM Treasury released a consultation paper outlining the UK regulatory approach to cryptoassets.[9] This consultation is a continuation of the government's commitment to introduce a new regulatory regime for cryptoassets, which was announced in April 2022. The focus of the consultation is on the future UK regulatory framework for cryptoassets used within financial services, rather than the broader application of DLT in financial services or the use of cryptoassets outside the financial sector. The regulation of cryptoassets is to be carried out in a phased approach, prioritising areas with the highest risks and opportunities.

19.10 FSMA 2023 implements phase 1 of the regulatory regime to target digital settlement assets (DSAs) and fiat-backed stablecoins.[10] Phase 2 will cover additional areas such as:[11]

(a) admitting a cryptoasset to a cryptoasset trading venue;

(b) making a public offer of a cryptoasset;

(c) operation of crypto trading venues;

(d) dealing with cryptoassets as principal or agent;

(e) arranging cryptoasset deals;

(f) making arrangements with a view to cryptoasset deals;

(g) Operating a cryptoasset lending platform; and

(h) Safeguarding and/administering activities other than fiat-backed stablecoins.

Other areas of future regulation include:[12]

(a) further post-trade activities in cryptoassets;

(b) further regulation on advice and management of cryptassets;

(c) mining or validation transactions, or operating a node on a blockchain; and

(d) using cryptoassets to run a validator node on PoS network.

19.11 HM Treasury is also proposing a market abuse regime for cryptoassets, modelled after elements of the UK Market Abuse Regulation (UK MAR) for financial instruments. The proposed regime would apply to persons engaging in market abuse with respect to a cryptoasset intended for trading on a UK trading venue.[13] Additionally, the consultation paper includes a call for evidence on DeFi, other cryptoasset activities, and sustainability.

9 HM Treasury, 'Future financial services regulatory regime for cryptoassets' (n 1 above).
10 *Ibid* [3.12]–[3.16], Table 3.A.
11 *Ibid* Table 4.A: Proposed scope of cryptoasset activities to be regulated.
12 *Ibid.*
13 *Ibid* [9.16] Table 9A.

HMRC consultation reforms to DeFi taxation

19.12 On 5 July 2022 HMRC initiated a call for evidence regarding the taxation of DeFi transactions.[14] The call for evidence proposed that cryptoassets lending and staking in DeFi might be treated similarly to other assets. HMRC suggested including cryptoassets as securities or extending the tax treatment used for repos and stock lending to cryptoassets, or devising a specific regime for cryptoassets.

19.13 On 27 April 2023, HMRC published a summary of responses to the call for evidence and launched a new consultation on a proposed taxation regime for DeFi transactions.[15] The proposed regime aims to cover CeFi transactions as well, where lenders expect a return while staking or lending their tokens and retain an economic interest in the cryptoassets.

19.14 The consultation focuses on the CGT treatment of lending and staking transactions in DeFi, which currently does not fully represent the underlying transactions' true nature. HMRC proposes a tailored regime to more accurately reflect the economic ownership of the assets involved and legislate separate rules for DeFi lending and staking, along the lines of those applicable to repos and stock lending.

19.15 The possible new regime would operate as follows:

(a) Transfers of beneficial ownership of tokens will be disregarded for capital gains purposes if they are loaned directly to a borrower, and the borrower has an obligation to return the same tokens or through a smart contract that allows the lender to withdraw the same tokens. The tokens can be returned at the lender's or borrower's request or at the end of the term.

(b) Any returns received by the lender during the term or at the end of the term will be subject to tax when received, and a new category of miscellaneous income could be created for cryptoasset transactions to simplify tax reporting for participants. The amount of the return is the market value of the additional tokens or other assets constituting the return at the time they are received.

(c) If the rights relating to the lent tokens are sold, this is treated as a disposal of the tokens for CGT purposes. The rules will regard the disposal of the rights as a disposal of the relevant cryptoassets at the time the rights are sold.

14 HMRC, 'Call for Evidence: The taxation of decentralised finance involving the lending and staking of cryptoassets' (5 July 2022) www.gov.uk/government/consultations/call-for-evidence-the-taxation-of-decentralised-finance-involving-the-lending-and-staking-of-cryptoassets [accessed 6 October 2023].

15 HMRC, 'The taxation of decentralised finance (DeFi) involving the lending and staking of cryptoassets' (27 April 2023) www.gov.uk/government/consultations/the-taxation-of-decentralised-finance-involving-the-lending-and-staking-of-cryptoassets/the-taxation-of-decentralised-finance-defi-involving-the-lending-and-staking-of-cryptoassets [accessed 6 October 2023].

(d) If the borrower cannot return the lent tokens, it is treated as a disposal of those tokens by the lender at when the default arises. The consideration is the amount received from the borrower as compensation for the tokens that cannot be returned.

(e) At the end of the term, when the tokens are returned to the lender or staker, it generally will not have any consequences for CGT.

19.16 The consultation includes practical examples of how the new regime might work. If implemented, the new tax regime is intended to apply to transactions after the commencement date. DeFi transactions that have started before the implementation date will continue to be taxed under the general CGT rules.

UK regulatory future for cryptoassets

19.17 The regulatory landscape for cryptoasset businesses in the UK has experienced significant transformation over the number of years and further changes are anticipated in light of the Markets in Crypto-Assets Regulation (MiCA) to align more closely with the EU, albeit not exactly. As the UK wishes to become a global cryptoasset technology hub,[16] the government is likely to take a collaborative approach with the industry to ensure that regulatory requirements are fit for purpose. Regulatory areas that are likely to be focused on include: [17]

(a) **Incorporation requirement**: imposing a condition for all cryptoasset issuers to establish themselves as legal entities. Currently, issuers are often characterised by their anonymous and decentralised nature. Such a requirement, with its implications, could significantly impact the fundamental principles underlying various schemes.

(b) **White Paper publication**: requiring all cryptoasset issuers to publish comprehensive white papers adhering to prescribed content and format and submitting them to competent authorities. This would mark a significant departure from the current practice of relying on high-level white papers with limited detail and no regulatory oversight.

(c) **Expanded regulatory scope**: clarifying and broadening the authorisation and supervision regime to include crypto assets currently beyond the UK's regulatory scope.

(d) **Market abuse prevention**: introducing measures to prevent market abuse and ensure the integrity of crypto asset markets.

16 'Government sets out plan to make UK a global cryptoasset technology hub' (4 April 2022) www.gov.uk/government/news/government-sets-out-plan-to-make-uk-a-global-cryptoasset-technology-hub [accessed 6 October 2023].

17 Mary Young and Jill Lorimer, 'Developments in the UK crypto-asset landscape', (2021) 2 IBLJ 241–254, 245–247.

19.18 Meanwhile, the FCA's ongoing efforts to provide guidance on how cryptoassets fit into the existing regulatory framework have allowed industry participants to now have some understanding of the FCA's perspective on regulated and non-regulated products. HMRC have also provided thorough initial guidance on taxation treatment. Both the FCA and HMRC's treatment of cryptoassets will be refined with legislation.

19.19 On 2 October 2023, the Policy Exchange published a report indicating that the UK has an opportunity to attract crypto firms leaving the US due to increased regulation and outlined 10 recommendations to the government regarding the UK regulatory framework:[18]

(a) HM Treasury's secondary legislation and regulation implementing a new cryptoasset framework should embrace, and set a high bar for, decentralisation to ensure that customers are protected against legacy risks of centralisation and so that innovative projects can issue tokens to appropriately broaden ownership of new networks.

(b) The government, with the help of the Law Commission, should clarify legal protections and liability for DAOs and their members.

(c) The FCA's risk-based AML program requirements should be flexible and fit-for-purpose in order to account for technological and behavioural differences between blockchain transactions and fiat currency transactions and to allow for innovative AML solutions.

(d) Regulation should not undermine digital self-hosted wallets.

(e) The FCA should require clear disclosures to consumers about which stablecoins are actually 'stable.'

(f) The FCA should not regulate proof-of-stake services as a financial service.

(g) HMRC should create a tax wrapper for the exchange of cryptoassets.

(h) The Department for Science, Innovation and Technology and the FCA should create a joint sandbox with input from HMRC and HM Treasury.

(i) The BoE should promote a flourishing stablecoin market in the UK by allowing stablecoin reserves to be placed at the central bank.

(j) The government should recruit digital fellows who help the government upgrade public services with cutting-edge technology.

19.20 The defining attributes of cryptoassets, such as anonymity, lack of transparency, and freedom from state oversight, have been significantly reduced as cryptoasset providers integrate more closely with mainstream financial institutions. This shift has prompted operators aiming to maintain these

18 Aria Babu, 'Web3: Democratising the Internet' (Policy Exchange, 2 October 2023) https://policyexchange.org.uk/wp-content/uploads/Web3.pdf [accessed 7 October 2023].

characteristics or unable to meet the costs of new regulatory expectations to seek less stringent jurisdictions outside the UK and EU. Nonetheless, the potential for regulatory arbitrage is gradually waning as international standards evolve to elevate consistency, promote higher standards, and spotlight jurisdictions falling behind. Amidst these changes, the increasingly regulated UK regime has opened new avenues for established institutions operating in the mainstream and new entrants willing to coexist with established players.

INTERNATIONAL COLLABORATION AND STANDARDS

Group of Seven and Group of Twenty

19.21 The Group of Seven (G7) is an informal bloc of industrialised democracies formed of the United States, Canada, France, Germany, Italy, Japan, and the UK that meets annually to discuss issues such as global economic governance, international security, and energy policy. Unlike the United Nations or the North Atlantic Treaty Organization (NATO), the G7 is not a formal institution with a charter and a secretariat. The presidency, which rotates annually among member states, is responsible for setting the agenda of each year's summit and arranging logistics for it.[19]

19.22 At the G7 Hiroshima Summit 2023, the participants confirmed the following:[20]

(a) They recognised the importance of effective monitoring and regulation to mitigate financial stability and integrity risks associated with cryptoassets in line with the Financial Stability Board (FSB) recommendations to be delivered July 2023.

(b) They committed to establishing robust regulatory and supervisory frameworks for cryptoasset activities, market operations, and stablecoin arrangements. These frameworks will align with the FSB's standards and the guidance provided by standard-setting bodies (SSBs). They encouraged global consistency in implementing these recommendations to prevent regulatory loopholes.

(c) They endorsed the FSB and SSBs' efforts to further examine DeFi and multifunction cryptoasset intermediaries, acknowledging the increasing threats posed by illicit activities, including state actors' involvement. This includes cryptoasset theft for proliferation financing, ransomware attacks, terrorist financing, and sanctions evasion.

19 Council on Foreign Relations, 'Backgrounder: What Does the G7 Do?' (28 June 2023) www.cfr.org/backgrounder/what-does-g7-do [accessed 8 September 2023].

20 G7 Finance Ministers and Central Bank Governors Meeting Communiqué (Niigata, Japan, 13 May 2023), 10 www.mof.go.jp/policy/international_policy/convention/g7/g7_20230513_2.pdf [accessed 8 September 2023].

(d) They support the Financial Action Task Force (FATF) in expediting the global adoption of FATF Standards for virtual assets, including the 'Travel Rule,' and in addressing emerging risks from DeFi and peer-to-peer transactions. They eagerly await the FATF's fourth progress report on virtual assets and ongoing initiatives in this area.

19.23 The Group of Twenty (G20) comprises 19 countries (Argentina, Australia, Brazil, Canada, China, France, Germany, India, Indonesia, Italy, Japan, Republic of Korea, Mexico, Russia, Saudi Arabia, South Africa, Turkey, UK, and United States), the African Union and the EU. The G20 is the premier forum for international economic cooperation, and it plays an important role in shaping and strengthening global architecture and governance on all major international economic issues. The G20 does not have a permanent secretariat or staff. Like the G7, the G20 Presidency rotates annually among the members and is selected from a different regional grouping of countries.

19.24 At the 2023 G20 Summit in India, the following was agreed and stated in relation to cryptoassets:[21]

(a) To closely monitor of risks in the cryptoasset ecosystem.

(b) Endorsment of the FSB's high level recommendations for cryptoassets regulation and oversight and global stablecoin arrangements. Asked the FSB and SSBs to promote the effective and timely implementation of these recommendations in a consistent manner globally to avoid regulatory arbitrage.

(c) Welcomed the IMF-FSB Synthesis Paper which includes a Roadmap for a coordinated and comprehensive policy and regulatory framework and ongoing global implementation of FATF standards to address money laundering and terrorism financing risks. The G20 Finance Ministers and Central Bank Governors will discuss taking forward the Roadmap at the meeting in October 2023.

(d) Welcomed the BIS Report on The Crypto Ecosystem: Key Elements and Risks.

(e) Welcomed discussions on the potential macro-financial implications arising from the introduction and adoption of CBDCs, notably on cross-border payments as well as on the international monetary and financial system.

(f) Welcomed the BIS Innovation Hub Report on Lessons Learnt on CBDCs and look forward to the IMF Report on Potential macro-financial implications of widespread adoption of CBDCs to advance the discussion on this issue.

21 G20, 'New Delhi Leaders' Declaration' (New Delhi, India, 9–10 September 2023), 23 www.g20.org/content/dam/gtwenty/gtwenty_new/document/G20-New-Delhi-Leaders-Declaration.pdf [accessed 6 October 2023].

European Union

The Markets in Crypto-Assets Regulation

19.25 In this section of the book the EU term 'crypto-asset' will be used when referring to MiCA instead of the UK term 'cryptoasset.'

19.26 The Markets in Crypto-Assets Regulation (MiCA) entered into force in June 2023. The regulation includes a substantial number of Level 2 and Level 3 measures that must be developed before the entry into application of the new regime (within a 12- to 18-month deadline depending on the mandate). This regulation is part of Europe's strategy to facilitate the financial sector's adoption of DLT and to regulate the issuance and usage of crypto-assets. The MiCA Regulation governs the issuance of crypto-assets within the EU and regulates their issuers and related service providers.

19.27 Under MiCA the term 'crypto-asset' is defined as 'a digital representation of a value or of a right that is able to be transferred and stored electronically using distributed ledger technology or similar technology'.[22] Importantly, the MiCA Regulation does not encompass e-money as defined in second Electronic Money Directive[23] (EMD2), nor does it include financial instruments defined in MIFID II.

19.28 The MiCA Regulation categorises crypto-assets into three sub-categories:[24]

(a) **E-money tokens (EMT)**: crypto-assets that aim to stabilise their value by referencing only one official currency. The function of such crypto-assets is very similar to the function of 'electronic money' as defined in EMD2. Like electronic money, such crypto-assets are electronic surrogates for coins and banknotes and are likely to be used for making payments.

(b) **Asset-referenced tokens (ART)**: a type of crypto-asset that is not an electronic money token and that aims to maintain a stable value by referencing another value or right or a combination thereof, including one or more official currencies.

(c) **Utility tokens**: a type of crypto-asset that is only intended to provide access to a good or a service supplied by its issuer.

19.29 Under MiCA, issuers of EMT must comply with the requirements of EMD2, as well as the requirements in Title IV of MiCA.[25]

22 MiCA, Art 3(1)(5).
23 Council Directive 2009/110/EC of 16 September 2009 on the taking up, pursuit and prudential supervision of the business of electronic money institutions amending Directives 2005/60/EC and 2006/48/EC and repealing Directive 2000/46/EC [2009] OJ L267/7.
24 MiCA, Recital 18.
25 MiCA, Art 48(1).

19.30 MiCA also contains a class of crypto-asset identified as 'significant token' which is is a type of ART or EMT that the Commission considers poses significant risks for financial stability and consumer protection across the EU. As a result, they are subject to enhanced rules under Articles 43–47 and Articles 56–58 respectively. The European Banking Authority (EBA) is mandated under MiCA to identify tokens as 'significant' according to specified criteria.

Public offerings

19.31 The public offering of crypto-assets is subject to a sophisticated regulatory regime under the MiCA. The requirements under the MiCA vary depending on whether the offering relates to (i) other crypto-assets, (ii) the ART, or (iii) the EMT.

19.32 For crypto-assets that do not qualify as ARTs or EMTs, the MiCA introduces a notification requirement to competent authorities and focuses on obligations for those offering or seeking admission to trade these assets.[26]

19.33 To conduct a public offering or gain admission to trading, the regulation mandates the creation, notification, and publication of a crypto-asset white paper (CAWP).[27] The MiCA lays out specific requirements for both the content and format of this white paper.[28] It also establishes liability for the information provided in a CAWP,[29] and requires notification of the CAWP and marketing communications to the competent authority.[30] Public offerings to fewer than 150 individuals in each Member State and public offerings of crypto-assets totalling less than €1 million over the last 12 months are exempt from these requirements.[31]

19.34 The public offering and trading admission of ARTs come with stricter regulations outlined in Title III.[32]

19.35 In addition to the requirements related to the CAWP, firms involved in offering ARTs to the public or seeking trading admission must seek authorisation[33] and meet specific fit and proper criteria.[34] Credit institutions under the Capital Requirements Regulation[35] issuing ARTs are exempt from authorisation but

26 MiCA, title II, Arts 4–15.
27 MiCA, Art 4.
28 MiCA, art 6.
29 MiCA, Art 15.
30 MiCA, Art 8.
31 MiCA, Art 4(2).
32 MiCA, Arts 16-47.
33 MiCA, Art 16.
34 MiCA, Art 21.
35 Council Regulation (EU) No 575/2013 of 26 June 2013 on prudential requirements for credit institutions and investment firms and amending Regulation (EU) No 648/2012 [2013] OJ L176/1.

must notify competent authorities at least 90 working days before their first ART issuance.[36]

19.36 ART issuers must maintain adequate own funds[37] and a reserve of assets meeting specific criteria, properly managed.[38] These reserve assets must be held in custody according to a custody policy.[39] Issuers must also establish a recovery plan for significant operational disruptions and a redemption plan for each ART,[40] both of which must be communicated to the competent authority. Significant ARTs face supervision by the EBA and must adhere to liquidity requirements.[41] However, exemptions apply to ARTs with an average value not exceeding €5 million over 12 months and those exclusively offered to qualified investors and held solely by them.[42]

19.37 The regulations for EMTs, including their public offering, admission to trading, and issuer requirements, are outlined in Title IV of MiCA.[43] Unlike ARTs, firms seeking to issue and offer EMTs must obtain authorisation as either a Capital Requirements Regulation (CRR) credit institution or an electronic money institution under the EMD.[44] No authorisation under MiCA is available for this purpose.

19.38 EMTs are subject to specific issuance and redeemability requirements under MiCA, not the EMD.[45] MiCA strictly prohibits the payment of interest in connection with EMTs.[46] Providing incomplete, unfair, unclear, or misleading information in the CAWP can result in liability for both the issuer and its management.[47] Similar to ARTs and other cryptoassets, offering EMTs to the public and gaining admission to trading require firms to notify the CAWP, meeting detailed content and form requirements specified by the competent authority.[48]

19.39 EMT issuers must deposit at least 30 per cent of received funds in separate accounts in credit institutions and invest the remaining funds in secure, low-risk assets qualifying as highly liquid financial instruments.[49] Like ART issuers, EMT issuers must develop and notify recovery and redemption plans to the competent authority.[50] The EBA will supervise EMT issuers categorised as

36 MiCA, Art 17.
37 MiCA, Art 35.
38 MiCA, Art 36.
39 MiCA, Art 37.
40 MiCA, Arts 46 and 47.
41 MiCA, Art 43.
42 MiCA, Art 16(2).
43 MiCA, Art 48–58.
44 MiCA, Art 48(1).
45 MiCA, Art 49.
46 MiCA, Art 50.
47 MiCA, Art 52.
48 MiCA, Art 51.
49 MiCA, Art 54.
50 MiCA, Art 55.

significant, subjecting them to additional requirements. Issuers have the option to voluntarily classify their EMT as significant.

Crypto-asset service providers

19.40 The MiCA establishes a unified framework for crypto-asset service providers (CASP) under Title V.[51] CASP are entities or businesses whose primary activity involves offering professional crypto-asset services to clients. These crypto-asset services include:

(a) **Operation of crypto-asset trading platforms**: this involves managing systems that facilitate the exchange of multiple third-party interests in crypto-assets, leading to contractual agreements, either trading crypto-assets for funds or swapping crypto-assets for other crypto-assets.[52] While the definition does not specify non-discretionary rules, Article 76(1)(e) mandates non-discretionary rules for fair and orderly trading and efficient order execution.

(b) **Custody and administration of crypto-assets**: CASP safeguard and control crypto-assets or access means, including private cryptographic keys, on behalf of clients.[53] Custody involves securing crypto-assets, while administration aids in exercising associated rights.

(c) **Exchange of crypto-assets for funds or other crypto-assets**: this service involves executing purchase or sale contracts for crypto-assets with clients using proprietary capital.[54] It resembles dealing on own accounts under MiFID II but is client-focused.

(d) **Execution of orders for crypto-assets**: CASP execute agreements for clients to buy or sell crypto-assets, ensuring the best interest of the client and optimal execution.[55]

(e) **Reception and transmission of orders for crypto-assets**: These providers receive orders from individuals and transmit them to third parties for execution, acting as intermediaries.[56]

(f) **Providing advice on crypto-assets**: CASP offer personalised recommendations regarding crypto-asset transactions or services based on clients' needs or provider initiatives.[57]

(g) **Placing of crypto-assets**: this involves marketing crypto-assets on behalf of the issuer or related parties.[58] Unlike MiFID II placement, it is purely a marketing service for the issuer.

51 MiCA, Arts 59–85.
52 MiCA, Art 3(1) no 18.
53 MiCA, Art 3(1) no 17.
54 MiCA, Art 3(1) no 19 and 20.
55 MiCA, Art 3(1) no 21.
56 MiCA, Art 3(1) no 23.
57 MiCA, Art 3(1) no 24.
58 MiCA, Art 3(1) no 22.

(h) **Providing portfolio management of crypto-assets**: CASP manage portfolios with crypto-assets as per client mandates on a discretionary basis.[59]

(i) **Providing transfer services for crypto-assets**: this service transfers crypto-assets between ledger addresses or accounts on behalf of natural or legal persons.[60] It is distinct from MiFID II and relates to settlement transactions in crypto-assets.

Licensing and EU passport for CASPs

19.41 CASPs must obtain a licence to offer crypto-asset services.[61] To secure this licence under MiCA, CASPs need to satisfy specific criteria, including fitness, governance, and prudential requirements.[62] These prudential conditions include maintaining a permanent minimum capital ranging from €50,000 to €150,000, depending on the type of crypto-asset service offered.[63] Additionally, CASPs must maintain prudential safeguards equal to a quarter of the previous year's fixed overhead (if it exceeds the permanent minimum capital).[64] Governance standards encompass suitability requirements for members of the management body[65] and the establishment of effective anti-money laundering and anti-terrorist financing systems.[66]

19.42 Certain financial institutions, such as CRR credit institutions, central securities depositories (CSDs), MiFID investment firms, electronic money institutions, and UCITS managers, can provide specific crypto-asset services after notifying the competent authority at least 40 working days before their initial service provision.[67]

19.43 CASPs can operate crypto-asset services across the European Economic Area (EEA) via establishment rights (including branches) or by offering services on a cross-border basis. To begin providing these services in other EEA Member States, firms must inform their home Member State's competent authority as outlined in Article 65 of MiCA.

Ownership control procedure

19.44 Proposed acquisitions of crypto-asset service providers must undergo an ownership control process. This process evaluates the reputation and financial

59 MiCA, Art 3(1) no 25.
60 MiCA, Art 3(1) no 26.
61 MiCA, Art 59.
62 MiCA, Art 63(10).
63 MiCA, Art 67(1)(a) and Annex IV.
64 MiCA, Art 67(1)(b).
65 MiCA, Art 68(1).
66 MiCA, Art 68(8).
67 MiCA, Art 60(1)–(5).

stability of the acquiring entity and assesses the potential impact on the target's ability to comply with regulatory requirements as a result of the acquisition.[68]

Conduct of business rules and service-specific obligations

19.45 Similar to MiFID II, MiCA mandates that CASPs act honestly, fairly, and professionally in the best interests of their clients.[69] They must also provide clients with clear, non-misleading information[70] and warn them about the risks associated with crypto-asset transactions.[71]

19.46 Moreover, CASPs face tailored requirements for each crypto-asset service:

(a) operating a crypto-asset trading platform;[72]

(b) custody and administration of crypto-assets on behalf of clients;[73]

(c) exchanging crypto-assets for funds or other crypto-assets;[74]

(d) executing orders for crypto-assets on behalf of clients;[75]

(e) receiving and transmitting orders for crypto-assets on behalf of clients;[76]

(f) providing advice on crypto-assets and/or portfolio management;[77]

(g) placing crypto-assets;[78] and

(h) providing transfer services for crypto-assets on behalf of clients.[79]

Market integrity and abuse

19.47 Title VI of MiCA establishes a regulatory framework focused on safeguarding market integrity and preventing market abuse.[80] It encompasses requirements concerning the handling of inside information related to crypto-assets, the public disclosure of such information, and the prohibition of insider trading and market manipulation.

68 MiCA, Arts 83–84.
69 MiCA, Art 66(1).
70 MiCA, Art 66(2).
71 MiCA, Art 66(3).
72 MiCA, Art 76.
73 MiCA, Art 75.
74 MiCA, Art 77.
75 MiCA, Art 78.
76 MiCA, Art 80.
77 MiCA, Art 81.
78 MiCA, Art 79.
79 MiCA, Art 82.
80 MiCA, Art 86–92.

Digital operational resilience for the financial sector

19.48 The Digital Operational Resilience Act (DORA) will apply in member states from 17 January 2025. DORA is designed to consolidate and upgrade ICT risk requirements throughout the financial sector to ensure that all financial system participants comply with a common set of standards to mitigate ICT risks for their operations and ensure the smooth functioning of the internal market. It aims to bring legal clarity on the applicable ICT risk provisions (especially in the case of cross-border financial entities), reduce regulatory complexity and lower the financial and administrative burdens resulting from diverse rules that apply across the EU.

19.49 DORA covers a broad range of financial entities, from credit institutions and investment funds to cryptoasset service providers,[81] to ensure that ICT risks are managed in a homogenous and coherent way.[82]

The Transfer of Funds Regulation

19.50 On 20 April 2023, the European Parliament officially approved the draft Regulation concerning the transfer of information for both funds and crypto-assets, referred to as the EU Travel Rule Regulation.[83]

19.51 Under the EU Wire Transfer Regulation[84] (EU WTR), European payment service providers are required to ensure that information about the sender and recipient accompanies fund transfers. These funds can be in various forms, including banknotes, coins, scriptural money, and electronic money which does not include virtual assets. The EU Travel Rule Regulation builds upon this by extending the same requirements to crypto-assets.[85] This means that CASPs will need to furnish information about the sender and recipient for any transfers involving crypto-assets, whether they are domestic or cross-border.[86] However, these obligations will not be applicable to person-to-person transfers of crypto-assets where CASPs are not involved, or when both the sender and recipient are CASPs conducting transfers on their own behalf.[87]

19.52 Upon enactment, the EU Travel Rule Regulation will replace the EU WTR and the current requirements related to information accompanying fund

81 DORA Regulation, Art 2(1)(f).
82 For further detail see **10.78–10.83**.
83 Council Regulation (EU) 2023/1113 of 31 May 2023 on information accompanying transfers of funds and certain crypto-assets and amending Directive (EU) 2015/849 [2023] OJ L150/1.
84 Council Regulation (EU) 2015/847 of 20 May 2015 on information accompanying transfers of funds and repealing Regulation (EC) No 1781/2006 [2015] OJ L141/1.
85 EU Travel Rule Regulation, Art 2(1).
86 EU Travel Rule Regulation, Arts 4–6.
87 EU Travel Rule Regulation, Art 2(4).

transfers will be carried over to the new Regulation.[88] This new Regulation will take effect simultaneously with the MiCA Regulation, from 30 December 2024.[89]

The Organisation for Economic Cooperation and Development: crypto-asset reporting framework and updated common reporting standards

19.53 The predecessor to the Organisation for Economic Cooperation and Development (OECD) was the Organisation for European Economic Co-operation (OEEC), which was set up to administer American and Canadian aid under the Marshall Plan for the reconstruction of Europe after World War II. The OEEC was transformed into the OECD in December 1960 and entered into force in September 1961. Since that date the OECD's mission has been to deliver greater well-being worldwide by advising governments on policies that support resilient, inclusive and sustainable growth. They provide evidence-based policy analysis and recommendations, standards and global policy networks, and closely collaborate with the G7 and the G20. Their remit spans the public policy horizon including tax transparency.[90] Since the CRS was adopted in 2014 over 100 jurisdictions have implemented the CRS.

19.54 As governments and tax authorities are concerned about regulating cryptoassets not only from a financial services perspective but also to protect the tax base due to the rapid adoption of cryptoassets for investment and financial activities, the OECD has adopted rules and commentary for the global transparency framework called the Crypto-Asset Reporting Framework (CARF) and amendments to the CRS. The CARF rules and commentary were approved in August 2022, and the draft CARF rules and CRS amendments were presented to the G20 in October 2022.[91] On 8 June 2023, the OECD published its International Standards for Automatic Exchange of Information in Tax Matters: Crypto-asset Framework and 2023 Updated to the Common Reporting Standard.[92] This has resulted in a new tax transparency framework that provides for the automatic exchange of tax information on transactions in cryptoassets in a standardised manner with the jurisdictions of residence of taxpayers (referred to as CARF) and a set of amendments to the CRS. The rule book is not binding, but OECD member countries may choose to ratify the provisions into their legal systems.

88 EU Travel Rule Regulation, Art 39.

89 MiCA, Art 148; EU Travel Rule Regulation, Art 40.

90 OECD, '60 Years' www.oecd.org/60-years/ [accessed 6 October 2023].

91 OECD, 'Crypto-Asset Reporting Framework and Amendments to the Common Reporting Standard' (Paris 2022) www.oecd.org/tax/exchange-of-tax-information/crypto-asset-reporting-framework-and-amendments-to-the-common-reporting-standard.pdf [accessed 6 October 2023].

92 OECD, 'International Standards for Automatic Exchange of Information in Tax Matters: Crypto-asset Framework and 2023 Updated to the Common Reporting Standard' (Paris 2022) www.oecd-ilibrary.org/taxation/international-standards-for-automatic-exchange-of-information-in-tax-matters_896d79d1-en [accessed 6 October 2023].

19.55 The CARF consists of three distinct components:[93]

(a) Rules and related Commentary that can be transposed into domestic law to collect information from Reporting Crypto-Asset Service Providers (RCASP) with a relevant nexus to the jurisdiction implementing the CARF;

(b) a Multilateral Competent Authority Agreement on Automatic Exchange of Information pursuant to the CARF (CARF MCAA) and related Commentary (or bilateral agreements or arrangements); and

(c) an electronic format (XML schema) to be used by Competent Authorities for purposes of exchanging the CARF information, as well as by RCASP to report CARF information to tax administrations (as permitted by domestic law).

19.56 Key features of the CARF include:

(a) A broad definition of 'Crypto-Asset' as 'a digital representation of value that relies on a cryptographically secured distributed ledger or a similar technology to validate and secure transactions', to align reporting with existing AML obligations. A 'Relevant Crypto-Asset' (RCA) is:

> '… any Crypto-Asset that is not a Central Bank Digital Currency, a Specified Electronic Money Product or any Crypto-Asset for which the Reporting CryptoAsset Service Provider has adequately determined that it cannot be used for payment or investment purposes.'[94]

Certain limited risk assets and closed-loop cryptoassets are also excluded.[95]

(b) Reporting obligations for RCASP means 'any individual or Entity that, as a business, provides a service effectuating exchange transactions for or on behalf of customers, including by acting as a counterparty, or as an intermediary, to such exchange transactions, or by making available a trading platform'[96] which would include exchanges, brokers, operators of crypto-asset ATMs, and DeFi platforms. Reporting is linked to factors such as tax residence, place of incorporation, or management. The framework specifies the information to be provided, including wallet addresses for cryptoasset transfers.[97]

(c) A 'Reportable Retail Payment Transaction' excludes cryptoassets transactions for goods and services below US$50,000.[98]

(d) Reportable relevant transactions under CARF include exchanges of cryptoassets for other cryptoassets or fiat currency and certain retail payment

93 *Ibid* 12 [8].
94 *Ibid* 22.
95 *Ibid* 51–52.
96 *Ibid* 22.
97 *Ibid* 18.
98 *Ibid* 22. Further information on de minimis reportable retail payment transactions can be found at 34–35.

transactions. Due diligence procedures build on the self-certification process of the CRS and reflect the 2012 FAFT recommendations.[99]

(e) RCASP must, with respect to its reportable cryptoasset users,[100] provide information such as identifying information, tax residence, place of incorporation or management, and transactions. The framework specifies the information to be provided, including wallet addresses for cryptoasset transfers.[101]

(f) It is anticipated that the OECD will continue developing guidance to support the consistent application of the CARF, including the definition of RCAs and future amendments.[102]

19.57 On 16 May 2023, the EU Economic and Financial Affairs Council reached agreement on a general approach consistent with the OECD CARF, to amend Directive 2011/16/EU on Administrative Cooperation in the Field of Taxation (DAC8)[103] with a proposed date for introduction of January 2026. The legislative proposal requires unanimous support and is in the process of being considered by the EU Parliament.[104] At the time of writing the UK government has not indicated a position on legislative implementation.

International Monetary Fund and Financial Stability Board

19.58 The International Monetary Fund (IMF) was established in 1944 in order to build a framework for international economic cooperation; its membership includes 190 countries and it is governed by and accountable to those countries.

19.59 The Financial Stability Board (FSB) was established by the G20 in April 2009 as the successor to the Financial Stability Forum. The UK is a member. The FSB coordinates at international level the work of national financial authorities and international standard-setting bodies and develops and promotes the implementation of effective regulatory, supervisory, and other financial sector policies in the interest of financial stability. It brings together national authorities

99 *Ibid* 13. See FATF, 'International Standards on Combating Money Laundering and the Financing of Terrorism & Proliferation' (Paris France 2012–2023), 135 www.fatf-gafi.org/content/dam/fatf-gafi/recommendations/FATF%20Recommendations%202012.pdf.coredownload.inline.pdf [accessed 26 September 2023].

100 *Ibid* 22, for definition of 'crypto-asset users'.

101 *Ibid* 18–19.

102 *Ibid* 12.

103 Council Directive 2011/16/EU of 15 February 2011 on administrative cooperation in the field of taxation and repealing Directive 77/799/EEC [2011] OJ L64/1.

104 www.consilium.europa.eu/en/press/press-releases/2023/05/16/cooperation-between-national-taxation-authorities-council-puts-the-spotlight-on-crypto-assets-and-the-wealthiest-individuals/ [accessed 7 September 2023]. See also Draft Council Directive amending Directive 2011/16/EU on administrative cooperation in the field of taxation (5 May 2023) https://data.consilium.europa.eu/doc/document/ST-8730-2023-INIT/en/pdf [accessed 21 November 2023].

responsible for financial stability in 24 countries and jurisdictions, international financial institutions, sector-specific international groupings of regulators and supervisors, and committees of central bank experts.[105] The FSB has assumed a key role in promoting the reform of international financial regulation and supervision.[106] The IMF has three missions: furthering international monetary cooperation, encouraging the expansion of trade and economic growth, and discouraging policies that would harm prosperity. IMF member countries work collaboratively with each other and with other international bodies to achieve this.[107]

19.60 In February 2022, the FSB published its Assessment of Risks to Financial Stability from Cryptoassets.[108] In February 2023, the IMF proposed Elements of Effective Policies for Crypto-assets.[109] In July 2023, the FSB published two high sets of High Level Recommendations for regulation of cryptoasset activities and markets[110] and global stablecoin (GSC) arrangements.[111] This was synthesised into one joint policy paper by the IMF and FSB.[112] This policy paper outlines the macroeconomic and global financial stability and regulatory risks and outlines a policy implementation roadmap involving the Committee on Payments and Market Infrastructures and International Organization of Securities Commissions (CPMI-IOSCO), FSB, IMF, FATF, SSBs and the World Bank.[113] The road map includes:[114]

(a) implementation of policy frameworks;

(b) outreach beyond G20 jurisdictions;

(c) global coordination, cooperation, and information sharing; and

(d) addressing data gaps.

19.61 In relation to cryptoasset activities and markets, the FSB's recommendations were as follows:[115]

105 FSB, 'Members of the FSB' www.fsb.org/about/organisation-and-governance/members-of-the-financial-stability-board/ [accessed 6 October 2023].

106 FSB, 'History of the FSB' www.fsb.org/about/history-of-the-fsb/ [accessed 6 October 2023].

107 IMF, 'IMF at a Glance' www.imf.org/en/About/Factsheets/IMF-at-a-Glance [accessed 7 September 2023].

108 FSB, 'Assessment of Risks to Financial Stability from Crypto-assets' (16 February 2022) www.fsb.org/wp-content/uploads/P160222.pdf [accessed 7 September 2023].

109 IMF, 'Elements of Effective Policies for Crypto Assets' (Policy Paper No 2023/004, 23 February 2023) IMF https://www.imf.org/en/Publications/Policy-Papers/Issues/2023/02/23/Elements-of-Effective-Policies-for-Crypto-Assets-530092 [accessed 7 September 2023].

110 FSB, 'High-level Recommendations for the Regulation, Supervision and Oversight of Crypto-Asset Activities and Markets' (Final Report, 17 July 2023) www.fsb.org/wp-content/uploads/P170723-2.pdf [accessed 6 October 2023].

111 *Ibid.*

112 IMF and FSB, 'IMF-FSB Synthesis Paper: Policies for Crypto-Assets' (7 September 2023) www.fsb.org/wp-content/uploads/R070923-1.pdf [accessed 7 September 2023].

113 *Ibid* 24–26.

114 *Ibid* 24.

115 *Ibid* 33–34.

(a) **Regulatory powers and tools**: authorities should have and utilise the appropriate powers and tools, and adequate resources to regulate, supervise, and oversee crypto-asset activities and markets, and enforce relevant laws and regulations effectively, as appropriate.

(b) **General regulatory framework**: authorities should apply comprehensive and effective regulation, supervision, and oversight to cryptoasset activities and markets – including cryptoasset issuers and service providers – on a functional basis and proportionate to the financial stability risk they pose, or potentially pose, and consistent with authorities' respective mandates in line with the principle 'same activity, same risk, same regulation'.

(c) **Cross-border cooperation, coordination and information sharing**: authorities should cooperate and coordinate with each other, both domestically and internationally, to foster efficient and effective communication, information sharing and consultation in order to support each other as appropriate in fulfilling their respective mandates and to encourage consistency of regulatory and supervisory outcomes.

(d) **Governance**: authorities, as appropriate, should require that cryptoasset issuers and service providers have in place and disclose a comprehensive governance framework with clear and direct lines of responsibility and accountability for all functions and activities they are conducting. The governance framework should be proportionate to their risk, size, complexity and systemic importance, and to the financial stability risk that may be posed by activity or market in which the cryptoasset issuers and service providers are participating. It should provide for clear and direct lines of responsibility and accountability for the functions and activities they are conducting.

(e) **Risk management**: authorities, as appropriate, should require cryptoasset service providers to have an effective risk management framework in place that comprehensively addresses all material risks associated with their activities. The framework should be proportionate to the risk, size, complexity, and systemic importance, and to the financial stability risk that may be posed by the activity or market in which they are participating. Authorities should, to the extent necessary to achieve regulatory outcomes comparable to those in traditional finance, require cryptoasset issuers to address the financial stability risk that may be posed by the activity or market in which they are participating.

(f) **Data collection, recording and reporting**: authorities, as appropriate, should require that cryptoasset issuers and service providers have in place robust frameworks, including systems and processes, for collecting, storing, safeguarding, and the timely and accurate reporting of data, including relevant policies, procedures and infrastructures needed, in each case proportionate to their risk, size, complexity and systemic importance. Authorities should have access to the data as necessary and appropriate to fulfil their regulatory, supervisory and oversight mandates.

(g) **Disclosures**: authorities should require that cryptoasset issuers and service providers disclose to users and relevant stakeholders comprehensive, clear and transparent information regarding their governance framework, operations, risk profiles and financial conditions, as well as the products they provide and activities they conduct.

(h) **Addressing financial stability risks arising from interconnections and interdependencies**: authorities should identify and monitor the relevant interconnections, both within the cryptoasset ecosystem, as well as between the cryptoasset ecosystem and the wider financial system. Authorities should address financial stability risks that arise from these interconnections and interdependencies.

(i) **Comprehensive regulation of cryptoasset service providers with multiple functions**: Authorities should ensure that crypto-asset service providers and their affiliates that combine multiple functions and activities, where permissible, are subject to appropriate regulation, supervision and oversight that comprehensively address the risks associated with individual functions and the risks arising from the combination of functions, including but not limited to requirements regarding conflicts of interest and separation of certain functions, activities, or incorporation, as appropriate.

19.62 In relation to global stablecoin (GSC) arrangements, the FSB's recommendations were as follows:[116]

(a) **Authorities' readiness to regulate and supervise GSC arrangements**: authorities should have and utilise the appropriate powers and tools, and adequate resources, to comprehensively regulate, supervise, and oversee a GSC arrangement and its associated functions and activities, and enforce relevant laws and regulations effectively.

(b) **Comprehensive oversight of GSC activities and functions**: authorities should apply comprehensive and effective regulatory, supervisory, and oversight requirements consistent with international standards to GSC arrangements on a functional basis and proportionate to their risks insofar as such requirements are consistent with their respective mandates.

(c) **Cross-border cooperation, coordination, and information sharing**: authorities should cooperate and coordinate with each other, both domestically and internationally, to foster efficient and effective communication, information sharing, and consultation in order to support each other in fulfilling their respective mandates and to ensure comprehensive regulation, supervision, and oversight of a GSC arrangement across borders and sectors, and to encourage consistency of regulatory and supervisory outcomes.

(d) **Governance structures and decentralised operations**: authorities should require that GSC arrangements have in place and disclose a comprehensive governance framework with clear and direct lines of responsibility and accountability for all functions and activities within the GSC arrangement.

116 *Ibid* 34–36.

(e) **Risk management**: authorities should require that GSC arrangements have effective risk management frameworks in place that comprehensively address all material risks associated with their functions and activities, especially with regard to operational resilience, cyber security safeguards, and AML/CFT measures, as well as 'fit and proper' requirements, if applicable, and consistent with jurisdictions' laws and regulations.

(f) **Data storage and access to data**: authorities should require that GSC arrangements have in place robust frameworks, including systems and processes for the collecting, storing, safeguarding, and timely and accurate reporting of data. Authorities should have access to the data as necessary and appropriate to fulfil their regulatory, supervisory, and oversight mandates.

(g) **Recovery and resolution of the GSC**: authorities should require that GSC arrangements have appropriate recovery and resolution plans.

(h) **Disclosures**: authorities should require that GSC issuers and, where applicable, other participants in the GSC arrangements provide all users and relevant stakeholders with comprehensive and transparent information to understand the functioning of the GSC arrangement, including the governance framework, any conflicts of interest and their management, redemption rights, stabilisation mechanism, operations, risk management framework, and financial condition.

(i) **Redemption rights, stabilisation, and prudential requirements**: authorities should require that GSC arrangements provide a robust legal claim to all users against the issuer and/or underlying reserve assets and guarantee timely redemption. For GSCs referenced to a single fiat currency, redemption should be at par into fiat. To maintain a stable value at all times and mitigate the risks of runs, authorities should require GSC arrangements to have an effective stabilisation mechanism, clear redemption rights and meet prudential requirements.

(j) **Conformance with regulatory, supervisory and oversight requirements before commencing operations**: authorities should require that GSC arrangements meet all applicable regulatory, supervisory, and oversight requirements of a particular jurisdiction before commencing any operations in that jurisdiction and adapt to new regulatory requirements as necessary and as appropriate.

19.63 Annex 3 of the IMF-FSB Synthesis Paper contains a shared work plan for FSB and SSBs in the coming years.[117]

Bank for International Settlements

19.64 In December 2022, the Group of Central Bank Governors and Heads of Supervision (GHOS), the oversight body of the Basel Committee on Banking Supervision, endorsed a finalised prudential standard on banks' crypto-asset

117 *Ibid* 37–41.

exposures known as SCO60. The standard provides a robust and prudent global regulatory framework for internationally active banks' exposures to cryptoassets to be implemented by 1 January 2025.[118]

19.65 In July 2023, the Bank for International Settlements (BIS) submitted a report to the G20 Finance Ministers and Central Bank Governors entitled 'The crypto ecosystem: key elements and risks'[119] concluding that due to 'inherent structural flaws' it is unsuitable to play a constructive role in the monetary system. The key takeaways from the report are:[120]

(a) The crypto ecosystem is subject to a high degree of fragmentation and is characterised by congestion and high fees. These structural flaws derive from the underlying economics of incentives of validators rather than from technology and while crypto has offered some elements of genuine innovation, these can be replicated or embedded in the safer and more trusted traditional finance system.

(b) Despite an original ethos of decentralisation, crypto and DeFi often feature substantial de facto centralisation, which introduces various pain points such as stablecoins, which piggyback on the credibility of the central bank's unit of account and may pose risks to monetary sovereignty.

(c) While DeFi mostly replicates services offered by the traditional financial system, it does not finance any activity in the real economy but amplifies known risks. Crypto and DeFi pose substantial risks to (especially retail) investors as growth is driven mainly by the speculative influx of new users hoping for high returns.

Financial Action Task Force

19.66 In June 2023, the Financial Action Task Force (FATF) conducted a targeted review of the implementation of its Standards on Virtual Assets and Virtual Asset Service Providers, which includes the Travel Rule. They also provided an update on emerging risks and market developments in this domain. The report reveals that worldwide adoption of these enhanced measures is still quite inadequate. This lack of regulation creates significant opportunities for criminals to take advantage of. It is crucial to urgently address these regulatory gaps on a global scale, and this will be a key priority as part of the FATF's Roadmap.[121]

118 See **4.5–4.30**.

119 BIS, 'The crypto ecosystem: key elements and risks Report submitted to the G20 Finance Ministers and Central Bank Governors' (July 2023) www.bis.org/publ/othp72.pdf [accessed 7 October 2023].

120 *Ibid* 1.

121 FATF, 'Targeted update on the implementation of the FATF Standards on Virtual Assets and Virtual Asset Service Providers' (Paris, June 2023) www.fatf-gafi.org/content/dam/fatf-gafi/guidance/June2023-Targeted-Update-VA-VASP.pdf.coredownload.inline.pdf [accessed 7 October 2023].

International Organization of Securities Commissions

19.67 In July 2022, the CPMI-IOSCO issued guidance regarding the application of the Principles for Financial Market Infrastructures (PFMI) to systemically important stablecoin arrangements.[122] In May 2023, IOSCO issued for consultation detailed policy recommendations to jurisdictions across the globe as to how to regulate crypto-assets service providers. The Recommendations in IOSCO's Consultation Report set expectations and guardrails to regulate and supervise cryptoasset markets. [123] The proposed recommendations are principles-based and outcomes-focused and are aimed at the activities performed by CASPs. They apply IOSCO's widely accepted global standards for securities markets regulation to address key issues and risks identified in cryptoasset markets. The proposed recommendations are activities-based and follow a 'lifecycle' approach in addressing the key risks identified in this report. They cover the range of activities in cryptoasset markets that involve CASPs from offering, admission to trading, ongoing trading, settlement, market surveillance and custody as well as marketing and distribution (covering advised and non-advised sales) to retail investors. The proposed recommendations do not cover activities, products or services provided in DeFi area.

19.68 In September 2023, IOSCO published its policy recommendations for Defi.[124] Their recommendations follow a principles-based and outcomes-focused approach, targeting DeFi products, services, arrangements, and activities. These recommendations align with IOSCO's globally accepted standards for regulating securities markets. IOSCO emphasises the importance of consistent regulation of cryptoasset markets and securities markets within each IOSCO jurisdiction, adhering to the principle of 'same activity, same risk, same regulatory outcome.'

19.69 Additionally, the proposed recommendations emphasise the need for increased cooperation among regulators to effectively coordinate responses to cross-border challenges in enforcement and supervision. They also address concerns related to regulatory arbitrage, which arises due to the global, cross-border nature of DeFi participants offering their products and services across multiple jurisdictions.[125]

Future directions and challenges

19.70 The UK is likely to witness continued evolution of international regulatory frameworks to keep pace with technological advancements and

122 COPMI-IOSCO, 'Application of the Principles for Financial Market Infrastructures to Stablecoin Arrangements' (IOSCO, July 2022) www.iosco.org/library/pubdocs/pdf/IOSCOPD707.pdf [accessed 7 October 2023].

123 IOSCO, 'Policy Recommendations for Crypto and Digital Asset Markets' (CR01/2023, May 2023) www.iosco.org/library/pubdocs/pdf/IOSCOPD734.pdf [accessed 8 September 2023].

124 IOSCO, 'Policy Recommendations for Decentralised Finance' (CR/04/2023, September 2023) www.iosco.org/library/pubdocs/pdf/IOSCOPD744.pdf [accessed 8 September 2023].

125 *Ibid* 16–42.

emerging risks. Regulations will be introduced and refined to address specific areas such as CBDCs, DeFi, DAOs, stablecoins and NFTs.

19.71 Collaboration among regulators globally will be crucial to establish consistent regulatory standards, promote interoperability, and mitigate regulatory arbitrage. Efforts to harmonise regulatory approaches across jurisdictions will shape the future of the legal landscape for cryptocurrencies.

19.72 The recent uniform legal framework for cryptoassets provided by MiCA will have a significant comprehensive impact on the EU market in cryptoassets, since it will allow firms to offer cryptoassets and provide related services across the Member States seamlessly. HM Treasury is currently implementing a similar phased strategy to MiCA.

CONCLUSION

19.73 The UK's legal and regulatory outlook for cryptoassets and DLT is dynamic. The cryptoasset ecosystem along with CBDCs are a global political agenda issue as can be seen from the G7 and G20 communiques.

19.74 Regulatory oversight and compliance with international standards is a priority for the UK and it is important for policymakers, businesses and individuals involved in the cryptocurrency ecosystem to stay informed about regulatory developments both domestically and internationally. Given the decentralised cross-border nature of cryptoassets, assessing applicable laws and ensuring legal compliance will remain a major issue for the foreseeable future.

Chapter 20

The Future of Cryptocurrency

INTRODUCTION

20.1 Cryptocurrencies have gained significant attention and adoption worldwide, and the UK is no exception. This chapter explores the future of cryptocurrencies in the UK, discussing potential trends, challenges, and opportunities that may shape the landscape in the coming years.

20.2 A prominent emerging trend stems from the existing legal clarifications that have already been initiated and are currently underway. These clarifications have primarily surfaced within the financial sector, driven by an exploration of the potential of distributed ledger technology (DLT) to lower intermediary costs, enhance efficiency and profitability. This trend entails a series of technological shifts within information systems that financial institutions are either experimenting with or planning to implement.

20.3 While the financial sector is at the forefront, other industries are also exploring DLT's capabilities. Sectors such as automotive, energy, luxury goods, and retail have initiated trials of blockchain applications to potentially shift their supply chains and traceability processes onto this protocol. The significance of these migrations, which could gain broader momentum, revolves around two key aspects: interoperability and legal assurance.[1]

20.4 To navigate this evolving landscape, we can identify three distinct categories of actors in developing the crypto ecosystem:[2]

(a) The first category encompasses individuals or entities responsible for developing and advocating DLT protocols themselves.

(b) The second category comprises actors dedicated to enhancing transaction security. Within a decentralised context, trust assumes paramount importance.

(c) The third group encompasses platforms offering services related to digital assets.

20.5 There is potential for the widespread adoption of digital tokens, cryptoassets, virtual currencies, or simply 'tokens' or 'coins,' collectively

1 Franck Guiader, 'Blockchain, crypto-assets, tokenisation: myth or plur(e)ality?' (2023) 29(3) Int TLR 133, 135.

2 *Ibid* 136–137.

referred to as the tokenisation of the economy. While these cryptoassets serve various purposes within different sub-categories, they all issued through a DLT. Cryptoassets possess attributes such as traceability and cryptography that position them as potential instruments for exchange, tracking, and loyalty in the future, without relying on a central controlling authority. These digital assets might find applications across several economic sectors due to their perceived security and potential cost benefits in enabling exchanges. This shift could reshape traditional business dynamics among producers, distributors, and payment infrastructures.[3]

FINANCIAL SERVICES

20.6 Cryptocurrency is revolutionising various aspects of the financial industry, ushering in innovative changes across securitised products, derivatives, securities financing, enablement use cases, debt markets, equity markets, and asset management.

Equity markets

20.7 In the realm of equity markets, while traditional operations and infrastructure in public equity markets are often deemed efficient by market participants and service providers, a diverse array of entities are venturing into or introducing DLT-based or smart contract solutions. These innovations aim to:[4]

(a) enhance flexibility in clearing and settlement timelines;

(b) minimise or eradicate settlement-related risks; and

(c) tackle the operational complexities linked to data silos within post-trade processing.

20.8 However, given the extensive transformation required to fully realise the potential benefits of most DLT-based solutions within centralised public equities markets, these initiatives are primarily in their nascent stages. In contrast, privately held equities, which lack the advantages of centralised infrastructure, standardised procedures, and abundant liquidity seen in public markets, remain a focal point for numerous stakeholders.[5]

20.9 Many of the evolving solutions seek to extend the efficiencies characteristic of public equity markets to the realm of private and SME shares through the implementation of DLT and tokenisation.[6]

3 *Ibid* 135–136.

4 World Economic Forum (WEF), 'Digital Assets, Distributed Ledger Technology and the Future of Capital Markets' (May 2021), 35 www3.weforum.org/docs/WEF_Digital_Assets_Distributed_Ledger_Technology_2021.pdf [accessed 7 October 2023].

5 *Ibid.*

6 *Ibid.*

20.10 Examples of DLT enabled equity markets include:[7]

(a) post-trade infrastructure – existing post-trade infrastructure is revamped using cryptocurrency;

(b) supplementary infrastructure – blockchain supplements post-trade processes;

(c) securities lifecycle – digital platforms cover the entire securities lifecycle; and

(d) equity tokens – cryptocurrency enables the issuance of equity tokens.

Debt markets

20.11 The realm of fixed income, especially bonds, has captured the attention of numerous observers and participants as an asset class ripe for substantial digital transformation. Several major DLT-based projects are already underway, with some high-profile 'blockchain bonds' having been issued in recent years. While the fixed-income landscape exhibits considerable diversity in market characteristics and operation, the challenges that DLT-based digitalisation could potentially address encompass:[8]

(a) inefficiencies in the processes of issuance, trading, and post-trade procedures;

(b) liquidity issues in secondary markets and the restricted issuance in primary markets; and

(c) limited market accessibility owing to high minimum transaction sizes.

20.12 In response to these challenges, various institutions are actively pursuing solutions, ranging from comprehensive end-to-end platforms to more specialised approaches targeting specific components of the value chain. Given the segmented, over-the-counter nature of secondary market trading, bonds are perceived as both more likely to benefit from DLT-based innovations and more amenable to transformation, without the necessity for an entire market overhaul.[9]

20.13 Examples of DLT debt markets include:[10]

(a) **Digital bond issuance**: cryptocurrency platforms facilitate the issuance of digital bonds.

(b) **Bond trading**: distributed order books on blockchain for bond trading.

7 *Ibid* 13.
8 *Ibid* 46.
9 *Ibid*.
10 *Ibid* 13.

(c) **Corporate bond lifecycle**: platforms cover the complete lifecycle of corporate bonds.

(d) **Retail bond issuance**: retail bonds are issued and distributed on blockchain.

(e) **Blockchain bonds**: stand-alone blockchain-based bond issuance gains prominence.

Derivatives

20.14 Derivatives contract management is a multifaceted process involving the coordination of numerous stakeholders. Despite a partial shift toward digital solutions in the industry, inefficiencies, particularly in the ongoing reconciliation of position-related data, continue to plague operations. Consequently, many market participants and service providers have embarked on initiatives to develop or investigate DLT-based solutions aimed at remedying these inefficiencies and mitigating risks. Several of these solutions are already active in the market and enable shared sources of truth and mutualised processing across ecosystems or within institutions.[11]

20.15 These innovative approaches include:[12]

(a) establishing a unified platform for the management of the post-trade life cycle of derivatives across counterparties;

(b) replacing existing post-trade infrastructure with a DLT-based system, particularly in markets with pre-existing central infrastructures;

(c) creating a versatile platform for institutions to oversee their margin and collateral pledging workflows across all derivatives counterparties; and

(d) developing a platform to mutualise data and streamline workflows for finalising derivatives trades.

20.16 Examples of DLT Derivatives include:[13]

(a) **OTC derivatives on DLT**: cryptocurrency platforms support post-trade processes for over-the-counter (OTC) derivatives, replacing traditional infrastructure with blockchain technology.

(b) **Collateral management**: DLT-based platforms manage collateral for cleared derivatives.

(c) **Exchange-traded derivatives**: cryptocurrency platforms oversee the complete trade lifecycle of exchange-traded derivatives.

11 *Ibid* 64.
12 *Ibid.*
13 *Ibid* 13.

Securities financing

20.17 Securities financing transactions, including repurchase agreements and securities lending, represent an arena where DLT can play a pivotal role. These transactions are typically operationally intricate, involving collateral, cash, and margin exchanges. Furthermore, they operate within tight time frames and are often characterised by relatively low profit margins. As a result, there is a growing interest in DLT-based solutions that:[14]

(a) alleviate the operational complexities associated with these transactions;

(b) reduce settlement timelines and associated risks; and

(c) enhance collateral management and its fluidity.

20.18 DLT and smart contract use cases have been developed to leverage the capabilities of this technology, achieving these objectives without necessitating a complete market-wide transformation (eg issuing digital securities). Consequently, many market participants view the digitalisation of collateral-based transactions as a catalyst for broader market digitalisation in the future, as institutions recognise the advantages while becoming more familiar and comfortable with the technology.[15]

20.19 Examples of DLT securities financing include:[16]

(a) **Repurchase agreements**: DLT underpins platforms for repurchase agreements.

(b) **Collateral swaps**: securities swaps occur across various collateral pools.

(c) **Securities lending**: traditional securities lending infrastructure is revamped on blockchain technology.

Securitised products

20.20 Securitised product markets are characterised by their substantial heterogeneity, stemming from variations in the underlying loans of mortgage-backed securities, asset-backed securities, collateralised loan obligations, and other financial instruments. Nevertheless, a common thread of widely recognised inefficiencies tied to manual processes and limited inter-institutional data trust runs through these markets. In addition to the shared challenges inherent in other securities markets, securitised products confront a distinctive set of issues as these securities effectively bundle the cash flows and risks of numerous underlying loans.[17]

14 *Ibid* 72.
15 *Ibid*.
16 *Ibid* 13.
17 *Ibid* 56.

20.21 While many agree on the significant potential for technology to enhance the entire value chain of securitised products, a substantial number of observers and market participants believe that DLT could offer distinct advantages to these markets. Specifically, DLT-based solutions have the potential to grant all relevant stakeholders in the value chain real-time access to identical data regarding underlying loans. This capability could significantly reduce the necessity for data verification and auditing throughout the life cycle of these securities.[18]

20.22 Examples of DLT securitised products include:[19]

(a) **End-to-end tokenisation**: cryptocurrency enables end-to-end origination, securitisation, and servicing platforms, allowing assets to be tokenised for efficient data management.

(b) **Loan tokenisation**: loans are tokenised for streamlined servicing and data handling.

(c) **Security servicing on DLT**: DLT facilitates secure servicing of securitised products.

Asset management

20.23 Asset management stands as a pivotal pillar within the global capital markets, commanding a substantial portion of global investment capital. These entities not only actively participate in the broader markets poised for transformation by DLT and related technologies but also grapple with inefficiencies and challenges. Here, distributed ledgers and smart contracts emerge as potential solutions. These solutions span a wide spectrum and include:[20]

(a) optimising the client onboarding and fund share issuance procedures;

(b) enhancing data sharing among various participants within the ecosystem; and

(c) undertaking comprehensive transformations of 'back-office' asset management operations.

20.24 While asset managers have begun offering cryptocurrency-based products, this section concentrates on solutions dedicated to enhancing operations and client services within traditional fund products. As financial assets continue to undergo tokenisation and digitisation, the asset management industry is poised for further transformation. Potential innovations may involve tokenised fund shares directly linked to underlying asset pools through smart contracts and the substitution of conventional fund structures with entirely customisable portfolios.[21]

18 *Ibid.*
19 *Ibid* 13.
20 *Ibid* 79.
21 *Ibid.*

20.25 Examples of DLT asset management include:[22]

(a) **Fund distribution**: DLT-based platforms streamline fund distribution and maintain registers.

(b) **Tokenised funds**: investor-facing platforms handle end-to-end processes for tokenised funds.

(c) **Fund administration**: cryptocurrency platforms support fund administration and servicing networks.

Enablement use cases

20.26 While numerous institutions are primarily focused on directly revolutionising specific securities and derivatives markets, others are diligently crafting technological solutions and infrastructure geared towards catalysing digitisation throughout the capital markets. Some are venturing into technological solutions in adjacent areas within the financial services ecosystem. Collectively, these use cases hold the potential to be the driving forces behind transformation in the capital markets. They encompass:[23]

(a) products originating in areas adjacent to the capital markets, yet upon which many capital markets operations rely (eg wholesale payments);

(b) solutions allowing institutions to seamlessly adapt to a DLT environment (eg institutional custody for digital assets); and

(c) Tools that enable institutions to fully harness the potential advantages offered by this technology (eg digital identity and document sharing).

These use cases defy easy categorisation into asset class divisions and often serve as indispensable components of solutions explored elsewhere in this report.

20.27 Some examples of DLT enablement use cases include:[24]

(a) **Wholesale payments**: cryptocurrency facilitates efficient wholesale payment systems.

(b) **Capital markets digitisation**: capital markets embrace digital transformation with cryptocurrency.

(c) **Custody services**: digital assets find secure custody services on blockchain platforms.

(d) **Digital asset issuance**: platforms enable the issuance of digital assets.

22 *Ibid* 13.
23 *Ibid* 84.
24 *Ibid* 13.

Strategic considerations for various capital markets stakeholders

Corporate issuer

20.28 Embracing crypto and DLT presents a promising opportunity for corporate issuers. It opens doors to a potentially lower cost of funding, stemming from a wider investment base, heightened secondary market liquidity, reduced transaction costs, and even direct participation in capital markets. This shift could substantially enhance their financial efficiency.

Investment bank

20.29 Investment banks can tap into new revenue streams thanks to the emergence of novel asset classes and parallel markets. Additionally, they stand to gain significant cost savings through streamlined and automated processes, potentially revitalising their operations. However, there is a risk of losing business if issuers start accessing markets directly, bypassing traditional intermediaries.

Broker/dealer

20.30 Broker/dealers can benefit from substantial cost savings as well, thanks to more efficient and automated processes. They can also unlock capital and liquidity savings through flexible settlement solutions. However, there is a counterbalance in the form of potential business loss resulting from a shift toward greater market concentration in over-the-counter markets.

Custodian bank

20.31 Custodian banks are presented with opportunities for cost savings driven by streamlined operations and processes. Furthermore, the potential for enhanced capital and liquidity management is on the horizon, primarily due to the increased flexibility in settlement. Nevertheless, they must be wary of potential risks to their traditional 'custody' role if a radical change in the industry occurs.

Asset manager

20.32 Asset managers can diversify their portfolio of services by leveraging new asset classes and parallel markets that crypto and DLT enable. They also stand to gain from cost reductions via streamlined operations, including lower custody costs. The enhanced flexibility in settlement contributes to capital and liquidity savings.

Asset owner/investor

20.33 Asset owners and investors have a unique opportunity to enjoy improved liquidity in secondary markets for specific asset classes. Moreover, they can explore investments in previously inaccessible asset classes, parallel markets, or markets that were traditionally challenging to access.

Exchange

20.34 Exchanges are well-positioned to expand their role within the value chain, potentially venturing into additional asset classes. They can capitalise on the evolving landscape driven by crypto and DLT to broaden their market presence.

Infrastructure provider

20.35 Infrastructure providers face potential risks to their traditional business models as markets gravitate away from conventional central securities depositories. However, regulatory support in favour of maintaining their role as systemic infrastructure remains robust. This situation offers an opportunity to diversify into governing decentralised platforms and smart contracts.

Other institutions (eg trustees, transfer agents, registrars)

20.36 Institutions outside of the core financial intermediaries might experience some turbulence due to increased transparency in securities and the automation of reporting and life-cycle activities. Nonetheless, the legal and regulatory foundations for their roles remain intact, offering stability. Additionally, there's potential for new lines of business by providing value-added services in this evolving landscape.[25]

WEB 3.0

20.37 The first generation of the World Wide Web, invented by Tim Berners-Lee in 1989 was a 'read-only' web where individuals and companies could broadcast information to audiences. There were some streaming and downloadable multimedia, limited forms of interactivity such as chatrooms, forums and browser-based games. Members of the public could make their own websites but it required a basic level of technical expertise.

20.38 The second generation, starting in 2004 and accelerating in the 2000s with more people in the Global North gaining access to broadband and mobile internet, transformed into a 'read-write' web. Web 2.0 focused on harnessing network effects to share, create and interact with content as well as consume it. Blogging, social media, platforms, APIs, web services, apps, and online

25 *Ibid* 28.

communities made it easy for everyone to take part and easier for large technology companies to centralise and control traffic.

20.39 The third generation of the internet, semantic web, or the decentralised internet all mean the same thing. The concept is that instead of linking information or documents for humans and computers to read, Web 3.0 links data or objects with highly structured semantic connections. At its most basic, it implies a distributed infrastructure for the internet with less reliance on tech companies, governments and payment processors. Users would control their own data and use a single personalised account for all their internet activities (including their phone and 'smart home'). The blockchain could act as an anonymous public ledger to record all that activity – not the individual's government ID, credit card, or biometrics. The state and private sector would have no control over the user's digital identity.

20.40 The original vision for the web was for it to be much more open and transparent, with no corporate control. Web 3.0's goal is to revert to this paradigm using smart contracts for automated trust between users, to control user data and transactions, instead of centralised organisations. Part of this will involve the use of open source apps and advanced AI so that people build their own tech services without needing to code or pay someone else to do it. This paradigm envisages new social networks, search engines, and marketplaces forming with no companies involved. However, it may end up being similar to Web 2.0 but less regulation and more fragmentation.

20.41 Most of current Web 3.0 projects focus on gambling and speculation while DAOs and other Web 3.0 projects have governance issues. Based on their share of ownership of a platform or organisation, users can sometimes hold governance tokens that entitle them to vote on the rules that govern it. These rules are then executed by smart contracts. Older internet protocols (such as TCP/IP and HTML) are governed via the multistakeholder model. Web 3.0 protocols might have the same reach and play a similar infrastructural role as these Web 1.0 protocols, but they have privatised governance structures like the tech companies of Web 2.0. The foundations of the new internet are in private control and can prioritise specific use cases.

20.42 Decentralised governance can be difficult and time-consuming, and comes with responsibility, investors and founders do not always know what legal rights, responsibilities or opportunities they ultimately hold. Delegating decision-making to expert individuals, private companies like Coinbase and Rainbow, or specialist agencies also has risks.

20.43 Coordinated inauthentic behaviour is a real problem that will only grow with distributed networks, reduced content moderation and more platforms to monitor. With Web 3.0, the illusion of community governance and transparency can make people feel secure with no regulatory safeguards.[26]

26 Phoenix CS Andrews, 'Privacy, Security, Citizen Rights and Transparency in Web 3.0' (Blair Institute of Global Change Briefing, 24 March 2022) www.institute.global/insights/tech-and-digitalisation/privacy-security-citizen-rights-and-transparency-web-30 [accessed 8 September 2023].

20.44 Legal policy issues include:[27]

(a) **Libel, harassment, defamation and dispute resolution**: cases are pursued or threatened in England and Wales that would not meet the legal threshold in other jurisdictions, even following the Defamation Act 2013. Legal systems are based on geography, which does not operate smoothly in a decentralised world. Location and identity can be more fluid online, and a decentralised organisation cannot even be said to be owned by individuals based in one physical place, nor a distributed entity hosted in a single physical server location. Guarantees offered by platforms or a specific country's laws can be difficult to uphold and disagreements between users over content or ownership and disputes between users and platforms cannot simply be resolved using smart contracts or existing laws. Harassment by a network (ie multiple perpetrators making individual comments at a single person or minority group) is not something that policymakers have fully addressed.

(b) **Online safety**: the duty of care principle in the Online Safety Act 2023 does not apply to platforms below a certain size. New and emerging crypto-enabled social media platforms may launch with no content moderation or blocking facilities. Crypto gambling mechanics within games and productivity apps are not regulated.

(c) **Money laundering**: there are multiple ways in which money laundering happens in Web 3.0 (such as chain hopping, shell VASPs, and programmatic money laundering); these can be detected via techniques such as cross-chain analytics, owner analytics and behavioural analytics, but the potential to act is limited and financial crime, AML/CTF laws and FATF requirements will probably need to be updated to take into account Web 3.0 innovations, as decentralised providers cannot easily be tied to a single jurisdiction.

GOVERNMENT

CBDCs

20.45 Governments and central banks are exploring the concept of issuing their own digital currencies, known as CBDCs. CBDCs could modernise payment systems, enhance financial inclusion, and offer new tools for monetary policy and governance.[28]

Realtime payments

20.46 Cryptocurrencies offer a feature called streaming payments, where funds flow continuously from one account to another, with intervals as short as

27 *Ibid.*
28 See **18.1–18.41**.

one second. These payments are facilitated by smart contracts, which are self-executing code stored on the blockchain, triggered by preset conditions. DApps on blockchains like Solana and Ethereum, such as StreamFlow and Sablier, enable users to set up streaming payments to recipients with crypto wallets.

20.47 CBDCs have the potential to enhance efficiency, security, and accessibility in payments, especially as cash transactions decline and digital payments rise in retail. Retail CBDCs, in particular, can address challenges in implementing real-time payments due to their specific characteristics:

(a) **Efficiency**: CBDCs can lower transaction costs and speed up payments, benefiting gig workers by providing real-time, low-cost earnings transfers, and reducing reliance on credit.

(b) **Trust and liquidity**: CBDCs, backed by the central bank, inspire trust and stability compared to other payment methods, like cryptocurrencies. They offer more stability and liquidity as they derive value from the national currency, which is crucial for supporting large gig payments.

(c) **Accessibility**: CBDCs can grant access to digital financial services for unbanked and underbanked populations, enhancing inclusion in the gig economy, even for those without consistent internet access, smartphones, or traditional bank accounts.

(d) **Cross-border payments**: CBDCs can facilitate faster and more seamless cross-border payments, enabling gig workers to explore opportunities globally. Interoperability among CBDCs could revolutionise international transfers, reducing fees and fragmentation.

(e) **Innovation**: CBDCs can drive financial innovation, encouraging participation from existing financial institutions and citizens, similar to the advancements seen with blockchain and cryptocurrencies.

(f) **Security**: CBDCs, issued and backed by central banks, offer a secure alternative to existing payment methods. Policymakers must decide between centralised and distributed ledger systems for recording CBDC transactions, each with its own security and efficiency considerations.

20.48 Policymakers will likely consider how CBDCs can benefit the 'gig economy' by making payments faster and more reliable. CBDCs should offer clear value to users compared to existing payment methods, with features like real-time and streaming payments that meet user preferences. CBDC design efforts will need to align with other nations to facilitate global participation along with robust security measures to protect CBDC payment systems from cyberattacks and exploitation.

20.49 Challenges lie in creating incentives for financial intermediaries to distribute and adopt CBDCs while finding a balance between user privacy and oversight to counter illicit financing, technological measures to protect personal data. These principles should consider the needs and concerns of all stakeholders, including workers, central banks, governments, and the private sector.[29]

Universal basic income

20.50 Universal basic income (UBI) is a social-economic programme where all citizens regularly receive money from the government without any conditions. While current methods like progressive taxation and social programmes address economic inequality to some extent, their impact is limited. Additionally, these approaches are costly to administer, and the resources available for redistribution are decreasing.

20.51 CBDCs can serve as the foundation for a UBI programme in a digital economy. If a digital transaction network is adopted nationwide for most economic activities, a small fee can be collected from each transaction and distributed equally to citizens as UBI.

20.52 The key features of this digital UBI design include:

(a) **network coverage**: a digital transaction network handling most domestic economic transactions;

(b) **automated fee collection**: automatically collecting a fixed percentage of fees from each transaction;

(c) **account coverage**: every citizen having a unique account on the network; and

(d) **automated UBI delivery**: distributing the collected fees periodically to citizens' accounts as UBI.

This design allows citizens to directly benefit from economic activity. The UBI amount fluctuates with economic growth and inflation, as fees are based on transaction volumes.

20.53 The UBI amount depends on network adoption, transaction-fee percentage, and economic activity. Additional features, like allowing citizens to save and accumulate wealth through staking their UBI or providing newborns with UBI that accumulates until adulthood, can enhance the programme. In essence, digital UBI, facilitated by CBDCs and a comprehensive transaction network, offers a promising approach to addressing economic inequality, and promoting financial inclusion.[30]

29 Mohit Chawdhry, 'Revolutionising Gig Payments Using CBDCs' (Paper, Tony Blair Institute of Global Change (TBIGC), 10 March 2023) www.institute.global/insights/tech-and-digitalisation/revolutionising-gig-payments-using-cbdcs [accessed 7 October 2023].

30 Tascha Che, 'A Proposal for Web3-Based Universal Basic Income' (TBIGC, 10 March 2023) www.institute.global/insights/tech-and-digitalisation/proposal-web3-based-universal-basic-income [accessed 7 October 2023].

Government budgets

20.54 Blockchain technology is being explored as a means to enhance financial transparency in government operations. It aims to improve public understanding of budget allocation, enable real-time tracking of public spending, reduce corruption, enhance government efficiency, and rebuild trust in government institutions. Corruption, encompassing misappropriation of funds, bribery, embezzlement, and tax evasion, hinders government service delivery and escalates public expenditure costs.

20.55 Globally, open data portals have transformed paper documents into machine-readable data or APIs. These portals provide access to data related to demographics, economics, healthcare, climate, education, energy, and government operations. This practice promotes standard data publishing procedures and encourages agencies to make data publicly accessible. Despite open data initiatives and procurement portals, real-time tracking of financial transactions, ranging from large procurement projects to microtransactions, remains elusive to the public and government departments. Budget reports are often inadequately shared, concealing the extent of government spending.

20.56 Blockchain technology is increasingly applied to government operations, potentially leading to the emergence of government applications known as 'gApps.' These applications may utilise consensus mechanisms like delegated PoS or PoA, which require less computational power and can be maintained by a limited number of approved node validators. Centralised blockchains with permissioned settings ensure data permanence and accessibility, minimising downtime. Governments have employed centralised blockchain applications in various sectors, including land registries, vehicle titling, digital currencies, credential validation, vaccine verification, loan and grant tracking, tax monitoring, and blockchain-based voting.

20.57 Implementing blockchain for financial transactions enables real-time accounting of government entities. In such a scenario, every monetary transaction is recorded on the blockchain, providing unprecedented transparency. Public wallet addresses are linked to agencies or individuals, making their financial transactions visible to anyone with internet access.

20.58 Blockchain-based transaction data are perpetually searchable. Public users would be able to instantly query financial data, and specialised search engines for government financial tracking may emerge. Transactions could be searched using labels, names, department tags, addresses, and other criteria. Bots equipped with red-flag alert systems could identify suspicious transactions and emerging patterns. Machine learning techniques applied to procurement data could predict corruption trends and provide insights into inefficient spending.

20.59 Machine learning tools can extend beyond identifying suspicious activity to improving efficiency and reducing waste. Spending trends and transaction records are immutable, preventing data manipulation without consensus among node validators.

20.60 A public-sector blockchain typically comprises a three-tier system:

(a) **Layer-1**: a protocol base layer establishing data and standards, featuring a PoA consensus model;

(b) **Layer-2**: a complementary sidechain; and

(c) **Layer-3**: an application with a user-friendly interface that utilises the blockchain.

20.61 As such, a minimal viable public-sector blockchain requires a protocol base layer with standardised tokens, employing a PoA consensus model. A digital treasury, external validators, and a one-to-one exchange mechanism ensure currency stability and transparency. Treasury issuance is tied to local currency deposits, ensuring currency stability. This model, while centralised, offers an unparalleled level of transparency, preventing token creation or wallet management by external parties.[31]

Identity management

20.62 Blockchain's inherent security features make it an attractive solution for digital identity management. Self-sovereign identity systems are emerging, allowing individuals to control and share their personal data securely while minimising the risk of identity theft.

20.63 With 'big-tech' user accounts, signing into online services can be very easy and allows you to sign into multiple different sites. As a user you can get an account relatively quickly obtain services and will not have to create an account when you return. However, this frictionless user flow is not always seen when accessing government services. The registration process is much slower and there is not a shared view of the user using the services requiring repetition of a lot of information in registration forms. The UK's Government Digital Service (GDS) team identified this issue and is looking at ways to try to improve the user's experience; they have focused on the siloed continued re-registration process, lack of linked data, and difficulty in knowing where the most up-to-date information is.

20.64 Linked data on the semantic web has the potential not only to improve citizens' experience of using government service, but also to enable better, data-informed decision-making across all levels of government. Berners-Lee has put forward the idea of using personal data 'pods' which will be maintained by the user and can move between different services—rather like moving social media platforms

31 Emil Skandul, 'Budgets on the Blockchain: Maximally Transparent Transactions' (TBIGC, 10 March 2023) www.institute.global/insights/tech-and-digitalisation/budgets-blockchain-maximally-transparent-transactions[accessed 7 October 2023].

and taking your friend list with you or moving doctors and taking your medical history with you. GDS is using Tim Berners-Lee's start-up, Solid, to help with its national identity work. Solid is based on the concept of personal data pods that give users control over the data they share. The National Data Strategy and Geospatial Commission Strategy show interest in making government data more interoperable between departments. The Covid-19 pandemic has highlighted the benefits of linking healthcare data and spurred work to continue through NHS Digital. Work from the GDS continues to build on the 'Government as a Platform' concept and combines user research with technical software work to make government services easier to access. Other programmes such as National Digital Twin draw on similar concepts, creating individual data objects, connected via standards.[32]

20.65 The Connecting Europe Facility (CEF) is working on the European Blockchain Services Infrastructure (EBSI), which is being put together by the European Commission in close cooperation with the European Blockchain Partnership (EBP). Like eDelivery, eSignature, and eID, EBSI is another strategy in digital transformation of EU public services. This would allow users to create and control their own identity (using the European Self-Sovereign Identity Framework) across borders without relying on centralised authorities, while at the same time being in control of their educational credentials. In practical terms, this means that blockchain can facilitate checks on the integrity and origin of official documents without the need to contact their issuing entity each time.[33]

Voting

20.66 Blockchain's transparency and tamper-resistant properties are being explored for secure and verifiable voting systems, enabling more inclusive and trustworthy elections.[34] Additionally, blockchain-based governance models are being implemented in various organisations and projects to enhance transparency and decision-making processes. United Nations (UN) Internet Governance Forum (IGF) Dynamic Coalition on Blockchain Assurance and Standardization has distributed a suite of blockchain standards authored by the Government Blockchain Association (GBA), including standards for the use of blockchain technology in elections.[35] The GBA Voting Working Group, comprising election

32 Yusuf Sohoye, 'Just Semantics: How Web 3.0 Can Make Digital Government a Reality' (Paper, TBIGC, 8 December 2021) www.institute.global/insights/tech-and-digitalisation/just-semantics-how-web-30-can-make-digital-government-reality [accessed 8 September 2023].

33 European Commission, 'Digital Europe: eIDAS enablers – Distributed Ledger Technologies Shaping the Future of Digital Governments' (Building Blocks) https://ec.europa.eu/digital-building-blocks/wikis/pages/viewpage.action?pageId=533365462 [accessed 7 October 2023].

34 Uzma Jafar, Mohd Juzaiddin Ab Aziz, and Zarina Shukur, 'Blockchain for Electronic Voting System – Review and Open Research Challenges', (2021) 21(17) Sensors 5874.

35 GBA, 'Request for Comments: Blockchain Based Voting Standards' (29 June 2023) https://gbaglobal.org/blog/2023/07/29/request-for-comments-blockchain-based-voting-standards/ [accessed 9 September 2023]; GBA, Draft BMM Voting System Supplement (17 August 2023) https://gbaglobal.org/wp-content/uploads/2023/08/BMM-Voting-Supplement-v0.9.1.pdf [accessed 9 September 2023].

officials, election system vendors, and global DLT experts, aims to make elections trustworthy and accessible. [36]

CityCoins

20.67 Web 3.0 fosters community creation beyond the control of the state and large corporations, and initiatives like CityCoins show how these tools can engage communities with traditional institutions, such as city governments. CityCoins, are powered by Stacks blockchain technology. They enable people to invest in cities while cities gain funding. CityCoins promote civic engagement by allocating a portion of mining profits to a specific city, allowing cities to experiment with new financial approaches.

20.68 CityCoins are generated by miners who transfer Stacks Tokens (STX) to a CityCoins contract. Existing CityCoins users who stack their tokens receive 70 per cent of STX profits, while 30 per cent go to a digital wallet for the city. Cities cannot hold cryptocurrencies directly due to regulations; the 30 per cent contribution is later converted into fiat currency. CityCoins do not involve cities in their creation or management. Anyone can vote to select the next city for a CityCoin, and anyone can mine CityCoins. These tokens are based on Bitcoin to leverage its global currency potential.

20.69 CityCoins share similarities with local currencies aimed at boosting a city's economy. However, they differ in their intended use and value stability. CityCoins are not designed as local currencies but as a way for people to hold 'stock' in a city. They aim to reward civic involvement and commitment rather than facilitating local transactions.

20.70 CityCoins' value volatility, similar to Bitcoin's, could hinder their use as a practical currency. Users might prefer holding and trading CityCoins for speculative purposes rather than using them for everyday transactions. Several technical questions remain unanswered for CityCoins. These include how STX in the city's wallet will be converted to fiat currency, decentralisation plans, and environmental impacts. If CityCoins gain traction, policymakers will closely monitor their usage, balance their monetary and civic aspects, and address technical and environmental concerns.[37]

36 GBA, 'UN Blockchain Dynamic Coalition' https://gbaglobal.org/voting-resources/ [accessed 9 September 2023].

37 Lauren Packard and Henry Fingerhut, 'CityCoins: Civic Engagement for the Crypto Era' (TBIGC, Explainer, 8 January 2022) www.institute.global/insights/tech-and-digitalisation/citycoins-civic-engagement-crypto-era [accessed 7 October 2023].

Network State

20.71 In 2022, Balaji Srinivasan, the former Chief Technical Officer of Coinbase proposed the concept of the 'Network State' in his book of the same name.[38] Srinivasan defines a Network State in the following terms:[39]

> 'A network state is a highly aligned online community with a capacity for collective action that crowdfunds territory around the world and eventually gains diplomatic recognition from pre-existing states.'

20.72 This proposed novel form of government has the following key elements:[40]

(a) **Social network**: it requires a group of connected individuals bound by a smart contract, akin to Rousseau's 'social contract,' forming a cooperative network.

(b) **Moral innovation**: this society must have a clear and purpose-driven ethos to thrive, focusing on a shared set of values or a common goal.

(c) **National consciousness**: citizens should recognise their choice to unite and cooperate in building a decentralised but cohesive nation.

(d) **Recognised founder**: founders play a vital early role in providing direction and legitimacy to the project, though leadership may later decentralise.

(e) **Capacity for collective action**: a transparent blockchain-based structure facilitates decision-making and cooperative efforts, similar to a 'network union'.

(f) **Interpersonal civility**: a respectful and friendly online environment fosters a high-trust society where people choose to stay.

(g) **Integrated cryptocurrency**: a recognised cryptocurrency, along with a secure and transparent blockchain, empowers citizens and ensures economic sovereignty.

(h) **Consensual government**: citizens opt-in voluntarily, and smart contracts define the limited authority of the network state.

(i) **Archipelago of crowdfunded territory**: while starting online, network states may eventually acquire physical territory for in-person interactions, crucial for diplomatic recognition.

(j) **Virtual capital**: an online hub, like a virtual reality environment or platform, serves as the virtual capital for citizens.

38 Balaji Srinivasan, 'The Network State: How to Start a New Country' (The Network State, July 2022) https://thenetworkstate.com/ [accessed 7 October 2023].

39 Srinivasan, 'The Network State in One Sentence' (The Network State, July 2022) https://thenetworkstate.com/the-network-state-in-one-sentence [accessed 7 October 2023].

40 Srinivasan, 'On Network States' (The Network State, July 2022) https://thenetworkstate.com/on-network-states [accessed 7 October 2023].

(k) **On-chain census**: diplomatic recognition is achieved when the society proves its population, territory, and income via a rigorous and auditable Web3 system and social smart contracts.

20.73 While a Network State has yet to materialise there have been small experiments such as Zuzalu in Montenegro which was funded by Vitalik Buterin, the founder of Ethereum.[41]

INTERNET OF THINGS

20.74 The internet of things (IoT) connects people, places, and products, creating opportunities for value creation and capture. IoT involves embedding advanced chips, sensors, and actuators in physical items that transmit data to the network. Analytics within IoT turns data into actionable insights, impacting business processes and fostering innovation. Nevertheless, there remain unresolved technical and security issues.

20.75 IoT operates across devices owned by different organisations, making it challenging to trace data leaks during cyberattacks. Data ownership is often unclear due to multiple stakeholders. Blockchain can address IoT's security and scalability concerns in several ways:

(a) Blockchain's tamper-proof distributed ledger eliminates the need for trust among parties and secures IoT data.

(b) It adds an additional layer of security, making it difficult for hackers to breach the network.

(c) Blockchain offers transparency, enabling authorised users to track past transactions and identify the source of data leaks.

(d) It supports fast transaction processing and coordination among countless connected devices.

(e) By fostering trust, blockchain reduces costs associated with IoT gateways.

20.76 Smart contracts stored on DLT automate contractual agreements based on predefined criteria, streamlining processes. Emerging DLT-IoT players and their use cases demonstrate the potential for data-driven value creation.

20.77 Current IoT systems with a centralised architecture face security vulnerabilities. DLT mitigates this by decentralising decision-making. However, when integrating IoT devices with blockchain, three key challenges must be addressed:

41 Alexandra McCarroll, 'Crypto Social Experiments: A Beginners Guide To Network States And Vitalik Buterin's Initiative In Montenegro' (Forbes, 26 May 2023) www.forbes.com/sites/alexandramccarroll/2023/05/26/crypto-social-experiments-a-beginners-guide-to-network-states-and-vitalik-buterins-initiative-in-montenegro/ [accessed 10 September 2023]; See also Zuzalu City, 'Zuzalu City' https://zuzalu.city/ [accessed 10 September 2023].

(a) **Scalability**: handling vast IoT data requires a clear data model to prevent performance issues.

(b) **Network privacy and transaction confidentiality**: public DLTs may compromise privacy, necessitating consideration of hybrid or private DLT.

(c) **Sensor integrity**: ensuring IoT sensor reliability is crucial for data accuracy and security.

20.78 In conclusion, DLT and IoT are promising technologies but face adoption challenges due to technical and security issues. Companies are exploring combined use cases to minimise risks and enhance security in this evolving landscape.[42]

ARTIFICIAL INTELLIGENCE

20.79 Artificial Intelligence (AI) and DLT technologies are likely to merge, creating new platforms, products, and services. When combined with IoT, these technologies offer even greater possibilities. In this convergence, IoT would act as the 'sensing' part, AI as the 'thinking' part, and blockchain as the 'remembering' part. This convergence has potential applications in smart cities, improving urban life through better infrastructure and safety.

20.80 IoT and DLT play crucial roles in enabling AI by providing the large datasets needed for AI learning. IoT generates and collects data, and as IoT devices become more affordable and widespread, they contribute significantly to data availability. DLT acts as a vast repository of validated records, supporting AI learning. Together, IoT and DLT reduce data collection costs, preventing AI from being dominated by a few large players. Blockchain's decentralised network addresses security, privacy, and resilience needs in the context of AI and IoT. As IoT gathers more consumer data, society's demand for security and data protection increases. Blockchain can enhance IoT infrastructure scalability, provide secure data audit trails, and improve IoT device interoperability with a trusted, common communication layer. Additionally, it can facilitate open, decentralised markets where data producers can sell, rent, or share their data, AI models, and resources.

20.81 The combination of AI, DLT and IoT can open new operational and commercial opportunities. Potential future examples of combined applications include:[43]

42 Deloitte, 'Can blockchain accelerate Internet of Things (IoT) adoption?' https://www2.deloitte.com/ch/en/pages/innovation/articles/blockchain-accelerate-iot-adoption.html [accessed 7 October 2023].

43 Arnold Verbeek and Maria Lundqvist, 'Artificial intelligence, blockchain and the future of Europe: How disruptive technologies create opportunities for a green and digital economy' (European Commission and European Investment Bank Main Report, June 2021), 37 www.eib.org/attachments/thematic/artificial_intelligence_blockchain_and_the_future_of_europe_report_en.pdf [accessed 7 October 2023].

(a) **Retail**: AI can enable predictive action based on data collected from IoT devices (eg ordering food), while DLT can support secure transaction processing.

(b) **Healthcare**: AI can enable monitoring of medical data, early detection of abnormalities and automatic scheduling of appointments, while DLT can provide a secure, accurate medical history.

(c) **Cybersecurity**: AI can enable fast, accurate data analysis, making logical decisions and taking autonomous actions, while DLT can store a secure record of potential evidence.

(d) **Manufacturing**: AI can enable comprehensive remote status and performance monitoring of machines across the globe, machine learning-powered proactive maintenance, and the assignment of the most suitable technician with replacement parts, while DLT can provide a secure way of purchasing.

SUSTAINABLE AND GREEN DLT SOLUTIONS

20.82 The energy consumption of certain blockchain networks, especially those using proof of work (PoW) consensus mechanisms, has raised concerns about environmental sustainability. Innovations like proof of stake (PoS)and Layer 2 scaling solutions aim to reduce energy consumption and make blockchain more eco-friendly.

20.83 Technological advancements can reduce the energy consumption of cryptocurrency networks. The energy usage of a cryptocurrency largely depends on whether it employs a blockchain and, if so, the consensus mechanism it uses. Several consensus mechanisms are more energy efficient than PoW. PoS is one such mechanism, where validators lock up cryptocurrency as 'stake' to validate transactions. Ethereum plans to transition to PoS, anticipating a 99.95 per cent reduction in energy consumption. Many top cryptocurrencies already use energy-efficient protocols, and Optical proof-of-work aims to eliminate energy as the primary mining cost by using light-based computing. Beyond blockchain, technologies like Directed Acyclic Graph and public hashgraphs offer promising alternatives for specific crypto applications, focusing on energy efficiency and scalability.

20.84 The challenge lies in convincing existing crypto miners to adopt more energy-efficient solutions, especially for well-established networks like Bitcoin. Transitioning such networks to energy-efficient mechanisms requires buy-in from a large and dispersed miner community. Additionally, creating entirely new, energy-efficient, and scalable crypto networks presents substantial challenges, as many promising protocols are still in early development stages. Policymakers will likely explore incentive structures to encourage the adoption of energy-efficient alternatives. Ethereum's transition to PoS highlights the need for governance frameworks to mitigate risks in ambitious projects like DeFi insurance.

20.85 Apart from consensus mechanisms and ledger technology, improving miners' operational models can enhance efficiency. Techniques like transaction batching and second-layer transactions reduce the overall number of transactions, enhancing mining efficiency. Miners can leverage waste heat generated by mining equipment for heating buildings. Immersion cooling offers higher energy efficiency. However, some coolants, like fluorocarbons, have environmental impacts. Achieving efficiency gains often necessitates new hardware and software, leading to electronic waste (e-waste) concerns. Hardware upgrades can quickly render previous models obsolete, contributing to substantial e-waste generation.

20.86 Policymakers can support circular economy initiatives to address e-waste resulting from crypto mining and encourage demonstrations and proofs-of-concept for innovative solutions in this field.[44]

BLOCKCHAIN FOR SUPPLY CHAIN AND TRACEABILITY

20.87 Industries such as agriculture, pharmaceuticals, and luxury goods are leveraging blockchain to enhance transparency and traceability within their supply chains. DLT's immutable ledgers ensure the authenticity and provenance of products, reducing fraud, and improving consumer trust.

20.88 DLT technology offers valuable applications in supply chains, which are intricate networks of interconnected companies. It records transactions, encompassing information, goods, services, and finances, on a shared, unchangeable ledger. This enables data capture, validation, and sharing among these businesses, providing a seamless exchange of value and a singular source of fact. Blockchain enhances global supply chains by predicting risks, improving visibility, ensuring data accuracy, and bolstering trust. It can also integrate with emerging technologies like IoT, smart contracts, and AI.

20.89 Blockchain can create substantial benefits by reducing supply chain risks, enhancing visibility, and fostering trust within a complex ecosystem. Importantly, it complements existing systems like enterprise resource planning software. Here are three examples of how blockchain delivers tangible benefits:

(a) **Risk mitigation**: supply chain risks, whether in sourcing, transport, facility, or distribution, can disrupt operations. DLT provides access to reliable data, enabling timely issue identification and alternative solutions. It eliminates data silos, ensures data trustworthiness, and facilitates data sharing among supply chain parties. For instance, DLT integrated with AI and IoT can monitor and identify bottlenecks, mitigating transport risks.

44 Ariana Kiran Singh, Olamide Oguntoye, Lauren Packard, 'Cleaning Up Crypto's Emissions: Why Policy Shouldn't Be Binary' (Paper, TBIGC, 3 August 2022) www.institute.global/insights/tech-and-digitalisation/cleaning-cryptos-emissions-why-policy-shouldnt-be-binary [accessed 7 October 2023].

(b) **Facility management**: using satellites, IoT devices, and cellular networks connected to blockchain, businesses can monitor inventory levels and disruptions in facilities. This real-time data, captured as immutable records, helps trace and address disruptions, reducing potential insurance disputes through smart contracts.

(c) **Distribution optimisation**: DLT aids in managing distribution risks by creating accurate, immutable digital inventories. By integrating AI, it provides real-time insights into demand shifts and patterns, enabling informed planning and efficient inventory management down to the last mile.

20.90 As DLT matures, universal interoperability standards are needed. 'Bridges' currently facilitate cross-chain interoperability, but trade-offs exist. Trust among participants is crucial in choosing bridge relayers. Scalability factors affect public blockchains, and enterprises may prefer private blockchains. Solutions include high-capacity layer 1 blockchains, layer 2 blockchains, and lightweight consensus mechanisms for private chains.

20.91 All technological solutions come with security and privacy risks. In the case of DLT and supply chain, these risks can be categorised into four main areas: confidentiality, integrity, consensus mechanisms, and smart contracts. As a result of the foregoing, adoption of DLT in global supply chains is still in its early stages.[45]

BLOCKCHAIN IN HEALTHCARE

20.92 Blockchain technology is being explored for securely managing and sharing medical records, clinical trial data, and health information. Its decentralised nature and strong security features can enhance data privacy and facilitate interoperability between healthcare systems.

20.93 Healthcare records are currently fragmented due to the lack of common standards. Each healthcare provider maintains its own database of patient information, resulting in a disconnected system. To address this issue, healthcare organisations could utilise DLT as a transaction layer to share standardised, non-sensitive information securely. This DLT-based system would improve data accessibility for healthcare organisations and research institutions while maintaining patient privacy. NHS Digital is currently exploring blockchain applications to healthcare and it was used to assist in the roll out of the Covid-19 vaccine programme in 2021.[46]

45 Wendy Henry, Rachana Kathawate, Erkik Chen and Josh Coulter, 'Using blockchain to drive blockchain transparency' (Perspectives, Deloitte, June 2023) www2.deloitte.com/us/en/pages/operations/articles/blockchain-supply-chain-innovation.html [accessed 7 October 2023].

46 See **20.60**; Tom Wilson, 'British hospitals use blockchain to track COVID-19 vaccines' (Reuters, 19 January 2021) www.reuters.com/article/uk-health-coronavirus-blockchain-idUSKBN29O0RW [accessed 7 October 2023].

20.94 DLT can store information in two ways: directly on the blockchain (on-chain) or by using links stored on the DLT to point to data in traditional databases (off-chain). Storing data on-chain offers better security but may slow down processing. Off-chain links are more efficient for large data files but require secure external databases. Organisations will have to carefully assess where and how to store data based on technical and confidentiality considerations.

20.95 Interoperability demands smooth data submission and access. DLT can serve as a unified platform for organisations to submit and share data securely. Standardised data, including demographics, medical history, and services rendered, could be stored directly on DLT. Smart contracts could enforce rules for data submission and storage.

20.96 DLT enhances data integrity and patient digital identities by using public/private key encryption. Each participant would have a private key that unlocks their identity when necessary, reducing vulnerabilities associated with storing personally identifiable information (PII) across multiple entities. Hacking a single patient's private key would have limited impact, as it requires hacking each user individually to access PII.

20.97 DLT's distributed ledger ensures data security, as changes to historical blocks require consensus among 51 per cent of network participants. This safeguards against malicious activity and maintains data integrity.

20.98 Smart contracts can serve as gateways for standardised data storage and retrieval, allowing organisations to easily integrate with DLT through APIs. These APIs enable querying specific blocks or submitting predefined queries.

20.99 Blockchain's transaction layer can provide standardised, non-patient identifiable information for research and initiatives like the Precision Medicine Initiative (PMI). This data can be analysed using 'Big Data' analytics and machine learning.

20.100 DLT has the potential to create a trusted healthcare data exchange, improve patient care, and support value-based healthcare. It can enhance transparency, trust, and data access, benefiting various stakeholders in the healthcare ecosystem.[47]

20.101 Legislators and regulators need to clarify how the General Data Protection Regulation (GDPR) applies to the use of blockchain technology in healthcare data processing. There is ongoing confusion about GDPR's interpretation in the

47 RJ Krawiec, Dan Housman, Mark White, Mariya Filipova, Florian Quarre, Dan Barr, Allen Nesbitt, Kate Fedosova, Jason Killmeyer, Adam Israel and Lindsay Tsai, 'Blockchain: Opportunities for health care' (White Paper, Deloitte, August 2016) www2.deloitte.com/us/en/pages/public-sector/articles/blockchain-opportunities-for-health-care.html [accessed 7 October 2023].

context of blockchain, and calls have been made for GDPR revisions to account for emerging technologies and data risks.

20.102 A European Parliament resolution of 3 October 2018 on distributed ledger technologies and blockchains acknowledges the potential benefits of blockchain in healthcare but emphasises the need for current blockchain technologies to align with GDPR. It recommends that the European Commission and European Data Protection Supervisor provide guidance on when data protections are necessary when using DLT.

20.103 Blockchain and GDPR compliance issues exist, particularly in public blockchains, affecting aspects like controller responsibility and the right to erasure. While some GDPR requirements can be addressed with the right blockchain architecture, certain grey areas pose compliance challenges.[48]

CONCLUSION

20.104 Cryptocurrencies are gradually gaining acceptance among governments, financial institutions, businesses, and consumers. More companies may start accepting cryptocurrencies as a form of payment, and traditional financial institutions may integrate cryptocurrency services into their offerings, providing users with greater accessibility and convenience.

20.105 The growth of DeFi presents new opportunities for individuals to access financial services, such as lending, borrowing, and asset management, without intermediaries. The UK may see an expansion of DeFi platforms and services, which could contribute to greater financial inclusion and innovation. The UK's proposed introduction of a CBDC may transform the economy, banking and governance.

20.106 As blockchain and cryptoassets gain broader recognition, governments and regulatory bodies are working to establish clear legal frameworks and standards. The goal is to balance innovation with consumer protection, preventing illicit activities while fostering the growth of the industry.

20.107 As cryptocurrencies continue to gain traction, scalability remains a challenge. Interoperability protocols and cross-chain solutions are being developed to enable seamless interaction and transfer of assets between different blockchain networks. As the cryptocurrency ecosystem evolves, it is crucial to implement robust security measures to safeguard user funds and protect against hacking and fraudulent activities. Improved security protocols, multi-factor

48 Kristina Livitckaia, Wendy Charles, Urko Larrañaga Piedra, Matthew Niemerg, Anton Hasselgren and Elsa Papadopoulou, 'Blockchain Applications in the Healthcare Sector' (EU Blockchain Observatory and Forum, April 2022), [3.2] www.eublockchainforum.eu/sites/default/files/reports/eubof_healthcare_2022_FINAL_pdf.pdf [accessed 7 October 2023].

authentication, and advanced encryption techniques are expected to become more prevalent.

20.108 Education and awareness campaigns may play a significant role in promoting responsible cryptocurrency use and protecting consumers from scams and fraudulent schemes. Regulators and industry stakeholders may collaborate to enhance consumer education initiatives and establish effective dispute resolution mechanisms.

20.109 Collaboration among international regulators is essential to establish consistent regulatory standards and promote cross-border interoperability. The UK may actively participate in global discussions and initiatives to develop harmonised frameworks for cryptocurrencies, addressing challenges such as cross-border transactions and investor protection.

20.110 The future of cryptocurrencies in the UK holds immense potential for innovation, financial inclusion, and technological advancements. As the regulatory landscape continues to evolve and market participants adapt to emerging trends, the UK is likely to witness increased adoption, integration, and maturity of the cryptocurrency ecosystem.

Part VI

Conclusion

Chapter 21

Key Takeaways

21.1 The legal aspects of cryptocurrency in the UK are complex and ever-evolving, reflecting the dynamic nature of this digital asset class. Throughout this comprehensive exploration of the legal landscape surrounding cryptocurrencies in the UK, several key takeaways emerge:

(a) **Regulatory framework**: the UK has taken significant strides in establishing a regulatory framework for cryptocurrencies. The FCA plays a central role in overseeing cryptocurrency-related activities, while other regulatory bodies address specific aspects such as AML/CFT and data privacy. The regulatory landscape for cryptocurrencies in the UK and internationally is continually evolving. Regulators are actively engaging with industry stakeholders, exploring regulatory adaptations, and collaborating with international counterparts to address emerging challenges and foster innovation.

(b) **Investor protection**: enhancing investor protection is a priority for regulators. Measures such as AML/CTF requirements are in place to mitigate risks associated with illicit activities. Regulators also emphasise consumer education and dispute resolution mechanisms to safeguard the interests of cryptocurrency users.

(c) **CBDC**: stablecoins and CBDCs are gaining prominence in the UK and internationally. Regulators are taking action to mitigate financial stability and consumer protection risks posed by stablecoins. The exploration of a CBDC by the Bank of England highlights the UK's interest in the benefits and implications of central bank-backed digital currencies which may open up new monetary policy tools.

(d) **Privacy and data protection**: UK GDPR and the Data Protection Act 2018 apply to cryptoasset businesses that handle personal data. Protecting user privacy and ensuring compliance with data protection laws are crucial considerations for cryptocurrency operators.

(e) **Taxation**: cryptocurrency taxation is an important aspect for individuals and businesses operating in the UK and is an evolving area. Tax obligations can arise from activities such as trading, investments, and converting cryptoassets into fiat currency. Understanding and complying with tax regulations is essential to avoid potential legal issues.

(f) **Technological advancements and challenges**: the UK legal landscape must adapt to technological advancements and emerging challenges associated with cryptoassets. Areas such as smart contracts, DeFi, and tokenisation present legal considerations that may require further regulatory clarity.

(g) **International collaboration**: the UK actively participates in global discussions and collaborations to establish consistent regulatory standards for cryptocurrencies. Cooperation with international counterparts helps address cross-border challenges, promote regulatory harmonisation, and combat illicit activities.

21.2 The legal aspects of cryptocurrency in the UK will continue to evolve as technology, market dynamics, and regulatory priorities develop. Market participants, businesses, and individuals involved in the cryptocurrency ecosystem should stay informed of innovations, remain compliant with relevant regulations, and seek legal advice when necessary. The UK's approach reflects a balance between fostering innovation, ensuring investor protection, and addressing regulatory concerns. With a robust regulatory framework, ongoing collaborations, and a commitment to adaptability, the UK can position itself as a leading jurisdiction for cryptocurrency-related activities.

Index

References are to paragraph number.

D